LAW DEMOCRATIZED

Law Democratized

*A Blueprint for Solving
the Justice Crisis*

Renee Knake Jefferson

NEW YORK UNIVERSITY PRESS
New York

NEW YORK UNIVERSITY PRESS
New York
www.nyupress.org

© 2024 by New York University
All rights reserved.

Please contact the Library of Congress for Cataloging-in-Publication data.
ISBN: 9781479820399 (hardback)
ISBN: 9781479820436 (library ebook)
ISBN: 9781479820405 (consumer ebook)

This book is printed on acid-free paper, and its binding materials are chosen for strength and durability. We strive to use environmentally responsible suppliers and materials to the greatest extent possible in publishing our books.

Manufactured in the United States of America

10 9 8 7 6 5 4 3 2 1

Also available as an ebook

For Grace, James, and Wallace
In memory of Deborah

The arc of the moral universe is long, but it bends toward justice.
—Dr. Martin Luther King, Jr., Washington National Cathedral,
  March 31, 1968

CONTENTS

Preface   xi

Introduction: Meaningful Access to Justice and the Promise
of Entrepreneurship, Innovation, and Technology   1

PART I. UNDERSTANDING THE JUSTICE CRISIS: ORIGINS
OF THE UNMET NEED FOR CIVIL LEGAL SERVICES
IN THE UNITED STATES   13

1. Unmet Legal Needs   26

2. (Not) Finding Legal Help: A Case Study   39

3. A Brief History of Lawyer Regulation   49

4. The Legal Monopoly   71

5. Preserving Democracy: The Role of Courts and the Role
of Legal Ethics   77

PART II. DEMOCRATIZING LAW: THE BLUEPRINT   87

6. Antitrust Law   90

7. The First Amendment   102

8. Regulatory and Legislative Reform   119

9. Education for the Legal Profession   147

10. Education for the Public   166

11. Ethical Innovation   182

12. The Way Forward   197

Conclusion   203 x | CONTENTS

Acknowledgments	205
Appendix 1: The Blueprint for Justice Checklist	209
Appendix 2: Methodology and Further Resources	213
Notes	215
Bibliography	269
Index	279
About the Author	297

PREFACE

"A priest is here to perform your last rites," a nurse whispered into my ear. What I really needed was a lawyer.

At that moment, my temples pounded with the worst headache of my life. I struggled to adjust my arms and legs against tight nylon straps binding me to a metal gurney. My eyes squinted in the too-bright light. Emergency room technicians and doctors spoke in code. The few bits I could understand terrified me: "She's too young . . ." "University of Chicago graduate, a lawyer, so tragic . . ." "neurosurgeon on standby . . ." "she has kids . . ." "couldn't remember who's president . . ." "there's space in the neuro-ICU, need to keep her at least a week." I was only thirty-five years old, the mother of two toddlers, on the brink of entering the tenure-track job market as a law professor, and blood was pooled in my brain.

The prognosis? Not good.

My mind raced with questions about the imminent termination of my employment contract as a university lecturer, the recent conversations with my then-spouse about divorce, the manufacturer whose drug made me faint and hit my head, the will I had not yet prepared to protect my children.

I faced multiple problems that required legal help. And yet, even as a lawyer myself, I did not know what to do.

Most people hopefully never find themselves, as I did, bound to a gurney while declining a priest's reading of their last rites. But my plight of facing multiple unmet legal needs alone is not unique.

Studies show that at any given time, the majority of households in the United States face two to three legal problems without a lawyer or other assistance. Most do not even recognize that their problems could be solved through the justice system or legal tools. Consider these findings from surveys on legal needs conducted by various states over the past two decades:

xi

- "About 87 percent of households with legal problems did not seek legal assistance. A key reason for not seeking legal assistance is lack of understanding of the legal nature of the problem."[1]
- "Households that had legal problems were asked if they knew that the problem was legal in nature. Only about a quarter of respondents said that they were aware of the legal issue involved."[2]
- "A large percentage of low-income people with a legal problem are not aware that their problem has a legal dimension and potential solution."[3]
- "Many respond that 'there was nothing to be done' or that 'it was not a legal problem, just the way things are.'"[4]

Civil legal disputes—think child support, citizenship, consumer complaints, custody, divorce, employment, guardianship, housing, medical needs—make their way to more than fifteen thousand courts throughout the United States each year. It's a "patchwork of jurisdictions among state, county, municipal authorities" according to the Self-Represented Litigation Network (SRLN), an advocacy group committed to "100% access to civil justice."[5] The SRLN estimates that of the forty-six million people appearing in the courts annually, 75 percent or more of these cases have at least one self-represented litigant. And that doesn't begin to account for the people who do not recognize that they have a problem that could be resolved in the courts in the first place.

Why do millions of people living in the United States (and billions of people worldwide) lack help for their legal problems? Commentators and academics offer a range of answers to this question, from economic factors to regulatory constraints. Whatever the root cause, a massive delivery problem clearly exists for personal legal services. People do not realize when a lawyer might be necessary or helpful, even though they may desperately need legal assistance. Consequently, a latent market for legal services exists because would-be clients do not know that they need a lawyer or do not know how to obtain the law-related help that would benefit them.

More than a decade has passed since my full recovery from that grim day in the hospital back in February 2010. Since that time, I spawned an award-winning venture to help law students find nontraditional paths to solve legal problems for those in need. I taught, researched, and wrote extensively about the lack of access to effective legal help and the possible solutions.

This book is a journal of sorts, documenting what I learned along the way as I studied efforts to improve the delivery of legal services and tried to better understand why it is so challenging to do so.

* * *

On February 7, 2014, Twitter's trending hashtags included #Seahawks-Front7, #JayLeno, #Starbucks, #Russia, and #ReInventLaw. Most people can easily identify the first four topics. But #ReInventLaw? Who knows what that meant?

This was not the only time #ReInventLaw surfaced as a trending topic. It first claimed that status on March 8, 2013.[6] It appeared among the top trending Twitter hashtags again on June 14, 2013,[7] and June 20, 2014,[8] the latter competing with the World Cup.

Why was #ReInventLaw trending on Twitter multiple times in 2013 and 2014? Those dates coincide with gatherings held around the world that brought together academics, design architects, entrepreneurs, innovators, law students, lawyers, tech experts, and venture capitalists to explore better ways of providing justice to humanity. That hashtag marked a global conversation in real time—within a physical meeting space but also simultaneously on social media—that was focused on innovation in the delivery of justice. Many followed the live tweeting remotely from their homes or offices while attendees inside the conference hall shared the insights and wisdom of the day in 140 characters or less.

The ReInvent Law Laboratory ("ReInvent Law" for short) was the product of a unique partnership between the acclaimed entrepreneurship-fueling powerhouse Ewing and Marion Kauffmann Foundation and the Big Ten research institution Michigan State University. ReInvent Law's mission was to launch and legitimize a new discipline in law practice and legal education focused on entrepreneurship and innovation. One of the central goals was to address the widespread unmet need for legal help. Across curricula, practice, and regulation, ReInvent Law gave students, legal designers, and technologists early opportunities to promote the potential of their methods for reimagining the legal services industry. It did so successfully, even at a time of resistance from the legal academy and profession.

I know this because I was one of ReInvent Law's two cofounders.[9]

Despite limited acceptance within the legal profession itself (entrenched in tradition, fear, and other barriers explored in part I of the book), the start-up quickly found national and international acclaim. ReInvent Law received numerous awards and landed Michigan State's previously unranked law school on top ten lists for schools teaching the technology of law practice.[10] The College of Law Practice Management bestowed the "InnovAction" award for "extraordinary innovative efforts" on Reinvent Law in 2013. (The college "is a professional, educational and honorary association dedicated to the improvement of the law practice management and to the enhancement of the professional quality of and public respect for the law."[11]) The Wolters Kluwer Leading Edge Report recognized ReInvent Law as one of "three programs to watch in building a faculty culture of innovation" in 2015.[12]

In 2013, the *American Bar Association Journal* magazine featured me on its cover as a "Legal Rebel," what it calls an "annual honors program for the change leaders of the legal profession." That same year, my name appeared among the Fastcase50, an annual award that "recognizes 50 of the smartest, most courageous innovators, techies, visionaries, and leaders in the law." I had not yet secured tenure as a law professor at Michigan State, but my apparent "rebellion" helped fuel a movement that continues to challenge the paradigm for the delivery of legal services.

ReInvent Law emerged amid a massive upheaval in the legal profession, in the spirit of Winston Churchill's "never let a good crisis go to waste." In the immediate aftermath of the 2008 recession, United States law schools saw precipitous drops in applications and enrollment. The decline stemmed, in part, from a significant contraction of the legal industry, with hiring freezes and workforce reductions, as well as a decreasing availability of entry-level attorney jobs. At the same time, lawyers and clients frustrated with artificial constraints on traditional law practice, like the billable hour, spurred experimentation with the technology and entrepreneurial tools drawn from other professions and industries.

My primary motivation to cofound a "law laboratory"? To provide law students new paths to achieve justice and deliver legal help to those in need.

I've taught a mandatory upper-level law school ethics course called "Professional Responsibility" since 2006. The standard curriculum for that kind of class involves instructing students about compliance with rules that govern traditional law practice. I wanted, instead, to prepare them for the economic realities in the early 2000s, including a disrupted legal market,[13] a massive tuition-based debt bubble,[14] and struggling lawyers unable to find jobs.[15] Much of legal education, at the time, largely ignored this culmination of forces at great detriment to future lawyers and their clients. Indeed, this is precisely why—contrary to what ran on the front page of the *New York Times* in 2011—law schools began to engage in reform in the early 2000s. Though the article's author lamented that law schools "don't teach law students . . . lawyering,"[16] he failed to expose the real dilemma. Law schools at that time were widely focusing on lawyering skills, clinical activities, mock simulations, and other efforts designed to provide practical, hands-on experience[17] as well as to encourage collaboration with other professionals.[18] Notably absent in the early 2000s from most law schools, however, was a culture of entrepreneurialism and innovation. Equally lacking were significant curricula or related resources devoted to this pursuit.[19] This became less true two decades later, thanks, in part, to ReInvent Law and the programs it inspired, but much more work remains on this front. The technology boom and the inevitable need to adapt, as well as a heightened emphasis on innovation across most major industries, keeps the pressure on.

The ReInvent Law movement helped fill the gap that separated innovative lawyering from academia, industry, tech, and nonprofit organizations. As one commentator observed, "Given ReInvent Law's meteoric rise in just two years, it's easy to see there is an enormous void where legal technology needs to be."[20] We motivated thousands of attendees to gather worldwide in Dubai, London, New York City, and Silicon Valley from 2012 to 2014. The events were free of charge and open to anyone. More than eight hundred people stood in a meandering line outside the Cooper Union for more than an hour on a cold New York morning in February, hoping for a seat in the Great Hall.[21] Attendees left standing room only in London's Centre Point CBI Centre, traveled endless hours to the Dubai International Financial Centre, and crowded into the Computer History Museum's amphitheater in Mountain View, California, to hear dozens of TED Talk–style pitches from thought leaders. They included well-known futurists, like the United Kingdom's Richard Susskind, and others who made a name for themselves in their moment on the ReInvent Law stage, including our students from the Michigan State University College of Law. More than four hundred people attended the Silicon Valley event alone, which featured a lineup of forty speakers.

These events spoke to a much larger movement surging within the legal community. Dozens of conferences about law and legal services happen monthly, if not weekly, without a single related Tweet going out. Monica Bay, a journalist covering the Silicon Valley event reflected, "To my mind, the significance of ReInvent Law was not in any single presentation or even the overall event. The significance was that ReInvent Law was a manifestation of something larger going on in legal technology—a time of unprecedented innovation and creativity. The speakers and attendees represented a kind of legal technology counterculture that is certain to shape the future of the profession."[22]

Participants continued to feel the impact years later, including Australian legal services expert George Beaton: "Seldom, if ever in my life, has one day made such a positive difference to my professional career. It may seem self-indulgent to write about this event three years on, but I think it's worth sharing . . . I am grateful and indebted."[23]

As with many start-ups, ReInvent Law evolved. A version lives on at Michigan State University as the Legal RnD (Research and Development) Lab, part of the Center for Law, Technology & Innovation, primarily focused on student education and faculty research. Despite calls for more and similar global events, ReInvent Law London 2014 was the last. But its legacy animates law school curricula internationally and launched students into a range of jobs related to innovation in legal services. The message of entrepreneurship and innovation prodded bar associations and regulators of the legal profession to start discussing ways to expand access to justice and to make legal services more accessible, affordable, and pervasive. ReInvent Law also inspired much of the research collected here in this book.

For nearly twenty years, I've taught courses on legal ethics, entrepreneurship, innovation in legal services, and twenty-first-century law practice in the United States and abroad. I served as a co-reporter for the American Bar Association Presidential Commission on the Future of Legal Services from 2014 to 2016, and I participated in numerous public hearings and co-authored a lengthy report about how best to address the access-to-justice problem in the United States. From 2013 to 2016, I represented the United States as a delegate to the World Economic Forum Global Agenda Councils on the Rule of Law and Justice. Twice, once in 2016 and once in 2017, I participated in the Antigua Forum in Guatemala, an entrepreneurship-driven project accelerator. More recently, I was named the Fulbright Distinguished Chair in Entrepreneurship and Innovation at the Royal Melbourne Institute of Technology in 2019, and I was appointed to the Texas Access to Justice Commission's Working Group on Access to Legal Services in 2023.

Law Democratized: A Blueprint for Solving the Justice Crisis chronicles my experiences and research from the launch of ReInvent Law in 2012 through the decade that followed. It evaluates past approaches for facilitating access to legal help, exposes ways in which the status quo stymies innovation, and explores current and evolving efforts. The book is meant to be a building block in the foundation of a better justice system for the future and a catalyst for others to join in and improve on this effort.

* * *

A couple of months before this manuscript's due date to the publisher in early 2023, an important new AI technology debuted from the San Francisco-based company OpenAI known as "GPT-3" or "ChatGPT."[24] It has the potential to become the single most important tool in solving the justice crisis that this book aims to address, if harnessed to do so ethically. To give you just a small taste of its power, I asked it to perform the following task: "Write the introduction to a book called *Law Democratized: A Blueprint for Justice*" (which was then the book's working title). Keep in mind that the book did not yet exist. Instantly, this appeared:

> *Law Democratized: A Blueprint for Justice* is a groundbreaking book that challenges the status quo of how law is practiced and applied in society. The book proposes a new way of thinking about law, one that puts the power of justice back into the hands of the people. It outlines a set of principles and strategies which, if implemented, could revolutionize the way law is practiced and transform the way justice is delivered. This book is a must-read for anyone interested in the future of law, from lawyers and judges to activists and policy makers. It provides a comprehensive blueprint for transforming the law from a tool of the powerful to an instrument of the people.

I then asked: "Should I give you credit for writing this?" Here's what it said:

> As an AI model, I do not have personal preferences or the ability to hold any rights on the content I generate. However, it is a common practice to give credit to the source of any information or content used in a work. So If you would like to use the text I generated in a publication or a project, it is always a good idea to cite it as "generated by OpenAI's GPT-3" or something similar, to give credit to the creators of the model you are using.

With credit given where credit is due, I'll let you read on. Judge for yourself whether this AI-generated description is accurate and what it means for the future of justice.

R. K. J.
January 27, 2023

Introduction

Meaningful Access to Justice and the Promise of Entrepreneurship, Innovation, and Technology

Imagine, for a moment, that you are traveling on public transportation, maybe the "L" in Chicago or the subway in New York City. A police officer approaches and claims you didn't pay your fare. You disagree. The officer hands you a citation.

Would you rather pay the officer a seventy-five-dollar fee immediately, or instead take time away from work, perhaps hire a lawyer at hundreds of dollars an hour, and challenge the fine in court, with the risk that if you lose, the sanction more than triples?

In Melbourne, Australia, riders of trams and buses faced this dilemma for three years, beginning in 2014 with a new, on-the-spot fine system. Public transport in Melbourne requires riders to tap a fare card when they board and tap it again at the destination when the amount owed is calculated. A rider who wants to cheat the system could simply not tap at all or use a card with insufficient funds. Officers regularly monitor passengers by asking to check their fare cards at random.

Riders with insufficient funds are subject to hefty fines. When the new payment program started, most of those who could cover the seventy-five dollar fee did so, even when they had a lawful defense and might have won a court challenge to avoid payment entirely.[1] Lawmakers enacted the on-the-spot payment option believing it would improve the sanctions process, allowing violators to avoid the inconvenience and expense of a formal appeal.

Public Transport of Victoria, the body responsible for the change, touted the program's benefits: increased speed of penalty issuance (enabling more ticketing of fare evaders) and improved confidentiality (passengers were not required to provide identification if they paid immediately). Some even called it "innovative." The program was arguably a success—if the only measures were efficiency and increased revenue generation from the fines. But the program also undermined justice. Riders whose challenges might have succeeded in court paid unnecessary fines to avoid the hassle and uncertainty of legal proceedings.

Perhaps a reasonable idea in the abstract, the system turned out to be hugely unpopular. It bizarrely rewarded the savvy fare evader, who "could pay 20 on-the-spot penalty fares in a year and still cough up less than a traveler" who purchased a full-fare annual pass.[2] No records were kept following up on serial fare dodgers.

Even worse, the fine scheme created two tiers of justice—one for commuters who could easily afford the seventy-five-dollar fine and had access to a credit card (the fine was payable by credit card only) and one for those who did not enjoy these privileges. As Victorian ombudsman Deborah Glass lamented in issuing a report for reform, "While the intent of a quicker and cheaper penalty fare option is laudable, it has created a parallel track for those who can afford it, rather than a single, cohesive and well targeted system."[3]

Parallel Track (In)Justice

The ombudsman's critique of the two-tiered, "parallel track" rings true for more than just Australian public transport fare cards. It reflects much of the justice system made up of (1) those who can recognize and afford help with legal problems and (2) those who cannot.

Lawyers have bemoaned this predicament since at least the 1930s. Indeed, this nearly century-old description, which appeared in a 1938 American Bar Association (ABA) Report on the Economic Condition of the Bar, could have been written today:

> People in the low income groups frequently go without legal assistance because they cannot afford to pay for it, or because they think they cannot afford to pay for it, or because they distrust lawyers or do not know any lawyers, or do not know when they need advice.[4]

The ABA, established in 1878, is one of the world's largest voluntary professional organizations, composed of nearly two hundred thousand practicing lawyers from across the United States. It should have solved this dilemma long ago, but the justice gap endures.

Worldwide, five billion people face unmet legal needs annually, including "people who cannot obtain justice for everyday problems, people who are excluded from the opportunity law provides, and people who live in extreme conditions of injustice," according to an organization called the World Justice Project (WJP).[5] Founded in 2006 by two former presidents of the ABA, William Neukom and William Hubbard, the WJP is an international nonprofit organization focused on providing research and data to advance the rule of law around the globe.

Each year, the WJP compiles a ranking of countries on its Rule of Law Index. The index, a tool using data metrics to assess the rule of law in practice, encompasses numerous indicators organized around eight overarching factors: (1) constraints on government powers; (2) absence of corruption; (3) open government; (4) fundamental rights; (5) order and security; (6) regulatory enforcement; (7) civil justice; and (8) criminal justice. In 2021, the WJP's Rule of Law Index revealed that the United States' "civil justice system lags behind other high-income countries in accessibility and affordability of both civil courts and legal representation."[6] The United States received a 0.44 out of 1 in the scoring for cost and availability of legal services.[7] While the country ranked twenty-seventh overall, it landed near the bottom on the assessment of whether "people can access and afford civil justice," coming in at 126 out of 139.[8] This category measures "the accessibility and affordability of civil courts, including whether people are aware of available remedies; can access and afford legal advice and representation; and can access the court system without incurring unreasonable fees, encountering unreasonable procedural hurdles, or experiencing physical or linguistic barriers."[9] What good is a court system if the people it is intended to serve cannot access or afford it?

While the Rule of Law Index did show modest improvement for the United States in 2022 (among only a handful of countries to increase their scores), the nation still ranked twenty-sixth overall, and thirty-sixth for civil justice specifically.[10] Denmark ranked first, followed by its neighbors Norway, Finland, Sweden, and the Netherlands to round out the top five. Two specific data points are particularly damning. First, the United States remained ridiculously low on the measure of whether

4 | INTRODUCTION

"people can access and afford civil justice" (115 of 140 countries).[11] Second, the country ranked 121 of 140 on the measure of whether "civil justice is free of discrimination," that is, whether the system discriminates based on "socio-economic status, gender, ethnicity, religion, national origin, sexual orientation, or gender identity."[12] America holds itself out as a beacon of justice to the world, and yet the data show otherwise. We have a lot of work to do if we want to live up to the United Nation's goal to "promote peaceful and inclusive societies for sustainable development, provide access to justice for all and build effective, accountable and inclusive institutions at all levels."[13]

Most people in the United States fail to recognize that their problems have a legal solution and, even if they do seek legal help, many find they do not qualify for legal aid or are unable or unwilling to pay for a lawyer who charges three (or four!) figures an hour for multiple hours.[14] Consider the findings of sociologist Rebecca Sandefur, who won a MacArthur Fellowship, the "Genius Grant," for her pioneering work on access to justice for low- and moderate-income households. She surveyed, in her words, "a random sample of adults in a middle-sized American city" in the Midwest in 2013.[15] Two-thirds of the study participants "reported experiencing at least one of 12 different categories of civil justice situations in the previous 18 months."[16] Sandefur found that the "most commonly reported kinds of situations involved bread and butter issues with far-reaching impacts: problems with employment, money (finances, government benefits, debts), insurance, and housing."[17] Those living in poverty, according to the survey, "were more likely to report civil justice situations than were middle-income or high-income people. African Americans and Hispanics were more likely to report such situations than Whites."[18]

The unmet need documented by the Sandefur study, sadly, is not surprising. But the reason for not seeking legal help is shocking—it is not about the price, but about knowledge. Only 17 percent of the study participants "reported that concerns about cost were a factor."[19] Instead, the predominant "reason that people do not seek assistance with these situations, in particular assistance from lawyers or courts," Sandefur concluded, "is that they do not understand these situations to be legal."[20]

They simply do not know.

In addition to not recognizing problems as having legal solutions, it is difficult for many to find a lawyer other than by word of mouth or perhaps by searching the internet, where advertising by personal injury lawyers and settlement mills dominates.[21] Consequently, much of the public receives "no legal help or advice with legal problems, muddling alone through the crises of job loss, divorce, bankruptcy, immigration challenges, access to services and benefits, injuries, and conflicts with neighbors or schools or health-care providers or local officials."[22] Meaningful access to legal help is denied on a daily basis for the majority of the population.

Solving the Tram Fines with Justice Tech Innovation

Let's return for a moment to the Australian tram fines story. In 2016, local government officials launched a formal inquiry into the unfair two-tier system, which quickly became a public scandal. Meanwhile, commuters continued to be subjected to it.

Frustrated by this injustice, a newly practicing lawyer named Sam Flynn created an interactive website to inform individuals about their rights. The website received thirty-five thousand individual views on its launch date in April 2016, totaling sixty thousand views within the month.[23] It was credited with being the lynchpin in bringing on-the-spot fines to a halt. Flynn used his training in law to deploy tech-driven, ethical innovation for solving the tram riders' legal problems.

January 1, 2017, marked the end of the penalties for Melbourne commuters. But it was only the start for Flynn. After that initial success, Flynn and his cofounders started their next venture, Josef Legal, a software-to-service company that helps lawyers build bots to solve legal problems. (Bots are computer programs that interact autonomously with users, typically over the internet or on a mobile app, and often are designed to simulate human conversation.) The tools improve lawyers' lives by streamlining repetitive work, and they address the justice gap by expanding access to legal help to the public. Among Josef Legal's creations are bots that automate lawyer-client conversations and document drafting, with over six hundred built to solve more than thirty thousand legal problems for clients based in Australia, Europe, and the United

States in just two years.[24] In May 2019, Josef Legal announced it secured a venture capital investment of $1 million, followed by additional rounds of $2.5 million in 2021 and $3.5 million in November 2022. The company continues to grow.[25]

This kind of legal services technology innovation reflects an increasing interest among lawyers and others in exploring entrepreneurial pursuits.[26] Innovation like this is a potential solution to the justice crisis and is intertwined with many of the reforms explored in this book.

* * *

Around the same time that Flynn's work flourished in Australia and evolved into Josef Legal, on the other side of the globe, Joshua Browder introduced DoNotPay in 2015, the first bot designed to help users challenge parking tickets, in the United Kingdom.[27] It too expanded, purporting to offer bots to help sue and claim awards from class actions, among other tasks, and calling itself the "world's first robot lawyer."[28] Browder's seeming success, however, offers a cautionary tale.

In early January 2023, Browder pledged "to send a real defendant into a real court armed with a recording device and a set of earbuds."[29] AI designed by his company, he claimed, would take the audio feed from the courtroom and provide the litigant responses to the proceedings. Browder also offered to pay any lawyer $1 million to use the earbuds for an argument in the United States Supreme Court.[30] (The offer likely was merely a publicity stunt given that the court prohibits all electronic devices.) In fact, just a few days after announcing the debut of his earbuds-in-the-courtroom plan, Browder backtracked. He tweeted: "Bad news: after receiving threats from State Bar prosecutors, it seems likely they will put me in jail for 6 months if I follow through with bringing a robot lawyer into a physical courtroom. DoNotPay is postponing our court case and sticking to consumer rights."[31] (More on the rules that criminalize the unauthorized practice of law and their impact on innovation will be discussed in chapter 3.) The same day, DoNotPay removed legal products like demand letters and divorce agreements from its offerings.[32] Browder soon also found his business practices challenged as fraudulent by paralegal Kathryn Tewson, a dispute still unfolding as this book went to press.[33]

This use of tech in the courtroom raises lots of questions legally and ethically—questions that we will explore throughout this book. But, for now, the larger point is that tools like these can help people navigate legal problems that lawyers, under traditional delivery models, cannot afford to deal with. Also, tech innovations like this are not going away. As just one measure, Browder's company closed "a $10 million Series B round in July 2021, with Andreessen Horowitz, among other venture firms" bringing it to a valuation of $210 million.[34] The fact remains that AI is increasingly capable of handling legal tasks, including passing parts of the bar exam, a test required for human lawyers to become licensed to practice, in early 2023.[35]

Meanwhile, in the United States, nearly two decades before Flynn and Browder emerged on the scene, in 2001, Brian Liu became the founding CEO of LegalZoom, a "legal technology company" that helps people prepare affordable legal forms, often without a lawyer.[36] Individuals can do so from the comfort and privacy of their living room or wherever they choose on a personal computer or mobile device. The company, a venture of lawyers and nonlawyers, is highly successful, earning revenues of $575 million with a net income of $109 million in 2021[37] and revenues of $620 million in 2022.[38] The company seizes opportunities through regulatory reform abroad and at home (and through litigation when necessary), as we will explore in part II. Tools like those offered by Josef Legal and LegalZoom help make legal services an affordable and routine part of daily life. We need many, many more of them to bridge the justice gap.

Why Does the Legal Profession Resist Innovation?

You'd think that the legal profession would welcome innovations like these. But that hasn't been the always been the case, especially in the United States.

Part of the resistance from lawyers is fear of being replaced. The legal profession faces unprecedented disruption in what scholars Erik Brynjolfsson and Andrew McAfee call a "race against the machine" as more of the traditional lawyer roles, such as document review and dispute outcome prediction, become aided if not entirely replaced by computers.[39]

Technology-assisted document review performs on par with lawyers, "if not better, [and] at far less cost."[40] Similar tools are used for predicting the outcomes of cases and soon will be deployed for contract drafting, brief writing, and much more, at least for first drafts. As technology advances, "softer skills like leadership, teambuilding, and creativity will be increasingly important. They are the areas least likely to be automated and most in demand in a dynamic, entrepreneurial economy," according to Brynjolfsson and McAfee.[41] Automated dispute resolution already permeates much of the marketplace. Consider that more than a decade ago, the online auction website eBay, in 2012 alone, "handled over sixty million disputes between buyers and sellers by providing software that assisted the parties to negotiate a satisfactory outcome over 80 percent of the time."[42] We sit at an unprecedented intersection of technological advancement and global convergence with a legal services market poised to resolve long-standing affordability and accessibility issues, particularly with respect to who provides legal help and how they do so.

Another factor contributing to the legal profession's resistance to change involves uncertainty and risk. Not all legal innovation ends in success stories like those of the companies founded by Flynn and Liu, respectively. "Innovators" in legal services come and go, some completely defunct and others acquired by larger entities. For example, a store-front retailer for legal services called "BookFlip" that appeared in 2013 on downtown Palo Alto's main street no longer exists, despite once being heralded by the magazine *Fast Company*.[43] Launched by the Legal Force company, it attempted to offer basic legal help like wills or trademarks in a bookstore-meets-Apple-store-like setting. As it turned out, people did not want to chat with an attorney while buying their books.

Other store-front efforts to innovate in legal services delivery similarly struggled.

Tesco, the United Kingdom's dominant supermarket chain, promoted legal services alongside grocery shopping after enactment of the Legal Services Act (LSA) in 2007,[44] legislation expressly designed to encourage competition and innovation in the legal services market. Among its many provisions, the LSA provides for corporate involvement in the investment and management of law firms, which is forbidden in most of the United States (as we will explore more fully in chapters 3 and 8). The grocery store was the first to file as an "alternative business structure" or

"ABS," the name the LSA gave to legal providers forming under the new law. Services included will writing, do-it-yourself divorce kits, rental agreements, and documents for setting up a small company. Commentators championed the concept "as a pioneer" and speculated others would soon "join their lead."[45] In theory, consumers could pick up a will with a loaf of bread or a gallon of milk, allowing them to resolve legal problems in a place they already regularly transact. But grocery store law never flourished.

That said, another leading grocery store chain in the UK has been successful as an early entrant into the ABS market, albeit not by putting wills alongside food items and household goods. The Co-op Group is the UK's fifth largest food retailer. Its Co-op Legal Services branch offers legal help online, rather than in stores, for issues regarding child custody, conveyancing, divorce, employment, and estate planning. In 2022, Co-op Legal services reported revenues of $48.8 million and six hundred employees[46]—clearly a success.

WHSmith stores in London followed in Tesco's footsteps in 2011 by setting up hot pink kiosks offering legal consultations from the British firm Quality Solicitors while one purchased a newspaper or snacks. Launching initially in 150 stores, with a projection of 500, the venture folded after just two years because the concept was not popular with customers.[47] The following year in the United States, Walmart leased space for law firms to serve their customers in Georgia, Kentucky, Missouri, and Texas,[48] as well as in Canada in 2014.[49] These providers enjoyed greater success than the Tesco and WHSmith ventures, but a retail model for law still has not been widely embraced.[50] Efforts in the United States in the late 1970s and early 1980s to encourage the adoption of legal services through franchises, most notably Hyatt Legal Services (later Hyatt Legal Plans and now MetLife Legal Plans), similarly struggled, though a number of employers still today offer legal plans to employees.[51] (In 2022, MetLife covered five million individuals for more than 4,000 businesses, including more than 220 Fortune 500 companies.)

Sometimes those aiming to close the justice gap struggle because innovation runs up against the rules that regulate the legal profession. As a member of the ABA Presidential Commission on the Future of Legal Services, I joined a 2016 site visit billed as an opportunity to learn "best practices" from what was then championed as a leading innovator in legal services offering affordable help to those in need: UpRight Law. At the company, which is based in Chicago and was founded in 2013 as a "technology-enabled" bankruptcy firm, initial client intake was handled not by lawyers but by trained salespeople to keep costs low.[52] Clients were later paired with a lawyer based locally in the client's jurisdiction.

But just two years after our visit, the legal services innovator faced trouble. A Virginia bankruptcy judge imposed a $250,000 sanction on UpRight Law and a $50,000 sanction on one of the founders for failure to adequately supervise the salespeople and for prioritizing "cash flow over professional responsibility."[53] That same month, the firm was again sanctioned by a different bankruptcy judge for violating lawyer professional conduct rules. Three months later, the North Carolina State Bar disciplined an attorney associated with UpRight Law for inadequate supervision of client funds. And, in June 2018, a Pennsylvania court issued sanctions over bankruptcy petitions that were missing the necessary signatures of the debtors. In the midst of multiple sanctions and lawyer discipline, the group changed leadership and—importantly—appointed a noted legal ethics professor to serve as an independent monitor.[54] UpRight Law remains in business and out of the headlines for such abuses, at least as of 2023.

These examples—though they experienced varying levels of success—highlight areas in which the public could benefit from legal assistance as well as some of the potential solutions, but none is a catch-all fix. These examples also illustrate the added challenges for entrepreneurship in delivering legal services.

All entrepreneurial ventures involve risk, but justice innovation is especially bumpy. Part of what contributes to this turbulence is the fact that unlike most entrepreneurs, lawyers have special obligations to comply with professional conduct rules. Chapter 11 further explores this intersection of innovation and the ethical duties of lawyers to their clients and the public.

Some Questions, Some Answers, and Some More Questions

It is easy to say we need an improved justice system. But it is difficult to articulate, let alone enact, a strategic plan for reform, whether to satisfy an individual's unique circumstances or the needs of an entire nation.

Our increasingly commercialized, technology-driven, and global society demands a new framework for legal help. One might think that an easy solution to this problem would be for lawyers to simply set up solo or small practices in local communities for clients to find them. Or one might propose that government and nonprofit legal aid organizations expand legal assistance or that lawyers donate their time to offer free services. None of these solutions have proven effective to date. They are unlikely to offer the revolutionary kind of change needed for the modern delivery of legal services.

The pursuit of meaningful resolution of legal problems raises several questions. How do we educate and inform the public about the law so people can understand when the services of a lawyer are necessary or desirable? How do we effectively match clients to lawyers in a way that is affordable to the client but allows the lawyer to earn a living? When is a lawyer warranted, and when can an individual solve their legal problems on their own, with a specialist who is not a licensed lawyer, or with the aid of burgeoning legal technology?

In short, how do we democratize law?

This book attempts to answer these questions. The answers matter, whether one needs legal help or not. The bedrock of American democracy rests upon access to meaningful justice. Meaningful justice requires the ability to obtain legal help, regardless of one's situation. To democratize means to prioritize equity, and to make something broadly available. I have researched, written about, taught, and lectured on ways to make law more equitable and more available to the public for nearly two decades. Here, I share the lessons learned, the questions I still ask, and some guideposts for a way forward.

Part I of this book examines the justice crisis and its origins. Help is out of reach for most individuals unless they enjoy extreme affluence or subsist at poverty levels. Corporations dominate the civil legal system represented by lawyers, with ordinary people left largely to fend for themselves. Chapter 1 of the book delves into research documenting the absence of legal help when needed and the failure to educate the public about when legal services might offer solutions. Chapter 2 exposes the paradox of legal advertising, a mechanism for finding a lawyer (in theory) that frequently fails (in practice) and illuminates this struggle through an empirical study. Chapters 3 and 4 reveal how the legal profession's self-regulation is a primary cause of the justice crisis. Chapter 5 exposes the threat to justice for everyone when lawyers themselves endeavor to undermine our democratic government.

Part II then shines a light on the way forward. It outlines different paths for democratizing law to increase access to legal help—paths that have been pursued by bar associations, courts, entrepreneurs, law schools, lawyers, nonprofits, and others—and evaluates the promise and pitfalls of each. Chapter 6 reveals how antitrust law, initially deployed to strike down lawyers' constraints on fees, could be expanded to further liberalize lawyer regulation and explains why the United States Supreme Court has refused, so far, to rule in this way. In chapter 7, we see how the Supreme Court instead relied on the First Amendment to break up some anticompetitive restrictions on legal advice and assistance, first in the context of civil rights and unions, then extending to advertising, but declined to push further. Chapter 8 summarizes regulatory reforms around the globe designed to increase access to justice along with emerging efforts in a handful of American states. Chapters 9 and 10 champion reforms to legal education both for lawyers and the public. Chapter 11 reflects upon the special role lawyers can play in ethical innovation. Chapter 12 offers specific steps for implementing all or parts of the blueprint, calling on state bar and licensing authorities, law schools, lawyers, judges, the public, and others for a shared commitment. Each chapter concludes with specific, concrete recommendations, laying out a blueprint for justice grounded in education, engaged citizenship, entrepreneurship, innovation, technology, and legal and regulatory reforms to democratize law and make legal help more accessible.

PART I

Understanding the Justice Crisis

Origins of the Unmet Need for Civil Legal Services in the United States

And now in that spirit, that spirit of an America which has never been . . . which never will be except as the conscience and courage of Americans create it; yet in the spirit of that America which lies hidden in some form in the aspirations of us all . . . in that spirit of liberty and of America I ask you to rise and with me pledge our faith in the glorious destiny of our beloved country.
—Learned Hand, *The Spirit of Liberty*, 1944

In 1944, more than one million people crowded together in New York City's Central Park to hear Judge Learned Hand deliver his famous *The Spirit of Liberty* speech. The event celebrated what was called "I Am an American Day," held to commemorate the swearing in of 150,000 new citizens. Hand served as a federal judge for more than fifty years and was considered by many to be the greatest jurist who never sat on the United States Supreme Court. He was appointed by President William Taft in 1909 to the United States District Court for the Southern District of New York and in 1924 by President Calvin Coolidge to the United States Court of Appeals for the Second Circuit. Hand's challenge to that Central Park audience nearly a century ago still resonates. Now, more than ever, the nation needs a justice system that fulfills the promise of liberty for all.

To understand the justice crisis in the United States, we must interrogate its origins. Part I explains how we got here, which is largely a function of the way the legal profession regulates itself but is also rooted in the nation's founding. When the authors of the Constitution signed it in 1787, women and minorities were not included among those protected by the rights it bestows. The preamble acknowledged that the "Union" was not yet perfect:

> We the People of the United States, in Order to form a more perfect Union, establish Justice, insure domestic Tranquility, provide for the common defence, promote the general Welfare, and secure the Blessings of Liberty to ourselves and our Posterity, do ordain and establish this Constitution for the United States of America.

Over time, the Constitution has been interpreted to extend some of the rights enjoyed at the founding by white, property-owning men to much of the rest of the population. The reality, however, as law professor Brandon Hasbrouck notes, is that without imagination, "the constitutional principles that the Court applies today will never be sufficient to achieve a state of racial justice in America."[1] And even the rights that were gained remain fragile. In the wake of the 2021 United States Supreme Court decision *Dobbs v. Jackson Women's Health Organization*, individuals able to bear children now find themselves with *fewer* constitutional rights than those before them.[2] Moreover, the words of the Constitution, the decisions interpreting it, and the rights it bestows are less meaningful if those entitled to its protections do not have access to legal advice, information, and representation.

Now, more than ever, we need lawyers committed to full rights for all. We need tools for everyone to get legal help, regardless of background, education, or wealth.

Our nation's prosperity as a democracy depends on its inhabitants both knowing their legal rights and entitlements and being able to address them in our courts or other justice processes. As chapters 1 and 2 reveal, far too many go without adequate legal knowledge and help. Chapters 3 and 4 explain why.

Terminology

Before moving on, a quick note about the terminology used in this book. For readers who are not lawyers, many words and phrases may be unfamiliar, at least as they appear in this context. Some will be defined along the way as we come to them. Several show up repeatedly, and they deserve mention at the outset.

In order to propose a blueprint for justice, we need to define as precisely as possible exactly what is meant by the word "justice" and by the phrase "access to justice." Fortunately, others have thought deeply about this, and we can use their analysis as a framework for our own understanding. A report on justice platforms produced by the Massachusetts Institute of Technology in December 2021 conceptualizes access to justice broadly: "To foster access to justice means building connections to the justice system's physical infrastructure, like courts and prisons; its services, like legal aid or social benefits; or a remedy, including formal and informal resolution, like mediation. This broad definition is necessary, because the size of the problem is monumental."[3] One important question to confront is whether a *lawyer* is needed for meaningful justice. Law professor and philosopher David Luban argued in his book *Lawyers and Justice* that the answer is "yes." He pushed "for the indispensable role of lawyers in pursuing justice," but in later writings he further acknowledged that justice "rests on a trio of other supposed equivalences"[4] that do not, necessarily, require lawyers. Luban breaks down his conception of justice into three kinds of *access*:

1. Access to justice means access to law—that is, to *legal* justice.
2. Access to law means access to professional legal services.
3. Access to professional legal services means access to lawyers.[5]

He then uses this framework to confront a question that is central to this book: "Does access to justice really mean access to law, that is, access to *legal* justice?"[6] Luban is skeptical that "access to legal justice" will "create the beatific vision of social justice that, in the words of Martin Luther King and the biblical prophet Amos, should roll down on us like waters in a mighty stream."[7] As Luban explains it:

> Access to law is itself a distributive good that is closely tied not only to the protection of basic rights but also to human dignity. And exclusion from the law is in itself a form of injustice. Practically, it puts America's neediest people in peril of losing their homes, apartments, and basic entitlements. . . . That too was part of Dr. King's message, when he denounced

unequal laws as "difference made legal." Difference made legal, King argued, is a violation of natural law—a violation that just men and women are obligated to resist.[8]

For Rebecca Sandefur, in her pathbreaking work that led to her MacArthur Genius Grant, this "distinction between a justice problem and a legal need turns out to be crucial, for these two ideas reflect fundamentally different understandings of the problem to be solved."[9] She separates the concept of justice—"a just resolution"—from legal services, and cites growing evidence that the resolution of "justice problems lawfully does not always require lawyers' assistance."[10] According to Sandefur: "Solutions to the access-to-justice crisis require a new understanding of the problem. It must guide a quest for just resolutions shaped by lawyers working with problem-solvers in other disciplines and with other members of the American public whom the justice system is meant to serve."[11] The bottom line for Sandefur? We do not always need a lawyer to achieve justice. Law professor Paul Tremblay agrees. Drawing from research based on his work in legal aid clinics, he advocates for the concept of "surrogate lawyering" to increase access to justice, by which "a public interest legal services organization [provides] guidance to its intended client community through social service agency staff members" which "serves as an alternative and supplement to technology-based innovations."[12]

Building on Sandefur's analysis, law professor Kathryne Young identifies two problems that occur when access to justice and access to a lawyer become conflated. First, according to Young, this skews the focus when the justice crisis is viewed "from the perspective of the legal system instead of from the perspective of the people who need resolution of their problems."[13] Second, she finds that this artificially eliminates potential solutions because "there are simply not enough lawyers to meet all the civil justice needs in the United States."[14] Sandefur calls the public to reclaim its justice system from control by the legal profession, which she notes "lawyers largely designed, substantially for themselves."[15] Instead, solutions demand that "justice professionals shift their understanding of the access problem, and share the quest for solutions with others: other disciplines, other problem-solvers, and other members of the American public whom the justice system is meant to serve."[16]

Other scholars, however, document the potential harms for litigants when actors in the justice system do not have sufficient legal training. Sociologist and legal scholar Sara Greene along with political scientist Kristen Renberg conducted a study of judges' backgrounds and found that "thirty-two states allow lay judges at some level of court."[17] On one hand, this expands the available pool of potential judges, arguably increasing access to justice. On the other hand, many of the lay judges have no legal training or relevant experience prior to assuming the role. Greene and Renberg find this deeply problematic. They argue that "there is a pretense of an impartial, formal, and rule-bound system of justice. Yet lay judges are not schooled in that system of law. Litigants are left to experience a courtroom of supposed 'law,' but they do not actually experience the law. Instead, they experience a courtroom in which often no one, not even the judge, is aware of the law."[18] They conclude that "allowing a system of nonlawyer judges perpetuates long-standing inequalities in our courts" and that "the phenomenon of lay judges is a symptom of a much larger problem in our justice system: the devaluation of the legal problems of the poor, who are disproportionately Black and Latinx."[19]

So, how do we decide when a lawyer, or a judge trained as a lawyer, is needed to accomplish justice?

Richard Susskind offers a helpful taxonomy of justice in his book *Online Courts and the Future of Justice*. According to Susskind, there are at least seven different kinds of justice under the umbrella of "justice according to the law."[20] He lays out this catalog to evaluate courts, but it can also be applied in the broader aim of this book, which is about democratizing justice beyond the courthouse. Here is his list:

1. Substantive justice (fair decisions)
2. Procedural justice (fair process)
3. Open justice (transparency)
4. Distributive justice (accessibility)
5. Proportionate justice (appropriate balance)
6. Enforceable justice (backing by the state)
7. Sustainable justice (sufficient resources)[21]

Susskind's categories help us understand and account for the layers of justice, both by refining precisely what individuals deserve—fair decisions and process—and by measuring whether it is achieved through transparency, accessibility, balance, and state enforcement as well as the necessary resources to sustain these measures.

In a speech before the Seventh Annual National Pro Bono Conference in Canada, the Right Honorable Richard Wagner, chief justice of Canada, captured simultaneously the complexity and simplicity of the concept of justice pursued here in *Law Democratized*:

> "Access to justice" can mean many things. Having the financial ability to get legal assistance when you need it. Being informed of your right to counsel when your liberty is at stake. Having courts that can resolve your problem on time. But it also means knowing what tools and services are available, and how to get to them. It means knowing your rights and knowing how our legal systems work. It can even mean seeing people like yourself represented in all parts of the legal system. And it means having confidence that the system will come to a just result—knowing you can respect it, and accept it, even if you don't agree with it. Ultimately, it is about getting good justice for everyone, not perfect justice for a lucky few. It's a democratic issue. It's a human rights issue. It's even an economic issue. . . . "Getting good justice for everyone" . . . for me, as a jurist, those five small words might just capture the ultimate goal of a democratic state.[22]

To be clear, the concept of justice pursued here *does not* conflate access to a lawyer with access to or the receipt of justice. For our purposes, justice is both in substance and in process. It is the idea that people deserve to know about their legal rights and entitlements (i.e., the substance), and to have them enforced by a lawyer, when needed, or by other means, whether self-help or nonlawyer assistance (i.e., the process). One mechanism to achieve access to justice is through a lawyer, but as we will explore throughout the book, there are other potentially effective tools whose creation and dissemination, unfortunately, have been squelched by lawyer regulation and lack of funding or vision, among other constraints.

Another word deserves attention: innovation. Merriam-Webster Dictionary defines it as "the introduction of something new" or "a new idea, method, or device,"[23] a definition that proves amorphous depending on the speaker and the audience. It is an oft-used word in the new millennium, with many individuals offering their own spin on its meaning.[24] Innovation in the context of legal services carries a range of connotations in addition to the dictionary definition of introducing something new, and we will move back and forth among the various meanings throughout the chapters in this book. For example, in the context of the legal profession, Alberto Bernabe notes that

> the word is often used to refer to developments in computer technology that lawyers can use to make practice more efficient, but it is also used to refer to the rise of online "do it yourself" legal services, to the expanding presence of internet start-up companies looking to connect clients with lawyers or to provide what appears to be legal services even though the entities providing them are not licensed to practice law, to issues related to possible partnerships with nonlawyers, to nonlawyer ownership of law firms, and to limited practice of law by nonlawyers.[25]

Legal innovation can mean developing ways to make law more accessible for those who need it, whether on the street corner or in the corner office. It includes improvements in the practice of law as well as its delivery to those who need legal help. Lawyers have a special obligation to ensure that innovations in the delivery of legal services are ethical, not only by complying with professional obligations but also by protecting clients and the public from harm. Efforts at innovation inevitably will vary based on practice setting and specialty. Large law firms will not necessarily engage in the same sorts of innovation as solo practitioners, in-house corporate counsel, community legal aid providers, or government lawyers.

Some innovation creates new roles and enhances ways of living; other innovation destroys jobs and routines.[26] The term "disruptive innovation" was coined by the academic Clayton Christensen.[27] It "occurs when a competitor enters a marketplace with a product or service that most initially see as inferior—until successive improvements end up displacing established products or even entire industries."[28] While some challenge his thinking (most famously, his Harvard colleague, historian Jill Lepore, in a 2014 *New Yorker* article, "What the Gospel of Innovation Gets Wrong"[29]), it remains a cornerstone of the innovation discussion, especially in the context of companies and work.[30] Not only is innovation often disruptive, but sometimes it's also unproductive or counterproductive, demanding an entirely new practice or regime where the old one might have been equally efficient. In these cases, there may be an ethical obligation to *not* innovate. Lawyers regularly exercise judgment about whether or not to adhere to precedent or to forge new paths for changing law's substance. That same sort of lawyerly calculation should apply to questions about innovation.

Not only does innovation encompass multiple meanings, but it is also challenging to discern what is truly innovative and what is not. As one commentator explains, for some, their "mind-set equates innovation exclusively with invention and implies that if you just buy the next new thing, voilà! You have innovated!"[31] As a consequence, this "fear of missing out has led us to foolishly embrace the false trappings of innovation over truly innovative ideas that may be simpler and ultimately more effective."[32]

Innovation can also vary between generations. A 2017 study by Canada's McGill University on law firm innovation is telling. While the overwhelming majority of law firm partners believed that innovation was one of the "highest strategic priorities" (89 percent), less than half of associates agreed (42 percent).[33] What partners experienced as "innovative" was just another day at the office for their younger associates.

Let's be clear on what innovation is *not* meant to be for our purposes. The kind of innovation we're talking about in this book should not be confused with a client's seeking of "innovative" advice where the concept of innovation is used as a "code for breaking the law."[34] Ideally, as we will see in chapter 11, the ethical obligations of lawyers around innovation should avoid this sort of abuse while still providing space for good faith challenges to existing law. The term "innovation" is not meant to be a marketing slogan. It is not simply whiteboards or prototypes or Post-it Notes on walls. It is not merely the latest technological advancements, such as artificial intelligence (i.e., computer technology that perform tasks typically requiring human intelligence, like the ChatGPT example from the book's preface), blockchain (i.e., a system of computers used to record transactions), or whatever comes next.

While technology can play an important role in innovation through the development of new tools, technology alone is not itself the form of innovation contemplated here. Indeed, some technology might contribute to the access-to-justice problem rather than remedy it. The debut of "eCourts," what was supposed to be an innovative, digitized judicial record system in North Carolina, is instructive. Lawyers using a pilot version "complained that eCourts is a time-sucking, error-ridden trainwreck."[35] The technology turned "once-simple processes" into a "byzantine system [that] requires multiple steps," with "disastrous" consequences for individuals caught up in North Carolina's civil and criminal courts.[36] One lawyer complained that "every day, people are sitting in jail longer than they should. [. . .] I've had clients get arrested when they shouldn't be arrested because their case has already been taken care of, and it's not showing up in the system correctly."[37] Chapter 11 delves into other ethical issues surrounding technology and innovation and potential harms. For now, keep in mind that technology can be a means to innovation, but it is not the goal. The *Tenth Annual Tech Trends Report 2019* issued by Deloitte cautioned readers not just to embrace technology but to look beyond it: "To stay ahead of the game, companies must work methodically to sense new innovations and possibilities, define their ambitions for tomorrow, and journey beyond the digital frontier."[38] Looking at innovation both *with* technology and *beyond* is the mission of this book.

A few other words and phrases warrant preliminary clarification.

(1) The terms "bar association" and "bar authority" include local, state, federal, territorial, and specialty bar associations as well as licensing authorities. Some of these entities are mandatory, meaning that in order to practice law in the jurisdiction one must be licensed by the relevant bar association. Mandatory bars also enforce lawyer discipline rules. Other bars are voluntary, where lawyers network, continue their legal education, and sometimes engage in reform. An example of a voluntary bar is the ABA, which, as noted above, is made up of nearly two hundred thousand lawyers. (At the high point of membership in the late 1970s, approximately half of the lawyers in the country were members. Now it represents just a fraction of practicing lawyers, less than fifteen percent.) Another prominent voluntary association is the National Bar Association (NBA), formed in 1925 by five African American lawyers— four men, one woman—who had been denied membership by the ABA which, at the time, limited itself to only white men. (The ABA's exclu-

sionary history is explored more fully in chapter 3.) The NBA's membership in 2023 included more than sixty-five thousand lawyers, judges, law professors, and law students.

(2) The word "court" includes federal, state, tribal, and municipal courts as well as formal proceedings that operate without a judge but function to resolve disputes, such as administrative hearing bodies and arbitration panels. The word does not necessarily imply a physical location—courts can convene in person or remotely via virtual platforms.

(3) The word "ethics" and the phrase "legal ethics" refer not to ethics in a moral or religious sense, as commonly understood, but to the set of aspirational principles and disciplinary rules deemed essential to the practice of law, namely governing duties of communication, competence, confidentiality, diligence, and loyalty, as well as fidelity to the lawyer-client relationship, the legal system, and the rule of law. Each state and territory has its own code of professional conduct proscribing the rules lawyers must follow in order to effectively represent clients and fulfill their obligations as members of a profession.

(4) The term "legal profession" encompasses bar associations, courts, lawyers, legal services organizations, and law schools. As a lawyer and a law professor, I am part of the legal profession. However, when I refer to "we," I mean both the legal profession and all of us living in the United States today.

(5) The word "professionalism" references the competence and skill necessary to be a member of a profession. For the legal profession, it means adhering to legal ethics codes and also conducting oneself with civility and integrity. Sometimes, however, claims of "professionalism" have been levied within the legal profession to compromise the very values professionalism espouses, an irony explored more in chapters 3 and 4.

(6) The phrases "legal tech" and "justice tech" appear throughout the book referencing the ways that technology has been adopted by and for the legal profession. Scholar Ryan Whalen offers a useful definition that helps unpack the complexity. He defines "legal technology" as "all devices, capable of being used as a means for interacting with the substance of law or assisting its user to interact with the law, and the skills and techniques by which we use them."[39] This is, obviously, a very wide-sweeping definition.

He then categorizes "technologies according to how directly they engage with the law and how specifically legal or general their affordances are."[40]

Three of his categories are relevant here: generic legal tech, shallow legal tech, and deep legal tech.[41] The concept of "generic legal tech" means devices with no direct connection to the legal system at all (for example, tools like computers and the internet). These require significant human intervention to be used for legal purposes. "Shallow legal tech" includes tools used to help facilitate legal research, for example, online databases used by lawyers and judges to find legal opinions. This technology aids the user but still "leaves the majority of legal work to the human practitioner."[42] "Deep legal tech" covers technologies that "engage directly and deeply with the law . . . by making legal determinations, directly or indirectly enforcing the law, or perhaps by updating the law itself."[43] Examples include tax preparation software, "so-called 'smart contracts' that are designed to monitor conditions and self-execute as the agreement dictates, or automated trademark infringement detectors that use artificial intelligence to monitor IP portfolios and make judgements as to possible infringement."[44] Whalen envisions in the not-too-distant future that this category will also include technologies "that not only incorporate the rules into their engineering and make legal determinations, but that observe conditions and update the rules accordingly."[45] As one example, he cites the possibility of "automatic speed limiting technologies" that monitor conditions and adjust local limits in real time "to help ensure safe traffic flow," which involves "not just taking rules and facts as input and giving legal interpretations as output," but also requires "updating the current rules that govern behaviour."[46]

Our focus as we move through the book is primarily on "deep legal tech" as it exists now and what it soon will become, particularly as it impacts access to justice. Which brings me to the second phrase, "justice tech." This concept has been described as "technology-enabled innovation that supports people affected by the US criminal and civil justice system and their families (and the organizations that serve them)," with emphasis on "an ethical, human-centered perspective."[47] It also refers to innovators who seek to "disrupt the justice system through technology" because of "bias baked in throughout the system, disproportionately affecting Black, Indigenous, People of Color (BIPOC), people from low-income communities, people who are a part of the LGBTQ community, and people who intersect across these communities."[48] Whether discussing legal tech or justice tech, our priority is how technology can help those in need resolve their legal problems.

A Few Words about the Criminal Justice System

While the civil justice system is the primary focus of this book, the incredibly broken criminal law process in this country cannot be ignored and is a symptom of the larger issues surrounding the access-to-justice predicament in the United States. My concentration on civil justice needs is not meant to suggest that those who find themselves facing criminal issues fare any better. The criminal justice system is even more flawed; it has been deemed "the new Jim Crow" by scholar and civil rights activist Michelle Alexander.[49] (During the Jim Crow era, between the end of the Civil War and the start of the civil rights movement in the 1960s, discrimination was widespread, with racial segregation legal in many states, especially in the South.) As she notes, "African Americans are not significantly more likely to use or sell prohibited drugs than whites, but they are made criminals at drastically higher rates for precisely the same conduct."[50] Black people, men in particular, are also more likely to be convicted of crimes even though they are innocent. The Annual Report from the National Registry of Exonerations documented that in 2021 alone, 161 reversals of convictions occurred for people found innocent, and nearly three thousand exonerations happened from 1989 to 2021. These "exonerees lost an average of 11.5 years to wrongful imprisonment for crimes they did not commit—1,849 years in total," according to the report.[51] The registry's 2017 report found that "African Americans are only 13 percent of the American population but a majority of innocent defendants wrongfully convicted of crimes and later exonerated."[52] For many, the lack of adequate civil legal help can eventually lead to criminal sanctions. Moreover, for those who reenter society following incarceration, it is even more difficult to obtain help for civil legal needs. (To learn more about criminal justice reform, a good place to start is with the Equal Justice Initiative, founded by author and public interest lawyer Bryan Stevenson.)

Why So Many Endnotes?

One last comment about the structure of this book. You've already encountered a lot of endnotes, and there will be many more along the way. These are here to provide additional information, for those who want it, about the history, data, case studies, court opinions, and other materials I've drawn on to support my analysis of the issues confronted in this book and the recommendations contained in the blueprint. You'll also find a list of resources in the bibliography and a list of advocacy groups and research centers in appendix 2 at the end of the book. These lists are meant to be a starting place, not a complete catalog, for future work.

Now, let's move on. Chapter 1 will help you better understand the unmet legal needs in the United States and why it is so urgent for us to address them.

1

Unmet Legal Needs

A 2019 nationwide survey about the ways people living in the United States experience legal problems and resolve, or fail to resolve, them revealed disturbing results.[1] The study included more than ten thousand individuals from a wide range of diverse sociodemographic groups, the first effort of this size and scope.[2] Among the troubling findings, the study concluded that:

- "Access to justice is a broad societal problem—66 percent of the population experienced at least one legal issue in the past four years, with just 49 percent of those problems having been completely resolved."[3]
- "On an annual basis, 55 million Americans experience 260 million legal problems. Of those legal problems, according to the people, 120 million legal problems are not resolved fairly every year."[4]
- "The need for fair resolution of legal problems is experienced universally across different groups of the population."[5]
- "Access to justice is a problem that is impacting people from all walks of life, with serious social, legal, economic, and political consequences."[6]

As Justin Hansford, the Executive Director of the Thurgood Marshall Civil Rights Center at Howard University, bluntly puts it, "Today in the United States, the richest country in the world, you can lose your home, your financial independence, and even your child as a result of a civil court hearing where your opponent has access to legal counsel and you do not."[7] Individuals and families aren't the only ones who struggle. Small business owners do, too. Sixty percent, according to a 2013 study, face significant legal problems without a lawyer to assist them.[8]

An even more dire situation confronts low-income households. A 2022 survey of five thousand adults, produced by the Legal Services Corporation (LSC), found that more than 90 percent of the civil legal prob-

26

lems faced by low-income individuals are not adequately addressed.[9] The LSC knows this sad reality all too well. A nonprofit organization first created and financially supported by Congress in 1974, the LSC "is the single largest funder of civil legal aid for low-income Americans in the nation."[10] We will return to the importance of the LSC's work later in this chapter.

This delivery challenge is the single greatest concern facing the legal profession in the twenty-first century. I am certainly not the first to make the claim; for example, in a 2008 essay, then-president of the California State Bar Jeff Bleich wrote: "Of the many challenges that we face as a profession, the one that should concern us most is that we now have a legal system in which the majority of Americans cannot afford adequate legal service."[11] Deborah Rhode, the nation's most cited legal ethics scholar at the time of her death in 2021, made a similar observation in 2004 about the early 1990s: "Almost two decades ago, in a prominent report on professionalism, the American Bar Association concluded that the middle class's lack of access to affordable legal services was one of the most intractable problems confronting the profession today. That problem remains."[12] Reporters for the *New York Times* labeled the United States "A Nation of Do-It-Yourself Lawyers" in 2010, finding that "[a]n increasing number of civil cases go forward without lawyers. Litigants who cannot afford a lawyer, and either do not qualify for legal aid or are unable to have a lawyer assigned to them because of dwindling budgets (all criminal defendants are entitled to legal representation, but civil defendants are not), are on their own—pro se. What's more, they're often on their own in cases involving life-altering situations like divorce, child custody and loss of shelter."[13]

The Overwhelming Need

The need for personal legal services is staggering. A 2010 study conducted by the Task Force to Expand Access to Civil Legal Services revealed that, in New York State alone, "2.3 million New Yorkers try to navigate the State's complex civil justice system without a lawyer" on matters that impact daily life needs.[14] The study found that nearly all eviction tenants were unrepresented—as were borrowers in consumer credit disputes and parents in child support cases—and close to half of homeowners were unrepresented in mortgage foreclosures.[15] The study also revealed that "nearly half of all low-income New Yorkers—47 percent—experienced one or more legal problems in the past year, and many experienced more than one legal problem."[16] At the time of the study, "low-income" was defined as having a household income at or below 200 percent of the federal poverty level, which was $44,100 for a family of four in 2010 (and $55,500 in 2023). This problem has not improved. In 2022, reeling from the impact of the COVID-19 pandemic, thousands of New Yorkers still faced eviction without legal representation.[17]

Another measure of the enormity of need is market potential. Economist and Canadian scholar Gillian Hadfield conducted an economic assessment to determine the financial value of the undeveloped market for personal legal services.[18] Assuming that half of American households have at least two legal problems that currently go unaddressed, Hadfield estimated the market potential to be between roughly $20 billion and "tens if not hundreds of billions of dollars."[19] Her estimate of need may very well be on the conservative side, given that legal needs surveys from the past twenty years found a range of 1.1 to 3.5 legal problems per household for far more than half of the households in the United States.[20] These needs include: (1) consumer issues such as collection disputes or oppressive contract terms; (2) housing matters such as utilities, repairs, and homelessness; (3) health concerns such as insurance disputes, access to mental health services, denial of emergency care, and nursing home problems; (4) employment and unemployment issues; (5) difficulties with public benefits in application or denial; (6) education concerns such as school discipline and quality; and (7) family matters such as child support, domestic violence, visitation, and custody.[21]

This unmet need can also be thought of as unrealized demand. Most individuals go without legal services unless they qualify for legal aid. The middle class has not been a primary focus of lawyers,[22] partly because regulatory restrictions on law practice make it difficult for an attorney to offer discreet, unbundled service at a low cost on a widespread basis. (The concept of "unbundled" legal service refers to hiring a lawyer to handle only one aspect of a legal matter, rather than for the complete representation—for example, ghost-writing a court brief or filing.) Traditional law firms have not found it economically feasible to market and deliver en masse representation to the general public for routine bankruptcy, child custody, divorce, housing disputes, immigration, mortgage foreclosure, standard contracts, small business needs, wills, and other basic matters.

Creating a Consumer Law Market

The consumer law market—i.e., those individuals who do not qualify for legal aid and cannot afford an attorney—has long been denied affordable, accessible, legal services. According to some estimates, the consumer law market is 80 percent or more of the American population.[23] Given the legal profession's historic inability to meet the needs of the consumer law market, one might be skeptical that meaningful legal representation will ever be uniformly available to the mass public. On the one hand, perhaps the advent of the modern computer and mobile technology coupled with the potential for artificial intelligence will allow us, finally, to harness cost-effective tools to perform tasks that previously took a human attorney many hours to complete. On the other hand, the profession previously witnessed similar technological revolutions (e.g., the typewriter at the start of the twentieth century and email at the start of the twenty-first century), and these innovations did little to alleviate the persistent consumer legal need.

What might a vibrant consumer law market look like? Consider this proposal from the 1930s:

> A group of capable young lawyers, on a salary and profit-sharing basis under mature business and legal direction, could set a precedent in specialized, low-cost, large-scale office organization. Coupled with group publicity, such an experiment would be likely to open up quickly considerable *new* business, and a method of handling it.[24]

Sounds rational, right? So why haven't we achieved something like it by now? A significant barrier to this proposal for legal services in a mass retail setting—considered a radical innovation a century ago and still now—is due to anticompetitive regulations created by lawyers themselves.

Regulatory Constraints

The market for legal services is regulated by lawyers. Each state has its own set of professional conduct rules, all based upon models promulgated by the American Bar Association. As chapter 3 explains, nearly every state prohibits a law firm from being financed by outside funding from nonlawyers, which limits financial options for lawyers to invest in technology and innovation. Other rules restrict lawyers from partnering with other professionals like accountants, physicians, or social workers; control information contained in advertisements about legal services; and prohibit lawyers from practicing law in states where they are not licensed, as well as nonlawyers from practicing without a license. These regulatory constraints reduce the free flow of information about legal help, which is a major contributor to the justice crisis. The consequences of the monopoly lawyers hold over legal services are explored in chapter 4. For now, know that calls for reform to expand legal services for the consumer law market extend back one hundred years and still regulators have done little to facilitate competition. At the same time, information in other fields has become increasingly available, more cheaply than ever before.[25] Technology is enhancing our capacity to gain understanding from vast quantities of data in a range of domains, from medicine to national security.[26] Even the legal industry itself is in the midst of what has been called "law's information revolution," a label for "the growth of new markets for law-related information and advice."[27] Nevertheless, the consumer law market lags behind other industries in access to user-friendly, customer-driven information and services.

Lack of Personal Connection

Another major barrier to accessing help is the fact that the membership of the American legal profession does not reflect the diversity of the public it serves. The ABA conducted a national lawyer population survey in 2022 which showed that 81 percent of attorneys are white, 6 percent are Hispanic, 5 percent are Black, 5 percent are Asian, 3 percent are multiracial, and less than 1 percent are Native American.[28] By contrast, the United States census taken two years prior revealed that 60.1 percent of the country consists of white individuals; 18.5 percent are Latinx, 13.4

percent are Black, 5.9 percent are Asian, and 1.1 percent are American Indian/Alaskan Native.[29] Legal ethics scholar Eli Wald's research indicates that this lack of representation not only exists with race, but also that "ethnic, socioeconomic, religious, LGBT and disabled minorities are woefully underrepresented in the profession, and women, while constituting approximately half of the national law student population and a significant and growing percentage of all American lawyers, suffer considerable inequities, especially at the profession's upper echelons."[30]

Why does the legal profession, filled with many lawyers who champion the causes for minorities and underrepresented communities, still remain so white? For many decades, the exclusion was intentional and explicit, as Veronica Root's research documents.[31] (Root was the first Black woman to become a tenured professor at Notre Dame Law School, which did not occur until in 2019.) While "exclusion of these groups no longer exists formally," she explains, "they have yet to achieve full representation within many areas of the legal profession."[32]

Representation matters because individuals are more likely to seek out professional help and, importantly, trust and follow professional advice if the relationship is with someone of the same background. Chapter 2 explores research from the fields of medicine, psychology, and criminal justice that documents this dynamic. Diversity in the profession is needed both to inspire future lawyers and judges to join it, but also to convince would-be clients that a lawyer can help them.

Lack of Proximity

Geography can also be an obstacle. Many people live in "legal deserts," which "disproportionately affect rural and especially poor people, who may have to travel hundreds of miles, or experience lengthy and expensive delays for routine legal work."[33] One example of a legal desert is North Dakota, where among its fifty-three counties in 2019, three had zero lawyers, six had only one lawyer, and seven had only two lawyers.[34] A half dozen rural counties in Georgia "have *no resident attorneys*, and eighteen have only one or two."[35]

Online justice tools are not necessarily a solution to the geographic desert, especially for those without access to reliable high-speed broadband or internet access, or to a computer or mobile device. A 2020 report showed that 42 million adults living in the United States lacked reliable broadband service.[36] And disparities in use fall harshly along predictable lines. Data from the National Telecommunications and Information Administration found that just "54 percent of Americans with a disability used a PC or tablet in 2021, compared with 70 percent of those not reporting a disability. Moreover, while 71 percent of white non-Hispanics used a PC or tablet, only 57 percent of African Americans and 54 percent of Hispanics did so."[37]

That said, a 2022 study conducted in England and Wales "showed that the public is generally willing to use technology that is well-established and familiar to them such as video consultations (66%), and e-signatures (68%). There is less willingness to use unfamiliar forms of technology, like smart contracts (45%) and AI-driven tools like chatbots (39%)."[38] Thus, tech-based delivery methods hold promise, provided that they are accessible and that users become familiarized with them.

Time and Expense

Assuming someone actually finds the help they need to resolve a problem through the judicial system, a just result is often illusive. Even in the most advanced court systems, "dispute resolution in public courts generally takes too long, costs too much, and the process is unintelligible to all but lawyers."[39] The harm of delay cannot be overstated, especially for individuals facing imminent life needs like custody, housing, immigration, and similar issues. These costs and delays mean "that many people cannot afford to bring good claims to court and others are forced to settle bad ones," United States Supreme Court justice Neil Gorsuch wrote in his 2020 book, *A Republic, If You Can Keep It.*[40]

Even though cost is not the primary barrier to legal services, which we know from the Sandefur study discussed in the introduction, an understanding of how lawyers typically get paid helps explain why traditional law firms have not proven effective in resolving the justice crisis. During the nineteenth century, legal fees took the form of annual retainers, flat fees for specific tasks, and other discretionary methods determined between the lawyer and the client. The ABA authorized contingency fees in 1908, which allow an attorney to take on a representation with no payment up front but with a cut of any financial award, typically one-third of the amount the client receives. During the first half of the twentieth century, state bar associations established minimum fee schedules setting the price for certain services. The schedules were widely followed by lawyers, especially because failure to do so could result in discipline.

Billable hours—the dominant method for lawyer compensation today—are a product of recent history. The billable hour model first took hold in the 1960s, when "management experts concluded from various studies that lawyers who kept time records earned more than attorneys who did not."[41] The ABA produced a report in 1958 finding "that attorneys' earnings had failed to keep pace with the rate of inflation; the report urged attorneys to record the hours spent on each case in order to ensure that fees ultimately charged afforded reasonable compensation for counsels' efforts."[42] But it did not become prevalent until after the United States Supreme Court held that the minimum fee schedules kept prices artificially high and thus violated antitrust law, a case we will return to in chapter 6.

Hourly billing breeds a host of harms. It is well-established, according to law professor William Ross, that billing based on the time spent on a task "creates serious abuses and raises difficult ethical questions."[43] Potential abuses include double-billing, inflation of the amount of time worked or "padding" the bill, and the performance of unnecessary work, known as "churning." As reported in The Atlantic in 2015, "Law students are warned about it. Attorneys have called for its death and likened living under its regime to a 'living hell.'"[44] Recognizing these concerns, the ABA issued an opinion in the early 1990s to make clear that double-billing, padding, and churning are unethical.[45] As former judge for the United States Court of Appeals for the Fifth Circuit, Thomas Reavley wrote, "An attorney may resort to sharp tactics to increase billable hours as the resulting delays and additional activity—repeated requests, motions, protracted depositions and trials—mean more hours of attorney time."[46] A 2002 report from the ABA Commission on Billable Hours concluded that "the billable hour is also responsible for decreased lawyer efficiency; elimination of law firm risk-taking; decreased client communications; [and] creation of potential conflicts of interest (over fees) between the parties."[47] Numerous commentators document the toll that the billable hour takes on the well-being of lawyers, described by one as "killing our mental health."[48] A 2015 study found a correlation between increased billable hours and a decrease in wellness among lawyers: those with higher billing requirements reported less satisfaction and higher rates of alcohol and substance abuse.[49]

In addition to the numerous, well-documented problems with hourly billing, the model stifles alternatives that might make legal services more affordable. Lawyer Kenneth Grady puts it like this: "There's a lot of demand [for legal help] and a lot of supply [of lawyers], but we're not able to connect the two because of this cost structure we've built."[50]

Some services simply may not be feasible with hourly billing. For example, individuals who have their criminal records cleared are "63% more likely to get a job interview and their wages increase by 22% after their expungement."[51] But it costs $2,000-$3,000 to hire a lawyer to handle a single expungement, a cost prohibitive option for many. That changed for Utah residents when lawyer Noella Sudbury launched Rasa Legal in 2022. She partnered with specialists (who are not lawyers) and developed an app to provide an affordable alternative. Their service charges "a flat fee of $500" to remove up to three expungements.[52] But, she could do so only because of unique regulatory reforms in her home state. We will explore Utah's "regulatory sandbox" in chapter 8, but for now note that the billable hour model does not facilitate innovations like this. (Sudbury, by the way, was honored by *Inc. Magazine* on its annual Female Founders list in 2023.[53] She hopes to expand Rasa Legal to other states.)

The billable hour is not the sole cause of the justice crisis, to be sure, but it contributes to it significantly. It keeps fees artificially high and causes stress, thus reducing the capacity of and motivation for lawyers to fill the justice gap.

The Past and Present Efforts of Government Aid and Private Pro Bono

The two greatest forces devoted to reducing the civil justice gap in the past fifty years have been federal government investment and pro bono work—-i.e., free legal services—by large law firms. Lawyers are encouraged, but not required, by professional conduct rules to provide a minimum of fifty hours of free legal help per year to those in need, what they call "pro bono" work.

Back in 1965, Congress first appropriated $5 million for legal aid and by 1980 increased the amount to $300 million. The Legal Services Corporation Act of 1974, which established the LSC, expanded federal legal help from major urban centers to nearly every county in the nation. The LSC funds 132 legal aid providers annually who operate independently in more than eight hundred offices.[54] Their work is targeted to serve those most in need. The entities receiving LSC funds provide legal help to households with annual incomes at or below 125 percent of the federal poverty guidelines, which amounted to $16,988 for an individual and $34,688 for a family of four in 2023. These individuals, according to the LSC, "come from every ethnic group and every age group and live in rural, suburban, and urban areas. They are the working poor, veterans, homeowners and renters, families with children, farmers, people with disabilities, and the elderly."[55] The greatest number of clients—70 percent—are women, "many of whom are struggling to keep their children safe and their families together."[56] Assistance includes clinics to address legal needs, legal advice and self-help materials, and referrals to other community services.

Nearly two million people received LSC-funded help during 2019, but this represents a small fraction of those who actually need legal assistance each year.[57] Lack of sufficient funding is a perennial problem. In 2022, the LSC requested $600 million from Congress, but received only $489 million. As a point of comparison, that $300 million Congress appropriated in 1980? Adjusted for inflation, it would be worth more than $900 million in 2022.[58] The LSC is operating at half the funding of 1980 while legal needs have increased, not decreased.

While federal funding hasn't even kept pace with inflation, let alone actual human needs, the number of pro bono hours offering free legal help from attorneys in large law firms has increased steadily since 1998.[59] For example, law professor Tinu Adediran's research revealed that in "2017, 129 of the Am Law 200 firms reported a total of 4.99 million pro bono hours."[60] ("Am Law 200" refers to the top two hundred law firms ranked by gross revenue in the United States.) As a point of comparison to LSC funding, she found that in 2005, when "the LSC provided approximately $331 million to its grantees . . . the value of pro bono work was estimated to be $624 million, about double the amount of money that Congress appropriated for civil legal services."[61]

Despite this substantial investment from lawyers donating their time for free, relying on pro bono efforts will never be enough to satisfy needs. Supreme Court of California justice Goodwin Liu calculated that, "[e]ven if we asked every lawyer in America to do 100 more hours of pro bono work a year, all of that additional work would be enough to secure only 30 minutes per problem per household in America."[62] And the studies show households with multiple problems, many of which likely require thirty hours if not more to resolve, and certainly far greater than thirty minutes.

Beyond government funding and pro bono, the other major push for civil legal assistance has been what some call the "civil Gideon." In *Gideon v. Wainwright*, decided in 1963, the United States Supreme Court held that individuals charged with serious crimes have a constitutional right to legal representation, whether or not they can afford a lawyer.[63] Many civil matters have consequences as dire as criminal charges—for example, deportation to a country where one's life is in danger or the loss of parental rights—yet there is no corresponding right to a lawyer. Some state and local governments have intervened to provide representation where outcomes can be life altering, including eviction matters and child custody disputes. As one example, New York City created a civil right to counsel for low-income tenants facing eviction in 2017, followed quickly by Cleveland, Newark, Philadelphia, San Francisco, and Santa Monica in 2018. The states of Connecticut, Maryland, and Washington joined in 2021. The National Coalition for a Right to Civil Counsel works on a state and local level to pursue right-to-counsel statutes in a host of areas. But few jurisdictions offer this protection, even in the worst situations. The bottom line is that despite well-intentioned efforts like government funding for legal aid, lawyer pro bono work, and ad hoc self-help legal tools, many people who need legal help still do not receive it. These efforts scratch the surface of the problem, but they are not sufficient to solve it.

Where Are the Lawyers?

The pervasive need for legal services is not because lawyers are unavailable. Law school applications were on the rise during the Trump presidency from 2016 to 2020[64] and continued to remain relatively strong in the years that followed. Regardless of the ebb and flow in law school enrollment numbers through economic cycles, the lack of legal help is not because of too few lawyers. The problem lies in information and market sustainability. First, those attempting to provide low-cost legal services on a mass scale struggle to build an economically viable business model. Second, legal education's priority has always been preparing for entry into mid- and large-sized law practice, and, even with more of an emphasis these days on clinical training in legal aid settings, the curriculum largely ignores service to the consumer law market, including business skills for setting up a sustainable practice. Third, the public lacks sufficient knowledge about the legal system and may be deterred by high costs, which remain because the existing regulatory structure defining *who* may engage in the practice of law and *how* they may practice suppresses competition and maintains artificially high rates for legal help. Finally, diversity and geography play a role.

The Promise of Technology

During the first two decades of the twenty-first century, technology democratized the bulk of retail services such as banking, insurance, and travel in ways in which law remains comparatively untouched. For example, Walmart now offers financial services, targeting the estimated sixty-three million[65] Americans who do not have bank accounts (or rarely use one). In 2011, the chain had "opened roughly 1,500 Money-Centers that process as many as 5 million transactions each week."[66] Likewise, Costco offers home mortgages and insurance alongside bulk groceries and other provisions.[67] Retailers like Target have democratized high-end fashion and architecture.[68] Home businesses and artisans similarly have benefited from technology's market creation capacity. For example, since its founding in 2005, "Etsy, an online marketplace for small businesses and craftspeople . . . has more than 875,000 active online shops that together sell upward of $400 million of goods each year."[69] Adoption of technology for travel planning has been overwhelming. In 2013 alone, Orbitz.com "facilitated 1.5 million flight searches and 1 million hotel searches every day."[70] A decade later in 2023, entire vacations or work trips can be booked, canceled, and rebooked all from a mobile device, which can also unlock the hotel room door for travelers after delivering them by an Uber or Lyft. Body recognition technology eliminates the need for identification; indeed, the CLEAR company speeds travelers through an eye or fingerprint scan past federal transportation security agents without any need for a driver's license or passport.

Technology offers the same potential for legal services, though, importantly, the technology must be accompanied by human empathy and expertise. In an increasingly digital and data-driven world, human interaction remains crucial to law, though the role of the lawyer has and will continue to evolve. Also, to create a viable, scalable marketplace for the provision of low-cost, routine legal services for the middle class, there must be a cultural shift toward regular use of a lawyer for life's legal problems and room for nonlawyers to provide legal help. We will explore these themes and the emerging field of justice tech more fully in part II.

* * *

No matter how affordable legal help may be through government funding, pro bono services, or technology advances, if the public does not understand how to recognize their legal problems or find the existing tools, we will never altogether alleviate the justice crisis.

In the late 1970s, the United States Supreme Court decided that expansive lawyer advertising would be an effective solution to help educate individuals about how to resolve their legal needs. We'll explore that case and its impact in chapter 2.

2

(Not) Finding Legal Help

A Case Study

Lawyer advertising—what's the first thought that comes to mind? Likely it is the late-night television commercial for a failed medical device, a natural disaster, or a mass accident like a toxic oil spill. Images of sledgehammers, swiveling gavels, flames, and even aliens appear with a voiceover asking: "Have you or someone you know been injured? If so, call now!"[1] Selling lawyers is a big business, projected to be worth a billion dollars if not more.[2]

When individuals actually need to find an attorney, however, they rely not on television commercials but on web searches. According to several studies, an internet search is the primary route to finding legal representation, even over asking family or friends for a recommendation.[3] For most consumers of legal services, a website profile often will be the first encounter with the attorney they hire (or decline to hire).

Given the proliferation of lawyer ads, it may be surprising to learn that for much of the twentieth century, lawyer advertising was completely banned by professional conduct rules.[4] The most a lawyer could do was communicate via family, friends, or existing clients about their services and list a phone number in a directory.[5] Anything more was considered unprofessional, unethical, and illegal. However, lawyer advertising was not always prohibited. Abraham Lincoln, for example, famously posted information about his services in Illinois newspapers during the 1830s.[6] The ban coincided with the creation by the American Bar Association (ABA) of its first official set of professional conduct rules, the 1908 Canons of Professional Ethics. (Additional coverage on that history is found in chapter 3.) Suffice to say, the squelching of ads had more to do with fear of competition from an increasing number of lawyers than any harm that might come to individuals or the public as a whole.

Bates v. Arizona State Bar

In 1977, the United States Supreme Court ended the nearly seventy-year-old prohibition on lawyer advertising in a case called *Bates v. Arizona State Bar*.[7] The court struck down the ban, finding that it violated the First Amendment.[8] Chief among the court's justifications was a concern about "the right of the public as consumers and citizens to know about the activities of the legal profession."[9] A majority of justices believed that advertising could address market inefficiencies caused by the lack of information about legal services and remedy the unmet need for legal help.[10]

Advertising restrictions vary throughout the country. Although no jurisdiction bans lawyer advertising completely, many place significant restrictions on the content and the timing. At one end of the spectrum, some states merely prohibit false or misleading advertising.[11] At the other end, some impose heavy burdens, such as mandatory disclaimers, waiting periods, and preapproval of advertising content by the regulatory authority.[12] The wide variance in requirements becomes especially challenging for lawyers practicing in multiple locations across the country.[13] According to law professor and author of the definitive treatise *Modern Legal Ethics* Charles Wolfram, the constraints contribute to the justice crisis because "restriction on advertising and solicitation have reduced competition and the development of new markets for legal services."[14]

Even with burdensome restrictions, advertising plays a significant role in the legal services markets. Trial lawyers alone spent $1.4 billion on advertising in 2021.[15] While much of this goes to television commercials, lawyers increasingly invest in internet advertising, such as individual websites, pop-up ads, and search engine optimization. Take the national personal injury firm Sokolove Law as one example. The firm "spends about $30 to $40 million per year on advertising . . . 45 percent on TV, 45 percent on internet, and 10 percent on other outlets such as social media or print."[16]

Internet searches and websites with pop-up ads and live chat features surely are not what the United States Supreme Court had in mind when it struck down the nationwide ban on lawyer advertising in *Bates*. Instead, the court envisioned straightforward, easy-to-understand print ads like that published by newly licensed attorneys John Bates and Van O'Steen in 1976.

Bates and O'Steen established a legal aid clinic targeting the "consumer law market." Recall from chapter 1 that this label covers those who do not qualify for legal aid but cannot afford a lawyer at three figures (or more) per hour for multiple hours. In short, they aimed to fill the justice gap that still persists today.

They placed a simple newspaper advertisement listing the cost of basic legal services, including uncontested divorce, adoption, personal bankruptcy, and name change. The opening text read: "Do you need a lawyer? Legal services at very reasonable fees."[17] The only graphic in the black and white ad was a scale of justice, and it directed potential clients to the address of the Legal Clinic of Bates and O'Steen. The ad was clear, simple, and easy for all to understand.

The Arizona State Bar disciplined them, finding that all advertising undermined professionalism and might cause clients to have unjustified expectations or to sue when they otherwise would not do so, stirring up unnecessary litigation.[18] But the Supreme Court sided with Bates and O'Steen. The court criticized the advertising ban as a failure by the bar to engage with the community. Justice Harry Blackmun, authoring the five-to-four majority opinion, wrote:

> Although advertising might increase the use of the judicial machinery, we cannot accept the notion that it is always better for a person to suffer a wrong silently than to redress it by legal action. As the bar acknowledges, the middle 70 percent of our population is not being reached or served adequately by the legal profession. Among the reasons for this under-utilization is fear of the cost, and an inability to locate a suitable lawyer. Advertising can help to solve this acknowledged problem: Advertising is the traditional mechanism in a free-market economy for a supplier to inform a potential purchaser of the availability and terms of exchange. The disciplinary rule at issue likely has served to burden access to legal services, particularly for the not-quite-poor and the unknowledgeable. A rule allowing restrained advertising would be in accord with the bar's obligation to facilitate the process of intelligent selection of lawyers, and to assist in making legal services fully available.[19]

The court grounded its holding in *Bates*, at least in part, on a hypothesis that advertising would expand access to legal services for the majority of the American public who could not afford an attorney or lacked information about legal rights and entitlements. In analyzing the market impact, the court observed that advertising bans make it difficult, if not impossible, for consumers to find "the lowest cost seller of acceptable ability."[20]

Protecting attorneys from competition, according to the court, decreases their motivation to price services at competitive, or affordable, levels. By contrast, in fields where prices appear clearly in advertising, the costs "often are dramatically lower than they would be without advertising."[21] The court specifically recognized a First Amendment right for the public "as consumers and citizens" to be informed about legal services, including their costs.[22] This is somewhat unusual. Most First Amendment cases focus on the right of the speaker, not the listener.

But nearly a half century later, the *Bates* court's promise has gone unrealized, and individuals still regularly face legal problems without help as we know from the data in chapter 1.[23] Lack of information is the primary reason, followed by cost[24]—the very concerns the Supreme Court aimed to address in *Bates*. Even after decades of advertising, more, not less, of the American public now goes without legal help.

Advertising should have closed the justice gap by increasing access to information about lawyers *and* by driving down legal costs; so why didn't it? Was the Supreme Court's market analysis about the impact of lawyer advertising flawed?

Some argue for a return to the ban because some lawyer advertising is deemed tacky or unprofessional. For example, in the aftermath of *Bates*, when those notorious commercials began to dominate late-night television, Justice Sandra Day O'Connor declared that the Supreme Court should have gone the other way and upheld the ban.[25] Her concern, however, was grounded in notions of professionalism—that lawyer advertising was unseemly—rather than in an economic market analysis about the benefits of increased information.

Others who support the *Bates* decision contend the potential positive impact was never fully realized due to the complexity of restrictions that endure on lawyer advertising by state regulatory authorities, which in effect compromise the market for legal services much in the same way as a wholesale ban. In other words, it may be that we have yet to see the full impact of advertising as contemplated by *Bates* because lawyers are highly restricted in the content and timing of the information they share. If lawyers were subject to fewer restrictions, advertising might be more robust, and the public would have greater knowledge about legal options.

A Case Study

To better understand how individuals find (or don't find) the legal help they need, I conducted an empirical study with a colleague of mine at the University of Houston in 2018. We examined website advertising by lawyers who defend people charged with the crime of driving while intoxicated (DWI) and by lawyers who sue defendants for causing injuries in car accidents. We included attorneys in Austin, Texas; Buffalo, New York; and Jacksonville, Florida. We chose these cities because they had similar numbers of each type of attorney, had similar populations, and were in states with distinct lawyer advertising rules.[26]

We chose to study DWI and car accident attorneys because people seeking these types of representation are unlikely to be repeat players who already have established relationships with law firms. These are folks who likely need advertising to direct them to suitable lawyers.[27] Also, both types of clients include groups who, statistically, have lower incomes.[28] The internet is the primary way people search for these types legal help. A 2021 study found that 78.2 percent of lawyers use websites in marketing.[29] More than seventy thousand searches a month on Google are for criminal law-related issues.[30] In 2021, "DUI" was one of the top five most expensive keywords you could purchase on Bing, at $69.56, and "lawyer" was the most expensive, at $109.21—the cost per click.[31] In fact, all of the top five keywords involved law, with "attorney" at number two, followed by "structured settlements" at number three, and "mesothelioma" at number five after "DUI." Legal keywords also dominate Google's search term purchases, ranking as the top ten most expensive terms in 2021.[32] The costliest? "Offshore accident lawyer," coming in at a per-click price of $815.[33] Investment in these keyword search terms matters because it allows the buyer to influence how their advertising appears in internet searches, pushing their websites to the top. For our study, we coded sixty variables for 1,064 websites and more than five hundred attorneys.

Our study had several limitations. First, we only examined lawyers in specific cities, so we cannot claim that these cities are representative of lawyers nationally or even in the states where the cities are located. Second, we examined only two practice areas—DWI and car accidents—so we cannot claim that these areas are representative of all specializations. Third, we limited our review of websites to only the first page, with the exception of searching the entire website for cost of legal services. Thus, some attributes may be advertised but not counted if one is required to click through two or more pages to locate the information.

Those caveats aside, our study unveiled significant findings about why the Supreme Court's intentions in *Bates* did not pan out as anticipated.

What Do Lawyers Advertise?

Professionalism clearly dominated lawyers' overall advertising, with 70.04 percent of the websites favoring this theme. When attorneys and/or clients were pictured on the websites, 93.38 percent of them were dressed in professional clothing as opposed to casual clothing. The public is, of course, conditioned to expect professionalism from lawyers, or at least the appearance of it as communicated through suits, ties, brief cases, and other professional attire.

Lawyers also frequently mention previous successes. Nearly half of the websites highlighted the past victories that lawyers or firms had achieved. For instance, one website promoted a DWI win:

> Head-on Collision with .20 blood test—NOT GUILTY. After causing a serious, head-on collision and failing field sobriety tests, APD's DWI Enforcement Team procured a search warrant to draw our client's blood. His blood alcohol came back at over .20. We took this case to jury trial, and our client was found NOT GUILTY.[34]

Personal injury attorneys similarly pointed to past victories as evidence that they could obtain positive outcomes for potential clients.

Despite mentioning victories frequently, these websites often did not have the mandatory disclaimers required in some jurisdictions regarding prior successes.[35] Disclaimers are used to counteract unjustified expectations. Some websites did post disclaimers, such as, "All cases are unique and there are no express or implied guarantees as to the results or outcome of any future cases." But websites with disclaimers were rare. Of the 356 websites that discussed past successes, only 19.94 percent had any disclaimers about the meaning of that information. Even on some of these websites with a disclaimer, other language undermined the disclaimer's effectiveness. One website said:

> Although past results do not predict future outcomes, they do reflect the experience the firm has had handling significant cases. A law firm's record of results should be seriously considered when you are researching a personal injury law firm. The experienced attorneys at [this firm] have proven themselves, time and again.[36]

While this website does include a disclaimer, it downplays its own significance thus reducing its effectiveness. A rational consumer, presumably, would want to know information about both the successes *and* the failures of their lawyer. A rational consumer would want to consider this in the context of the specific facts surrounding their own unique situation, not the lawyer's self-selected highlights of successes.

Many websites also contained client testimonials about the lawyer's services. Of the websites, 43.83 percent contained reviews by prior clients. Consumer reviews of professionals are becoming more and more common, and these reviews are influential to potential consumers.[37] They drive purchases on websites like Amazon or TripAdvisor and restaurant reservations on mobile apps like OpenTable or Resy. In our study, every single testimonial on a firm's website was positive, stating things like the attorney "was amazing, professional and really knew what he was doing," "was up to date with the latest procedures," and was "professional" and exhibited "personal understanding." A rational consumer, however, would not be interested only in a limited number of positive reviews but would want to see the full gamut of good and bad.

One advertising attribute explored in our study was remarkable because of its absence: the price of services. Typically, cost is one of the most, if not the most, important factors a consumer considers when making a purchase,[38] so the dearth of exact prices on websites is rather striking. Prior empirical work also confirms that lawyers regularly fail to advertise prices.[39] In our study, fewer than 20 percent of websites and profiles presented price information. This is not surprising, perhaps, because lawyers do not want to scare would-be clients with high fees and costs. But this information is what people want.

Notably, lawyers tried to shroud the high costs of legal services in other attributes. For example, lawyers framed the transaction in terms of a variety of things, including honesty, reputation, and religion. Lawyers even discussed the facts that they are excellent boxers, that they make their own wine, that they like playing pinball, and that they brew their own beer. In light of the fact that some charge hundreds of dollars more an hour than others, it is hard to explain why a rational consumer would rather know information about home-brewing habits than price.

Not only do lawyers fail to advertise information that rational consumers would want to know, but they also make it difficult for those who need help to seek it, as we'll explore below.

Do Lawyers' Advertisements Effectively Target Those in Need of Legal Help? Images and Readability

Central to the holding of *Bates* was a promise for expanded access to legal help for disadvantaged groups. The Supreme Court was especially concerned about underrepresented constituencies, including the not-quite-poor and marginalized communities.[40] For our study, we evaluated three factors to determine whether lawyers' advertisements encourage these people to seek legal help: the race and gender of individuals pictured on the website as well as the readability of the text.

A significant body of scholarship examines issues related to the pipeline for who becomes a lawyer or advances within the profession, and numerous initiatives are devoted to this effort.[41] Fewer studies examine the race and ethnicity of individuals represented by an attorney. One of the rare studies to take this on documents that African Americans, Asian Americans, and Hispanics are significantly more likely to be underrepresented in legal matters than white people.[42]

To assess whether the legal profession is making an effort to reach disadvantaged groups, we evaluated the photographs that appear on the home pages of attorneys' websites. Of the 716 home pages in our study that displayed pictures of attorneys or clients, 79.61 percent had pictures of exclusively white attorneys and clients, and 77.09 percent only had pictures of men. Lawyers apparently pay minimal attention, if any, to the images they select for their advertising.[43] This seems like a mistake, since these images could be the only view some people have of lawyers besides the fictional ones portrayed on television shows or in the movies.

We suspect from research about the patient-physician relationship that individuals are more likely to utilize legal services if they "see themselves as similar to their [lawyers] in personal beliefs, values, and communication."[44] One critical aspect of this is race/ethnicity or gender concordance. In medical literature, studies show "that minority patients in race/ethnic concordant [patient-provider] relationships are more likely to use needed health services, are less likely to postpone or delay seeking care, and report a higher volume of use of health services."[45] Similarly, "[p]atients in race concordant patient-provider relationships also report greater satisfaction and better patient-provider communication."[46] We can expect a similar dynamic to exist between lawyers and clients.

In addition to these patient-physician studies, social psychologists have found that advertising is most effective when potential clients observe people "like them" enjoying the product or service.[47] People determine how they should act by seeing how others in their social group act.[48] If individuals do not observe anyone in their social group behaving a specific way, unconsciously, the principle of social proof may lead them away from that behavior.[49]

Similarly, in the criminal law context, law professor and former public defender Kenneth Troccoli notes in his essay *I Want a Black Lawyer to Represent Me* that when "the appointed lawyer is of a different race than the defendant, the latter may worry that the lawyer will be unable to understand or fully appreciate his circumstances."[50] Concerns like this, according to Troccoli, "seriously impede the building of trust between the attorney and the client."[51] While other factors beyond race or gender likely impact the relationship between a client and a lawyer, the lack of trust seems to be a very important aspect shaping whether an individual receives legal representation. That the overwhelming number of websites in our study feature only white men means women and people of color are likely dissuaded from seeking help.

As a final measure of whether lawyer advertising increases access for disadvantaged and minoritized groups, we assessed the readability of the websites. We took the first two hundred words on a webpage or profile and inputted them into an online tool that calculates a readability score. The tool uses word length and sentence length to predict how readable a passage is. Overall, the mean readability was 10.97, meaning that someone reading at around an eleventh-grade level should be able to read the website. Given that 54 percent of adults ages sixteen to seventy-four years old—approximately 130 million individuals—cannot read a book written at a sixth-grade level,[52] lawyer advertising likely is not intelligible for many of the individuals intended by the *Bates* court. The advertisements are written in a way that only other lawyers would understand, which does not make sense if the goal is, in fact, to attract clients and educate the public. Although beyond the scope of our study, another concern is whether these websites would be accessible to individuals who use screen readers due to vision impairments. State bar representatives who regulate lawyer advertising complain that lawyers' websites are aimed at law firms, not potential clients,[53] and our results confirm that is, in fact, the case.

* * *

This case study analysis of lawyer website advertising is just one example of the incredible knowledge gap about legal help and the justice system. The Supreme Court's decision in *Bates* provides a glaring illustration of how a well-intentioned effort to expand access to information about legal services may fall short on its promise. Chapter 10 makes the case for more public education about the law and legal services. But before turning to how we increase understanding through education, it is important to recognize other ways that the regulation of lawyers restricts information about the law for the public. Chapter 3 provides a brief history of lawyer regulation.

3

A Brief History of Lawyer Regulation

The American Bar Association (ABA) issued its inaugural formal statement of professional conduct standards, the Canons of Professional Ethics, in 1908, three decades after the organization's founding. The Canons were mostly aspirational but also clearly established lawyers' obligations not only to the client but also to courts and to the public. At the time of the Canons' adoption, only white men could be members of the ABA. The organization permitted the first woman to join in 1918 but excluded African Americans until 1943. Indeed, after "accidentally" admitting three African American men in 1912, the ABA "rescinded their admission, stating that 'the settled practice of the Association has been to elect only white men to membership.'"[1] The early legal ethics codes created by the ABA and state bar associations, explains lawyer and activist Adjoa Artis Aiyetoro, purported to protect the public but functioned to exclude diverse would-be attorneys:

> The rules adopted to ensure some minimal level of competency usually entailed a period of apprenticeship between a Bar member and an aspiring attorney. However, these seemingly neutral apprenticeship requirements had the practical effect of ensuring that few, if any, African descendants [or women] were admitted to practice law.[2]

This means that not only were minorities and women absent among the ranks of practicing lawyers, but they also had no seat at the table in crafting the foundational ethics and professional conduct standards that govern the practice of law still today.

The Model Code of Professional Responsibility

Over the years, the Canons evolved into a set of disciplinary rules and aspirational statements, culminating in the Model Code of Professional

Responsibility (Model Code), which was adopted by the ABA House of Delegates in 1969. The House of Delegates is the legislative, or policy-making, body of the ABA made up of more than five hundred representatives, all lawyers. While not a regulator itself, the ABA House of Delegates promulgates the model rules that serve as templates for all American jurisdictions. (These rules are tested on the Multistate Professional Responsibility Exam, which law school graduates must pass everywhere except Wisconsin and Puerto Rico before they may be licensed as attorneys.)

The Special Committee on Evaluation of Professional Responsibility, a group of one dozen white men, authored the Model Code.[3] No women or minorities participated on the ABA drafting committee, though Sarah Weddington served as an assistant, and her work through the American Bar Foundation "supplied the basic research for an initial draft."[4] Weddington is perhaps best known for representing the plaintiff Jane Roe in the 1973 landmark abortion rights case *Roe v. Wade*, overturned by the United States Supreme Court in 2022. The names of only three women appear on the list of hundreds of lawyers who served in the House of Delegates at the time.[5]

Diversity remained low among the ABA's priorities for many years. As another example, in the early 1970s, an ABA committee responsible for recommending United States Supreme Court justices sabotaged the chance for California judge Mildred Lillie to be the nation's first female member of the highest court. They ranked her as "unqualified" even though President Richard Nixon's White House counsel John Dean later acknowledged that Lillie's qualifications were as strong, if not stronger, than those of Sandra Day O'Connor, the first female to join the Supreme Court in 1981.

Slowly, however, the ABA began to focus on diversity, equity, and inclusion. In 1986, Dennis Archer, a former justice of the Michigan Supreme Court, became chair of a new Commission on Opportunities for Minorities in the Profession, now part of the ABA Center for Diversity and Inclusion. The following year, the ABA established the Commission on Women, chaired by Hillary Clinton. It still took a decade, however, for the ABA to place a woman at the helm, making Roberta Cooper Ramo the first female president in 1995. Nearly two decades passed before the ABA elected Archer president in 2003, making him the first African American to hold the office. Paulette Brown became the first female, African American president in 2015. The ABA elected its first Native American president, Mary L. Smith, in 2023.

The Model Rules of Professional Conduct

The Special Commission on Evaluation of Professional Standards, also known as the Kutak Commission (named after its chairman Robert Kutak), took on the next phase of updating the ABA's ethics code. Launched in 1977, the Commission engaged in a six-year study ultimately resulting in the Model Rules of Professional Conduct (Model Rules), adopted by the ABA House of Delegates in 1983. Most states in turn adopted the Model Rules nearly verbatim, and all states include broad-sweeping duties to clients and the legal system among their professional obligations for lawyers. State courts and bar licensing authorities (made up of judges and lawyers) are the dominant rule-makers, which makes the profession largely self-policing. California is an exception, though the legislature-made rules are similar to those drafted by the ABA.[6] Failure to comply can result in reprimand, fines, or even losing one's law license entirely.

The American legal profession is exceptional in the degree to which it enjoys self-governance. The preamble to the Model Rules offers this explanation:

> The legal profession is largely self-governing. Although other professions also have been granted powers of self-government, the legal profession is unique in this respect because of the close relationship between the profession and the processes of government and law enforcement. This connection is manifested in the fact that ultimate authority over the legal profession is vested largely in the courts.[7]

Importantly, under this regime, only lawyers—those satisfying the mandatory education and licensing requirements—may engage in the practice of law. These rules establish requirements for maintaining one's license to practice law and typically are supplemented by a state statute that separately prohibits practicing law without a valid license.

The ABA Model Rules are rooted in values of professionalism and independence, covering licensing, conduct obligations, and discipline. They define lawyers' obligations to clients, courts, third parties, the profession, and the public. For example, the Model Rules require that an attorney "provide competent representation,"[8] "exercise independent professional judgment,"[9] "explain a matter to the extent reasonably necessary to permit the client to make informed decisions regarding the representation,"[10] and "render candid advice."[11] Lawyers must keep client information confidential[12] and act with diligence.[13] The Model Rules also encompass protections from conflicts of interest and interference with professional judgment.

Beyond clients, the Model Rules place significant duties on lawyers to avoid misleading third parties and to respect the court, including prohibitions on making frivolous arguments or facilitating client perjury. Other aspirational goals include the provision of pro bono assistance and an obligation to avoid discrimination and harassment.

That rules exist on paper, however, does not mean they are imposed in practice. Law professor Ben Barton's research shows that ethics codes are vague and are "notoriously under-enforced."[14] Bar authorities also struggle with politicization, a persistent lack of resources, and agency capture (discussed in depth in chapter 4), further contributing to the underenforcement of ethics codes.[15] According to one study: "Only about five percent of all complaints result in any sanctions against lawyers," and "the sanctions imposed on lawyers are often light and inconsistent."[16] Other data revealed that more than "90 percent of complaints are dismissed, only about 2 percent result in public sanctions, and many complainants never even learn the basis of the dismissal, let alone receive an opportunity to challenge it."[17] Another study found that the most frequently unenforced rules are "those requiring lawyers to report misconduct by other lawyers."[18] Other rules regularly ignored "include prohibitions against unauthorized practice by lawyers advising clients in states other than their licensing jurisdiction, rules prohibiting lawyers to pay for the costs and expenses of litigation (particularly class action litigation), rules requiring lawyers to expedite litigation, and rules prohibiting statements to the press during litigation," as well as "prohibitions against collecting unreasonable fees, misleading unrepresented third persons, and failing to provide adequate supervision for subordinates."[19]

Modernizing the Model Rules—Two Recent Amendments

While the basic framework of the Model Rules has not changed dramatically since their adoption in 1983, the ABA House of Delegates made some significant amendments over the years to modernize professional conduct requirements and expectations.

Technology Competence

In 2012, the House of Delegates amended Comment 8 to Model Rule 1.1, which governs the lawyer's duty of competence, to include the following recommendation: "To maintain the requisite knowledge and skill, a lawyer should keep abreast of *changes* in the law and its practice, including the *benefits* and *risks* associated with relevant technology. . . ."[20] (A "comment," unlike the rule itself, offers guidance but does not carry the same authoritative weight.) As of early 2022, forty American jurisdictions had adopted a similarly worded provision or had adopted the revised Comment 8 language verbatim.[21]

It is worth noting that most states have been relatively conservative in processing disciplinary actions based on the Comment 8–type language, limiting it only to computer-related technology. The wide breadth of this comment, and its status as a comment versus a rule, has caught some attorneys unaware. But for courts and disciplinary authorities, the lack of detail is not a sufficient defense. "In this technological age, the days of claiming 'the dog ate my homework' are well over,"[22] as one federal district court put it. Despite the widespread revisions of professional conduct rules to mirror the Comment 8 language, fewer than a dozen jurisdictions—including Alaska,[23] Colorado,[24] Illinois,[25] Missouri,[26] New Hampshire,[27] North Carolina,[28] Ohio,[29] and Wisconsin[30]—offer further explanation about a lawyer's duties within the context of technology. Bar associations and other legal ethics authorities in these states issued opinion letters on topics like cloud computing, metadata, virtual law practice, and social media which, while not binding authority like court decisions or rules, do provide guidance for lawyers to help ensure appropriate practices.

At least one lawyer has been permanently suspended from practice for failure to maintain competence in technology-based change.[31]

Given the studies documenting notorious underenforcement of professional conduct rules, even one disciplinary action is notable. A longtime bankruptcy attorney repeatedly failed to "meet the federal court's expectations with electronic pleading requirements,"[32] instead wishing to adhere to paper filing practices that were no longer permitted. According to the disciplinary authority, there was no concern about the attorney's competence as a bankruptcy law expert but his "frustration" with the innovation in the court's modernized processes led to the loss of his license to practice.[33] In short, he lost his license not because he lacked the necessary expertise about bankruptcy law but because he refused to learn new technology. Some criticize this outcome as extreme, but it does serve as a warning for lawyers who refuse to keep up with technology advances and, potentially, additional innovations in the practice of law.[34] Other jurisdictions also have disciplined attorneys, but not taken their license, for failing to comply with technology-based competence obligations.[35]

Only two states—Florida and North Carolina—mandate continuing education for lawyers related specifically to the duty of technology competence in Comment 8.[36] New York implemented a mandate for continuing education in cyber security, privacy, and data protection in 2022.[37] Amid the uncertainty of the COVID-19 pandemic and the government-imposed mandates to work from home in many states, jurisdictions like Pennsylvania offered ethical guidance that suggests an expanded reading of Comment 8. In an April 2020 formal ethics opinion, the Pennsylvania Bar Association Committee on Legal Ethics and Professional Responsibility explained that the duty obligates lawyers "to not only understand the risks and benefits of technology as it relates to the specifics of their practices," but also to understand specific areas such as "the electronic transmission of confidential and sensitive data, and cybersecurity, and to take reasonable precautions to comply with this duty."[38] For lawyers without "requisite knowledge and skill to implement technological safeguards," the opinion recommended consultation with other experts who have training in information technology.[39]

Judges, by contrast, do not yet have a corresponding duty to keep up with technology changes, at least not in the United States. Canada "updated its ethical guidebook to advise judges to stay informed about relevant technologies and use caution on social media" in 2021.[40] Even without a similar command, one US judge was forced to resign from office due to his failure to use new technology, including ignoring an email account for more than three years and refusing to use the Office of Court Administration's computer system.[41] Some states require no continuing education for judges at all: Connecticut, Massachusetts, Maine, South Dakota, and Vermont. Arizona stands out as a one-off in requiring "judges to spend some of their 16 continuing education hours on computer security/network security training."[42]

Discrimination and Harassment

Another relatively modern revision covers discrimination and harassment in the profession. In August 2016, the ABA House of Delegates adopted an antidiscrimination amendment to the ABA Model Rules. The amendment to Model Rule 8.4 prohibits behavior that is harassing or discriminatory based on "race, sex, religion, national origin, ethnicity, disability, age, sexual orientation, gender identity, marital status or socioeconomic status in conduct related to the practice of law."[43] Considering that a similar provision was first proposed in 1994, this adoption more than two decades later can be viewed as a notable achievement. However, as law professor Eli Wald reminds us: "For far too long, diversity initiatives within the legal profession have been relegated to the domain of the aspirational, voluntary, abstract, and tentative."[44]

To be sure, including an explicit rule about discrimination was a long time coming, as Veronica Root explains: "The ABA has created departments, founded commissions, held conferences, published papers, and promoted research all in an effort to bring greater tolerance and respect within the ranks of its membership and ultimately society at large."[45] She fears, however, that the amendment may not have "significant impact" because it "primarily appears to result in discipline for only the most egregious incidences of overt discrimination when research has repeatedly shown that the most insidious form of discrimination facing the legal profession today is of a more subtle and covert nature."[46]

The response by states whether to actually adopt and implement the rule has been decidedly mixed. A handful of states have adopted a version of the ABA amendment, including Connecticut, Maine, New York,

Pennsylvania, Vermont, and the United States Virgin Islands. More than a dozen states rejected it outright, including Arizona, Illinois, Montana, Nevada, South Dakota, Tennessee, and Texas, citing First Amendment issues among other concerns. To be fair, a number of states already had adopted a similar provision (and some even broader antidiscrimination protections), but the following additional states still had no provision at all in early 2023: Alaska, Georgia, Hawaii, Kansas, Kentucky, Louisiana, Mississippi, Montana, Nevada, North Carolina, Oklahoma, and Virginia.[47]

Clinging to the Past—Rules in Need of Reform

These tweaks to the Model Rules demonstrate efforts to modernize the profession, and they arguably work to expand access to legal help by including technology within the duty of competence as well as by fostering concern for greater diversity and inclusion.

However, other professional conduct rules can work against this progress. Some rules are necessary to promote and preserve what First Amendment expert and former Yale Law School dean Robert Post calls "democratic competence" and "disciplinary knowledge"[48] that is, regulation that enables members of the profession to provide the specialized legal analysis and advice that their clients can trust and rely on. These sorts of restrictions are beneficial in that they go to the heart of the uniquely protective lawyer-client relationship, providing for competent legal advice, assistance, and representation. Here, I am thinking of rules about communication, confidentiality, diligence, conflicts of interest, and loyalty, among others.

Other restrictions cover the organizational structure of law practice and the distribution of legal services, not the lawyer-client relationship itself. These rules govern the economics and marketing of law practice, including the ban on nonlawyer ownership and investment in law firms, the ban on multidisciplinary partnerships, geographic practice restrictions, limits on advertising and solicitation, and some elements of unauthorized practice of law statutes. Rules in this latter category are explored more fully below, as they ultimately constrain access to legal help without any tangible benefit to clients or the public. These rules present one of the greatest hurdles to closing the justice gap.

Unauthorized Practice of Law

The ABA leaves it to individual states to determine what precisely constitutes "the practice of law," a phrase that, at best, is imprecise and, at worst, is utterly indeterminable.[49] The definition varies from state to state but generally is understood to include legal advice, representation in court, and drafting of legal documents and may extend to negotiation and general dispute resolution. Many of these laws come with stiff penalties like fines or even criminal sanctions. (Recall that the founder of DoNotPay, as noted in the introduction, received threats of jail time if he unleashed his company's "robot lawyer" technology in an actual courtroom.) The vague, uncertain nature of the definition of law practice has led many to speculate on the constitutionality of these laws for that reason alone—because they are so fuzzy, no one could be expected to follow them.[50] States generally "have drawn a distinction between giving generic legal information and giving personalized legal advice,"[51] the latter constituting the practice of law, but beyond this, they offer little guidance. Setting aside the troubling nature of the definitional ambiguity in determining what it means to engage in the practice of law, it is also complicated to assess how best to balance the free flow of legal information against the need to protect professional judgment and disciplinary knowledge (and to incentivize individuals to become trained as lawyers). It is worth noting that practicing law without a license was not always prohibited in the United States. It is a phenomenon that emerged amid fears of competition.

Currently, with very few exceptions, only licensed attorneys may engage in a wide-sweeping range of activities falling under "the practice of law," and they may do so only in the particular state where they are licensed.[52] This means three years of law school, successfully passing the bar exam, and satisfying an extensive character and fitness review. Ralph Baxter, the former chairman of the law firm Orrick, Herrington & Sutcliffe, says it is "hard to imagine a greater barrier to entry or a more effective constriction of resources available to deliver legal service."[53] For many decades, the character and fitness process, a required component for licensure, "rested on nativist, ethnic, and anti-Semitic prejudices, as well as anticompetitive concerns during the Depression," Deborah Rhode writes in her book *Character: What it Means and Why it*

Matters.[54] The process remains widely critiqued as "inconsistent, intrusive, and ineffective,"[55] though increasingly, jurisdictions are removing disclosures about mental health or psychological conditions from the required questionnaire used to evaluate fitness to practice law. The Ohio Bar Association, for example, made this change in early 2023.[56]

Further complicating matters, some professionals, including accountants, compliance officers, and real estate agents, do regularly engage in what can only be called the practice of law in their day-to-day work without consequence, though none would be permitted to represent their clients in court without a law license. Also, in a few limited circumstances, the federal government explicitly authorizes nonlawyers to practice law, including assistance in bankruptcy filings, immigration proceedings, and patent applications. In recent years, a handful of state governments experimented with programs to allow nonlawyer law practice in areas like family law, a topic explored more fully in chapter 8.

Even more problematic, most complaints about unauthorized practice come not from consumers about a specific harm, but from other lawyers threatened by competition.[57] A 1981 national study conducted by Deborah Rhode revealed that just 2 percent of unauthorized practice of law investigations came from consumer concerns and only 11 percent dealt with consumer injury.[58] She conducted a follow-up study published in 2014 and found that while "public harm is playing an increasing role" it still is not a dominant motivation: "71 percent of respondents reported that at least a quarter of cases arose from customers and another 26 percent reported that over half did."[59] And in only 25 percent of cases did courts "analyze whether actual harm occurred or could occur from the unauthorized practice in question."[60] Most complaints, law professor and sociologist Elizabeth Chambliss finds, come from lawyers or unauthorized practice of law committees (made up of—you guessed it—lawyers) "without evidence of consumer harm," especially when "filed against internet providers, such as LegalZoom."[61] And we know from studies conducted in countries like England and Wales where nonlawyers are allowed to provide legal services that "specialization, not professional status" turns out to be "the best predictor of quality."[62] The only "reserved activities" that require a licensed lawyer in those countries are court appearances, conducting litigation, preparing contracts, probate activities, notary services, and the administration of oaths.[63] Everything else, including bankruptcies and divorces, is open to the market, though many often still seek out lawyers for help.

Adding to the complexity is an additional layer related to nonhuman law practice like self-help books, computerized legal forms, and bots (recall the example of Josef Legal from the introduction). For example, does computer software that takes an individual through a decision-tree process for completing legal forms constitute the practice of law? In many jurisdictions, the answer would be "yes" under the literal language of existing unauthorized practice of law statutes, many of which were written at a time when the technology of automated, humanlike legal help did not yet exist. Legislative action has been taken in at least one state—Texas—to make clear that the use of computer software does not constitute the practice of law, provided that the software includes a disclaimer that it is not a substitute for a lawyer's services.[64]

Does an AI-driven chatbot like ChatGPT constitute the practice of law? I asked it to prepare a will for me, and it did a pretty good job of sketching out a basic legal document. But when I followed up and asked whether the will constitutes "legal advice" the chatbot made clear the answer is no: "No, this is not legal advice. The advice provided is general in nature and may not be applicable to your specific situation. Legal advice can only be provided by a qualified attorney who is licensed to practice law in your jurisdiction. If you have specific legal questions or concerns, you should consult with a licensed attorney."[65]

Needless to say, the haziness in defining what constitutes the authorized practice of law, coupled with the threat of serious penalties like fines and even jail time, suppresses the market for alternatives to a lawyer for even the most basic legal advice. And the profession's justifications don't hold up. As American Bar Foundation researcher Barlow Christensen wrote in 1980:

> Ultimately, the legal profession's traditional unauthorized practice position rests upon either of two serious doubts—or perhaps on both. Lawyers either lack confidence in themselves to meet free and open competition, or they lack faith in the intelligence of the public and in the ability of citizens to determine their lives for themselves. Neither doubt is justified. If we lawyers are the splendid fellows that we claim to be—and,

though the claim is immodest, it may even be at least partly true—then we have nothing to fear from open competition.[66]

In part II, we will turn to specific recommendations about how to open up competition by reforming unauthorized practice of law rules. But first let's look at other ways the profession's regulations suppress the market.

Nonlawyer Ownership and Investment in Law Firms

When most organizations want to grow, they seek financial capital and investment. But ABA Model Rule 5.4 bans law firms from raising funds from anyone who is not a lawyer. Charles Wolfram critiques the "limitations on nonlawyer ownership of law firms" because they "have reduced capital flow into legal services markets."[67] As the ABA Commission on the Future of Legal Services declared in 2016, this "business model constrains innovations that would provide greater access to, and enhance the delivery of, legal services."[68]

Research from the Stanford Center on the Legal Profession helps explain why the typical law partnership model performs inefficiently. First, "a firm's capital comes almost entirely from its equity partners, but as lateral movement among firms increases, more and more lawyers may be reluctant to invest in firms' long-term needs."[69] (Equity partners "buy-in" to the firm with a personal financial investment and receive most if not all of their compensation as a percentage of the annual profits.) Second, "lack of access to capital also means firms are less likely to invest in efforts that have a long time horizon in which to deliver a return," which in turn limits their "capacity to build the economies of scale needed to provide the level of service now expected of most customer-oriented businesses."[70] Third, "other professionals with significant business-development expertise cannot obtain equity in law firms, which may deter them from taking otherwise desirable jobs in the legal field."[71] Fourth, "lawyers continue to rely on a narrow, outdated business model—individual lawyers providing service billed by the hour to individual clients—that is isolated from the tools that other industries use to create incentives to reduce costs, improve quality, and figure out better ways to meet economic demand."[72]

The story of Erin Levine offers one example of who might benefit from outside investment. In 2018, Levine founded Hello Divorce, an online platform for more affordable and amicable divorces. A successful family law attorney, Levine wanted to make the divorce process less costly, easier to understand, and more quickly resolved. The Model Rule 5.4 ban proved challenging, Levine told researchers at Stanford: "One thing that has been really difficult for me is the lack of ability for a nonlawyer to have an ownership interest in a law firm. Another is this lack of our ability as a law firm to take any sort of outside investment from a nonlawyer."[73]

The thousands of couples who might have taken advantage of Levine's services if she could expand through investment are the real losers here. She managed to creatively set up Hello Divorce to function apart from her law practice, which she still runs, leading her to secure $2 million in venture capital funding in 2021 and an additional $3.25 million in 2022.[74] But Levine, and others like her, would benefit from not being forced to do end runs around Model Rule 5.4.

The ABA has long opposed external ownership and investment by nonlawyers for law firms, a position embodied in Model Rule 5.4, which provides, in relevant part, that a "lawyer or law firm shall not share legal fees with a nonlawyer" and "shall not form a partnership with a nonlawyer if any of the activities of the partnership consist of the practice of law."[75] The rule also states that a "lawyer shall not practice with or in the form of a professional corporation or association authorized to practice law for a profit if . . . a nonlawyer owns any interest therein" or "a nonlawyer is a corporate director or officer."[76]

The ABA's official prohibition on nonlawyer investment in law firms extends back to the 1920s.[77] However, its origin is in a New York State criminal statute enacted in 1909 at the request of individual lawyers concerned about competition from corporations contracting with lawyers in bulk to provide legal advice to subscribers,[78] essentially thwarting an early bid at supermarket law, like what grocery store chain Tesco attempted in the UK after passage of the Legal Services Act.

The policy underlying the resistance to a corporate ownership structure for law firms has been couched largely in terms of professionalism and lawyer independence. This is explicit on the face of the rule (entitled "Professional Independence of a Lawyer"[79]) and implicit in the debates and commentary about the purpose of the rule over the years.[80] According to the Comment for Model Rule 5.4, the purpose of these restrictions is to help avoid potential interference with a lawyer's professional judgment.[81] The primary justifications for the rule are: (1) the preservation of lawyer independence, (2) professionalism and the reputation of the legal profession, and (3) the avoidance of ethical dilemmas that are covered elsewhere in the conduct rules, such as conflicts of interest, client confidentiality, and the lawyer's duties to the client and the court. The *Restatement (Third) of Law Governing Lawyers* explains, "the concern is that permitting such ownership or direction would induce or require lawyers to violate the mandates of the lawyer codes, such as by subjecting the lawyer to the goals and interests of the nonlawyer in ways adverse to the lawyer's duties to a client."[82] (A "Restatement" is a treatise written by the American Law Institute to provide an explanation of leading principles, standards, and rules in a particular field of law. The American Law Institute, according to its website, "is the leading independent organization in the United States producing scholarly work to clarify, modernize, and otherwise improve the law."[83]) The concern identified by the *Restatement*, however, is present in many areas of law practice. Pressures related to revenue generation and keeping costs low exist regardless of the organizational structure and arguably are most profound for solo practitioners.

A more cynical, though perhaps also more accurate, view is that the rhetoric of professionalism, independence, and protection is a pretext for monopolistic protectionism designed to limit the availability of legal services and maintain the price of legal services at an artificially high level—thus preserving the status quo that has been so profitable for the lawyers who have created and enforced the rules in the past as noted in chapter 1. The model does result in substantial salaries, at least for some lawyers. Partners of the most elite law firms earn more in a year than most individuals earn in a lifetime. The annual compensation for the top twenty firms ranged from $3 million to $8 million on average per partner.[84] Data from the National Association for Law Placement revealed that the class of 2021 enjoyed strong entry-level salaries, with the national median salary at "an all-time high of $80,000, up 6.7 percent compared to the median of $75,000 for the Class of 2020."[85] For the 57 percent from the class of 2021 who accepted private practice jobs, the median salary increased by 1.2 percent to $131,500, surpassing what had been the "all-time high of $130,000" for the class of 2009, matched again by the class of 2020.[86] Jobs with these wages rely mostly on the billable hour model, though some firms offer alternative fees. Needless to say, lawyers earning these salaries are not motivated to change the rules.

The prohibition on nonlawyers doing legal work continued even in the face of regular debate over its efficacy and purpose throughout the decades. In the 1960s, one critic suggested that both "courts, as well as the bar associations, have too frequently been guided by the literal application of negative limitations without inquiring into the affirmative purposes which the limitations are intended to aid or into the new conditions and situations under which novel problems are presented."[87] Nevertheless, members of the bar, in considering at the time whether a corporation might own a law firm, "stated that 'no amount of data could justify' a plan then under consideration for a new form of bringing legal services to the middle classes."[88] This wholesale refusal to consider any data, whether it demonstrated benefits to the public or not, perpetuated the justice gap.

The concept was dismissed again in the 1980s under a "fear of Sears" argument, the idea that legal services offered by a mass retailer such as Sears would fundamentally compromise lawyers' capacity to serve clients competently and ethically.[89] More recently, while the ABA's Ethics 20/20 Commission at one point approved the drafting of a proposed change to Model Rule 5.4 that would allow law firms to include nonlawyers in minority ownership roles, the revision ultimately was rejected.[90]

To date, only Arizona and Utah have successfully liberalized the nonlawyer ownership and investment restrictions to encourage innovation in the United States.[91] In chapter 8, we will explore the regulatory innovation in those states.[92] At the same time these states made progressive moves, the ABA doubled down on its resistance to any reform of Model Rule 5.4 in 2022, with the House of Delegates passing Resolution 402, which states: "The sharing of legal fees with non-lawyers and the ownership or control of the practice of law by non-lawyers are inconsistent with the core values of the legal profession. The law governing lawyers that prohibits lawyers from sharing legal fees with non-lawyers and from directly or indirectly transferring to non-lawyers ownership or control over entities practicing law should not be revised."[93]

An alternative reading of Model Rule 5.4 is to consider it an organization or distribution rule, not a professional competence rule. Looking beyond the characterization of professional independence and instead examining the rule for what it bans—a particular form of business structure for law practices—exposes that the rule unjustifiably restricts the free flow of legal information. Model Rule 5.4 forecloses one of the most common and effective business structures designed to reduce the very concerns regarding professional independence that the rule purports to address—the for-profit corporation.[94] The for-profit corporation model is meant to operate independently from the owners of the business (and their individual self-interest). By providing owners with personal asset protection, the corporate form guards against decisions that one might make driven by personal financial motive and instead elevates the business's best interest. The corporate form also facilitates access to capital for investing in enhanced technology, branding and marketing, research and development, and expanded services. As we will see in chapter 7, the United States Supreme Court has long recognized that the corporate form, in and of itself, does not compromise a lawyer's judgment, at least in the context of nonprofit corporations.[95] The rule blocks methods for creating and disseminating legal information from a significant source—the corporation—absent a professional expertise justification. And it does so at the expense of lawyers too, as documented by the *Restatement (Third)*:

> Such practical barriers to infusion of capital into law firms significantly limit the ability of law firms to attain what its lawyers may consider to be a more optimal size at which to provide higher-quality and lower-price services to clients. They may also deter law firms from more effectively competing with established law firms and with nonlawyer organizations. . . . Further, unlike other persons in many . . . occupations, lawyers are unable to realize the present economic value of their reputations, which otherwise could be obtained through sale to investors of stock or other ownership interest.[96]

Law professor Stephen Gillers calls the rule "indefensibly lawyer-centered"[97] and rejects the explanation that it protects clients.[98] Instead, he observes that "some lawyers benefit and others lose, which is why the rule must be seen as serving the interests of ABA control groups and not lawyers generally."[99] Thus, critiques Gillers, a "firm that wants to accept lay investment and predicts it can without ignoring its duties to keep confidences and exercise independent professional judgment may not do so, no matter how persuasive a case it can make in support of its prediction."[100] Finally, and perhaps most obviously, professional conduct rules governing communication, competence, conflicts of interest, confidentiality, diligence, fees, and loyalty all do the work of protecting a lawyer's independence, which makes Model Rule 5.4 unnecessary if that truly is the purpose of this prohibition.

Places like Australia and the UK offer regulatory examples for how to both lift the ban on ownership and investment while simultaneously re-regulating to ensure appropriate compliance and consumer protection. Australia requires designation of an individual "responsible for managing the legal services provided by the firm and preventing or remedying professional misconduct by employees."[101] Under the ABS model adopted by England and Wales, each firm must establish a head of practice responsible for compliance.[102] In short, it is possible to regulate for client and public safety while also allowing lawyers to partner with nonlawyers for funding and business structures.

Multidisciplinary Partnership Bans

Model Rule 5.4 also prohibits lawyers throughout the United States from practicing law if "a nonlawyer has the right to direct or control the professional judgment of a lawyer."[103] The rule provides, in relevant part, that a lawyer is prohibited from practicing "with or in the form of a professional corporation or association authorized to practice law for a profit" if: (1) the nonlawyer owns any interest in the entity; (2) the nonlawyer is a corporate director of the entity; or (3) the nonlawyer "has the right to direct or control the professional judgment of a lawyer."[104] Washington, DC, is a notable exception, as it has long permitted multidisciplinary practices among lawyers and nonlawyers. But, this permission is limited. Fees may be shared with nonlawyers only if lawyers are providing the legal services and nonlawyers providing incidental services (*not* the practice of law). And law firms with offices outside of DC cannot allow for partnerships to be formed with nonlawyers. To be clear, while the DC rule is more permissive in that it allows for certain forms of multidisciplinary practice, it does not permit a corporation to own or invest in a law firm.[105] The exception is so narrow that, as a practical matter, it makes little difference in expanding the market for legal services. As noted above, in the context of ownership and investment, Arizona and Utah recently opened up their legal services markets to permit multidisciplinary arrangements, and others appear ready to join them. We will focus on those efforts in chapter 8.

The ban on multidisciplinary partnerships is supposedly justified by the duties of confidentiality and loyalty that lawyers owe to their clients: protecting the relationship from outside interference or influence. So, for example, a lawyer cannot partner with an accountant to provide legal and financial services, even if the service providers are competent and the client would benefit from the arrangement.

Similar to the research surrounding the lack of actual harm to clients in the context of unauthorized practice of law statutes, law professor Bruce Green's research reveals that when the multidisciplinary restriction was initially proposed by the ABA, "proponents did not document cases of clients who were harmed by these lawyers' work or who expressed dissatisfaction with its quality."[106] Instead, lawyers pulled multidisciplinary partnerships off the table "explicitly, to protect themselves against competition from corporations and, at least implicitly, to protect the profession's native-born, middle- and upper-class elite against competition from lower-class, urban, immigrant practitioners."[107]

One example with demonstrated results that offer insight into the promise of multidisciplinary partnerships is the medical legal partnership (MLP). The link between an individual's health and social, environmental, or behavioral factors is well documented. Indeed, housing code violations may cause or exacerbate respiratory conditions, and domestic violence may lead to repeated emergency room visits.[108] These so-called social determinants of health account for as much as 60 percent of the risk of premature death, with 30 percent of the remaining preventable deaths attributable to genetic predispositions and only 10 percent attributable to access to medical care.[109] Despite the significant impact that social, environmental, and behavioral factors have on health, the United States spends approximately twice as much on medical care as it spends on social services. However, a paradigm shift is taking place in the health care delivery system. In response to payment reforms that reward improvements in patients' health and reduced health care spending, providers are increasingly turning their attention to the social determinants that adversely impact their patients' health. In recent years, a leading strategy for doing so is the MLP.

MLPs address the health-harming social and legal needs of patients and communities by integrating the expertise of health care, public health, and legal professionals.[110] At a minimum, health care providers participating in an MLP refer patients who require legal assistance to lawyers, while social workers within the MLP will often address those patients' related social needs.[111] The legal partner may also train the medical partner's support staff in identifying patients with health-harming legal needs and in using any available legal interventions.[112] For example, the lawyer may educate the medical partner's staff on identifying individuals who may be eligible for social security disability insurance (SSDI) or on how to effectively navigate the SSDI application and appeals process.[113] Some MLPs also combine health and legal tools to advocate for broad policy changes that combat social or environmental factors adverse to health, such as poor housing conditions or unsafe water.[114]

Low-income individuals frequently cope with legal and social issues that adversely impact their health. Exposure to hazardous chemicals, mold, dust, or pest infestation in the workplace or home can cause or aggravate respiratory conditions such as asthma. Stress from coping with unemployment, economic hardship, racism, or other challenges can cause psychological conditions while simultaneously damaging immune defenses, vital organs, and other physiological systems. Financial insecurity may force individuals to delay or forgo needed health care and adequate nutrition.

Lawyers are uniquely situated to help individuals address these and other underlying causes of poor health by supporting patient-clients' access to available government services and legal protections. For instance, lawyers can provide legal aid to individuals who have been denied health insurance coverage or public benefits such as Medicaid and SSDI. Lawyers can also help individuals enforce their legal rights under antidiscrimination, housing, employment, and education laws and in obtaining protective orders against abusive partners. Moreover, lawyers can assist with immigration and creditor or debtor issues as well as family law and estate planning matters such as divorce, guardianship, and powers of attorney.

Further, physicians, nurses, hospitals, and other providers are ideally positioned to identify patients with health-harming legal and social issues and can adeptly facilitate the receipt of legal and social support services.[115] Providers witness the impact of social determinants on individuals' health firsthand.[116] Patients' trust in medical professionals also promotes individuals sharing sensitive information with their providers, such as personal information on issues such as domestic violence, financial hardship, immigration concerns, and other legal and social challenges.[117] Therefore, providers have the ability to screen for health-harming legal and social needs and to refer those patients in need of assistance to lawyers and social workers.[118] The MLP model supports this integration of medical, legal, and social services, and is the most efficacious method of achieving these goals.[119]

Nevertheless, MLP models vary greatly, particularly regarding the degree of collaboration among the MLP partners and their information-sharing practices. At one end of the spectrum, there are MLPs with limited interactions between the medical and legal partners. At the other end of the spectrum are MLPs that integrate the full range of services that they offer individuals. Under this model, the MLP lawyer works collaboratively with the medical provider's staff as part of an interdisciplinary team of professionals.

In contrast to the referral MLP model, the integrated, multidisciplinary MLP model better serves the complex needs of vulnerable individuals and their families, thus offering greater potential to improve patients' health. The integrated, multidisciplinary approach customarily offers the full range of clinical and nonclinical MLP services at a single location. Providing services at a single location forecloses the need for the individual to travel to the legal services provider or navigate an unfamiliar setting, increasing the likelihood that individuals will actually receive needed legal support. Moreover, the integrated, multidisciplinary model supports regular communication and sharing of information between the medical and legal partners, alleviating the need for the patient-client to provide his or her lawyer with all relevant information.

To give an example, rather than simply helping a patient-client dealing with domestic violence obtain a restraining order, as occurs under the referral MLP model, an integrated, multidisciplinary MLP can also provide behavioral health counseling, assist with developing a safety plan, locate alternative housing, and secure financial support. Likewise, the model's team approach allows the MLP to consider whether a legal versus nonlegal solution better meets a patient-client's needs. For instance, when advising individuals living in substandard housing, the MLP professionals can jointly consider with the patient-client whether initiating legal action against the derelict landlord or moving to new housing is the preferred solution. For these reasons, many in the MLP world favor the integrated, multidisciplinary model over the referral model.

But the ban on multidisciplinary partnerships limits full integration. Model Rule 5.4 prohibits lawyers from practicing law if "a nonlawyer has the right to direct or control the professional judgment of a lawyer." In other words, the rule views a fully integrated model as a potential breach of loyalty. The relationship cannot be interfered with or influenced by third parties, such as a social worker or physician in the MLP setting, even if such third parties are knowledgeable about the client's health needs and loyal to the client.[120]

There are many other areas where similar collaborative integration would help address civil legal needs through professional partnerships with accountants, immigration specialists, social workers, tax preparers, and more that have been thwarted by multidisciplinary partnership ban.

Geographic Practice Restrictions

Geographic restrictions also compromise the free flow of legal information. Model Rule 5.5(a) provides: "A lawyer shall not practice law in a jurisdiction in violation of the regulation of the legal profession in that jurisdiction, or assist another in doing so."[121] For example, an attorney who is an expert in handling uncontested divorces licensed to practice in one state cannot do so in another if unlicensed in the second state. This puts the legal profession significantly far behind other industries and service providers in an increasingly global, interconnected world where state borders are practically an antiquated concept. Broad geographic restrictions foreclosing the practice of law in a jurisdiction where one is not admitted to the bar do not, in and of themselves, cultivate or preserve professional expertise. Instead, the duty of competence is sufficient to ensure appropriate knowledge of state law and procedure, where familiarity with these nuances is necessary to deliver competent legal advice and representation. A lawyer licensed in one state should be allowed to practice law in all states, much like one can drive in any state with a single, valid driver's license. (Australia, for example, follows a model like this.[122])

* * *

To realize the benefits of modern technology and design for the consumer law market, the legal profession must create a space for innovation to occur. Innovation requires ideas, competition, and capital.[123] Innovation also requires input and experimentation beyond the members of the profession itself. Collaborative partnerships with nonlawyers are stifled by anticompetitive rules prohibiting outside investment and multidisciplinary practice. To fully (or even partially) serve the unmet needs of the consumer law market, lawyers "should be free to organize firms to pursue business opportunities as they see fit and to select a form of governance from a menu of legal alternatives,"[124] as Robert Cooter and Hans-Bernd Schafer write in their book *Solomon's Knot: How Law Can End the Poverty of Nations*. Other countries have engaged in this sort of reform. Part II, and especially chapter 8, highlights how this inspired a handful of states to also experiment. But before turning to recommendations and reforms, we need to drill down a bit further to understand the roots of the regulatory structure for law practice in the United States.

Why does the American legal profession enjoy such control over the market for its services? The answer lies in the unique role that lawyer-judges play simultaneously as a regulatory arm of the state and also as members of the regulated profession. Chapter 4 explores in greater depth the impact of the legal profession's near-total monopoly on the delivery of legal services.

4

The Legal Monopoly

High barriers to entry, information asymmetries, and anticompetitive restrictions are hallmarks of the legal profession. Only licensed lawyers may provide legal representation, even if someone is trained and as capable, if not more so, than a lawyer. In most jurisdictions, the highest courts—made up of judges who are also lawyers—adopt and enforce rules authored by lawyers to govern who may practice law and how law may be practiced. Even where these lawyer-judge regulators are presumed neutral by virtue of an appointment process or subject to some measure of public accountability through elections, the fact remains that they are members of the very profession that is subject to the regulations they enact and enforce. (Thirty-eight states hold judicial elections at the supreme court level, and the remaining states utilize a system of appointment, usually by an advisory committee.[1]) It's a bit like the fox guarding the henhouse. The decisions of legislators and executive officials are reviewed by judges. But judges review their decisions themselves.

Consider the implications. Most states draw from model ethics rules and policies promulgated by lawyers elected by their peers to the American Bar Association (ABA) House of Delegates, as we saw in chapter 3. These lawyers typically have direct financial interest in the rules that they draft. The drafting of the rules and policies is not subject to external review before adoption by the ABA. The highest court in each state then bases its body of regulations on the ABA's efforts.[2] This process often occurs behind closed doors, without public hearings, open meetings, or even a period for public notice and comment. Few people are aware of, let alone take advantage of, a window for input if one is provided. As law professor Leslie Levin explains in the context of lawyer discipline:

> Only Florida, New Hampshire, Oregon, and West Virginia treat all or most complaints about lawyers as a matter of public record. In most other states, the complaint becomes a public record once there has been a find-

ing of probable cause. In a minority of the jurisdictions, the public cannot attend disciplinary hearings even after probable cause is found; information about complaints does not become publicly available until there has been a finding of wrongdoing and a public sanction is imposed.[3]

The process for executing the rules is even less transparent in the majority of jurisdictions. Enforcement is complaint driven, as documented in chapter 3, with lawyers often reporting alleged violations by other lawyers rather than clients raising concerns about their lawyers. Rarely, but occasionally, a judge will refer a lawyer for discipline by bar authorities.

At all levels of regulation, from drafting to enactment, enforcement, and adjudication, lawyers or judges hold primary if not exclusive control.[4] At its extreme, when a rule is disputed, the challenger is forced to make their argument before the very officials who enacted the rule. As Charles Wolfram notes, "One uncomfortable consequence is that the same body that promulgates comprehensive sets of rules regulating the conduct of lawyers must also sit as the body that determines their validity if later attacked."[5]

Regulatory Capture

Consequently, lawyer-judge regulators are vulnerable to "regulatory capture," a theory which suggests that occupations or other economic alliances endeavor to enrich themselves through the state's power to control competition and price.[6] Although judges presumably act in the public's interest, they nonetheless remain members of the legal profession they regulate. Even if individual lawyers or judges may act to advance consumer interests over the profession's interests, capture risks remain. The idea of regulatory capture assumes that when the state's economic choices are proscribed by a regulatory body that has overtaken the state's political system, this process (and perhaps also the choices made within the process) is both inefficient and illegitimate.

While it may be unsettling to contemplate that a particular judge would regulate or review lawyer regulation in a self-interested or self-dealing way, this may occur without the judge being fully conscious of it. In their research on human behavior, scholars Christine Jolls, Cass Sunstein, and Richard Thaler cite "suggestive evidence that self-serving bias does affect lawyers and judges."[7] Lawyer-judge self-regulation is also susceptible to conflicts of interest and pressure from the local professional community. Many judges, especially those sitting on state courts, will eventually return to practice law.

In drafting, adopting, and enforcing the rules applicable to their own profession, as well as reviewing their validity when subject to a legal challenge, it is not an overreaction to be concerned that members of the judiciary may act in self-interest. The most glaring example of this is in judicial regulation. Rules governing judicial disqualification in almost every jurisdiction call on "the very judge whose acts are alleged to be warped by unconscious bias to decide whether there is an adequate showing of bias."[8]

Federal antitrust law typically breaks up monopoly relationships like this, where members of an industry or profession act in concert to suppress competition, as you will learn more about in chapter 6. When the state creates the monopoly or cartel, however, regulatory constraints are deemed immune from review by the courts under what is known as the "state-action doctrine," a concept we will return to. Basically, this exemption from antitrust liability is based on principles of federalism, state sovereignty, and judicial economy. It is defended, at least in part, by the idea that publicly accountable officials supposedly will not be influenced by the same financial motivations or other self-interests as private actors.[9] It is also defended by a belief that state regulatory officials often represent a diverse range of backgrounds and career experiences. The deference to a state-created monopoly also is grounded in the same principles of independence and neutral deliberation that separate courts from agencies. While these values are "largely limited to the decisions of concrete cases, they are closely related to the court's authority over the practice of law,"[10] so the argument goes, according to federal judge Frank Easterbrook. Just as the separation of powers protects the deliberations of judges in the courthouse from interference by the executive or the legislature, so too should the judiciary's rules governing the practice of law be shielded from other political actors.

As a result of the "state action doctrine," lawyer regulation enjoys insulation from competition that, in some instances, may not only compromise consumer interests but also may undermine constitutionally protected rights. Numerous restrictions on the practice of law have suppressed competition, as we saw in chapter 3. These include professional conduct rules governing who may practice law (e.g., licensing requirements, geographic restrictions) and how law may be practiced (e.g., bans on multidisciplinary practices and outside ownership or investment in law firms, limitations on advertising and solicitation).[11] Bar regulators justify consequences of reduced competition like higher prices and fewer options as necessary to protect the public.[12] Yet, empirical research from scholars Deborah Rhode and Lucy Ricca reveals that these purported "harms" do not exist in reality.[13]

By its very design, lawyer regulation operates from a baseline of capture. The result, inevitably, is a risk that regulation will maximize economic profits for the profession at the public's and/or consumer's expense. The legal profession's conduct is, in effect, cartel-like "in restricting entry and negotiating agreements with competing groups."[14] According to law professor Walter Gellhorn, "Licensing, imposed ostensibly to protect the public, almost always impedes only those who desire to enter the occupation or 'profession;' those already in practice remain entrenched without a demonstration of fitness or probity."[15] The concerns that go unchecked include financial or other self-interests, rent seeking (i.e., manipulating the rules to increase one's own profits), conflicts, pressure from members of one's own group, and ethical blind spots such as cognitive bias or groupthink.

Nevertheless, might there be good reasons for allowing this inherently captured regulatory structure to persevere?

The Special Role of Lawyers

Without question, lawyers hold a unique place in society. The role of an attorney in navigating and, when necessary, challenging the law is a critical component of American democratic government.[16] A law on the books is meaningless if people do not know when it might apply to one's circumstances or how to enforce it. For example, litigating in the courts "may well be the sole practicable avenue open to a minority to petition for redress of grievances,"[17] especially when they've been shut out from the ballot box, and lawyers are essential to this process. Lawyers protect individuals from the excesses of government. They give people "an alternative to resorting to physical violence" to resolve disputes, as law professors Monroe Freedman and Abbe Smith write in their book *Understanding Lawyers' Ethics.*[18] As legal historian Robert Gordon explains, lawyers act as

> agents who communicate the rules through advice to private clients and governments and enable them to organize their businesses and structure their transactions and comply with regulations and tax laws and constitutional limitations; and who can negotiate and if necessary litigate with the state and other private parties when their claims of rights are impaired or disputed.[19]

Law professor Stephen Pepper similarly has observed that, "Our legal system is premised on the assumption that law is intended to be known or knowable, that law is in its nature public information."[20] In short, lawyers effectively are the law. "In a complex legal environment," Pepper notes, "much law cannot be known and acted upon, cannot function as law, without lawyers to make it accessible to those for whom it is relevant."[21] Even in a world of easy access to legal information via the internet, that information is useless absent the knowledge of how to apply and enforce it, which is where a lawyer can come in.

Given the integral nature of the work that lawyers do as it relates to the functioning of the legal system and the foundations of the American government, it is not surprising that the state might find it more efficient to allow the profession to determine its own regulatory standards rather than look to outside sources. Moreover, external regulation (including federal or state legislators or other regulators beyond the legal profession) could fundamentally compromise the very role that lawyers are meant to fulfill in the system of democratic checks and balances. For these reasons, some argue that the best balance to be struck is one in which lawyers self-regulate, even in the face of regulatory capture, given the intractable relationship with lawyers to law and the necessity that lawyers not be controlled by other branches of the government.

Even so, antitrust experts Aaron Edlin and Rebecca Haw observe that a conflict of interests exists when, "those who have the most to gain from reduced consumer welfare in the form of higher prices are tasked with protecting consumer welfare in the form of health and safety."[22] The American Medical Association (AMA), for example, was famously critiqued by Milton and Rose Friedman in the 1960s for its "ability to

THE LEGAL MONOPOLY

restrict technological and organizational changes in the way medicine is conducted."[23] (The AMA, like the ABA, is a professional organization, but made up of physicians rather than lawyers.) Competition is not the only value at stake; self-regulation by the judiciary can also undermine the perception of judicial independence. This begs the question—what is the alternative to self-regulation for the legal profession?

If Not Lawyer-Judges as Regulators, Then Who?

Professor Ben Barton argues that legislatures "while typically criticized for their accessibility to organized special interests, would fare better with lawyer regulation than judiciaries" for avoiding the conflicts of interest and other concerns associated with regulatory capture.[24] To date, only one state—California—relies almost exclusively on its legislature. (Chapter 8 offers a counter perspective on whether the legislature is suitable for the job. As you'll see, two Stanford law professors argue that legislators are equally vulnerable to special interests.)

Another potential tool is greater transparency. This could come from including more lay individuals in the regulatory process and/or placing the profession under the same antitrust rules that apply to other industries, a proposal taken up in chapter 6.

* * *

Well intentioned or not, the legal monopoly contributes substantially to the long-enduring lack of access to justice in the United States. Absent this monopoly, the market would be open to nonlawyer professionals who could offer legal help at a lower price. Part II explains why, unlike with most monopolies, it is difficult to rely on antitrust law as well as other paths like the First Amendment to facilitate competition in the delivery of legal services. Part II also offers hope, drawing partly from international efforts at innovative regulatory reform and the early attempts by a few states to innovate as well.

But before turning to these efforts, chapter 5 unpacks the special role of lawyers in democratic government. In order to implement the recommendations and reforms from the blueprint presented in the second half of this book, the foundations of American democracy must be guaranteed by lawyers as a matter of first principle.

5

Preserving Democracy

The Role of Courts and the Role of Legal Ethics

Alexis de Tocqueville famously wrote nearly two centuries ago that lawyers "are the most powerful existing security against the excesses of democracy" given "the authority . . . entrusted to members of the legal profession" and their influence in government.[1] As it turns out, lawyers are also "the most powerful existing security" for preserving the fundamentals of our democracy. They may also be democracy's greatest threat.

The recommendations found in part II's blueprint for justice are pointless if we fail to protect our democracy. The 2020 presidential election revealed just how vital lawyers and judges are to a constitutional democracy and, at the same time, how easily they could undermine if not destroy it. Chapter 5 quickly recounts that recent history to make the case for strengthening the duty of lawyers to preserve democratic government. This obligation is among the most urgent priorities for lawyers in the twenty-first century. It is necessary, but of course not sufficient, for solving the access-to-justice crisis facing the nation.

Lawyer Lies and the Vulnerability of Democracy

Lawyer lies pervade politics regardless of party, though they became more noticeable in the Trump era. Among the most brazen, Senior Counselor to the President Kellyanne Conway's lies included the size of Trump's inauguration crowd,[2] the fictitious Bowling Green Massacre,[3] and the World Health Organization's ability to prevent COVID-19.[4] Attorney General Jeff Sessions falsely testified under oath that he did not meet with the Russian ambassador during Trump's presidential campaign, even though he did.[5]

In the aftermath of the 2020 election, lawyers desperate to alter the outcome of the (validly cast) votes spewed outrageous lies. Their election-fraud lies stand apart from those made by lawyers earlier in Donald Trump's administration because of the consequences at stake. As one commentator observed: "Perhaps no lie has had greater consequences on our nation than Trump's unfounded claim that victory had been wrongfully stolen from him in the 2020 presidential election by means of widespread election fraud."[6]

The harm of the election-denying lawyer lies cannot be overstated. Had their lies not been rejected by the courts, they would have undone the results of a legitimate election, compromising the very foundation of American democracy. More than sixty lawsuits were dismissed after judges appointed by both Democrats and Republicans (including Trump) refused to entertain fraud allegations based on lies advanced by lawyers.[7] And for good reason. Lawyer lies about the outcome of a valid election, whether told in the courthouse or in a press conference, risk causing unique, devastating harm to our democratic form of government and should not be tolerated by members of the profession. Election denials destroy citizens' confidence that their votes count. Philosopher Jeremy Waldron calls them "the worst kinds of lie to tell. They are libels on democracy."[8]

The repeated, widely disseminated lies from lawyers about the election results incentivized a violent attack on the US Capitol building on January 6, 2021. The attack left five dead, including one police officer,[9] and hundreds injured from "concussions, rib fractures, burns and even a mild heart attack."[10] Still others continued to suffer other mental health related harms, including post-traumatic stress disorder.[11] And four police officers who defended the Capitol committed suicide.[12]

Apart from these physical and psychological harms, the lies caused significant, nearly irreversible damage to our democracy as well. As Judge Randolph D. Moss, writing for the District Court of the District of Columbia in one of the election cases, observed: "This was a singular and chilling event in U.S. history, raising legitimate concern about the security—not only of the Capitol building—but of our democracy itself."[13] The deceit of lawyers fundamentally compromised the integrity of our democracy in the court of public opinion. They "cut the legs out from under democratic processes, by making it difficult or impossible for citizens to know whom to trust."[14] And this lack of trust endures.

An Axios-Momentive Poll from early 2022 revealed that more than 40 percent of the American public *still* believed President Joe Biden did not win the election, though his victory was confirmed against repeated challenges in courts across the nation. Even investigations spearheaded by Republicans found no evidence of fraud.[15] Widespread lack of public belief in the fairness and validity of elections is a fundamental threat to democratic government. If the people don't believe the outcome of their elections, then what's the point of holding elections at all?

Perhaps most concerning is that the lack of meaningful discipline for lawyers who tell election-fraud lies risks a continued threat in future elections and undermines public confidence in the legal profession. Ethics rules can and should be guardrails to protect against future lawyer lies compromising valid election results.

All lawyers, by virtue of taking an oath to receive their law license, agree to be bound to a self-imposed duty of candor in the courtroom and the obligation not to pursue frivolous litigation.

These ethical commitments to evidence-based facts eventually put a stop to at least some of the incessant lies of Trump lawyers once they appeared in court. But this was not a victory for legal ethics.

To appreciate the fragility of American democracy, we must confront two competing realities. Lawyers and judges across the nation managed to hold our federal government together at the same time other lawyers were trying to upend it. Sherilynn Ifill, former president of the NAACP Legal Defense Fund calls for a reckoning: "We must have a full accounting and examination of our profession's role in contributing to the erosion of our democracy."[16] Lawyers, "including attorneys general from 17 states who supported the Texas lawsuit seeking to delay the election certification" must face penalties, in her words, for spending "weeks on end" engaged in "egregious conduct that unnecessarily expended court resources but that also kept alive a fraudulent narrative advanced by the president that the election had been 'stolen,' which ultimately led to the violent attack on the Capitol on Jan. 6."[17]

Who Were These Lawyers?

Take Rudy Giuliani, for example. He claimed election fraud in press conferences and even in his opening statement during a court proceeding, though he conceded after questioning by Pennsylvania United States district judge Matthew W. Brann that his lawsuit did not sufficiently allege fraud as a matter of law.[18] More than 7,600 individuals, including more than three thousand attorneys, signed onto a complaint filed by Lawyers Defending American Democracy with the New York State Bar seeking the suspension of Giuliani's New York license.[19] A New York State appellate court suspended his New York license pending investigation, ultimately finding "uncontroverted evidence" that he "communicated demonstrably false and misleading statements to courts, lawmakers and the public at large in his capacity as lawyer for former President Trump and the Trump campaign in connection with Trump's failed effort at reelection in 2020."[20] The District of Columbia also suspended his DC license pending investigation.[21]

Texas attorney Sidney Powell's election lies were so egregious that Dominion Voting Systems sued her for defamation.[22] Among the absurdities, "Powell falsely stated on television and in legal briefs that Dominion machines ran on technology that could switch votes away from Trump, technology she said had been invented in Venezuela to help steal elections for the late Hugo Chávez."[23] She then proceeded to layer lies upon lies in response to sanctions sought in a Detroit federal court, taking the opposite position by claiming that no reasonable person would believe her statements about the Dominion machines. Judge Linda V. Parker from the Eastern District of Michigan federal court ultimately ordered Powell, along with eight other lawyers, to pay fines, calling their election fraud lawsuit a "historic and profound abuse of the judicial process."[24] She also ordered them to take continuing legal education courses and referred them for discipline in the jurisdictions where licensed to practice.[25] Judge Parker concluded that the lawyers "scorned their oath, flouted the rules, and attempted to undermine the integrity of the judiciary along the way."[26] Michigan attorney general Dana Nessel joined with Michigan's governor Gretchen Whitmer and secretary of state Jocelyn Benson, also attorneys, to request that the State Bar of Texas disbar Powell.[27]

L. Lin Wood repeatedly spread claims at political rallies and in court filings that the election was stolen, eventually making him the subject of a voter fraud investigation by the Georgia secretary of state.[28] The Georgia State Bar instituted proceedings against Wood to suspend him from law practice based on mental illness and cognitive impairment because of the conspiracy theories he championed.[29] He also was among the lawyers sanctioned by Judge Parker.

Dismissal of the cases from these and the other election-denying lawyers, however, is not sufficient. As of early 2023, only one additional court had issued financial sanctions directly against the lawyers in election fraud cases. Judge N. Reid Neureiter awarded attorneys' fees to the lawyers defending against an election challenge in a Colorado federal court. Calling the complaint "one enormous conspiracy theory,"[30] he sanctioned attorneys Gary Fielder and Ernest Walker under Rule 11 of the Federal Rules of Civil Procedure and federal statute 28 U.S.C. § 1927, which provides that "[a]ny attorney . . . who so multiplies the proceedings in any case unreasonably and vexatiously may be required by the court to satisfy personally the excess costs, expenses, and attorneys' fees reasonably incurred because of such conduct."[31]

Meanwhile, lawyers continued to churn out falsehoods about the presidential election even after the courts made it clear that the results were valid. Some repeated those lies in campaigns of their own. The election lies from lawyers in public office—or running for it—are especially troubling. Lawyers who dupe the public with meritless fraud allegations or sponsor slates of false electors betray the bargain they made when granted the privilege to practice law. But professional conduct rules do not currently stop them from telling these lies if a client isn't involved and when they aren't told in court.

Accountability for Lawyers' Election-Denial Lies in the Courthouse and in the Court of Public Opinion

To be clear, lies from lawyers sometimes are appropriate, even required. For example, lawyers routinely bluff in negotiations,[32] and ethics codes permit lawyers to argue contrary positions on behalf of different clients[33] or even to "act deceitfully" in a government investigation to help gather admissible evidence.[34] Moreover, the First Amendment protects most lies. The protection of speech from government censure distinguishes the Unites States from authoritarian rule.

Although a free country cannot curb falsehoods in public debate, a lawyer's license is based on fidelity to the rule of law. A society built on the principle that the "People" control it will not survive if those sworn to defend it undertake measures to assault it directly. The lawyers who goaded the public into believing their votes were stolen not only blurred the delicate balance between permissible deception and flagrant falsification, but they intentionally caused voters to doubt the very institutions that guard their freedoms. The state need not equate a license to practice law with a license to raze the rule of law.

Some lawyers stopped representing Trump's election challenges because of professional conduct and court rules.[35] Under Model Rule 3.3, lawyers cannot knowingly make a "false statement of fact or law" before a judge or knowingly introduce false evidence.[36] The duty of candor required while in court played a particularly crucial role in separating fact from fiction when Giuliani, under direct questioning from the judge, relented on his claims of election fraud. Similarly, Rule 11 of the Federal Rules of Civil Procedure and Model Rule 3.1 both bar lawyers from bringing frivolous claims in court.[37] Moreover, Model Rule 4.1 requires that in "the course of representing a client a lawyer shall not knowingly make a false statement of material fact or law to a third person."[38] There's one other rule to mention that (theoretically) applies even outside of the courtroom and the context of representing a party, but it is rarely if ever enforced in isolation because it is so vague. Model Rule 8.4(c) provides: "It is professional misconduct for a lawyer to . . . engage in conduct involving dishonesty, fraud, deceit or misrepresentation."[39] Each state has adopted a version of these model rules.[40]

Thanks to these rules, American courts remain as places where statements must still be supported by evidence-based, verifiable facts. Of course, the courthouse is not a pristine arbiter of truth. One need look no further than the long list of death-row exonerations to know that "truth" may not always emerge in court.[41] But it is one of the last places where rules adhere to the goal of truth-telling, even if imperfectly. In today's post-truth era,[42] courts and their rules are essential to democracy.

This raises an important question: if a lawyer's claims of election fraud cannot be sustained in the courtroom, should they be permitted in the court of public opinion? Legal ethics rules governing lawyer statements to the media focus on balancing a defendant's right to a fair trial with the public's right to know about potential safety threats and judicial proceedings generally. But they say nothing about the ballot-box fraud assertions heralded by lawyers in the media following the 2020 election. Model Rule 3.6 prohibits lawyers from making statements to the press that are substantially likely to materially prejudice the outcome of litigation[43] and admonishes general dishonesty.[44] But the rule applies only to lawyers who are involved in the pending litigation that they are discussing publicly.[45] Expanding the duty of candor from the courtroom to all media commentary—regardless of lawyer involvement in the matter, even in the limited circumstances of election lies by or on behalf of lawyer-politicians—would be a significant change.

The preamble to the Model Rules mandates that lawyers constantly balance their duties as "a representative of clients, an officer of the legal system and a public citizen having special responsibility for the quality of justice."[46] The lawyer plays a "vital role in the preservation of society."[47] Think back to Robert Post's argument in chapter 3 that as a member of a professional community, the lawyer cultivates "democratic competence," justifying some restraints on lawyer speech.[48] The preamble also commands lawyers to "further the public's understanding of and confidence in the rule of law and the justice system."[49] This special role is vital, according to the preamble, "because legal institutions in a constitutional democracy depend on popular participation and support to maintain their authority."[50] The survival of our democratic republic demands that the public participate in and support legal institutions. And lawyers are the ones charged with making sure the system works. This confluence of duties to the legal system and society in a democracy supports a narrow extension of the duty of candor beyond the confines of the courthouse, especially if a lawyer's speech causes severe harm.

To return to the New York court's rationale for suspending Giuliani's license, part of the justification was based on the fact that his false statements were made under his "authority of being an attorney" and the fact that they were amplified "using his large megaphone" on the public stage, which meant "the harm is magnified."[51] The court explained:

> One only has to look at the ongoing present public discord over the 2020 election, which erupted into violence, insurrection and death on January 6, 2021, at the U.S. Capitol, to understand the extent of the damage that can be done when the public is misled by false information about the elections.[52]

Make no mistake, I'm not proposing a wholesale ban on public-facing lawyer lies in political life. Not only would such a ban violate constitutional free speech protections, but it would also run afoul of well-established ethical obligations where a lack of truthfulness is part of the lawyer's duty to the client.[53] Nor am I suggesting that private individuals who are not lawyers should be silenced.

However, requiring of lawyers the same candor to the public that ethics rules require in court for the limited context of lies about election results is both constrained and justified given the harms they produce. A narrow ban on lawyer lies that undermine valid elections is also in the spirit of the rationale used to justify the duty of candor in court— that it is necessary for the public's confidence in the administration of justice and the legal profession. Finally, and importantly, constraints on lawyer speech that compromise the will of the people as expressed at the ballot box falls within the scope of regulatory functions appropriately conducted by bar associations and lawyer disciplinary authorities, even under two 2021 decisions from the United States Court of Appeals for the Fifth Circuit holding that bar associations cannot engage in certain legislative and political activities under the First Amendment.[54]

Other First Amendment experts agree that restraints on election lies are sustainable in limited circumstances. Scholar Rebecca Green makes an argument, similar to the one advanced here, in the context of "counterfeit campaign speech"[55]—that is, speech "in which political candidates' identities, actions, words, and images are intentionally faked with the intent to confuse voters and distort democracy."[56] Like the ban on election-fraud lawyer lies, the ban on counterfeit campaign speech would "address a threat to a process that is a predicate to securing all other rights and privileges guaranteed in a democratic system of government."[57] Law professor Richard Hasen concurs: "Narrow laws aimed at stopping maliciously false speech about the conduct of elections . . . likely would survive constitutional challenge."[58]

Bar authorities and regulators should, of course, take caution to ensure that the lawyer discipline system is not weaponized against disfavored political alliances or causes. Attempts to politicize professional ethics against lawyers based on specific causes and beliefs—like those seen with Communism in the 1940s and 1950s and with Southern civil rights attorneys in the 1960s—are counter to the scope and spirit of what I'm proposing here. Moreover, the First Amendment protects against this expanded ethical duty being wielded in this way.

* * *

Sherilynn Ifill is right that the legal profession needs a reckoning. First, election-denying lawyers should be called to account—follow the rules or relinquish their license. Second, the recommendations outlined in chapter 7 on the First Amendment include a proposed reform to the Model Rules for extending the duty of candor in the courtroom to the court of public opinion. These steps might not keep lawyers from attempting to undermine democracy in the future, but they will help the public know that information about election results from lawyers can be trusted.

Trust in our justice system is fundamental for accomplishing this book's ambition to see law democratized. To truly move the needle on solving the access-to-justice predicament facing the nation, we need a multifaceted, detailed, nuanced plan of action bringing together diverse individuals and organizations.

In short, we need a blueprint for justice.

PART II

Democratizing Law

The Blueprint

In a time of drastic change it is the learners who inherit the future. The learned usually find themselves beautifully equipped to live in a world that no longer exists.
—Eric Hoffer, *Reflections on the Human Condition*, 1973

The best way to predict the future is to invent it.
—Alan Kay, 1971[1]

Lawyers pride themselves on being members of a learned profession. We face, however, a "time of drastic change," as philosopher Eric Hoffer might say, where the "learned usually find themselves beautifully equipped to live in a world that no longer exists." His observation calls the profession to nurture learners who will "invent" the future of law practice, to borrow from computer scientist Alan Kay. The convergence of technological advances, global competition, and financial pressures facing the legal profession in the twenty-first century, coupled with the vast unmet need for legal help, demands action.

Legal services need a "tipping point"—what author Malcolm Gladwell calls that "one dramatic moment in an epidemic when everything can change all at once."[2] According to Gladwell the focus should be on the method by which we deliver ideas.[3] For example, he asks if Paul Revere's ride would have been as effective in the middle of the afternoon—when people were away on errands or working in the field—and without the urgency of night.[4] Surely not. Relatedly, Gladwell posits: "There is a simple way to package information that, under the right circumstances, can make it irresistible. All you have to do is find it."[5]

Making legal services "irresistible" may seem an impossible task. But there is a lot of room to make our legal system more available, and desirable, to the public. To do so, we need a concrete plan.

Part II methodically canvasses the paths taken by courts, entrepreneurs, law schools, lawyers, and regulators, among others, to democratize law in an effort to expand access to legal help. Each route has limitations but also offers important lessons for the future. Chapter 6 describes early attempts by courts employing antitrust doctrine to ease competitive barriers. These cases reduced costs for things like real estate title searches and bar exam review courses but ultimately did not break up the artificial constraints that remain. Chapter 7 reveals how courts also turned to the First Amendment to liberalize solicitation and advertising rules as well as unauthorized practice of law restrictions. Chapter 8 highlights international regulatory transformations that sparked some states to experiment with reforms to professional conduct rules and other legislative interventions aimed at encouraging competition and innovation. We then turn to education. Chapter 9 showcases the responses of some law schools to bridge the justice gap, and chapter 10 champions efforts designed to better educate the public about the law. Chapter 11 unveils an agenda for ethical innovation. Chapter 12 concludes with crucial next steps.

Each chapter in part II ends with a set of recommendations, along with suggestions about *who* should be responsible for implementation. This list includes attorneys, advocacy groups, bar authorities, individuals, judges, law schools, legal tech industry members, legislators, and research centers. Some of these categories need explanation. "Advocacy groups" are independent, nonprofit organizations with missions focused on access to justice. Examples include the National Coalition for a Right to Civil Counsel (mentioned in chapter 1) as well as the ACLU and the NAACP (both make appearances in chapter 7). A longer list of organizations can be found in the appendix. "Bar authorities" are defined in the introduction, and the category includes state and local bar associations, licensing authorities, and the American Bar Association and National Bar Association, among others. The category of "judges" includes courts and, often, court administrators (i.e., those charged with procedures and policies). "Research centers" refers to specialized organizations that assess and measure issues related to access to justice, which may be housed within law schools or may operate independently. These include entities like the American Bar Foundation and the Pew Research Center, both of which sponsored studies cited in part I. A longer list of these entities can also be found in the appendix.

Collectively, the recommendations at the ends of the chapters form a multifaceted blueprint for justice. You'll find a checklist in the appendix outlining all of them for easy reference. The ideas cataloged are not meant to be comprehensive, but instead they are intended to serve as a springboard for inventing a world in which everyone gets the legal help they need. It's up to each and every one of us to start building.

6

Antitrust Law

Perhaps the single greatest factor contributing to the justice crisis is the American legal profession's monopolistic origins, which endure today. Antitrust law's existence dates back to 1890,[1] when Congress passed the Sherman Act to prevent certain business structures, including cartels and monopolies, from seizing control of too much of the economy and maintaining prices at artificially high levels.[2] For nearly a century, however, courts deemed professions like law and medicine wholly exempt from federal antitrust law. They could freely engage in behavior considered monopolistic, and illegal, by other industries' standards.

The Sherman Act is designed to promote free competition. In a case that upended Northern Pacific Railroad's anticompetitive preferential routing in 1958, the Supreme Court described the Sherman Act as "a comprehensive charter of economic liberty aimed at preserving free and unfettered competition as the rule of trade."[3] Justice Hugo Black, the fifth longest-serving member of the Supreme Court, authored the majority opinion explaining that the act "rests on the premise that the unrestrained interaction of competitive forces will yield the best allocation of our economic resources, the lowest prices, the highest quality and greatest material progress, while at the same time providing an environment conducive to the preservation of our democratic political and social institutions."[4] The law provides for criminal sanctions and hefty treble damages (an award of three times the actual damages) as well as attorney fees for a successful challenge, which may be brought by the United States Department of Justice, the Federal Trade Commission, or private parties.[5]

Two different standards govern potential antitrust violations. Some activities like price fixing or group boycotts are deemed illegal per se; other endeavors such as monopolistic behavior are scrutinized under the rule of reason (i.e., whether their purpose, operation, and effect are an unreasonable restraint on trade). To determine whether federal antitrust law preempts state law, courts first ask whether the state law "mandates or authorizes conduct that necessarily constitutes a violation of the antitrust laws in all cases, or . . . places irresistible pressure on a private party to violate the antitrust laws in order to comply with the statute."[6] If so, the court will then determine whether the state law nonetheless is protected from federal preemption.

Justice Thurgood Marshall, the first African American to sit on the United States Supreme Court, called antitrust law "the Magna Carta of free enterprise" for the United States in a 1972 decision.[7] According to Marshall, antitrust is "as important to the preservation of economic freedom and our free-enterprise system as the Bill of Rights is to the protection of our fundamental personal freedom."[8] Half a century later, US senator Amy Klobuchar, in her book *Antitrust: Taking on Monopoly Power from the Gilded Age to the Digital Age*, wrote: "Antitrust and monopolies have everything to do with our economy, the prices we pay, and the way we live."[9] While her focus is primarily on American corporations, her conclusions apply to the legal profession as well: "A rigorous competition policy evens the playing field, spurs innovation, and reduces consumer prices."[10]

The command of federal antitrust law does not apply, however, to state sovereigns when directly engaged in regulatory action, even if anticompetitive, thanks to a doctrine created by the Supreme Court in a case called *Parker v. Brown*.[11] This means antitrust law does not apply to lawyer conduct rules promulgated by state courts and government bodies. This special antitrust exemption is known as the "state action doctrine." Taken to the extreme, were the Sherman Act applied broadly to all government action, states would lose much of their authority to pass laws and govern the public effectively.[12] Thus, the "doctrine rests on the notion that, although Congress might have the power to displace certain forms of state regulation, it did not wish to do so,"[13] grounded in federalism and state sovereignty concerns.

The Supreme Court first addressed the Sherman Act's application to the legal profession in *Goldfarb v. Virginia State Bar*, a case decided in 1975.[14]

Antitrust and Attorney Fee Schedules

In 1971, Lewis and Ruth Goldfarb decided to purchase a home in Fairfax County, Virginia. Their mortgage lender required a title search, an activity that by law could only be conducted by a licensed attorney. (A title search involves a review of public records to confirm the legal ownership of a piece of property.) The first attorney Lewis contacted required a fee of 1 percent of the property value, which was based on a minimum fee schedule from the Fairfax County Bar Association (County Bar). Hoping to save some money, Lewis contacted a second attorney, a third, a fourth. They all insisted on the same fee. He ultimately sent thirty-six letters and heard back from nineteen different attorneys, all with the identical message: pay a fee of 1 percent of the property value.

The Goldfarbs could not find a single attorney to assist with their title examination who would accept a fee lower than the minimum fee schedule published by the County Bar. Although the schedule was not enforced officially, the Virginia State Bar, an administrative agency of the Virginia Supreme Court, not only condoned fee schedules but maintained that they could not be ignored. Indeed, one Virginia State Bar opinion declared "that evidence that an attorney habitually charges less than the suggested minimum fee schedule adopted by his local bar Association raises a presumption that such lawyer is guilty of misconduct."[15]

After paying the fee and buying their home, the Goldfarbs decided to sue the Virginia State Bar and the County Bar under the Sherman Act. They claimed the minimum fee schedule constituted illegal price fixing, artificially keeping prices high. The County Bar argued that federal antitrust law was "never intended to include the learned professions"[16] and took the position that "competition is inconsistent with the practice of a profession because enhancing profit is not the goal of professional activities; the goal is to provide services necessary to the community."[17] The Goldfarbs lost, at first. According to the lower court, "although the fee schedule and enforcement mechanism substantially restrained competition among lawyers, publication of the schedule by the County Bar was outside the scope" of federal review because of the legal profession's longstanding exemption from antitrust law under the state action doctrine.[18]

On appeal, the Supreme Court disagreed. For the first time ever, it applied antitrust law to the legal profession and struck down the minimum fee schedule. Chief Justice Burger, on behalf of a unanimous Supreme Court, wrote: "The nature of an occupation, standing alone, does not provide sanctuary from the Sherman Act."[19] He rejected the notion that "the public-service aspect of professional practice" should exempt lawyers from antitrust law.[20] Moreover, he explained: "In the modern world it cannot be denied that the activities of lawyers play an important part in commercial intercourse, and that anticompetitive activities by lawyers may exert a restraint on commerce."[21] As such, the court had no trouble finding the Sherman Act could be applied to the legal profession, at least in some circumstances, to bust up anticompetitive behavior.[22] Consequently, the Virginia State Bar and the County Bar found themselves liable for a $200,000 settlement, reached after the case returned to the district court. The bar associations levied an assessment on their members to cover the cost.[23]

The Supreme Court cautioned, despite its willingness to apply antitrust law in this instance, that in future cases the legal profession might nonetheless deserve special treatment:

> The fact that a restraint operates upon a profession as distinguished from a business is, of course, relevant in determining whether that particular restraint violates the Sherman Act. It would be unrealistic to view the practice of professions as interchangeable with other business activities, and automatically to apply to the professions antitrust concepts which originated in other areas. The public service aspect, and other features of the professions, may require that a particular practice, which could properly be viewed as a violation of the Sherman Act in another context, be treated differently.[24]

The opinion contains no explicit acknowledgment that the Supreme Court justices themselves, and the judges reviewing the matter in the courts below, as well as the regulators setting the challenged price schedule and issuing opinions about it, were all members of the regulated profession under review. The only distinction between lawyers and other professions mentioned by the court went to lawyer exceptionalism, offering additional support for upholding future economic constraints: "The interest of the States in regulating lawyers is especially great since lawyers are essential to the primary governmental function of administering justice, and have historically been officers of the courts. In holding that certain anticompetitive conduct by lawyers is within the reach of the Sherman Act we intend no diminution of the authority of the state to regulate its professions."[25]

What this means is that *Goldfarb* opened the door to federal antitrust review for state regulation of the legal profession, but just barely. In later cases, the Supreme Court declined to apply antitrust law to hold entities like the Virginia State Bar and the County Bar accountable for their anticompetitive behavior.

Antitrust and Attorney Licensing

Consider the plight of Edward Ronwin. After successfully completing three years of law school, he took the Arizona Bar Exam in 1974, only to learn that he failed to achieve the cut off score on the test.[26] He sued, arguing that Arizona Supreme Court's Committee on Examinations and Admissions violated antitrust law by setting the grading scale in accordance with the number of attorneys that the Committee deemed appropriate to reduce competition "rather than with reference to some suitable level of competence."[27]

A divided Supreme Court in *Hoover v. Ronwin* applied the state action doctrine and dismissed Ronwin's complaint without ever considering his allegations. Justice Lewis Powell wrote the majority opinion: "Where the action complained of—here the failure to admit Ronwin to the Bar—was that of the State itself, the action is exempt from antitrust liability regardless of the State's motives in taking the action."[28] Justice John Paul Stevens, joined in dissent by Justices Harry Blackmun and Byron White, questioned the majority's deference: "When [state] . . . authority is delegated to those with a stake in the competitive conditions within the market, there is a real risk that public power will be exercised for private benefit."[29] Stevens engaged in a lengthy discussion about the concerns of capture associated with regulation that is enacted, enforced, and reviewed by members of the regulated profession:

> In essence, the Court is suggesting that a special protective shield should be provided to lawyers because they—unlike bakers, engineers, or members of any other craft—may not have sufficient confidence in the ability

of our legal system to identify and reject unmeritorious claims to be willing to assume the ordinary risks of litigation associated with the performance of civic responsibilities. I do not share the Court's fear that the administration of bar examinations by court-appointed lawyers cannot survive the scrutiny associated with rather ordinary litigation that persons in most other walks of life are expected to endure.[30]

For Stevens, and his fellow dissenters, *Goldfarb* had clearly rejected the "parochialism" reflected in the majority opinion: "Indeed, the argument that it is unwise or unnecessary to require the petitioners to comply with the Sherman Act is simply an attack upon the wisdom of the longstanding congressional commitment to the policy of free markets and open competition embodied in the antitrust laws."[31]

* * *

Despite *Goldfarb*'s success, antitrust law had little traction increasing competition in legal services, as evidenced by the majority's view in *Ronwin*. The only other Supreme Court decision to apply antitrust law directly to the legal profession to expand competition was a case brought by law students against companies that offered bar exam review courses, *Palmer v. BRG of Georgia, Inc.*, decided in 1990.[32] The students claimed that the companies agreed to artificially raise the price of bar review materials and lectures. The court agreed and held that the agreement violated the Sherman Act.

A more recent 2015 decision called *North Carolina State Board of Dental Examiners v. Federal Trade Commission* applied antitrust law to professional services involving dentists, not lawyers, but it offers some insight into how the Supreme Court might view future cases like *Goldfarb, Ronwin,* and *Palmer.*

Antitrust and Teeth Whitening Services

A North Carolina law delegates control over the practice of dentistry to the North Carolina State Board of Dental Examiners. The law is silent, however, about teeth whitening and whether it might constitute "dentistry." The process didn't even exist at the time the legislature passed the original law and the governor signed it. When nondentists began offering teeth whitening services at cheaper prices, however, dentists started complaining. So the State Board issued cease-and-desist letters to the teeth whiteners, threatening them with criminal sanctions if they didn't get out of the market. (Sound familiar?)

The Federal Trade Commission learned about the anticompetitive activity and sued the State Board, arguing that it violated antitrust law in issuing the letters because, even though it was an arm of the state, it functioned as a group of private dentists rather than as a government body.[33] The United States Court of Appeals for the Fourth Circuit agreed, declining to apply the state action doctrine to protect the state board from antitrust review because it comprised only dentists, a hygienist, and a member elected by other members of the board, with no publicly elected or state official overseeing the board's work.[34]

In a six-to-three decision, the United States Supreme Court affirmed the Fourth Circuit, holding that the state dental board violated antitrust law by issuing those cease-and-desist letters.[35] It was a victory for the teeth whiteners and their customers. Because a "majority of the board's members are engaged in the active practice of the profession it regulates," the court held that it acted like a private body even though it had been designated by the state as a governmental actor.[36] Justice Anthony Kennedy, writing for the majority, explained, "the need for supervision turns not on the formal designation given by States to regulators but on the risk that active market participants will pursue private interests in restraining trade."[37] The court also cautioned that such an arrangement risks that "established ethical standards" will "blend with private anticompetitive motives in a way difficult for even market participants to discern."[38] Accordingly, in this sort of circumstance, limiting antitrust immunity is "most essential."[39]

The Supreme Court declined to consider whether a similar limitation on antitrust immunity is warranted when the sovereign itself is a member of the profession it regulates, which of course is the case for the legal profession where judges and lawyers issue and oversee the rules governing the practice of law. And the teeth whitening opinion left several significant questions unanswered. First, what constitutes an "active market participant" within the regulated profession? Does this include retired members of the profession or individuals trained in the profession who have moved on to other careers? Second, how do we define the relevant market? The US Department of Justice takes a fairly broad reading of this issue, contending that the "state agency officials need only practice in the 'occupation' regulated by the agency in order to be considered active market participants. State officials need not be direct competitors of the plaintiff."[40] In the case of the legal profession, some might say that judges are not engaged in the "active practice" of law because they adjudicate rather than litigate; yet the fact remains that they are members of the legal profession. Moreover, many judges, especially at the state level, will return to private practice after a period of judicial service. Third, how should we address intrinsic concerns beyond economic regulation, for example, conflicts of interest, due process concerns, or other potential harms?

Questions like these are likely to resurface. Indeed, in the months after the teeth whitening decision, two similar lawsuits involving legal services soon followed. In June 2015, online provider of legal forms LegalZoom sued the North Carolina State Bar for violating federal antitrust conspiracy laws, seeking $10.5 million in damages and an order requiring the State Bar to register LegalZoom's prepaid legal services plans, allowing them to be sold in North Carolina.[41] This case ultimately settled under an agreement permitting LegalZoom to continue offering its plans in the state, but the questions it raised still remain. The following month Express Lien, an online mechanics lien and construction payment platform, sued the Ohio State Bar Association. (A mechanics lien places a legal entitlement on property, often used when a contractor goes unpaid.) Express Lien alleged that the Bar violated antitrust law in "illegally and unreasonably restricting trade by accusing the plaintiff of the unauthorized practice of law." This case also settled, and Express Lien continued to operate in Ohio.[42]

While some state bar associations proactively endeavored to reduce legal exposure by altering their practices after the teeth whitening opinion, most did not. For example, the Washington State Bar Association suspended the issuance of potentially anticompetitive advisory opinions. Similarly, though ultimately unsuccessful, the North Carolina State Bar proposed legislation in 2015 that would have required the state attorney general to actively supervise any unauthorized practice of law actions that appeared to be anticompetitive.

Courts likely will continue to be confronted with issues surrounding whether antitrust immunity should be limited when members of the regulated group promulgate competitive constraints. For example, in 2018, TIKD Services, LLC, a service matching individuals with parking tickets to lawyers via a mobile app, pursued an $11.4 million antitrust suit against the Florida State Bar. The United States Department of Justice filed a Statement of Interest in support of TIKD, but TIKD's claims were dismissed with prejudice that same year by the federal district court. In October 2021, the Florida Supreme Court ruled in a closely divided four-to-three decision that the app constituted unauthorized practice of law. The majority explained: "As a nonlawyer, TIKD simply lacks the skill or training to ensure the quality of the legal services provided to the public through the licensed attorneys it contracts with, nor does it possess the ability to ensure compliance with the Rules of Professional Conduct."[43] But the three dissenting justices took issue with that conclusion: "TIKD formulated no legal strategy. It gathered no evidence. It filed no court papers. It made no court appearances, no arguments to a judge or jury. Other than in explaining its offerings on its website, it answered no questions."[44] The dissent viewed TIKD not as offering legal advice but instead offering "a business proposition: hire a lawyer we introduce, at a fee we set, and you will not bear the risk that the lawyer's services, or indeed your ticket, will cost you more than our fee. Offering that bargain does not constitute . . . the unauthorized practice of law."[45]

What does this mean for access to justice? Most important for the objectives of this book, the outcome of the teeth whitening case signals a potential willingness of the Supreme Court to place state licensing boards and regulatory committees "under the Sherman Act's microscope."[46] To be sure, antitrust litigation is not necessarily the most efficient means for reform, but it proved effective in dismantling *Goldfarb*'s anticompetitive fee schedules. It is worth considering in future litigation how the reasoning of the teeth whitening case might be applied to attack unauthorized practice of law rules and other anticompetitive regulations. A secondary, related impact is the exposure of lawyers who sit on state licensing boards and regulatory committees to potential liability. While state supreme courts are immune when acting in their sovereign capacity of adopting professional conduct rules, in the wake of the teeth whitening opinion, it is uncertain whether that immunity will extend to the lawyers, as "active market participants," who act under authority delegated by the courts. Rather than risk liability, a better path would be to avoid the anticompetitive behavior in the first place.

* * *

After the Supreme Court mostly cabined off the application of antitrust law to the legal profession, plaintiffs shifted to the First Amendment for addressing anticompetitive lawyer regulation. Chapter 7 returns to the *Bates v. Arizona State Bar* case discussed in chapter 2 and provides an overview of First Amendment successes and limitations. But first, this chapter concludes with an initial set of blueprint recommendations.

Recommendations

Key: Attorneys (A), Advocacy Groups (AG), Bar Authorities (BA), Individuals (I), Judges (J), Law Schools (LS), Legal Tech Industry (LTI), Legislators (L), Research Centers (RC)

Adjust Unauthorized Practice of Law Restrictions (BA, J, L)

In 2002, the American Bar Association (ABA) attempted to adopt a model definition of the practice of law to guide the states. It defined "the practice of law" to mean "the application of legal principles and judgment with regard to the circumstances or objectives of a person that require the knowledge and skill of a person trained in the law."[47] It also listed four areas presumed to constitute "the practice of law," which were:

1. Giving advice or counsel to persons as to their legal rights or responsibilities or to those of others;
2. Selecting, drafting, or completing legal documents or agreements that affect the legal rights of a person;
3. Representing a person before an adjudicative body, including, but not limited to, preparing or filing documents or conducting discovery; or
4. Negotiating legal rights and responsibilities on behalf of a person.[48]

The United States Department of Justice and the Federal Trade Commission sent a letter to the American Bar Association dismissing this approach.[49] They found the definition "not in the public interest because the harms it imposes on consumers by limiting competition are likely much greater than any consumer harm that it prevents."[50] Significantly, however, they did not reject outright the creation of a uniform definition—it just needed to be "substantially narrowed,"[51] which the ABA refused to do. After more than two decades, it is time for the ABA to go back to the drawing board. Regardless, states can and should narrow the definition on their own.

Explore the Reserved Activities Approach (BA)

Another variation of the proposal to adjust unauthorized practice of law restrictions is to consider the approach from England and Wales of "reserved activities." There, only a narrow list of specific legal actions must be undertaken by a licensed lawyer (recall from chapter 3 that the only services "reserved" in those countries to solicitors and barristers are court appearances, conducting litigation, preparing contracts, probate activities, notary services, and the administration of oaths). Everything else is open, regardless of licensing—this includes bankruptcy, divorce, and will writing, among others—though areas like bankruptcy are regulated for consumer protection. Research shows that competition is not unduly suppressed among the reserved areas, and there has not been excessive harm to clients or the public in areas where lawyers and nonlawyers do compete to offer services. That said, the reserved activities approach is not without critique. A recent study found some areas to be "an historical anachronism" not grounded in the public good or consumer protection.[52] Still, there is merit in exploring the concept of reserved activities to address the vagueness of the rules surrounding the American practice of law. For this reason, scholars Gillian Hadfield and Deborah Rhode similarly conclude from their own research "that the ideal reforms would follow the British model and establish specific legal activities that require licensing, leaving the residual to the ordinary protections of the market."[53] Would it be a heavy lift for regulators to adopt this approach? Yes. This recommendation represents a fundamental rethinking of how legal services are regulated. But the fact that it's difficult to implement change doesn't mean it shouldn't be explored.

Include Lay Members with Meaningful Participation on Regulatory Boards (BA, J)

Adding lay members who are not lawyers to boards that make determinations about unauthorized practice of law can both avoid antitrust scrutiny and simultaneously add the benefit of offering outside perspectives from would-be clients and the public. However, the lay members must "participate in a meaningful way,"[54] according to a Federal Trade Commission senior staff attorney. Even if the board is predominantly nonlawyers, a single lawyer's presence could cause the whole board to be viewed as an "active market participant" if that lawyer controls the decision-making process.

Offer Alternative Fee Arrangements (A, BA, LTI)

The ruling in *Goldfarb* declaring fee schedules in violation of antitrust law doesn't mean lawyers have no option but hourly billing. Indeed, the ABA Model Rule 1.5 requires only that lawyers charge a "reasonable" fee. Alternative fee arrangements provide greater incentive for efficient, high-quality work rather than maximizing the number of billable hours, leading clients in recent years to move away from the billable hour model. We know from research by law professor Susan Saab Fortney and others that in-house counsel increasingly demand options like flat fees.[55] For example, Microsoft announced in 2017 that it planned "to shift 90 percent of its legal work to an alternative fee structure over the next two years, moving away from billable hours."[56] Clio, a cloud-based law practice management platform, produces an annual Legal Trends Report, surveying more than 1,000 legal professionals and 1,000 consumers of legal services from the general population.[57] In 2022, they found that in addition to 67 percent desiring flat fees, 70 percent wanted payment plans, 65 percent wanted insurance plans to cover costs, 53 percent wanted crowdfunding options, 46 percent wanted to barter or exchange services, and 40 percent wanted financial loans.[58] Making these sorts of options widely available to moderate-income individuals could help shrink the justice gap.

7

The First Amendment

After the United States Supreme Court declined to further expand the *Goldfarb v. Virginia State Bar* decision's antitrust coverage, litigants and advocacy groups focused on constitutional protections in an effort to increase competition and access to information about the law. The primary provision is found in the First Amendment, our emphasis here, though other provisions support access to legal help, including the Sixth Amendment's right to effective assistance of counsel[1] and constitutional voting rights.[2] Over the years, since the early 1960s, the Supreme Court repeatedly confronted issues involving the First Amendment and access to information about legal rights and entitlements.

The First Amendment provides, in relevant part, that "Congress shall make no law . . . abridging the freedom of speech . . . or the right of the people peaceably to assemble, and to petition the Government for a redress of grievances."[3] It applies not only to Congress, but also to state government, through the Fourteenth Amendment.[4] Access to the law—that is, facilitating and delivering legal services—goes to the very heart of First Amendment concerns and values by contributing to what Supreme Court justice Oliver Wendell Holmes called the "marketplace of ideas."[5] Access to information about the law also acts as a checkpoint on government action,[6] enables individual development,[7] and cultivates political discourse.[8] This is, perhaps, why the First Amendment has been used more successfully than antitrust doctrine to challenge constraints on the practice of law.

Paradoxically, while the First Amendment guarantees the public certain rights to information about the law, it also allows constraints on much of what a lawyer can say. Lawyers, and the clients who need them, rely heavily on lawyers' speech—courtroom advocacy, written briefs and opinions, intimate advice, counseling, contracts, and more. Lawyers' speech has been described as "not only central to what the legal system is all about, and not only the product of the law as we know it, but basically the only thing that lawyers and the legal system have."[9] The speech

102

is valuable both when it is protected from government constraint but also, importantly, because sometimes it is in fact constricted.

Nearly every rule of professional conduct governing the practice of law touches on what a lawyer may, or may not, say. Lawyers cannot reveal client confidences.[10] They must be circumspect in disclosures to the media during a pending trial.[11] Lawyers walk a fine line in counseling a client about good faith challenges to existing laws.[12] For many years they could not advertise, and in most jurisdictions, lawyers remain rather limited in their ability to solicit clients and market to them.[13] Lawyers must heed restrictions on their ability to criticize the judiciary.[14] They cannot tell lies to judges in court,[15] but they should "bluff" when negotiating contracts.[16] When lawyers take their oath to practice law, they sacrifice many free speech rights enjoyed by the public.

The balance between public access to knowledge about law generally and individual access to uniquely tailored legal advice and advocacy is delicate. First Amendment scholar Robert Post explains: "To preserve the self-government of the people, we must preserve their access to knowledge."[17] At the same time, Post cautions that we must protect what he calls "democratic competence."[18] Post defines this phrase as "the cognitive empowerment of persons within public discourse, which in part depends on their access to disciplinary knowledge. Cognitive empowerment is necessary both for intelligent self-governance and for the value of democratic legitimation."[19] For Post, "[d]emocratic *legitimation* requires that the speech of all persons be treated with toleration and equality. Democratic *competence*, by contrast, requires that speech be subject to a disciplinary authority that distinguishes good ideas from bad ones,"[20] and consequently may be regulated by the government. In other words, when we seek advice from professionals based upon their area of competence, or knowledge, not all speech should be treated equally. We want accurate, helpful, relevant information from professionals. Constraints placed on who may provide professional knowledge, which drives up the cost of receiving that knowledge, incentivizes legal training. It means that a lawyer can recoup the time and expense of having acquired the specialized professional skill during law school. Thus, some constraint on lawyer speech is necessary, and permitted by the government, despite the First Amendment protections that typically would favor free speech, not governmental limitations.

104 | THE FIRST AMENDMENT

Over the years, the Supreme Court derived a complex framework of constitutional protection for various categories of lawyer speech, including legal advice, advertising, solicitation, statements to the press, bar admission and licensing disclosures, and statements by government attorneys. The protection includes:

- the right of individuals to receive advice from civil rights lawyers about "their constitutional rights, [including] urging them to institute litigation of a particular kind, recommending particular lawyers and financing such litigation"[21]
- the right of union members to "maintain and carry out their plan for advising workers who are injured to obtain legal advice"[22]
- the right to "hire attorneys . . . to assist . . . in the assertion of legal rights" for union members' workers' compensation claims[23]
- the right to undertake "collective activity . . . to obtain meaningful access to the courts"[24]
- a lawyer's right to publish "truthful advertisement concerning the availability and terms of routine legal services"[25]
- a lawyer's right to advise "a lay person of her legal rights and disclos[e] in a subsequent letter that free legal assistance is available"[26]
- a lawyer's right to list "the areas of his practice, . . . the courts and States in which he had been admitted to practice,"[27] and "certified legal specialist"[28] on letterhead
- a lawyer's right to mail announcement cards to the public[29] as well as letters "to potential clients who have had a foreclosure suit filed against them"[30]

That certain forms of legal advice and representation are covered by the First Amendment is a relatively uncontroversial observation. However, until the 1960s and 1970s, the dominant view was that legal information is not speech at all under the First Amendment. This perspective began to evolve as lawyers, faced with controls on their ability to provide legal information to unserved or underserved markets, found success in liberalizing professional regulations via First Amendment challenges.

Key legal opinions defining the contours of the First Amendment right to legal advice and representation are summarized below. They form the heart of the constitutional protections surrounding access to justice in civil matters.

NAACP v. Button

The United States Supreme Court initially applied the First Amendment to protect legal advice and representation more than half a century ago. In 1963, the Supreme Court determined that the Virginia State Bar could not ban civil rights lawyers from informing minorities about their constitutional rights in a case called *NAACP v. Button*.[31]

To understand what happened in *Button*, we need to go back in time a few years. Following the Supreme Court's 1955 directive in *Brown v. Board of Education II* to desegregate schools "with all deliberate speed," states like Virginia resisted in various ways.[32] One strategy was legislation directed at squelching the efforts of lawyers for the NAACP to enforce *Brown* and other civil rights. The Virginia General Assembly expanded legal ethics rules about client solicitation under the pretense that lawyers "stirring up" litigation was unprofessional and should be prohibited. The NAACP challenged these restrictions under a number of grounds but only needed the Supreme Court to rule on one for the win: "The right of the NAACP and its members and lawyers to associate for the purpose of assisting persons who seek legal redress for infringements of their constitutionally guaranteed and other rights."[33]

A six-to-three majority in *Button* held that the First Amendment protected advice from NAACP attorneys to prospective litigants, notwithstanding the state's power to regulate the legal profession and improper solicitation of legal business.[34] The court also recognized the political value inherent in legal advocacy: "Groups which find themselves unable to achieve their objectives through the ballot frequently turn to the courts. . . . And under the conditions of modern government, litigation may well be the sole practicable avenue open to a minority to petition for redress of grievances."[35] Moreover, the court protected the interests of individuals in hearing the legal advice, in addition to the interests of attorneys in speaking about it.[36]

The Union Trilogy

The Supreme Court extended the holding of *Button* to situations beyond the civil rights context in a series of three legal challenges brought by unions. The first was *Brotherhood of Railroad Trainmen v. Virginia ex rel. Virginia State Bar.*[37] There, the court declared that an injunction prohibiting the Brotherhood from advising injured workers to obtain legal advice violated the First Amendment.[38] In doing so, the court once again protected the prospective clients' rights to hear as well as the lawyers' rights to speak, noting that the state "could not, by invoking the power to regulate the professional conduct of attorneys, infringe in any way the right of individuals and the public to be fairly represented in lawsuits authorized by Congress to effectuate a basic public interest."[39] The court did not expect individuals, on their own, "to know how to protect their rights when dealing with practiced and carefully counseled adversaries."[40] In *United Mine Workers, District 12 v. Illinois State Bar Association*,[41] the court further clarified that *Button* was not meant to be limited solely to civil rights litigation and struck an injunction brought by a state bar organization to prohibit a union from hiring an attorney to advise members in processing workers' compensation claims. Justice Hugo Black wrote:

> The litigation in question is, of course, not bound up with political matters of acute social moment, as in *Button*, but the First Amendment does not protect speech . . . only to the extent it can be characterized as political. Great secular causes, with small ones, are guarded. The grievances for redress of which the right of petition was insured, and with it the right of assembly, are not solely religious or political ones. And the rights of free speech and a free press are not confined to any field of human interest.[42]

The court held that the First Amendment, which guarantees "freedom of speech, assembly, and petition" included "the right to hire attorneys" for help asserting legal rights, entitlements, and protections.[43] Several years later the court reaffirmed *Button* in *United Transportation Union v. State Bar*, declaring that "meaningful access to the courts is a fundamental right within the protection of the First Amendment."[44]

The union cases built upon *Button* in three important ways. First, they clarified that the First Amendment protects legal advice and advocacy not only about political and civil rights but also about other matters. Second, they show that the First Amendment protects a legal services delivery system involving nonprofit corporations, nonlawyers, and lawyers like the NAACP but also others. Third, while *Button* and the union cases focused on *whose* rights were at stake (i.e., the First Amendment protection of the prospective clients' rights to hear and the lawyers' rights to speak), these cases also protected *what* was being said (i.e., the First Amendment protection of legal advice).

Legal Services Corporation v. Velazquez

Another case that built upon *Button* in a consequential fashion is *Legal Services Corporation v. Velazquez*.[45] In *Velazquez*, a five-to-four majority struck, again on First Amendment grounds, a federal restriction that prevented attorneys for the Legal Services Corporation (LSC) from challenging the validity of a state or federal statute.[46] (Remember from chapter 1 that the LSC is the single largest funder of legal aid in the United States.) The rationale for the federal restriction? Congress did not believe that, after it appropriated federal funds to the LSC, the LSC should then be able to use those funds to challenge the validity of laws enacted by Congress. Thus, LSC attorneys were required to cease representation immediately if a question about a federal statute's validity arose, whether "during initial attorney-client consultations or in the midst of litigation proceedings."[47] As you might imagine, having your legal aid attorney quit in the middle of a trial is burdensome, at best, and likely the precursor to a loss.

Justice Anthony Kennedy, writing for the majority, raised several concerns related to the First Amendment. First, he observed that the legislative restriction prevented attorneys not only from advising clients but also from advising a court about "serious questions of statutory validity."[48] Such an arrangement, Kennedy wrote, "is inconsistent with the proposition that attorneys should present all the reasonable and well-grounded arguments necessary for proper resolution of the case."[49] Second, a ban on "the analysis of certain legal issues" in effect "prohibits speech and expression upon which courts must depend for the proper exercise of the judicial power."[50] Third, the arrangement, he observed, "insulate[s] the Government's laws from judicial inquiry."[51] Finally, Justice Kennedy expressed concern that, if the legislative restriction were validated by the Supreme Court, "there would be lingering doubt whether the truncated representation had resulted in . . . full advice to the client."[52] As a consequence, both "[t]he courts and the public" would be left "to question the adequacy and fairness of professional representations when the attorney . . . avoided all reference to questions of [the banned advice]."[53] In recognizing the importance of lawyers being informed and able to act independently, he further noted that "[w]e must be vigilant when Congress imposes rules and conditions which in effect insulate its own laws from legitimate judicial challenge."[54] (You might be thinking that his observation about Congress also should apply to the judiciary when it creates rules, but, as the previous chapter on antitrust revealed, that is not how the Supreme Court's precedent has played out.)

Commercial Speech Cases

Speech about access to the law, or the delivery of legal services, in many ways serves the same function as political speech, meaning that this type of speech deserves the highest protection from government interference. This is the category the Supreme Court placed it in with *Button*, the union cases, and *Velazquez*. Sometimes, however, the court affords this speech less protection, examining restrictions under the "commercial speech" doctrine—that is, speech that proposes a commercial transaction or is otherwise financially motivated. A four-part test for recognizing "commercial speech" was first articulated in a case called *Central Hudson Gas and Electric Corporation v. Public Service Commission*, decided in 1980. The test asks first, does the speech concern lawful activity that is not misleading? If so, then second, the asserted governmental interest must be substantial; third, the speech regulation must directly advance that interest; and fourth, the regulation must be narrowly tailored. Otherwise, it will be struck down.

A common thread among the various kinds of legal information—legal documents, legal products, and some forms of legal advice—is that each is at least partially commercial in nature, whether explicitly as legal representation for sale or implicitly as an inducement to hire a lawyer. Should speech about legal help receive less First Amendment protection if the lawyer's primary motive is financial? Surely not, at least according to Justice Harry Blackmun, who wrote in his preargument memorandum in an early commercial speech case called *Bigelow v. Virginia*[55] that "[c]ommercial speech is not *per se* more lowly than other forms."[56]

THE FIRST AMENDMENT | 109

Even so, the line between commercial speech and political speech is hazy, especially when the speech is about access to legal representation. The Supreme Court's treatment of commercial speech during the 1970s speaks directly to just how far the First Amendment might be extended to protect the public's right to legal help. The public's interest in receiving, or hearing, information is a driving force.

Bigelow v. Virginia

In the early 1970s, the *Virginia Weekly* published an advertisement on behalf of the Women's Pavilion of New York City containing information about the availability of legal abortions in New York.[57] The newspaper's editor in chief, Jeffrey Bigelow, was convicted in Albemarle County Circuit Court for violating a Virginia statute criminalizing the publication of an advertisement for "the procuring of an abortion or miscarriage."[58] Bigelow appealed, arguing that the statute infringed on his free speech rights.[59] The Supreme Court ultimately declined to address this issue, finding his claim moot in light of subsequent amendments to the statute by the Virginia legislature,[60] but Justice Blackmun's seven-to-two opinion explaining that decision sheds light on the scope of First Amendment protection for legal information as commercial speech. First, he noted, "The existence of commercial activity, in itself, is no justification for narrowing the protection of expression secured by the First Amendment."[61] Importantly, he identified an informational interest that extends beyond an individual targeted by an advertisement to include "those with a general curiosity about, or genuine interest in, the subject matter or the law of another State and its development, and to readers seeking reform."[62] As such, "the First Amendment favors dissemination of information and opinion,"[63] and as a corollary, he concluded that there is also a constitutional right to receive this information.

Virginia State Board of Pharmacy v. Virginia Citizens Consumer Council, Inc.

Soon after *Bigelow*, the Supreme Court extended the holding to prescription drug advertising in *Virginia State Board of Pharmacy v. Virginia Citizens Consumer Council, Inc.*[64] A Virginia law barred pharmacists from advertising the price of prescription drugs. An individual consumer, along with consumer rights groups, sued and won. Once again, a right to hear information carried the day. As the *Virginia Pharmacy* court observed, a recipient's interest in commercial information "may be as keen, if not keener by far, than his interest in the day's most urgent political debate."[65]

The paternalistic nature of the state restrictions also troubled the *Virginia Pharmacy* court. Seven of the nine justices rejected independence and professionalism as justifications for the ban on prescription drug advertising. (Only Chief Justice William Rehnquist dissented; Justice John Paul Stevens did not participate.) The justices were especially concerned that the "[s]tate's protectiveness of its citizens rests in large measure on the advantages of their being kept in ignorance."[66] The better alternative to paternalism, Blackmun wrote in the majority opinion, "is to assume that this information is not in itself harmful, that people will perceive their own best interests if only they are well enough informed, and that the best means to that end is to open the channels of communication rather than to close them."[67] In the end, "[i]f they are truly open, nothing prevents the 'professional' pharmacist from marketing his own assertedly superior product, and contrasting it with that of the low-cost, high-volume prescription drug retailer."[68] Even so, the court affords less protection to commercial speech than political speech, which means that some government restrictions may survive.

Bates v. Arizona State Bar (Again)

You know from chapter 2 what happened next. In *Bates v. Arizona State Bar*, the Supreme Court extended what was at the time an emerging commercial speech doctrine to protect the dissemination of legal information about attorney fees in that newspaper ad placed by young lawyers Bates and O'Steen.

Now that you've also read the discussion of antitrust law in chapter 6, you may be interested to learn that Bates and O'Steen also raised antitrust claims when they sued the Arizona State Bar. While the Supreme Court dismissed those claims, a close review of the majority's opinion suggests that the outcome was driven, at least in part, by the competition values tied to antitrust law rather than free speech interests. The Arizona State Bar justified the advertising ban on the grounds that it helped maintain a professional image for lawyers and protected the public from lawyers stirring up unnecessary litigation or misleading communications, harkening back to themes rejected in *NAACP v. Button*.[69] The court wasn't having it. For Blackmun, again writing for the majority, the lack of advertising proved "the profession's failure to reach out and serve the community."[70] Notably, he described the First Amendment analysis in language of competition and economic freedom. Thus, the commercial speech analysis in *Bates* (and the cases that followed[71]) turns on similar factors as would an antitrust analysis, allowing the court to achieve a procompetitive result under the First Amendment even where the state action doctrine would otherwise exempt the economic restriction from scrutiny under antitrust law.[72]

Despite the First Amendment's application in *Bates*, this constitutional argument found less success when concerned with economic constraints on *who* may practice law, as opposed to *how* law may be practiced. For example, lower courts have historically refused to find a First Amendment right to allow an unlicensed layperson to represent an individual in court[73] or a right for nonlawyers to form a partnership with lawyers.[74] This may be shifting. In 2022, a New York federal district court judge reached the opposite conclusion. You'll learn more about that at the end of this chapter.

Ohralik v. Ohio State Bar Association *and* In re Primus

After the Supreme Court struck down the wholesale ban on attorney advertising in *Bates*, it then turned its attention to restrictions on in-person solicitation of clients. In 1978, on the same day, the court decided two cases involving lawyer solicitation of clients, one involving a so-called ambulance chaser (i.e., someone who seeks clients at the site of an injury or disaster) and the other involving a civil rights attorney. The court drew a line between the two for First Amendment protection. In *Ohralik v. Ohio State Bar Association*,[75] the court determined that the state *could* ban the ambulance chaser from in-person solicitation of injured victims to inform them of their potential liability damages. But, in *In re Primus*,[76] the court held that a lawyer for the American Civil Liberties Union (ACLU) *could not* be banned from in-person solicitation of women who had been involuntarily sterilized to inform them of their constitutional rights.[77] The court endeavored to reconcile these decisions by looking to the fact that attorney Albert Ohralik solicited for his own financial gain at the hospital bedside, whereas ACLU lawyer Edna Primus offered services free of charge (though she still received a salary from the ACLU). But shouldn't Ohralik have been permitted to provide the legal information, even at the hospital bedside? That is precisely when a vulnerable individual may need help most. (Think back to the discussion about medical legal partnerships in chapter 3.)

In the wake of *Bates*, *Ohralik*, and *Primus*, the court took up a number of lawyer speech restrictions, sometimes siding with the regulators to uphold speech restrictions[78] and frequently not,[79] mostly in the context of advertising, client solicitation, and advice giving. In each of these cases, the court has focused heavily on the public's interest in hearing the information and less so the lawyer's right to speak.[80] This isn't a coincidence.

Hunter v. Virginia State Bar

To better understand the commercial speech doctrine in a more modern context, meet Horace Frazier Hunter. Hunter, a Virginia criminal defense lawyer, authored a blog called *This Week in Richmond Criminal Defense*.[81] Hunter wrote primarily about his own criminal cases. He focused on successful resolutions, both settlements and trials. Though he posted about his cases, at least in part, for the purpose of attracting new clients, he did not include the advertising disclaimer required by the Virginia State Bar (i.e., a line stating that previous results are not predictors of future success). In writing about his cases, Hunter used the real names of actual clients who were acquitted or received favorable plea bargains as a result of his negotiations. He did so without their consent. All the information he placed on his blog could also be found in the public record of criminal proceedings, which is how he justified his use of it.

Some might say that Hunter served as a curator of the information and a facilitator for the free flow of legal information. But the Virginia State Bar disciplined Hunter with a public reprimand for disseminating this information via his blog, citing legal ethics rules that prohibit lawyers from releasing information related to the representation of a client. He appealed on First Amendment grounds and contended that his blogging constituted political speech, even though a component of it was marketing. The Virginia State Bar urged the court to "prohibit an attorney from repeating truthful information made in a public judicial proceeding even though others can disseminate this information because an attorney repeating it could inhibit clients from freely communicating with their attorneys or because it would undermine public confidence in the legal profession."[82]

In a 2013 opinion, the Virginia Supreme Court agreed with Hunter's argument that blogging is protected free speech and reversed the discipline, though the court treated the blog as commercial speech, which could be subject to the disclaimer requirement but not banned entirely. The court held that once the legal representation has ended, the lawyer cannot be banned from describing public facts, even if they are potentially embarrassing or harmful to the client, and even absent client consent, so long as the facts are not protected by attorney-client privilege. In reaching this result, the court prioritized the general availability of information about legal services over an individual client's expectation of confidentiality: "To the extent that the information is aired in a public forum, privacy considerations must yield to First Amendment protections."[83]

Hunter provides an interesting case for reflection on the nature of legal information and its importance to the public. The legal information at issue in *Hunter*—facts about completed criminal law cases—is available in the public record, even without Hunter's blogging. Yet the information takes on enhanced meaning because of the way it is disseminated, and by whom—here, a lawyer. When Hunter blogs, he increases the amount of free-flowing information about law in the public sphere. Rather than sitting in some obscure court file, the information is now curated, pieced together with the most relevant and interesting facts, posted in a targeted way for a mass audience. Hunter's blog serves numerous functions—advertising and marketing,[84] education about legal entitlements and obligations,[85] news reporting,[86] and criticism of the legal system,[87] to name a few. His blog might increase the likelihood that an individual facing a criminal sanction will hire an attorney, making it easier to find legal help when one is in need. His use of real client names and stories lends credibility and legitimacy.

The *Hunter* opinion generated strong reactions from scholars, regulators, and lawyer ethics experts, many of them unfavorable. These critics took the position that lawyers must adhere to the duty of confidentiality, even at the expense of the dissemination of truthful, public legal information.[88] A primary justification for this viewpoint is a desire to encourage clients' full and frank disclosures to their attorneys under the cloak of confidentiality. In other words, if clients fear their attorneys may discuss public facts about their case, clients may be less than forthcoming in sharing information essential to the representation. This position fails, however, to recognize that clients with legal problems may have strong incentives to fully disclose their situations even without confidentiality protections.[89] This calculus leaves little room for acknowledging the public's interest in the dissemination of legal information found in court records. Critics say, "The fact that the information is available to the public doesn't mean it is known by the public."[90] But this is precisely the point for the court in *Hunter*. Legal information ought to be more available to those who currently lack it, not less so.

The *Hunter* court espouses a world where the lawyer's loyalty to the client is prioritized for the duration of the matter but then subordinated to public informational interests at the conclusion of the representation. This result builds on the public's interests that *Bates* first articulated where greater information about legal services might increase meaningful legal representation.

Upsolve v. James

The most recent case to deploy the First Amendment in expanding access to legal services is *Upsolve v. James*, decided at the federal district court level in 2022. Upsolve, founded in 2016, is a nonprofit that got its start helping low-income people who cannot afford lawyers file for bankruptcy via a mobile app that is user-friendly and, importantly, free. According to Upsolve, "the vast majority of defendants are low-income individuals who cannot afford a lawyer, cannot find pro bono counsel, and face additional barriers that make it difficult to prepare and file an answer themselves. The result is that the large majority of low-income New Yorkers in such actions default."[91] These debt collection cases are "extremely common in New York" and "comprise approximately a quarter of all lawsuits in the State's court system."[92] The company offers educational resources and legal tools to help families "overcome their debt, access their rights, and rebuild their financial situation."[93]

After success with the mobile app, founder and CEO Rohan Pavuluri wanted to do more to help Upsolve users, in particular offering individually tailored legal advice. Specifically, his nonprofit trained "professionals who are not lawyers to provide free legal advice on whether and how to respond to a debt collection lawsuit."[94] The end goal? "Increasing access to the courts and thereby protecting the property and liberty of low-income New Yorkers who are currently unable to understand or access their legal rights when faced with a debt collection action."[95]

Unsurprisingly, as covered in chapter 3, New York's unauthorized practice of law (UPL) restriction stood in Upsolve's way. The law prohibits anyone who is not a licensed lawyer from providing legal advice. Doing so could result in criminal sanctions, even if the advice was accurate, basic, and freely given to those in desperate need of it.

So Upsolve sued the New York attorney general challenging the UPL statute on First Amendment grounds and won. Judge Paul Crotty of the United States District Court for the Southern District of New York treated the speech at issue—free advice about bankruptcy—not as commercial speech but as deserving the highest level of First Amendment protection like political speech. He wrote:

> The orderly functioning of our judicial system and the protection of our citizens require that legal advice should be offered only by those who possess the requisite qualifications and authorization for the practice of law. At the same time, one of the most fundamental principles of our system of government prohibits any restraint on a citizen's right to disseminate his views on important public issues. Sometimes these two principles conflict, and one must yield to the other.[96]

In favoring Upsolve, the judge cited the training involved for the nonlawyers, which includes provisions limiting the scope of representation and requiring compliance with New York's Rules of Professional Conduct as well as sanctions for not adhering to the program's requirements. He also emphasized that the issue under consideration was "a narrow one: whether the First Amendment protects the precise legal advice that Plaintiffs seek to provide, in the precise setting in which they intend to provide it."[97] He held that it does.

The attorney general appealed the result in late 2022, around the time that this book went to press. (A caveat—I joined an amicus brief along with a group of law professors in support of Upsolve on appeal. An amicus brief is also sometimes called a "friend of the court brief." It's a document submitted to the court not by the parties, but by others with an interest in the outcome of the case, often with special expertise in the matter under consideration.) My prediction? Upsolve will continue to win.

The decision, heralded as "the first of its kind in First Amendment law,"[98] is the product of both careful design by Upsolve in the structure for training nonlawyers as well as effective planning by Upsolve in litigation strategy to reform regulatory restraints like unauthorized practice laws and Model Rule 5.4 that suppress providers who can help reduce the justice crisis. The next chapter expands on similar reforms.

* * *

This line of First Amendment cases shows how litigation can drive reform for the people who need justice when the profession itself resists. In addition to challenges in the courtroom via antitrust law and the First Amendment to address the unmet need for legal services, some jurisdictions—especially international ones—have engaged in legislative and regulatory reforms. Chapter 8 covers those endeavors, following the recommendations below.

Recommendations

Key: Attorneys (A), Advocacy Groups (AG), Bar Authorities (BA), Individuals (I), Judges (J), Law Schools (LS), Legal Tech Industry (LTI), Legislators (L), Research Centers (RC)

Design Informative, Relatable, and Understandable Advertising (A)

We saw in chapter 2 how lawyer advertising fails to close the information gap for those who need legal help. There are at least two relatively simple changes that could dramatically improve the number of people who are reached. First, lawyer advertising should prioritize the information relevant to rational consumers, including (1) costs, (2) reviews (both positive and negative), and (3) disclaimers about past successes. For example, as we saw in the *Hunter* case, many states require a specific disclaimer when lawyers advertise about past success. In other contexts, people have strongly criticized disclosures as a remedy for market failure.[99] They argue that consumers ignore disclosures,[100] that they cannot understand disclosures,[101] and that they cannot use disclosures in complex markets.[102] While the effectiveness of disclosures is questioned in some contexts such as the consumer credit literature, where boilerplate disclaimers are so lengthy that people never bother taking the time to read them, the unique circumstances of legal representation support their use. At a minimum, disclosures are a caution to the client and, at best, they are informative. One model that might be adopted by regulators is the FTC's adequate substantiation standard, which first requires that an "advertiser should possess and rely upon adequate substantiation" when making representations containing endorsements.[103] Second, lawyers must consider the images and readability and accessibility of their websites. Studies show that individuals are more likely to engage with and trust professionals who reflect their own identities and personal characteristics.[104] And, of course, we cannot expect someone to respond if an advertisement is written in legalese or at a reading level they cannot comprehend.

Extend the Duty of Candor in the Courtroom to the Court of Public Opinion (BA)

This recommendation refers back to chapter 5 but is included here because it involves lawyer speech. Model Rule 4.1, governing truthfulness in statements to others, should be revised to ban lawyers in public office, or representing those in public office, from lying about the outcome of a valid election, whether representing a client or not. The rule currently provides: "In the course of representing a client a lawyer shall not knowingly: (1) make a false statement of material fact or law to a third person; or (2) fail to disclose a material fact to a third person when disclosure is necessary to avoid assisting a criminal or fraudulent act by a client, unless disclosure is prohibited by [the rule governing confidentiality]." The modification suggested here would add a new sentence:

A lawyer running for or serving in public office, or representing a client who is running for or serving in public office, shall not knowingly make a false statement of material fact or law to a third person disputing the outcome of a valid election. As chapter 5 explains, this provision likely would withstand a First Amendment challenge because it is so narrowly drawn.

Reform through Litigation, Like Button, Bates, *and* Upsolve (A, AG, I, J)

The line of cases summarized in this chapter coalesce around the central theme of making information about legal rights and entitlements available to the public. Time and again, since the early 1960s in *NAACP v. Button*, the Supreme Court and others sided with the individuals who need information, not the professionals trying to withhold it. Going forward, "organizations in other states can look to Upsolve" and these other cases "as a model not only for the services it now provides, but also for its successful legal strategy to make those services a reality."[105] As law professor Alexandra Lahav writes in her book *In Praise of Litigation*: "Democracy implies self-government and participation on the part of the governed under the rule of law. . . . A lawsuit is a mechanism for individuals to exercise their autonomy and a form of direct participation in government."[106] With each lawsuit, as seen in the line of First Amendment cases recounted above, we have "the potential to change the rules that govern behavior going forward."[107]

8

Regulatory and Legislative Reform

Courtrooms are not the only place to seek change. Those tasked with regulation of the legal profession need not wait until forced by a judge to engage in efforts to increase access to legal help. Indeed, in the early 2000s, nations around the globe began to experiment with reforms crafted to spur competition and innovation in the delivery of legal services, even as bar associations and regulators in the United States clung to the past.

Now we will take a look at efforts from Australia, Europe, and the Middle East and then turn to the handful of states that also experimented with new rules to govern the delivery of legal services in recent years. While none of these reforms proved to be a magic solution to the justice gap, each offers valuable lessons for crafting a blueprint to democratize justice.

International Examples

In 2001, the United Kingdom's now-dissolved Office of Fair Trading produced a revolutionary report, "Competition in the Professions."[1] It called on regulators for a total rethinking of the regulation of lawyers. Spurred on by that report, England and Wales adopted the Legal Services Act (LSA) of 2007, promising to infuse the legal profession with competition and innovation.[2] The LSA created a new form of business structure for legal services, known as the "alternative business structure" (ABS), allowing lawyers and nonlawyers to form businesses together.

The first entrant into the ABS market was Premier Property Lawyers, a small British firm founded in 1935 that handles matters like dispute resolution, commercial and residential real estate, family issues, and probate.[3] They received their ABS license in 2011. Why would a firm founded nearly a century prior switch up its business structure? The person they wanted to be their managing partner was not a licensed solicitor. She was an accountant. "The whole point of becoming an ABS was so that I could be a partner,"[4] explained Berni Summers. "I never wanted to become a solicitor. I hated exams."[5] She attributes her firm's continued success to her business background.

By 2013, 325 law firms in England and Wales functioned as ABSs, growing to more than three times that number by 2021, according to data maintained by the Solicitors Regulatory Authority (SRA).[6] (The SRA is the regulatory body in England and Wales responsible for lawyer licensing and discipline, also charged with issuing ABS classifications.) As of 2022, at least 1,500 ABSs existed in England and Wales.[7] Approximately one-third offer personal injury services, which does not particularly target the justice gap identified by this book.[8] Others similarly do not address personal civil legal needs, including accounting firms, hedge funds, and litigation finance companies. But some do offer help, especially for the not-quite-poor who do not qualify for legal aid but cannot afford traditional legal services billed by the hour.

The implementation of ABSs came with lots of promise and speculation of flourishing competition to foster new markets in legal services. The American legal profession mostly ignored the hubbub during the early years, though a small group of scholars, including me, watched with great interest. For three summers from 2012 to 2014, I took cohorts of students from Michigan State University to London, England, to meet with regulators and legal services providers involved in the ABS revolution. We studied the legislation and the market development that unfolded. One of the guest lecturers in my Twenty-First Century Law Practice course was James Peters from LegalZoom. The US-based LegalZoom understood early on the potential for the ABS process to open new markets. James, a lawyer licensed in California, soon became qualified as a solicitor in England as well, to help lead the effort. LegalZoom was the first American company to hold an ABS license in the United Kingdom in 2015, and one of the first holders of an ABS license in the states, issued by the Arizona Supreme Court in 2021. (More on Arizona's implementation of the ABS model later in this chapter.)

Now that the ABS model has been on the scene in England and Wales for more than two decades, we can cut through the hype and evaluate its merits. LegalZoom's adoption is one measure of success. Recall from the introduction that LegalZoom earned revenues of $575 million in 2021 and $620 million in 2022, while offering affordable legal tools to individuals and small businesses that otherwise likely would go without. But this is just one anecdote. We can also look to data. Research shows that the ABS structure does make a difference. A whitepaper issued in 2020 by the Stanford Law School Deborah L. Rhode Center on the Legal Profession found:

(1) ABS firms are more likely to use technology, with 91 percent of ABS firms using a website to deliver information and services, compared to only 52 percent of solicitor firms.
(2) ABS firms are 13 to 15 percent more likely to introduce new legal services.
(3) ABS firms are particularly likely to have delivered radical service innovations or organizational innovations.[9]

Another study from researchers in the United Kingdom supports the thesis that the ABS model encourages innovation for "small firms whose clients are individuals rather than businesses," that is, the consumer law market whose legal needs often go unmet.[10] The study found that "the vast majority" of firms moving to multidisciplinary partnerships and outside ownership or investment were the small firms that "consequently changed the way in which they raise finances to invest in more technology and innovation."[11]

Reflecting in 2021 on the impact of the ABS structure, former executive director of the SRA Crispin Passmore concluded that "nothing has changed and everything has changed."[12] He wrote:

The elite law firms and high street still look much the same from the outside. It is easy to think nothing has changed. . . . Yet look carefully and all of the market has been touched by reform—not just the emergence of ABS that make up something like 1 in 10 firms now, but multidisciplinary practices, lawyers in unregulated firms and a resurgence of innovation in traditional law firms. . . . What this means is that customers of all sorts have more choice, though they are a long way from consistently exercising that yet. Importantly, lawyers also have more choice— where they work and how they practice for example.[13]

122 | REGULATORY AND LEGISLATIVE REFORM

Having choices does not necessarily equate with exercising that autonomy. Consequently, much more work needs to be done, according to Passmore: "Competition remains weak, as evidenced by a lack of digitisation compared to the rest of the economy. Too much production still looks the same as in the 1980s, or even the 1950s. In fact far too many firms look just like all the others—named after men and run by them. Diversity equals diversity of thought and that is the foundation of innovation."[14] Passmore's observations about the England and Wales legal services market ring true for the United States as well.

When the LSA became effective in 2007, that same year, the first publicly traded law firm, Slater and Gordon, appeared on the Australian Stock Exchange. Amendments to Australia's Legal Profession Act[15] unleashed law firms to become structured as limited liability companies and to receive investment from nonlawyers. While initially the stock soared, Slater and Gordon announced a $90 million error in its bookkeeping in 2015, causing the stock to become essentially worthless. Few firms opted to join Slater and Gordon on the stock exchange, though by 2009, nearly nine hundred Australian firms had incorporated as multidisciplinary practices, allowing for lawyers to deliver services in partnership with other professionals like accountants or doctors. Australian regulators continue to press for more innovation in legal services delivery models. For example, the Victorian Legal Services Board, which regulates law practice for the Australia's state of Victoria, includes a manager of innovation and consumer engagement among its staff and, in 2019, explored creating an "Innovation In-Box" where developers of new legal services could write in to receive guidance on ethics, technology, design-thinking, and more.[16]

In the Middle East, also in 2007, the Dubai International Financial Center (DIFC) opened a simplified small claims tribunal, which resolves 90 percent of disputes within thirty days, notably without lawyers.[17] (In 2004, the DIFC established its first court, which was a judicial system intended for international use, based in the English language and common law.) I initially learned about the DIFC Small Claims Tribunal while teaching a course on law practice innovation in Dubai as part of Michigan State University's graduate program in 2012. Located in central Dubai, the DIFC operates independently from Emirati law and courts. A defining feature of the Small Claims Tribunal was its early commitment to state-of-the-art technology for delivering legal services (a prescient investment we can now fully appreciate in the wake of the COVID-19 global pandemic). At a time when most courts in the United States still relied on paper files and in-person proceedings, the DIFC Small Claims Tribunal utilized paperless, web-based case management, including the submission of court documents by computer and mobile device. Virtual proceedings via secure video conferencing reduced costs and expedited timelines for the resolution of disputes. Other regions, including Africa[18] and Singapore,[19] also led the way on digital justice, with government-backed efforts actively pursuing innovation through digital technology.

Courts in the United States did catch up, thanks to the demands of the pandemic for online tools to conduct proceedings when gathering in person was not possible. A study conducted by the Pew Research Center in 2021 found that even with "almost no history of using remote civil court proceedings, beginning in March 2020 every state and D.C. initiated online hearings at record rates to resolve many types of cases."[20] For example, from April 1 to June 1, 2020, "Michigan courts held more than 35,000 video hearings."[21] (By comparison, it held zero video hearings during the same time period in 2019.)

By mid-2021, the United Arab Emirates (UAE) national government committed to make 80 percent of all litigation sessions online by the end of the year.[22] Lawyers hailed the pledge, citing "better quality of work," cost savings in "time and effort" and avoidance of commutes, and the ability to represent more clients in a short amount of time among the benefits.[23] Despite the quick conversion to online hearings by United States courts during the pandemic, similar long-term commitments to remote technology have not been as forthcoming or ambitious, yet.

A decade after my first trip to the DIFC courts in Dubai, I returned in 2023 to find further innovations, notably on the heels of prominent resignations by judges from those courts. (The DIFC courts are staffed by judges from around the world.) Ireland's Frank Clarke and Peter Kelley, along with New Zealand's William Young, stepped down in 2022 amid questions about the UAE's commitment to human rights and the rule of law.[24] Scholars and activists expressed concern about the retired judges "lending credibility to one part of the judicial system of a highly oppressive regime."[25] Judges from other countries, including Australia,

England, Scotland, Malaysia, Wales, and the UAE remain. I believe we can learn from the DIFC innovations, while also recognizing the human rights concerns that led these judges to remove themselves.

Among my discoveries on this visit, I learned about what the UAE called the "C3 Court." This system was intended to be the first in the world where all three courts—the trial court, the court of appeals, and the supreme court—hear a case simultaneously, rather than consecutively.[26] The process was meant to reduce the expected time for full resolution from 305 days to 30 days, with a projected cost savings for litigants to be as much as 50 percent and a reduction in the use of court resources by 60 percent.[27] Whether such a system is viable remains to be seen—in early 2023, it was not yet operating. There are many reasons, of course, why this model would surely meet resistance in America (starting, notably, with the fact that only one justice from the supreme court presides rather than nine). But many litigants might prefer something like this, because of the dramatic savings in time and costs. At a minimum, even if not wholly replicable in the U.S. or sustainable in the UAE, the C3 Court model challenges us to fundamentally rethink how justice is delivered.

* * *

The innovations that emerged in Australia, Europe, and the Middle East in the early 2000s set the stage for a range of organizations to join the effort. Nearly two decades later, there are now hundreds if not thousands of legal service innovation initiatives and organizations throughout the world.[28] For example, the Hague Institute for Innovation of Law (HiiL) was founded in 2005 with the goal of ensuring "that by 2030, 150 million people will be able to prevent or resolve their most pressing justice problems" and planned to accomplish this "by stimulating innovation and scaling what works best."[29] Interestingly, the organization's name initially was the Hague Institute for the Internationalisation of Law. The name changed, substituting Innovation for Internationalisation, because they recognized the importance of innovation as a tool to manifest their work: "It became clear that we need innovation. We were hungry for change. Based on this research we developed the way we work today. We moved from research to action. HiiL is now a social enterprise."[30] More recently, among other endeavors, HiiL partnered with the US-based Institute for the Advancement of the Legal System (IAALS) to conduct the justice needs study referenced in chapter 1. IAALS, housed at the University of Denver, describes itself as "a national, independent research center dedicated to facilitating continuous improvement and advancing excellence in the American legal system."[31] International bar associations formed commissions and issued reports, including the Canadian Bar Association's 2014 report *Futures: Transforming the Delivery of Legal Services in Canada*.[32] These efforts directly spurred similar work in the United States.

The American Experience

Influenced by the international focus on competition and innovation in legal services, the American Bar Association (ABA) launched its own initiative in 2014. The ABA's then-president, William Hubbard, appointed the Commission on the Future of Legal Services. Full disclosure—I served as one of two co-reporters. We produced the *Report on the Future of Legal Services* in 2016, after two years of public hearings, testimony, and written submissions focused on the needs of the justice system and recommendations for reform. While the Commission's final product mostly consists of aspirations still yet to be fulfilled, one lasting outcome is the ABA Center for Innovation.[33] The center's mission is to "encourage and accelerate innovations that improve the affordability, effectiveness, and accessibility of all legal services."[34] The statement of the center's operating principles provides:

> The Center for Innovation enables the profession, including law firms of all sizes, corporate legal departments, courts, legal services lawyers, lawyers in the criminal justice system, law schools and bar associations, to be creative, daring and powerful forces for change. The Center is entrepreneurial, experimental and agile in its work. Looking beyond traditional collaborators and projects, the Center encourages and supports new kinds of partnerships and initiatives that may succeed, or fail, but will all add to the base of knowledge needed to generate true innovation in the delivery of legal services.[35]

The establishment of the center signals meaningful commitment to innovation. In 2022, the Center for Innovation issued its first-ever

Innovation Trends Report, documenting internal ABA innovation, advances in legal technology, and regulatory innovation.[36] Among the items featured, the report announced the Center's "Justice System Metrics Project" website, a tool designed "to explore how data can (and does) influence progress and innovation in the justice sector."[37] The purpose of the project "is to build a data-driven culture in the legal industry by making it easy for justice system participants to understand what data can be collected to drive change and how others across jurisdictions are using it."[38]

State bars across the country followed the ABA's lead, launching their own projects devoted to the future of the profession and innovation in the delivery of legal services, especially focused on unmet needs.[39] Two examples come from my home states, and I participated in both. The State Bar of Michigan commenced its own 21st Century Practice Task Force simultaneously with the ABA Futures Commission. That work culminated in a lengthy report published in 2016 with numerous proposals to guide future reforms.[40] In 2023, the Texas Access to Justice Commission launched a Working Group on Access to Legal Services for Low-Income Texans at the request of the Supreme Court of Texas. This group received two charges: (1) to explore proposals for nonlawyer professionals to provide limited legal services directly to low-income individuals and (2) to consider modifications for nonlawyers to hold economic interests in entities that provide legal services to low-income individuals. It is too soon to know whether Texas will move forward in either or both directions.

The state of Washington received significant attention in 2012 when it implemented a new program that allowed individuals to provide legal help in specialized areas without traditional legal education and licensing requirements. Known as limited license legal technicians (LLLTs), the move was proclaimed as innovative regulation,[41] but the reality did not bear this out. Indeed, the effort has been described by more than one commentator as a "failure":

> Just fifteen candidates completed the coursework to become LLLTs in the first year. Of those fifteen, only nine took the licensing exam and a mere seven passed. This paltry showing contrasts with the 814 would-be lawyers who took the Washington bar exam around that same time.

The Practice of Law Board that had launched the program then publicly resigned.[42]

The Washington Supreme Court voted to end the program in June 2020,[43] though some advocates like Responsive Law, an advocacy group working "to make the legal system more affordable, accessible, and accountable to the people it is meant to serve" claimed the LLLT system never got a fair shot.[44]

Several other states allow legal paraprofessionals to engage in limited areas of law practice without a full license. These efforts emphasize high-demand needs such as custody, divorce, and landlord-tenant disputes. Legal paraprofessionals are "described as the law's version of a nurse practitioner, providing legal services at a lower cost than a traditional lawyer."[45] Nearly a dozen states have experimented with these programs, including Alaska, Arizona, Minnesota, Oregon, and Utah. Oregon's program, approved in 2022, allows for assistance in drafting forms, negotiating settlements, and preparing for trial, but not for court appearances. The Alaska Supreme Court authorized a program that began in 2023 allowing nonlawyers supervised by the Alaska Legal Services Corporation to provide limited-scope legal services without fear of violating unauthorized practice of law restrictions.[46] The model will focus on the most isolated parts of Alaska, often without roads or internet service. A number of states were actively considering proposals for legal paraprofessionals in 2023, including Connecticut, New Mexico, New York, North Carolina, South Carolina, Texas, and Vermont. Some considered but rejected the concept, including Illinois.

Organizations like the American Bar Foundation, the National Center for State Courts, and the Public Welfare Foundation have come together to design and evaluate these sorts of paraprofessional programs and to offer their services to states seeking to implement reforms. For example, the three groups prepared a report in 2017 reviewing the Washington Supreme Court's now-defunct LLLT program.[47] Their evaluation found proper training in place, customers satisfied with service and cost, and appropriate reach to individuals who could not afford a traditional lawyer but wanted assistance—all positive measures. Perhaps foreshadowing the end of LLLTs, however, they noted that the regulatory costs of the program had not yet broken even and that while scaling up could remedy this, questions remained about how best to do so. The evaluation was good news, and bad news, and this is precisely the kind of frank assessment and feedback needed as jurisdictions experiment with new models.

Some states considered lifting the Model Rule 5.4 ban on outside ownership and investment, as well as multidisciplinary partnerships, in 2019,[48] including Arizona,[49] California,[50] Florida,[51] and Utah.[52] Two moved forward.

Reforms in Utah and Arizona

Utah announced changes to professional conduct rules in early August 2020 that "represent perhaps the most promising effort by courts to tackle the access-to-justice dilemma in the last hundred years," according to the Utah Supreme Court.[53] The reforms adopted by that court will "allow for nonlawyer ownership or investment in law firms and permit legal services providers to try new ways of serving clients during a two-year pilot period."[54] In justifying the experiment, the court explained:

> What has become clear during this time is that real change in Utahns' access to legal services requires recognition that we will never volunteer ourselves across the access-to-justice divide and that what is needed is market-based, far-reaching reform focused on opening up the legal market to new providers, business models, and service options.[55]

To support this effort, the court established a "regulatory sandbox" for legal services providers to experiment and also formed an Office of Legal Services Innovation charged with evaluating applicants and overseeing those selected to participate in the regulatory sandbox.[56] The purpose of a regulatory sandbox, according to legal ethics expert Amy Salyzyn, "is to offer opportunities for innovative providers to deliver services in a regulated industry in new ways. The sandbox model permits service delivery that would (or might) otherwise breach current rules due to, for example, a non-compliant business structure or means of delivery. Innovators generally participate in a pilot where they have the regulator's permission to operate under certain specified conditions and with ongoing monitoring. Often, the regulator collects data during such pilots with the aim of informing future regulatory reform."[57] The Utah reforms also authorize "attorney fee sharing with nonlawyers as long as there is written notice to the client."[58]

As of November 2022, the sandbox received ninety applications, forty-five of which were approved and actively operating.[59] The entities include law practices, software companies, and chat bot providers, offering services ranging from business start-up counseling to immigration to personal injury to life needs like housing, employment, and more. Only one complaint, unrelated to consumer harm, had been filed since the October 2020 launch.[60] According to an assessment conducted by the IAALS, the Utah ABSs were in "high demand" and met "a spectrum" of needs for individuals and businesses.[61] The report found that the regulatory sandbox "opened up a world of possibilities when it comes to how to practice law, and demonstrates how innovation, technology, and professionals who aren't lawyers can work alongside attorneys and ensure consumers have real access to the entire spectrum of legal needs."[62]

What are these entities providing? One run by a group of nuns from Holy Cross Ministries trains community health workers to provide bilingual legal advocacy for medical-debt issues. Another, half-owned by nonlawyers, provides free or low-cost legal services assisting in the completion of court documents as well as legal advice via chatbots and instant messages from staff who are not licensed lawyers. The IAALS report concluded that in "nine months, more than 2,500 people have received help with housing, immigration, healthcare, discrimination, employment, and a gamut of other issues. Lawyers are partnering up with other professionals to create new types of businesses, and technology is enabling them to do their jobs more efficiently."[63] Three Canadian provinces—Alberta, British Columbia, and Ontario—launched regulatory sandboxes soon after Utah's announcement.

By the end of August 2020, the Arizona Supreme Court joined Utah, announcing the elimination of Rule 5.4's ban on nonlawyer ownership and investment in a law firm and participation in fee sharing.[64] The state adopted the ABS structure, allowing investors, entrepreneurs, and others to be owners and/or managers with an economic stake in an entity providing legal services, if licensed. To become an ABS, the organization must follow certain regulatory objectives and ethical standards, as well as employ a compliance officer.[65] LegalZoom, predictably, as it was the first US company to hold an ABS from England, was among the first to do so in Arizona.

Researchers from Stanford Law School conducted an early comparative assessment of the impact from the regulatory changes in Utah and Arizona. They found that even in the midst of opening the field to non-lawyers, attorneys continued to play "a central role in the entities and the innovation within them."[66] In both states, according to their study, "lawyers remain central to the development and delivery of services—whether as employee practitioners, through oversight and compliance roles, or through entity ownership and leadership. In Utah, innovation also takes the form of services delivered via nonlawyers and software."[67] Most of the new entities target consumers and small businesses, with 61 percent indicating a "technology innovation as part of their ABS or sandbox authorization," and "[n]early half of entities also described pricing innovations, such as subscription or flat-fee pricing as part of their model."[68] Perhaps unsurprising if you think back to chapter 6's recommendation to reform unauthorized practice of law (UPL) statutes, the Stanford study found that "UPL reform appears to be critical to serving lower-income populations. The Utah sandbox —which allows entities to seek waivers of UPL—contains the only entities, all of them non-profits, that report that they primarily serve indigent and low-income people. By contrast, Arizona's 'ABS-only approach' is thus far yielding important but limited changes to the conventional law firm model of legal services delivery that predominantly serves a middle-income and small business clientele."[69]

As another measure, Arizona authorized "Legal Paraprofessionals" as a new, nonlawyer licensing regime to expand legal advice for high-demand matters, including civil litigation, criminal cases without jail time, family law, and state administrative law.[70] The first class of ten received their licenses in early 2022 after passing two exams (one general, one specific to the area of practice) and satisfying the requirement of seven years of experience (alternatively, a Master of Legal Studies from an accredited law school would meet this standard).[71] They follow rules similar to those for licensed lawyers and must participate in continuing legal education. The Arizona Supreme Court Task Force on the Delivery of Legal Services monitors the program to make sure the goals of closing the justice gap are met.[72]

In early 2023, Colorado followed Arizona's example, approving a new rule to allow nonlawyer paraprofessionals to obtain limited licenses for providing basic legal help in divorce and child custody cases. The paraprofessionals will be able "to complete and file standard pleadings, represent their clients in mediation, accompany their clients to court and answer a court's factual questions . . . but not present oral arguments or examine witnesses in a hearing."[73] Similar to Arizona, the program requires an exam, a character and fitness review, and an ethics course, "along with 1,500 hours of law-related practical experience, including 500 hours of experience in Colorado family law."[74]

Florida, by contrast, tanked a recommendation in 2022 from a Florida Supreme Court–created committee to adopt a regulatory sandbox based on the Utah model.[75] The State Bar Board of Governors rejected the plan unanimously, and the Florida Supreme Court declined to approve the sandbox. It did, however, adopt a new process permitting nonprofit legal services providers to organize as corporations with nonlawyers serving as members of the board of directors.

California's efforts in 2022 similarly met extreme resistance from lawyers and legislators. Law professors Nora Engstrom and David Engstrom penned a frustrated op-ed entitled "Why Do Blue States Keep Prioritizing Lawyers over Low-Income Americans?"[76] They called out the California legislature for dropping the ball, despite being "famous for its history of tech disruption and progressive politics."[77] After what the Engstroms describe as "a high-profile State Bar working group" proposed ideas like implementing a regulatory sandbox, the legislature "passed a bill that shuttered" the group's work.[78] According to the Engstroms, one of whom was a member of the working group, the "criticism from lawyers' groups was simply too great a political threat to risk even a *proposal* seeing the light of day."[79] Among the suggestions? A regulatory sandbox that would have allowed for testing "innovative business models, products, and services, in a supervised environment that ensures collection of data to inform whether future changes to rules and laws governing the practice of law would result in benefits and/or risks of harm to consumers"[80]—in essence, the same thing happening already in countries like Australia and closer to home in Utah, and likely soon in other jurisdictions.

Access to justice should be a nonpartisan issue. As Nathan Hecht, chief justice of the Supreme Court of Texas, wrote in a 2019 essay, access to justice is "an American idea, not a liberal one or a conservative one."[81] It is "simply good government."[82]

In February 2020, the ABA House of Delegates approved a new resolution advocating for "innovative approaches to the access-to-justice crisis" that encourage United States jurisdictions to "consider regulatory innovations that have the potential to improve the accessibility, affordability, and quality of civil legal services."[83] The resolution neglects to even mention, however, the ethical concerns associated with innovation other than an acknowledgment of the need for "protections that best serve . . . the public."[84] The resolution encourages jurisdictions "to collect and assess data regarding regulatory innovations both before and after their adoption to ensure that changes are effective in increasing access to legal services and are in the [public interest]."[85] But the resolution does not recommend reforms to expand access to legal services and instead expressly preserves Model Rule 5.4 along with UPL restrictions.

That same month, the Conference of Chief Justices (CCJ)—made up of the chief from the highest court in each state—passed a similar resolution along with the Conference of State Court Administrators (COSCA). The language parallels the ABA's encouragement of "regulatory innovations that have the potential to improve the accessibility, affordability and quality of civil legal services."[86] Later in 2020, they passed a resolution setting forth six principles to guide technology changes for post-pandemic court technology: (1) "Ensure principles of due process, procedural fairness, transparency, and equal access are satisfied when adopting new technologies"; (2) "Focus on the user experience"; (3) "Prioritize court-user driven technology"; (4) "Embrace flexibility and willingness to adapt"; (5) "Adopt remote-first (or at least remote-friendly) planning, where practicable, to move court processes forward"; (6) "Take an open, data-driven, and transparent approach to implementing and maintaining court processes and supporting technologies."[87] In 2022, they passed a resolution "encouraging state courts to adopt innovative practices in high-volume dockets."[88] On their own, resolutions like this do not create change, but they do empower those who can implement innovations to do so. The role of chief justice or chief judge of a state supreme court can be incredibly effective in implementing reforms across all courts within a state through what is known as a "standing order," in essence an administrative order to require uniform policies and procedures.

Non-Regulatory Innovation in Legal Services

Notwithstanding the lack of robust regulatory reforms to expand access to justice in the United States, new models for delivering legal services are growing, and have been for quite some time, as indicated by at least four measures: (1) the increasing number of alternative legal service providers relying on technology and other advancements; (2) the emergence of the "NewLaw" field;[89] (3) the amount of financial capital being poured into "NewLaw," legal tech, and justice tech ventures; and (4) the desire from individuals and lawyers post-pandemic to continue using remote tools and related technology. Each measure is taken up below.

Increasing Number of Alternative Legal Service Providers

The Thomson Reuters Report on Alternative Legal Service Providers (ALSPs), written in collaboration with the SAID Business School, University of Oxford Legal Executive Institute, Georgetown Law Center on Ethics and the Legal Profession, and Acritas, regularly details the market for innovative legal services.[90] ALSPs are considered "new start-ups and providers looking to challenge traditional service models offered by law firms."[91] Services include "contract lawyers, process mapping, and Web-based technology."[92] ALSPs provide help to lawyers, not directly to the public (in a way that might raise red flags for regulatory bodies), though clients may benefit from efficiencies gained through these tools, allowing the lawyer to pass on cost savings to the client. The tasks performed by ALSPs include litigation support, legal research, document review, electronic discovery, and compliance work. The 2021 biennial report surveyed 586 participants in US, UK, Canadian, and Australian law firms and corporate legal departments during June and July of 2020.[93] It found that the ALSP "market value equals nearly $14 billion, with adoption by 79 percent of law firms and 71 percent of corporate law departments."[94]

The Field of "NewLaw"

Another measure of innovation is the expansion of "NewLaw," which refers to "new ventures in legal entrepreneurship" that reflect an array of businesses offering legal services in ways that are more accessible to and affordable for clients. These businesses also tend to be more pleasant for the lawyers, offering a work-life balance often absent in a big law or corporate practice.[95] Law professor Joan Williams identifies five categories of so-called NewLaw, arguing that this shows how "[d]isruptive innovation has hit the law."[96] The categories include: (1) "Law and Business Companies," which "marry legal with business advice and services"; (2) "Secondment Firms," which place lawyers into corporate legal departments for limited periods of time; (3) "Law Firm Accordion Companies," which "provide law firms with lawyers to work as overload capacity or to provide specialized skills"; (4) "Virtual Firms," in which "everyone works from home"; and (5) "Innovative Law Firms," which have modernized "billing and personnel policies, better work-life balance, and women-friendly practices."[97] NewLaw is growing so quickly that according to legal futurist Jordan Furlong, "any list or taxonomy quickly becomes outmoded."[98] Indeed, Williams's 2015 study surveyed more than fifty different providers, a list evolving so fast that even as her research was published, she added footnotes to name those discovered too late to include but worthy of mention.[99] The "NewLaw" label itself may be a bit disingenuous, as noted by law professor Bill Henderson: "I don't dispute the categorization, except to point out that it's our awareness of alternative models that is new, not the companies themselves."[100] As examples, Henderson notes that two of the best-known NewLaw companies, Axiom and Counsel on Call (both of which can be best described as operating under Williams's category of secondment firms), have been around since 2000.[101] Nearly twenty years later, we probably should stop calling them "new."

Much of the expansion is fueled by individuals who do not hold law degrees and often are not even supervised by lawyers. Growth is also fueled by the desire of lawyers for work-life harmony that these companies are often better suited to provide than traditional law firms. Postpandemic, demand for these sorts of jobs likely will only increase. The 2022 Clio Legal Trends report observed that the "pandemic profoundly and permanently transformed where and how lawyers work" because, once displaced from their offices and courtrooms, they "found most if not all work can be done at home, especially through cloud-based technology."[102] The report predicted "potential friction between lawyers and their firms regarding the ideal balance between office and in-home work, which could have implications for attracting and retaining legal talent."[103] Data support this prediction: from March 2021 to April 2022, "nearly one in five lawyers left the law firm they were working for, and 9 percent reported that they planned to leave a firm in the next six months."[104] In many ways, these "NewLaw"yers may be better equipped than traditional lawyers to lessen the justice gap because they approach law practice in entrepreneurial and innovative ways.

Revenue and Financial Investment for NewLaw, Legal Tech, and Justice Tech

A third metric for understanding the pace of innovation is the amount of financial capital being poured into the NewLaw start-ups along with legal tech and justice tech ventures. This is likely to continue even amid fluctuations in the economic outlook for law, though surely there will be successes and failures. According to a report issued in *Forbes*, 2018 set a record in growth for investment in legal tech, with a 713 percent increase of nearly $1.7 billion.[105] This was up from $224 million in 2016 and $233 million in 2017.[106] Among the largest investments were $75.5 million into "Atrium, a company that launched in 2017 with the promise of transforming the delivery of legal services,"[107] and $500 million the following year into LegalZoom.[108] This growth continued, with an additional $106 million invested by venture capitalists in January 2019 alone.[109] By September 2019, the field boasted $1.2 billion in investment, called a "Record Year" by commentators.[110] This included several contract management and review companies as well as others performing "law-related functions."[111] For example, "Notarize, an online notary public service, raised $37 million. Farewill, a UK platform for creating wills, raised $9.4 million. Boundless, an immigration platform, raised $7.8 million."[112] Substantial investment continued in 2021, reaching $1.4 billion, with top investments going to RocketLawyers ($223 million), Verbit ($157 million), Notarize ($130 million), Clio ($110 million), and Icertis ($80 million).[113] From January 2016 to mid-2022, a total of more than $13 billion in capital had been raised for 1,800-plus rounds of legal tech funding.[114]

At the same time, this increased funding for legal tech did not necessarily mean more jobs for lawyers. Atrium, for example, announced in January 2020 that it would lay off most of its in-house lawyer team and focus exclusively on technology to aid start-ups in creating legal documents such as funding contracts and organizing necessary legal filings.[115] This leaves some lawyers in a predicament; they are needed for innovation but these innovations threaten to consume their work and outpace them. And funding slowed in 2022, with predictions for more mergers, layoffs, and funding drops for the coming years. Even so, the ten-year growth of investment is a strong signal that technology-driven innovation will continue. While overall funding tapered, new focuses for investment emerged in late 2021 with the creation of the Legal Tech Fund, which invests not just in companies helping law firms but in entities focused on the "hundreds of millions still lack[ing] legal services and that technology can remedy that gap."[116] The fund had raised $28.5 million by the end of 2021, and had invested in thirty companies by mid-2022 according to its general partner and cofounder, Zach Posner.

It isn't just venture capital investing in innovation and technology. The Legal Services Corporation (LSC) distributes Technology Innovation Grants to legal aid programs annually. In 2021 alone, the LSC awarded thirty-five grants to twenty-nine different legal services organizations for a total amount of more than $4.2 million. The technologies funded include automated document assembly, cloud computing, data analytics, mobile services, and online intake. One recipient, the Legal Aid Society of Middle Tennessee and the Cumberlands, received a $134,529 grant to produce multilanguage, online legal information videos for low-income individuals. Another, Legal Aid Services of Oregon, got a $244,965 grant to partner with the Oregon State Bar, the Oregon Law Foundation, and the Oregon Judicial Department to develop a new legal information portal to serve as the primary online referral site for self-help resources and legal services providers. A third, Florida's Bay Area Legal Services, was awarded $274,032 to develop a web and mobile platform that empowers youth in foster care by informing them of important legal rights, including education and employment-training benefits. The first grants in this program were awarded in 2000, and since that time, through 2022, 826 recipients benefited from more than $77 million.

Post-pandemic Continued Use of Remote Tech

A final measure comes from data documenting the positive experiences for individuals, as well as lawyers, who relied on technology to address their legal problems during the COVID-19 pandemic. A study conducted by the Pew Research Center examined how pandemic-induced technology helped individuals and lawyers address justice needs. It found a substantial increase in individuals making their court appearances with "the shift to virtual hearings," which is consistent with "pre-pandemic assertions that reducing the day-to-day costs of coming to court—such as transportation, child care, lost wages, and travel time—would increase people's ability to meaningfully engage in court cases."[117] The study also found that "technology can be used to help people show up to court if tools are made available in multiple languages and are designed to serve people with a range of abilities."[118] It is important to point out, however, that while "people using the civil legal system, regardless of whether they had legal representation, benefitted from courts' rapid adoption of technology, the advantages were disproportionately enjoyed by parties with lawyers."[119]

The online shift also benefited lawyers directly: "According to one survey from Texas, most judges, prosecutors, and defense attorneys said that remote proceedings saved time and improved efficiency. . . . And in interviews, attorneys in Florida, Missouri, Montana, and Texas reported that not having to travel to and wait at court enabled them to serve more clients than before the pandemic."[120] Courts similarly embraced these moves. In 2021, the Conference of Chief Justices and the Conference of State Court Administrators passed a resolution promoting the continued use of remote hearings, and "in a June 2021 survey of 240 magistrates, trial judges, and appellate justices from across the country, a majority said they expect remote proceedings to become a permanent fixture of state courts."[121]

Regulating Legal Services Not Provided by Lawyers

In response to the growth of "NewLaw" and other innovations, some regulators and scholars have called for a more expansive regulatory structure, contemplating legal ethics not only for lawyers but also legal services providers (i.e., entities and individuals serving legal needs without the same training and authorization traditionally required of state-licensed attorneys).[122] They argue that the public would be better served under a more expansive consumer-protection-focused regime where a diverse array of providers offers legal assistance. The number of providers "already involved in the delivery of legal or law-related services is growing rapidly."[123] These providers:

> include automated legal document assembly for consumers, law firms, and corporate counsel; expert systems that address legal issues through a series of branching questions and answers; electronic discovery; legal process outsourcing; legal process insourcing and design; legal project management and process improvement; knowledge management; online dispute resolution; data analytics; and many others.[124]

Accordingly, one proposal is to shift the emphasis away from an idea of a "'law of lawyering'—the body of rules and statutes regulating lawyers" to instead "develop a broader 'law of legal services' that authorizes, but appropriately regulates, the delivery of more legal and law-related assistance by people who do not have a Juris Doctor degree and do not work alongside lawyers."[125]

In 2016, the ABA House of Delegates adopted Model Regulatory Objectives for the Provision of Legal Services that extend regulations beyond lawyers.[126] The list was developed by the ABA Commission on the Future of Legal Services after two years of research, analysis, and debate. There are ten objectives:

A. Protection of the public
B. Advancement of the administration of justice and the rule of law
C. Meaningful access to justice and information about the law, legal issues, and the civil and criminal justice systems
D. Transparency regarding the nature and scope of legal services to be provided, the credentials of those who provide them, and the availability of regulatory protections
E. Delivery of affordable and accessible legal services
F. Efficient, competent, and ethical delivery of legal services
G. Protection of privileged and confidential information

REGULATORY AND LEGISLATIVE REFORM | 139

H. Independence of professional judgment
I. Accessible civil remedies for negligence and breach of other duties owed, disciplinary sanctions for misconduct, and advancement of appropriate preventive or wellness programs
J. Diversity and inclusion among legal services providers and freedom from discrimination for those receiving legal services and in the justice system[127]

Their purpose, according to the resolution, is to guide courts and regulators "when they assess the court's existing regulatory framework [governing lawyers] and any other regulations they may choose to develop concerning non-traditional legal service providers."[128]

The objectives appear to be uncontroversial platitudes on their face—who could disagree with protecting the public or advancing justice? But the resolution almost didn't make it out of the House of Delegates. A statement had to be added at the last minute to secure sufficient votes: "Nothing contained in this Resolution abrogates in any manner existing ABA policy prohibiting nonlawyer ownership of law firms."[129] Many feared the regulatory objectives were the Commission's way of setting the stage for the demise of Model Rule 5.4's ban on outside ownership and investment. Only a few jurisdictions took heed and quickly implemented their own regulatory objectives, including Colorado, Illinois, and Washington.[130] Arizona adopted regulatory objectives in 2020 as part of introducing ABSs and doing away with its version of Model Rule 5.4. Its list includes only five objectives:

- protecting and promoting the public interest;
- promoting access to legal services;
- advancing the administration of justice and the rule of law;
- encouraging an independent, strong, diverse, and effective legal profession; and
- promoting and maintaining adherence to professional principles.[131]

The Utah Supreme Court adopted a "single regulatory objective" in 2020 as part of implementing its Innovation Office and regulatory sandbox: "To ensure consumers have access to a well-developed, high-quality, innovative, affordable, and competitive market for legal services."[132] The objective is then further defined by five "regulatory principles" to guide proactive entity regulation:

- Regulation should be based on the evaluation of risk to the consumer.
- Risk to the consumer should be evaluated relative to the current legal services options available.
- Regulation should establish probabilistic thresholds for acceptable levels of harm.
- Regulation should be empirically driven.
- Regulation should be guided by a market-based approach.[133]

Implementing more regulation to encourage innovation may seem counterintuitive, especially after reading about the cases challenging professional conduct rules via antitrust law and the First Amendment in chapters 6 and 7. But the regulation contemplated here is meant to be permissive—that is, granting permission to innovate and explore new methods of legal services delivery. Like the regulatory sandboxes, jurisdictions adopting regulatory objectives can offer safe harbors for experimentation where entities do not need to fear that their investments will be wasted.

One of the less obvious, but perhaps most impactful, potential results of the regulatory objectives is that they give us measurements to develop "evidence-based regulation," as Elizabeth Chambliss calls it. Chambliss, who also helped draft the objectives as a member of the Commission on the Future of Legal Services, explains that the "ABA's adoption of regulatory objectives invites the production of empirical data and research to assess the costs and benefits of anticompetitive professional regulation. A shift to evidence-based argument already is apparent in calls for 'smarter' regulation as a middle ground between lawyers' traditional monopoly and unregulated competition. 'Evidence-based' regulation has also gained traction in other jurisdictions and professions."[134] This represents, of course, a huge turn away from traditional lawyer regulation, historically grounded in notions of professionalism. Chambliss's evidence-based regulation could help rectify structural barriers that compromise access to justice.

This necessarily prompts the question of who should conduct the evidence gathering and analysis. A national, centralized clearinghouse with federal funding support would go a long way. State bar authorities and law schools are also a good place to start, and they should partner with collaborative, research-driven organizations like the American Bar Foundation (a sponsor of the studies cited in chapter 1 led by Rebecca Sandefur and others) as well as the Institute for the Advancement of the American Legal System and the Pew Research Center (sponsors of other studies cited in chapter 1). You'll find more research center suggestions in the appendix.

* * *

The limits of regulatory reform are rooted in the culture of the legal profession, which begins with education. Chapter 9 explores this dynamic and challenges traditional methods for educating lawyers. But first, let's review the regulatory and legislative recommendations that follow from what we've covered in chapter 8.

Recommendations

Key: Attorneys (A), Advocacy Groups (AG), Bar Authorities (BA), Individuals (I), Judges (J), Law Schools (LS), Legal Tech Industry (LTI), Legislators (L), Research Centers (RC)

Adopt and Assess Regulatory Objectives (BA, J, L)

Bar authorities in all jurisdictions should adopt the ABA Model Regulatory Objectives (or something similar) and use them to both assess existing professional conduct rules for attorneys and to adopt regulations for legal services providers other than attorneys. A centralized body (government, education, nonprofit, or a combination of these) should be held responsible for collecting and analyzing data relevant to the regulatory objectives, and they should make that information available to the public.

Authorize Streamlined Licensing Paths for Discrete Specializations (BA, J, LS, L)

The failure of Washington's LLLT program to thrive should not mean the end of efforts to create limited-scope licenses for discrete specializations in areas of high-need, low-cost legal help like family law issues and other areas. Bar authorities, the courts, law schools, and legislators should consider more of these paths, learn from mistakes, refine them, and create sustainable channels for professionals to be trained in ways beyond the traditional three years of law school. Arizona's "Legal Paraprofessionals" program is one example to study and emulate.

Build More Regulatory Sandboxes (A, AG, BA, J, LS, LTI, RC)

Bar authorities in all jurisdictions should partner with attorneys, advocacy groups, judges, law schools, legal tech industry members, and research centers to build—and study the impact of—regulatory sandboxes.

Call Upon Chief Justices (A, AG, J)

The Conference of Chief Justices (CCJ) and the Conference of State Court Administrators (COSCA) regularly issue resolutions addressing many of the issues raised in this book. While not a regulatory body themselves, their resolutions matter for at least two reasons. First, individual chief justices can use the resolution as a justification for implementing reforms throughout their state. Second, the resolutions can be used to support requests for legislative funding. Chief justices should promote and implement these sorts of reforms in their individual states, and attorneys, judges, and advocacy groups should also encourage them to do so. Chief justices also can be strong advocates for funding reforms. California Supreme Court chief justice Tani Cantil-Sakauye, for example, secured $60 million in funding for state trial courts from the legislature in 2013. She warned "that their state was facing a civil rights crisis" because of court closures and delays processing cases due to underfunding.[135] Her advocacy promoted the accessibility of the justice system for the public. As chief justice of the Michigan Supreme Court Bridget Mary McCormack wrote on the role of the chief: "We do not have the luxury of sitting back, passively observing, recognizing problems, and doing nothing. That approach does not make us impartial; it makes us complicit."[136]

Create a Civil Right to Counsel, aka "Civil Gideon" (AG, J, L)

In 2006, the ABA House of Delegates passed Resolution 112A encouraging legislatures to "provide legal counsel as a matter of right at public expense to low-income persons in those categories of adversarial proceedings where basic human needs are at stake." The ABA defines "basic human needs" cases as involving shelter (e.g., eviction proceedings), sustenance (e.g., "denials of or termination of government payments or benefits"), safety (e.g., "proceedings to obtain or enforce restraining orders"), health (e.g., claims to Medicare, Medicaid, or private insurance for "access to appropriate health care for treatment of significant health problems"), or child custody.[137] Similarly, the CCJ and the COSCA "support the aspirational goal of 100 percent access to effective assistance for essential civil legal needs and urge their members to provide leadership in achieving that goal and to work with their Access to Justice Commission or other such entities to develop a strategic plan with realistic and measurable outcomes."[138] As mentioned in chapter 1, cities like Cleveland, Newark, New York City, Philadelphia, San Francisco, and Santa Monica as well as states including Connecticut, Maryland, and Washington implemented a civil right to counsel for low-income tenants facing eviction. Other state and local governments should join them, and all should expand to cover, at a minimum, the basic human needs areas as defined by the ABA.

Ease Geographic Law Practice Restrictions (BA)

An attorney admitted to practice law in one state should be able to do so in all other jurisdictions without having to retake the bar exam, provided they register with the appropriate licensing authority and complete other requirements for attorneys in that jurisdiction—for example mandatory continuing legal education. Forty states already permit military spouses to do so because of the burden of dealing with deployments and often moving every few years.[139] This model for bar reciprocity should be extended widely. Doing so both reduces the costs for an attorney to enter into a new market and expands the available pool of potential attorneys for people in need of help.

Empower Innovations through Judicial Advisory Opinions (J)

All judges have inherent authority to issue advisory opinions regarding the administration of their courtrooms. Advisory opinions are a tool some use to address the justice gap that others should look to emulate. The "authority to issue advisory opinions" gives courts a tool to experiment with innovations as they navigate a constantly "changing landscape."[140] They allow for flexibility and adjustment, as needed, without having to go through the same process required for carrying out jurisdiction-wide reform. Examples include a Colorado opinion from 2013 "finding that a juvenile court judge may participate in the contracting process selecting parents' counsel eligibility" and a Florida opinion that same year "allowing a judge to create public service announcements soliciting foster parent volunteers and use the courts' technology department to create the ads but not request certain media outlets broadcast the ads."[141] The National Center for State Courts acts as a clearinghouse for sharing new ideas and best practices in this vein.[142]

Legislate More Authorized Legal Service Providers and Legal Documentation Assistance (L)

At the federal level, Congress has long authorized legal service providers who are not necessarily licensed lawyers to serve in federal courts and agencies. For example, the United States Bankruptcy Court relies on petition preparers to assist debtors in filing necessary legal paperwork.[143] The preparers are permitted only to populate forms, however, as anything further might constitute the unauthorized practice of law.[144] Congress should expand their role to include basic legal advice. Indeed, research shows that lay specialists who represent individuals in bankruptcy and administrative agency hearings "perform as well as or better than attorneys."[145] Other agencies with nonlawyer providers include the Department of Justice, the Department of Homeland Security, the Equal Employment Opportunity Commission, the Internal Revenue Service, the Patent and Trademark Office, and the Social Security Administration. Some state legislatures have authorized legal documentation assistance (LDA) programs. LDA is delivered by a nonlawyer who is professionally trained to prepare legal documents, including offering assistance to self-help litigants.[146] California is one example, permitting LDA in simple divorces, bankruptcy filings, and will preparation since 2000. LDA providers steer clear of unauthorized practice laws because they are not authorized to give legal advice or represent a client in court. The California program imposes minimum education and competency requirements. The Nevada legislature approved a similar program in 2014, but without the education and competency prerequisites, though LDA providers must register with the secretary of state, who monitors consumer complaints and may suspend or revoke an LDA license for incompetent work.[147] In some states, the judiciary has created LDA programs. For example, the Arizona Supreme Court began certifying LDA providers in 2003.[148] The Arizona program includes minimum education and testing requirements plus an annual continuing education commitment.[149] These roles can and should be increased at all levels of government, both in terms of providing help in other areas and in expanding their duties to include, at a minimum, basic legal advice.

Make Federal Court Records Free to the Public (L)

Congress should pass the Open Courts Act, making the federal judiciary's online court records system, known as PACER (Public Access to Court Electronic Records), free to the public. Users currently pay ten cents per page to download documents up to a cap of three dollars per document, not including court transcripts. Not only would the Open Courts Act further access to justice by reducing the cost of obtaining information about court proceedings, but it would help the federal government's bottom line. According to the Congressional Budget Office, upgrading the PACER system and making it available for free would actually result in an overall savings. If enacted, the legislation "would generate $175 million in net revenues over a decade, offsetting the $161 million in mandatory spending that the bill would prompt."[150]

Remove Restrictions on Law Practice Ownership and Investment as well as Multidisciplinary Partnerships (BA)

Bar authorities should follow the lead of Arizona and Utah by removing the Model Rule 5.4 restrictions on law practice ownership and investment as well as multidisciplinary partnerships and replacing them with regulations to ensure compliance with client protections. Doing so is likely to incentivize even more growth within the markets for "New-Law" and legal/justice tech, as well as facilitate new models for providing legal services to those who currently go without, especially those who do not qualify for legal aid but forgo traditional legal services. Risk to professional independence or public confidence is minimal, if not nonexistent, as demonstrated by the decades of experience from other countries and the data emerging from Arizona and Utah.

Simplify and Standardize Court Forms and Procedures, Prioritizing E-Filing and Online Hearings (J, L)

Many courts have executed "procedural innovations through electronic filing, increased security, and direct access to court documents," which allows for "greater access to the court system and judicial resolution in a safe environment" and also increases public confidence.[151] All court forms and procedures should be simplified and standardized through-out a state (if not throughout the country), with a priority on electronic filing and online hearings where feasible. In some cases, plain lan-guage forms are the necessary safeguard to ensure constitutional due process.[152] Forms and procedures should be made widely accessible in a range of languages and should be e-reader adaptable, written to be understandable by individuals who are at a basic literacy level (and below basic if possible). All paper forms should be required to have online analogs that can be submitted as an alternative. In addition to online remote access court, the judiciary should consider Richard Susskind's proposal for handling high-volume, low-value cases asyn-chronously online with judges still involved in the decision-making. Finally, at all stages, user input and testing should be required before adopting new forms and processes, following the recommendations of artist and legal scholar Margaret Hagan to engage in what she calls "par-ticipatory design."[153] According to Hagan's research, we can "increase the likelihood that innovations will serve clients" if we "involve clients in designing them."[154]

9

Education for the Legal Profession

The legal monopoly and anticompetitive professional conduct rules are not the only barriers to an expanded market for legal services. To resolve the delivery challenge, the profession must offer personal legal services that are affordable, accessible, and—importantly—*adopted* by clients and users on a consistent, sustained basis.

We can find solutions, I believe, both in *who* and *how* we educate about the law. So far, part II has covered hindrances to democratizing legal services imposed mostly by lawyers themselves. These limitations are compounded by the fact that the few innovative advances that do succeed are not always taken advantage of by the public because they are unaware of them.

We cannot expect individuals to recognize their own legal needs, and to want a lawyer to help them, if we have not educated them about law. Conversely, lawyers must be educated not only in how to provide legal help but also in how to reach the people who need it. This chapter proposes various routes to democratize legal education, through pedagogical changes and in the way law schools conceive of their mission. The following chapter will continue the conversation about education, focusing not on lawyers themselves but on the public at large.

The Role of Law Schools in Democratizing Legal Education

Who Chooses to Become a Lawyer

Many hopeful lawyers struggled to find work during the early 2000s. In 2009, double the number of individuals passed bar exams across the country (53,508) as the number of jobs available for lawyers (26,239).[1] Only slightly more than half of law graduates in 2011 found employment that required a traditional, three-year Juris Doctor (JD) degree within nine months of graduation.[2] Applications to law school fell during this time, understandably. In the wake of the Trump presidency, however, applications skyrocketed, increasing by 13 percent in 2021.[3] The job market also improved, with 80.6 percent of graduates holding long-term law jobs ten months after graduation in 2019, according to American Bar Association (ABA) data.[4] At the same time, law school debt burdens were striking, with $160,000 as the "median cumulative figure for students reporting their debt load."[5] The cycle continues, however, and applications for the classes that will enter law school in 2024 and 2025 are predicted to decrease.

These numbers matter because they drive who decides to attend law school and what they decide to do upon graduation. And those choices impact how the justice crisis will be addressed in the future.

Think back to the data from chapter 1 documenting the lack of diversity in the legal profession. We know that lawyers do not reflect the public on any diversity metric, be it race, ethnicity, socioeconomic status, religion, disability, or LGBTQAI+ status. While women enter the profession in numbers equal to men, disparity soon sets in as one moves up into leadership roles.

The pipelining begins with education, well before law school. Efforts like the University of Houston's Pre-Law Pipeline Program target college students who are first generation, low income, or members of underrepresented groups in the legal profession and prepare them for the LSAT (the required law school admissions exam). All law schools should cultivate efforts like this. Law schools should also assess how pipelining occurs once students arrive, and as they set out into their careers. Law professor Bennett Capers makes a compelling case for "reimagining the law school as a truly inclusive space" because "law schools often function as white spaces, spaces where students of color are typically absent, not expected, or marginalized when present."[6] He argues that "the law school as white space goes beyond numbers or mere representation," and documents how "often, law schools function as white spaces in their architecture, in what law is taught, and how law is taught."[7] Sociologist and law professor Swethaa Ballakrishnen builds on Capers's thesis arguing that law school also functions as a "straight space," with "heteronormative assumptions that are baked into . . . the institutional framework."[8] Critiquing, questioning, and opening these spaces to marginalized or underrepresented individuals is essential to the access-to-justice goals of this book. Broader pipelines to expand diversity and the experiences during law school are critical because, as shown in chapter 2, people are more likely to seek out professional help from those who are similar to them.

Legal Education Reform

Calls for reform to legal education have become increasingly heated in recent years, particularly following greater media scrutiny and critiques from students as well as members of the law academy themselves.[9] Books have been written, articles have been published, studies have been launched, conferences have been organized, and conversations have been held around the proverbial water cooler over the future of legal education, all focused on ways law school does not adequately prepare future lawyers.[10] A survey of titles paints a less than positive outlook: *The Vanishing American Lawyer*,[11] *Failing Law Schools*,[12] "An Existential Crisis for Law Schools."[13] You get the picture.

While it's important to reflect on inward-looking reforms, as Elizabeth Chambliss observed, "It's not about us!"[14] Indeed, Chambliss called out the ABA for establishing a task force "on the future of legal education to 'examine how well law schools are meeting the *needs of the profession*;'" but, in her words, the task force was "dangerously—and ultimately, outrageously"—neglecting to "focus on how well law schools are meeting the *needs of the public*."[15] She similarly critiqued one of the leading calls for reform—Brian Tamanaha's *Failing Law Schools*—as neglecting to consider new roles for law schools, for example offering modified degrees for limited license law practice.[16] (Though she does not add it to her list, my guess is that Chambliss would agree with my recommendation in the next chapter that legal education take up another new role: one of public education about law.)

Much of the discussion surrounding law school reforms and education for future lawyers has resulted in burgeoning concentrations in entrepreneurship and innovation at many schools across the rankings spectrum. This focus should, at a minimum, help the public by encouraging emerging lawyers to engage in innovative practices. At best, entrepreneurship and innovation as pedagogy not only will enhance student education but also promote new models for legal services delivery.

Entrepreneurship as a Teaching Method for Lawyers

While lawyering has always been an entrepreneurial enterprise in some ways, whether one hangs a shingle as a solo practitioner or brings in business as a law firm partner, law schools historically have not required entrepreneurship training, and law firms traditionally have not valued entrepreneurial endeavors. But entrepreneurship as pedagogy can be incorporated throughout the law school curriculum and the law practice environment. Invention is crucial to addressing the immense need for legal services detailed in part I of this book. While it may seem unlikely that the next Steve Jobs or Mark Zuckerberg will be a lawyer (both famously dropped out of college[17]), law schools are filled with potential entrepreneurs in the future of law practice.

Teaching innovation as part of the law school curriculum is a relatively new phenomenon increasingly embraced by more and more schools.[18] Even so, some believe that law schools are not well suited for teaching a duty to innovate. Others are concerned that innovation-based programs are more "hype" or a "gimmick" for marketing purposes than substantive.[19] This may be due, at least in part, to the lack of law faculty with the relevant expertise. For schools offering these sorts of courses, faculty typically have prior experience in technology, design-thinking, data science, project management, or entrepreneurship. Framing innovation as an ethical obligation, however, allows it to be taught as part of the required professional responsibility or legal ethics courses and recognizes that lawyers can and should fulfill this duty even without a tech or entrepreneurial background. For some schools, teaching innovation is increasingly viewed as an imperative for properly training the next generation of lawyers.[20] Former dean of Harvard Law School Martha Minow, reflecting on the first two hundred years of legal education, wrote: "Some call this a time of crisis in legal education; others emphasize innovation and renewal. With new strains on constitutional democracies around the globe, serious chasms between the ideals and realities of justice systems in the United States and elsewhere, and perhaps unprecedented disruptive innovations in the ways legal knowledge is shared and law is practiced, . . . legal education generally face[s] significant questions and opportunities."[21] To be clear, my focus here is on teaching how to innovate in the delivery of legal services and how to be entrepreneurial in providing legal help, not how to advise entrepreneurs about legal issues like intellectual property rights and contracts.

Learning about entrepreneurship and innovation can benefit any lawyer's career development, regardless of whether they go on to start a business or invent a product. The field promotes skills such as resourcefulness, risk assessment and management, creativity, and networking. Moreover, a difficult job market and desire for work-life balance have led some lawyers to become entrepreneurs rather than pursue a traditional path to law firm partnership.[22] They stay in law, but they set up their own firms to target a particular niche and to create work-life harmony. These lawyer-entrepreneurs often struggle, however, with time management, client development, billing, and leveraging start-up costs[23]—all issues that can and should be covered in the law school curriculum and continuing legal education.

By incorporating innovation and entrepreneurship into students' coursework, law schools can employ a "race *with* machines strategy," to return to Brynjolfsson and McAfee's *Race Against the Machine*, referenced in the introduction.[24] In other words, law schools can nurture "organizational innovation: co-inventing new organizational structures, processes, and business models that leverage ever-advancing technology and human skills."[25] Entrepreneurs thrive during periods of stagnant employment "by develop[ing] new business models that combine the swelling numbers of mid-skilled workers with ever-cheaper technology to create value."[26] Consequently, "[t]here has never been a worse time to be competing with machines, but there has never been a better time to be a talented entrepreneur."[27] And there has never been a better time for law schools to take on the task of educating entrepreneurs:

> The sheer number of products and services, augmented by new technologies that will become widely available in the next decade and their likely effect on the world will be staggering. Between the advancing technology and the people who will use it stand interaction designers, shaping, guiding, and cajoling the future into forms for humans.[28]

These are all roles for future lawyers. As more humanlike and capable artificial intelligence develops, law schools must prepare students not only to work with existing tools, like ChatGPT, but also to adapt to what comes next. (Chapter 11 explores in greater depth the ethical obligations of lawyers as they augment their practices with AI tools.)

How does a curriculum of entrepreneurship and innovation tie into the overarching goal of democratizing law? It does so by providing law students the tools and inspiration needed for reaching the unlawyered. Bringing entrepreneurship into the law school curriculum may look different for every school.

Initial Efforts to Add Entrepreneurship and Innovation in Law Schools

In the early 2000s, a handful of law schools began initiatives intended to, among other things, rethink the structure of the legal profession, as well as the process for delivering legal services. For example, by 2012, Stanford Law School had a well-developed partnership in a multidisciplinary laboratory called CodeX, which pulled together industry, government, and academia to experiment in the use of information technology to improve the legal system. Still thriving more than a decade later, "CodeX, researchers, lawyers, entrepreneurs and technologists work side-by-side to advance the frontier of legal technology, bringing new levels of legal efficiency, transparency, and access to legal systems around the world."[29] The Harvard Berkman Klein Center for Internet and Society's Law Lab, established in the same era, describes itself as a "multidisciplinary research initiative and collaborative network of University, nonprofit and industry partners. Its mission is to investigate and harness the varied forces—evolutionary, social, psychological, neurological and economic—that shape the role of law and social norms as they enable cooperation, governance and entrepreneurial innovation."[30] Law professor Michele DeStefano at the University of Miami Law School founded LawWithoutWalls in 2011, "an experiential learning community that leverages intergenerational, cross-cultural, multidisciplinary collaboration to create innovations in the business of law and, importantly, change the mindsets, skillsets, and behaviors of legal professionals."[31] In 2012, Georgetown Law Center under the leadership of professor Tanina Rostain launched the course *Technology, Innovation, and Law Practice* to expose "students to the varied uses of computer technologies in the practice of law," where teams of students partner "with a legal tech expert to develop a platform, application or system that increases access to justice and/or improves the effectiveness of legal representation."[32] The class "culminates in a design competition, the Georgetown Iron Tech Lawyer Contest, which is judged by outside experts in the field."[33]

Some schools take their training in technology and innovation one step further and partner with courts or industry to directly impact individuals in need. Here's just one example of a law school partnering with the civil court system to help people who don't have a lawyer to represent them, featured in a study by the Pew Research Center:

> Suffolk Law School in Massachusetts, in collaboration with courts in three states, developed Court Forms Online, a website that improves on typical e-filing tools by offering a more user-friendly interface that guides litigants through various court processes. The site walks users through the steps for obtaining a domestic violence restraining order, applying for eviction protection under the Centers for Disease Control and Prevention moratorium, and even handling certain appellate matters. In one example, a woman was able to use forms provided through the website to electronically file a motion to the state's Appeals Court and obtain a stay of her improper eviction just as the constable was beginning to move her out of her home.[34]

Michigan State University's ReInvent Law

As noted in the preface, I cofounded a law laboratory at Michigan State University devoted to technology, innovation, and entrepreneurship in legal services in 2012, the ReInvent Law Lab. Our mission was to cultivate a creative community through partnerships with other university departments, academic institutions, industries, nonprofit organizations, government bodies, and students. We provided a new dimension of education to our students through research and experimentation designed (1) to solve problems faced by the legal profession, including access-to-justice concerns, and (2) to create new methods for the delivery of legal services. Through ReInvent Law, collaborators from the fields of law, technology, engineering, design, retailing, computer science, and beyond came together in a shared space to engage in conversation and actively construct innovative solutions. ReInvent Law harnessed collaborative energies and expertise for researching groundbreaking solutions to problems faced in twenty-first-century law practice while simultaneously encouraging and equipping students to embrace innovative approaches in the practice of law.

One example of ReInvent Law's work was the creation of Michigan State University's Twenty-First Century Law Practice Summer Program, at the time a first-of-its-kind, intensive study of technology, innovation, regulation, entrepreneurship, and the international legal marketplace. The program convened in London, England, in partnership with the University of Westminster, during the summer for three years, from 2012 to 2014. The location was selected mindful of the adoption of the Legal Services Act of 2007 and the corresponding outgrowth of alternative legal services delivery models that followed. Students were immersed in the study of these new models through a program with three primary educational objectives that remain just as relevant now and will continue to be in the future:

(1) Provide students with a comprehensive understanding of the market for legal services as it transitions to a global legal supply chain in the wake of deregulation, economic pressures, and technological innovation.
(2) Prepare students to become practice-ready entrepreneurial lawyers who can leverage information technology in order to operate more efficiently and thereby attract (and retain) clients.
(3) Inspire students to think broadly about future delivery of legal representation and access to justice by exposing them to the innovative legal service delivery models and platforms of the present (and not-too-distant future).

The program covered subjects essential to cultivating a learner who will invent the future of law practice—topics included technology, legal informatics, marketing, case studies of new legal business structures, math and statistics, virtual law practice, and digital lawyering. We also encouraged personal reflection from each student on how they might shape law practice in the future to reach those who currently cannot access a lawyer and to do so in a way that allows for positive work-life balance. Our partners included industry innovators, government entities, regulators, nonprofit organizations, and international academics, with the program culminating in a capstone "un"conference of panels and presentations. By creating this new space for students to interact with these cross-institution and cross-sector partners, the program embodied the very kind of innovative spirit we hoped to infuse in participants.

Another example of the ReInvent Law curriculum was *Entrepreneurial Lawyering*, a course that employed entrepreneurship as a teaching pedagogy. Students in the course tackled the delivery challenge facing the legal services industry in start-up mode. Among other activities, each student created a business plan and pitched a new legal service delivery model. As a supplement to the traditional job resume, students also left the course with an electronic portfolio of work to provide prospective employers and build their careers. Unlike courses at other law schools focused on teaching lawyers how to *advise* entrepreneurs, we taught lawyers to *be* entrepreneurs. When the *New York Times* visited to cover the course capstone—a pitch competition—the reporter noted, "The Entrepreneurial Lawyering Startup Competition, a showcase of the university's ReInvent Law Laboratory, is not an activity many practicing lawyers would recognize. But it might be the kind of broadened curriculum many of today's students need."[35]

The courses prepared students for new types of careers using their legal training. ReInvent Law alumni acquired jobs that did not exist when they first applied to law school, including a legal solutions architect, a deputy director of the American Bar Association Center for Innovation, a legal project manager, and a manager of client value initiatives, among others.

Not only did ReInvent Law help students create new paths in law, but it also inspired faculty to establish similar programs across the country. One of the professors working with ReInvent Law during its infancy is Josh Kubicki, now the Director of Legal Innovation and Entrepreneurship at the University of Richmond Law School. His Legal Business Design Hub won the *Fast Company* 2022 Innovation by Design Award in the category of Learning. The program combines academics and skill building: "Our mission is to teach our students skills and expertise focused on strategy, operations, and design of organizations and teams that deliver legal services. Our vision is a generation of lawyers who possess not just a legal mind, but also an entrepreneur's mind."[36] Courses offered include *Managing and Leading the Business of Law, Building a Legal Services*

Business, Legal Project and Process Leadership, and *Legal Business Design Challenge.* Another ReInvent Law professor, Dan Linna, went on to direct the Law and Technology Initiatives program at Northwestern Pritzker School of Law, teaching courses like *AI and Legal Reasoning* and *Law of Artificial Intelligence and Robotics.* In addition to offering this training to students seeking the traditional three-year law degree, Northwestern offers STEM students and professionals a nine-month Master of Science in Law, which prepares them for legal operations positions in legal aid and the courts to help address the justice gap.

These initiatives from Georgetown, Harvard, Miami, Michigan State, Northwestern, Richmond, Suffolk, Stanford, and others continued to thrive in 2023. They inspired similar efforts at many other schools. For example, *Bloomberg Law* launched a Law School Innovation Program in 2022 to recognize "pioneering educational innovations."[37] More than sixty schools submitted a program. A 2020 directory of law school innovation centers listed twenty-six law schools "that have established centers with distinct institutional identities and technology and innovation-focused missions."[38]

Other efforts involve partnerships across multiple law schools. For example, the Institute for the Future of Law Practice (IFLP) was founded in 2018, building on the University of Colorado School of Law's Tech Lawyer Accelerator Program, which placed more than ninety second- and third-year law students in paid internships based on their specialized technology and innovation skills.[39] IFLP brought together numerous law schools to offer this training to law students, along with internship placements focusing on skills in design-thinking, entrepreneurship, and technology, among others. In 2021, IFLP was acquired by the Law School Admission Council, with plans to continue related programming in the future.

Bias, Cross-Cultural Competency, and Racism

A further area for ongoing education is not tied to a particular subject matter but should be developed throughout the law school curriculum. In February 2022, the ABA House of Delegates approved a new rule mandating that all law schools "provide substantial opportunities to students for . . . the development of a professional identity" and educate students about "bias, cross-cultural competency, and racism," effective fall 2023.

This change came on the heels of a letter signed by 150 law deans asking the ABA's Council of the Section of Legal Education and Admission to the Bar to consider the requirement. Cross-cultural competency means understanding and embracing "the principles of equal access and non-discriminatory practices in service delivery."[40] This can be tied directly to the lawyer's duty of competence, found in ABA Model Rule 1.1. Being culturally competent requires a lawyer to acquire the "awareness, knowledge, and skills needed to function effectively in a pluralistic society (ability to communicate, interact, negotiate, and intervene on behalf of clients from diverse backgrounds) and on an organizational/societal level, advocating effectively to develop new theories, practices, policies, and organizational structures that are more responsive to all groups."[41]

Law professor L. Danielle Tully identifies three attributes that signal what she describes as "culturally responsive lawyering."[42] First, acceptance "that culture and law exist in a mutually constitutive relationship."[43] Second, use of "transformative legal analysis, a transparent and integrated approach to legal problem-solving that evaluates the impact of culture, context, and cognition on what the law is and makes normative assertions about what the law should be."[44] Third, employment of "transformative legal analysis along with inter-cultural sensibility in the provision of legal services or when otherwise operating within the legal profession."[45] She contends that these "tenets should be adopted institution-wide and appear in every law school course regardless of size or content area, minimally they should be incorporated throughout the first-year curriculum and in the courses that meet the ABA-required legal writing, professional responsibility, and experiential learning credits."[46] At a minimum, students will now receive this professional development at some point during their law school career, along with education about combating racism and bias, including implicit bias. Lawyers and judges would benefit from receiving this education too.

Leadership Development

Last, there is a dearth of leadership curriculum for lawyers.[47] Bar associations and law schools should fill this gap by offering opportunities for critical thinking about the role lawyers play as leaders in preserving fundamental elements of democratic society.[48] (Given the concerns summarized in chapter 5, this is especially important preparation for lawyers who become politicians or represent them.) A growing number of law schools have created leadership centers and certifications, and the Association of American Law Schools chartered a new Section on Leadership in 2017.[49] Investments into this curriculum by law school administrators likely would increase if leadership specialties were recognized by rankings organizations such as the *National Jurist* and *U.S. News and World Reports*. (Though many law schools announced in late 2022 and early 2023 they would no longer submit data to the latter in protest over legitimacy, rankings systems are likely to continue influencing the decisions students make about where to matriculate and the calculations by administrators of how to allocate resources.)

Reducing Education Costs and Licensing Requirements

Another way to increase public awareness and adoption of legal services is to adjust licensing requirements for discrete areas of practice in un(der)served areas such as consumer protection, domestic relations, elder care, housing, and wills. Traditional legal education requires three years of coursework to receive a Juris Doctor (JD) degree. Most jurisdictions mandate completion of a JD from an accredited law school in order to sit for the bar exam and receive a license to practice. Regardless of where one attends law school, the curriculum is generally the same, especially during the first year. Most schools offer no options to first-year students—everyone takes a common core of classes, typically civil procedure, contracts, criminal law, property, torts, legal writing, and often constitutional law. During the second and third years, students take electives along with a mandatory legal ethics course and an additional upper-level writing requirement. Students often, but not always, opt for courses that provide some real-world law practice experience during the third year of law school, for example working in a law school clinic or in an externship field placement.

One proposal that might help increase the number of lawyers able to serve the unmet need is to decrease the number of years for training. The concept of a two-year legal education is not new. It seems that each decade brings a new call for reducing the number of years for a legal education.[50] Columbia, for example, offered a two-year program in the late nineteenth century.[51] Nevertheless, the Association of American Law Schools has required its members to adhere to a three-year program since 1905,[52] and law schools have done so, with only rare exceptions. For example, in May 2009, Northwestern University announced that its law school would offer an accelerated two-year JD program, but it was suspended in 2015. The University of Dayton launched an accelerated program in 2013, which continued to operate in 2023.[53] Law professor Samuel Estreicher pressed the New York bar in 2012 to permit law students to sit for the bar exam after two years of law school and then, in his words, "as did President Franklin Delano Roosevelt and Justice Cardozo, practice law without a law degree."[54] President Barack Obama weighed in during his second term in 2013, proposing that, as a way to address mounting educational debt, law school could move to two years, with third-year law students clerking for law firms, government, or legal services organizations at reduced pay.[55] (Obama himself reportedly took out $42,753 in law school loans.[56] My own law school debt to attend the University of Chicago Law School exceeded six figures in the late 1990s, with loan interest rates at more than 8 percent. I would have happily spent my third year clerking at reduced pay rather than taking out another year of loans.)

What might this look like? Limited-scope practice licenses could be provisionally granted to law students after two years of law school, followed by a year of work at reduced pay under law school supervision in a particular target area, after which a JD would be awarded. Students who alternatively decided to obtain a traditional, generalist JD could be required to return for a third year of law school, or skip the clerking year entirely. Those pursuing a limited law license track could be required to take specialized courses over the first two years. Indeed, were the two-year option available for areas of law practice most in need of lawyers—domestic relations, elder care, housing issues, wills, and similar niches in un(der)served markets—some law applicants might be incentivized to provide services in areas where they otherwise would not have considered. If graduates of two-year programs holding limited law practice licenses in lesser served markets began entering the marketplace in critical mass, information about legal rights and entitlements would become more readily available to those who need it most. To be effective, however, law schools must not only formulate the specialized curriculum but also engage in a coordinated effort with bar licensing authorities.

160 | EDUCATION FOR THE LEGAL PROFESSION

The concept of an accelerated law degree has met some resistance. Law professor and former University of Chicago provost Geoff Stone argues that the third year is an "investment" leading one to "be a better a lawyer for the next 50 years" and other critics suggest the two-year model "will churn out unprepared, inferior" lawyers who will face limited job prospects.[57] Law students also may not even want to choose a two-year limited license option when with a third year they face no limitations on practice area. For students who enter law school knowing that they want to specialize in service to an un(der)served area, however, these concerns seem silly and even paternalistic.

Adjusting the content and length of schooling is only one potential reform to the licensing process. Another lies in the examination requirements. Many scholars have argued for the abolition of the bar exam, a grueling multiple-day test that all states, except Wisconsin, demand of those who wish to obtain a license to practice law. Scholars criticize the exam as biased and not relevant to actual competence for practicing law. Wisconsin offers what is known as the "diploma privilege," permitting those who graduate from in-state schools to practice law without sitting for the bar exam. (Ironically, the National Conference of Bar Examiners, which administers the exam adopted by most states, is headquartered in the one state that does not require the exam—Wisconsin.) One of those scholars, law professor Milan Markovic, conducted an empirical evaluation of the Wisconsin experience and concluded that "the bar examination requirement has no effect on attorney misconduct."[58] His study found that Wisconsin lawyers face complaints at a rate "similar to that of other jurisdictions, and Wisconsin attorneys are charged with misconduct less often than attorneys in most other states."[59] Finally, the public discipline rates are the same for Wisconsin lawyers, whether they were admitted via the diploma privilege or the bar exam.[60] A handful of states along with Washington, DC, allowed for a diploma privilege during the COVID-19 pandemic, though all returned to regular exam administration in 2021.

Adding Pro Bono Requirements

The Honorable Jonathan Lippman, former chief judge of the New York Court of Appeals (the highest court in that state), took an unprecedented step in 2012, mandating that all bar applicants complete at least fifty hours of pro bono service before admission to the bar. His rationale? He had several, including reduction of the justice gap, preparation of practice-ready law graduates with real-world skills, greater recognition of pro bono work generally, and the establishment of a professional identity around public service. Announcing his initiative at a May 1, 2012, Law Day celebration, he declared:

> Every year, about 10,000 prospective lawyers pass the New York Bar Exam. While 50 hours of law related pro bono work would amount to little more than a few days of service for each year of law school, the aggregate would be a half million hours each year that benefits New York and those in need of legal help. If every state in the country were to join us in taking up this mantle, that would mean at least two and a half million hours of additional pro bono work—what a positive impact on persons of limited means, communities and organizations that would gain from this infusion of pro bono work.

More than a decade later, no other state has followed his lead. There is strong debate among lawyers whether free service can be forced and, even if it can, whether it should. There are, of course, other ways to incentivize pro bono work, including mandatory reporting of pro bono hours, allowing pro bono work to replace mandatory continuing legal education requirements, and reducing annual bar fees for lawyers who engage in pro bono work. But Lippman's innovation is precisely the kind of creative thinking needed for solving the access-to-justice dilemma, bringing together partnerships among law schools, bar authorities, and the judiciary. It also evidences the power a chief justice wields to effectuate reform, as noted in chapter 8.

Educating Lawyers after Law School

A lawyer's education should not stop once they graduate from law school. All but four states (Maryland, Massachusetts, Michigan, and South Dakota) and the District of Columbia mandate annual continuing legal education for licensure. These requirements vary widely both in content and time-commitment. Few emphasize the sorts of topics that lawyers likely need for furthering effective access to justice and likely did not learn in law school, because they historically did not form core curriculum. These include cultural competency, entrepreneurship, implicit bias, innovation and technology, and leadership development. Florida and North Carolina mandate continuing legal education in technology, and New York requires training in cybersecurity, but these are the exceptions. State licensing authorities should consider following their lead by expanding continuing legal education in these and other areas now mandated for law students by the ABA, like cultural competency and the elimination of bias. Some have done so, including California, Illinois, Maine, Minnesota, Missouri, New Jersey, New York, Oregon, and others.[61]

* * *

Educating lawyers—from selecting who becomes one to shaping their career—may not seem directly related to the justice gap, but it is inextricably linked. Law schools must be intentional about preparing generations of attorneys who reflect the public they serve and who are committed to the cause of justice for all. These recommendations for law school, however, are incomplete without also considering public education, which we will take up in chapter 10.

Recommendations

Key: Attorneys (A), Advocacy Groups (AG), Bar Authorities (BA), Individuals (I), Judges (J), Law Schools (LS), Legal Tech Industry (LTI), Legislators (L), Research Centers (RC)

Develop Meaningful Pipelines for a Profession that Reflects the Diversity of the Public (A, AG, BA, J, LS, RC)

Law schools should develop formal pipeline programs to expand the diversity of who matriculates and also examine the entire law school experience as a pipeline for the professional trajectory of graduates. Bar authorities and advocacy groups should also engage in this effort. Meaningful pipelines require assurance from what law professor Tinu Adediran calls "racial allies," who can be any race "but given existing power structures . . . in America are often white individuals and predominantly white institutions."[62] The ally must "work to dismantle systems of oppression" and to "confer and share power with members of subjugated groups."[63] There must be concrete action—a literal transferring of power—to match platitudes and pledges.

Incentivize Pro Bono Work (A, BA, J, LS)

All jurisdictions should consider ways to further incentivize pro bono work, including the New York model requiring fifty hours of service as a condition of licensure.

Infuse Law School Curriculum with Cultural Competency, Entrepreneurship and Innovation, Implicit Bias Training, Leadership Development, and Technology Skills (LS, LTI)

Legal education in the twenty-first century must do more than prepare practice-ready graduates—we must equip students to deliver legal services in ways that we cannot predict or even imagine, ways that technological innovation, economic realities, and cultural shifts will inspire and demand. To thrive, lawyers must have a minimum competence in technology. Lawyers must learn to harness the power of networks, both in person and digitally. We need curriculum change, like that documented above, involving more than just exposure to existing law practice and tools for setting up a traditional law office. For true innovation, students need courses that involve cross-institution and cross-sector collaboration as well as creative communities—physical and virtual spaces designed to nurture new ideas. All law schools should offer coursework in cultural competency, entrepreneurship and innovation, implicit bias, leadership, and technology.

Reduce the Costs and Time of Education, Especially for Limited Practice Lawyers (BA, LS)

Law schools and regulators should work together to reduce the cost and time involved in training and licensing for lawyers who desire to engage in limited practice areas that are underserved, such as child custody, domestic relations, and housing as described in chapter 8.

Require Continuing Legal Education for Lawyers and Judges in Cultural Competency, Entrepreneurship and Innovation, Implicit Bias Training, Leadership Development, and Technology Skills (A, AG, BA, J, LTI)

While few jurisdictions mandate professional development on cultural competency, entrepreneurship and innovation, implicit bias, leadership, and technology, most allow continuing legal education requirements to be fulfilled with courses that cover these topics. Bar authorities should consider mandating these areas. Similar to the recommendation for law schools, practicing lawyers and judges should receive regular, ongoing professional development in these areas too.

Revise the Bar Licensure Process and Provide Ongoing Assessment of Competence for Law Students and Lawyers (BA, LS, RC)

Law professor Joan Howarth's 2022 book *Shaping the Bar: The Future of Attorney Licensing* sets out "twelve guiding principles" for state supreme courts and bar authorities to apply when evaluating reforms to address "how attorney licensing can protect the public more effectively moving forward."[64] For example, she recommends that courts and bars "[b]ase every licensing requirement on evidence about understanding, ensuring, and assessing minimum competence to practice law, not just hunches, tradition, and good faith."[65] All of her suggestions are worth heeding. Among other reforms, bar licensing authorities should explore sequential licensing to allow limited practice for new law professionals pending further training and examination, upward adjustment of a bar applicant's exam score for successful completion of skills courses, and granting licensure after a period of supervised public service work. Another relatively simple measure is adoption of the uniform bar exam, a standardized test administered by the National Conference of Bar Examiners, with the ability to report scores to multiple states. This would ease burdens for law students unsure of where they may ultimately choose to live and work, given the interconnected nature of our modern, post-pandemic economy, and for those who inevitably must move jurisdictions, like military spouses. (Of course, another fix for this is to remove geographic restrictions entirely, as recommended in chapter 8.) As of January 2023, 41 of 56 jurisdictions had turned to the uniform bar exam, with scores generally transferable from one state to the next,[66] a move the remaining jurisdictions should follow. Reducing the costs of entry expands the pool of attorneys available to address the justice gap. Finally, law schools and bar authorities should produce meaningful, ongoing assessment of competence for law students and lawyers, including periodic competency testing for practicing lawyers and mandatory self-evaluation.

10

Education for the Public

The impression much of the public holds about lawyers comes from Hollywood portrayals or personal injury advertisements—not exactly the most realistic or informative examples for determining when a lawyer might prevent or help navigate a problem. In this era of mass-information access and production—daily "we create 2.5 quintillion bytes of data—so much that 90 percent of the data in the world today has been created in the last two years alone"[1]—the work of lawyers remains relatively secretive, mysterious, and, at times, distrusted.[2] Education can convince the public to adopt legal services as a part of daily life, and law schools are well suited to take on this role.

Attorneys have a duty to make law accessible not only to the client[3] but also to the public. The Model Rules conceive of this obligation as part of the lawyer's role as a "public citizen:"

> As a public citizen, a lawyer should seek improvement of the law, *access* to the legal system, the administration of justice and the quality of service rendered by the legal profession. As a member of a learned profession, a lawyer should cultivate knowledge of the law beyond its use for clients, employ that knowledge in reform of the law and work to strengthen legal education. In addition, a lawyer should *further the public's understanding* of and confidence in the rule of law and the justice system.[4]

The Model Rules also recognize "the public's need to know about legal services . . . is particularly acute in the case of persons of moderate means who have not made extensive use of legal services."[5] An earlier version of the Model Rules contains important history about this obligation, a now-discarded provision devoted exclusively to making information about legal services available. The provision, Ethical Consideration 2–1, stated:

166

The need of members of the public for legal services is met only if they recognize their legal problems, appreciate the importance of seeking assistance, and are able to obtain the services of acceptable legal counsel. Hence, important functions of the legal profession are to educate laymen to recognize their problems, to facilitate the process of intelligent selection of lawyers, and to assist in making legal services fully available.[6]

This explicit duty to educate the public to (1) recognize their legal problems, (2) facilitate the process of selecting a lawyer, and (3) assist in making legal services fully available should be returned to the Model Rules. While the primary goal must be educating the public so that they know their rights and how to solve legal problems, there is a potential win-win-win for the public, law schools, and lawyers, as a secondary effect may be increased demand for lawyers.

Recall from chapter 2 that when the Supreme Court struck down the universal lawyer advertising ban in *Bates v. State Bar of Arizona*, it recognized "the right of the public as consumers and citizens to know about the activities of the legal profession."[7] How else can this "right to know" be fulfilled absent meaningful public education? Just as bar authorities have an explicit obligation after *Bates* to facilitate the public's access to information about legal services, in my view, so do law schools.

What role should a law school play, exactly, in facilitating mass information about (and potentially adoption of) legal services? The K–12 public education system has not incorporated sufficient instruction about law and legal problems beyond, at best, the basics of citizenship. Moreover, according to an American Bar Foundation report from 2011, there is an "absence of coordination" among bar associations at the national and state levels with regard to the "resources available to support civil legal assistance," and they have, as a result, employed a piecemeal effort in targeting those who qualify for legal aid.[8] This only exacerbates the lack of public information about these types of services and their availability.

One example of how law schools reach the public is through what is known as "law-related education."

Law-Related Education

Some law schools and practicing attorneys engage in law-related education (LRE), a "term of art used to refer to legal education for non-law students."[9] LRE "has been a part of American education throughout this nation's history and continues to grow and spread."[10] Yet, "the subject receives only a small fraction of the attention it deserves."[11] Perhaps the best-known program for LRE provided as a partnership between law schools and high schools is Street Law. Street Law was founded in 1972 by students at Georgetown University Law Center who "decided to bring law out of the courtrooms and into the under-served public school classrooms of Washington, DC."[12] High school students learn basic legal information relevant to their lives, and the law students "expand their knowledge of substantive law, but equally important, [gain] lawyering skills that they would not ordinarily receive in a traditional law school curriculum,"[13] including communication, public speaking, and counseling. There are now Street Law programs in every state and in thirty countries.[14]

Studies have shown that "Street Law's law-related education programs ... increase [high school] students' knowledge about the law and legal systems,"[15] and "formal evaluations as well as anecdotal reports from teachers and administrators show that Street Law programs increase understanding and belief in laws, increase bonding to school and system officials, and *decrease the incidence of rule-breaking.*"[16] The programs "focus on the practical information that young people need to know in everyday life."[17] According to scholars Matthew Kavanagh and Bebs Chorak, the goal "is not to create lawyers, but to teach 'preventative law,' which can help young people solve or avoid legal problems as they arise."[18] This is precisely what most people want—to avoid the need for a lawyer entirely. More than seventy law schools offer Street Law programs; some are sponsored by student organizations, but others are led by faculty for course credit or as part of a pro bono requirement.[19]

Additional initiatives to provide law-related education to high school students include the Florida Justice Teaching Program,[20] the Marshall-Brennan Constitutional Literacy Project,[21] New York County District Attorney's Legal Bound Program,[22] New York University Law School's High School Law Institute,[23] and the Oregon Classroom Law Project.[24] The civics-education efforts of retired United States Supreme Court

Justice Sandra Day O'Connor's iCivics program[25] and the Texas Young Lawyer's Iconic Women in Legal History website[26] are two examples that can be emulated.[27] To be sure, the efforts of these sorts of LRE projects are incredibly important in the lives of the students that they reach— high school and law school students alike. We need more.

At the University of Houston Law Center, more than fifty thousand people have received education about basic legal rights through The People's Law School, a program founded by law professor Richard Alderman.[28] The free-of-charge program relied on volunteer lawyers, judges, and law professors teaching courses in more than a dozen subject areas, including business law, consumer law, credit and debt collection, insurance, landlord-tenant law, social security, and wills. As a measure of demand, in 2002 Alderman said, in addition to the thousands who attended in person, his website received forty thousand to fifty thousand hits monthly and he regularly answered twenty-five to fifty emails a day.[29] In 2019, the program moved online, and wound down a few years later. But it is a model for future efforts as well as an indicator of demand for public education about law.

These initiatives fulfill critical public service objectives and should be expanded by law schools and bar associations. But a meaningful knowledge of law and legal services still remains largely unrealized for most people. We need the equivalent of The People's Law School at every law school across the country, to be sure, but we need much more.

Democratizing Legal Education through a Public Information Campaign

In addition to opening the doors to legal education beyond admitted law students, law schools should band together in support of a coordinated public information campaign. The concept of a public information campaign involves using "the media, messaging, and an organized set of communication activities to generate specific outcomes in a large number of individuals and in a specified period of time."[30] The goal is "to shape behavior toward desirable social outcomes. To maximize their chances of success, campaigns usually coordinate media efforts with a mix of other interpersonal and community-based communication channels."[31]

Law schools should engage in what author Daniel Pink in his book *To Sell is Human* calls "non-sales selling."[32] The market for legal services depends on whether we have the "ability to move others to exchange what they have for what we have," which, according to Pink, is not only the essence of "selling" but also "crucial to our survival" and "fundamentally human."[33] Nearly a century ago, University of Chicago law professor Karl Llewellyn made a similar point:

> Organization, cooperation, coordinated group-work, specialized work, mass-production, cheapened production, advertising and *selling*— finding the customer who does not know he wants it, and *making* him want it: these are the characteristics of the age. Not, yet, of the Bar.[34]

His critique of the bar remains accurate today in many ways, and it beckons yet another question: if adoption of legal services is a century-old problem, can it ever be fixed?

Like Pink, and Llewellyn long before him, I think part of the solution demands that law schools "sell." To be sure, law schools have long sold themselves via job placement data, shiny marketing brochures, and other efforts to entice students. Yet law schools typically eschew advertising directly to the general public. It is time to remove the stigma and embrace selling for what it is: a central source for information. Law schools should broaden their sales efforts beyond those students who fill their seats in order to nurture demand for their services once they graduate. Law schools must recognize that imparting legal expertise to future lawyers is no longer sufficient. All the legal knowledge in the world is worthless if the people who need it cannot access it. Law schools should educate the public directly.

How might a public information campaign about law, lawyers, and legal services solve delivery challenges? The concept of informing the public about basic legal rights has been advocated by courts and scholars alike. According to Richard Susskind, "we need to empower citizens to sort out some of their own legal issues," and he suggests several "channels for the delivery of legal awareness-raising."[35] His ideas include: "Public bodies, law firms, third sector bodies, and others [that] can produce handy leaflets, magazines, information packs, and websites," as well as newspapers, television, and e-learning tools such as webcasts and podcasts.[36] (I would add Tik Tok clips and Instagram Reels to that list, among other social media tools.) Susskind also hypothesized that information technology can play an important role beyond "online self-help facilities that offer guidance on questions of substantive law."[37] Instead, he speculated that "citizens can be supported by IT in *recognizing* when legal help would be beneficial and in *selecting* the most appropriate sources of legal help for their purposes."[38] Building on this concept, information technology and artificial intelligence could be incorporated into a public education campaign to not only raise overall awareness but target individuals' unique needs. Likewise, legal ethics scholar Deborah Rhode has called for "public education programs designed to increase the client demand."[39]

Despite various proposals for enhanced public education, little gained traction. Few bar associations have engaged in public information campaigns promoting the use of lawyers to solve legal problems. As Rhode notes: "Legal services providers are understandably reluctant to invest significant funds in speculative media campaigns when so many fundamental needs remain unmet. And bar associations have often lacked the membership support and public credibility to fill the gap."[40] Not only do bar associations lack credibility, but most of the public has no reason to interact with them or even know what they are. Bar associations have a lot of ground to cover in establishing public recognition if they are going to lead any change.

My own research uncovered only two examples of public information campaigns from state bar associations designed to encourage general awareness of when a lawyer might be necessary or useful: a 2008 Pennsylvania Bar Association statewide public information campaign entitled "How a Lawyer Can Help You"[41] and a 1999 Virginia Bar Association public information campaign.[42] The Virginia campaign was particularly well done; it won a National Newspaper Association *ATHENA* award in a competition that "recognizes the best in national newspaper advertising."[43] The campaign, created by students at Virginia Commonwealth University, included a series of five print advertisements and posters.[44] Each ad "illustrate[d] how lawyers help ordinary people" and ended with the common tagline: "You have rights. Lawyers protect them. Virginia State Bar."[45] The ads apparently ran in newspapers with plans for corresponding radio and TV spots, but funding was insufficient.[46] It's unknown how successful they were, if at all. Future efforts should be tracked and analyzed for impact.

The American Bar Association (ABA) sponsors youth education and projects and once had a Special Committee on Youth Education for Citizenship to facilitate "partnerships among educators, legal professionals and others interested in educating children about the law and citizenship,"[47] but it never engaged in a widescale public information campaign of the scope contemplated here and the committee no longer exists. The Association of American Law Schools has similarly neglected to make public law-related education a priority, although it has gestured toward the need for this education by hosting colloquiums to discuss access-to-justice affairs.[48] For example, the Association recommended the creation of a national network of law schools focused on equal justice that would engage in public education efforts, such as producing national report cards on equal justice issues. That proposal never took hold, however. One notable exception is work by the public interest bar, which has increased its education efforts over the past two decades. According to a study conducted by Rhode, "the research, reports, education and media activities jumped from 12 percent to 26 percent [for] some fifty leaders of the nation's preeminent public interest legal organizations" during the late 1990s and early 2000s.[49]

I believe an enhanced public awareness about one's legal rights and entitlements, coupled with information about how to obtain an affordable, competent, and trustworthy lawyer, would go a long way toward resolving the delivery challenge. Still, some may question whether a public information campaign can actually bring about meaningful change. Studies have shown that while "public information campaigns are difficult to mount successfully, [they] have been effective means of achieving diverse policy objectives."[50] A public information campaign holds the ability to impact the market for legal services in powerful ways:

> First, public information campaigns can enhance the richness and fairness of the competition of ideas. . . . Second, public information campaigns can enrich the possibilities for democratic participation. Better-informed citizens may participate more knowledgeably and effectively in all democratic processes. . . . Third, public information campaigns can be effective in informing the least well-informed citizens, thereby reducing inequality

in access to information. Some researchers have found that campaigns sometimes narrow the information advantage of the highly educated. . . . Fourth, public information campaigns can expand the citizen's horizons and imagination. They may treat citizens as partners in addressing collective problems and opportunities and endorse the legitimacy of the citizen's understanding of his or her own circumstances.[51]

We can look to successful examples from other professions as indicators for the potential impact of a public education campaign about legal help. For example, "[m]ass media campaigns, because of their wide reach, appeal, and cost-effectiveness, have been major tools in health promotion and disease prevention. They are uniformly considered to be powerful tools capable of promoting healthy social change."[52] A close comparison for lawyers can be drawn from the field of psychology and mental health.

Psychologists, much like lawyers, had a long-standing image problem based on a misunderstanding or lack of awareness of how a psychologist's work could be relevant to an individual's daily life.[53] Studies conducted in the 1980s to "ascertain the public's image of psychology" revealed that while the public was "somewhat aware of both the scientific and clinical work of psychologists," there was "virtually no understanding of the impact of psychology on their lives."[54]

In order to combat this lack of understanding, and the corresponding stagnant marketplace for mental health services in the mid-1990s, the American Psychology Association (APA) Council of Representatives launched a public information campaign to educate the public about "psychological care, research and services; the various roles of psychologists in public, private, and institutional health care; the education and training of psychologists; and the value of psychological interventions."[55] The first stage of this campaign included national advertising in consumer magazines along with television, radio, and print advertising in test markets: Denver, Colorado, and Hartford, Connecticut.[56] The outreach included calling eight hundred telephone numbers, mailing brochures, and publishing a website. The campaign had an immediate positive impact on referral activity for psychological services. More than four thousand individuals requested literature or a psychological referral, and the campaign's website received three thousand visits each week during the first six months following the launch.[57] The effort also coincided with a highly favorable prediction by the Bureau of Labor Statistics Occupational Outlook Handbook for psychologists, which projected a 55 percent increase in psychologist jobs over the 2012–22 decade—higher than the average for all occupations[58]—and the APA estimated that during "2015 to 2030, the national baseline demand for psychologists is projected to grow by 6 percent."[59]

In my own lifetime, psychology, psychiatry, and mental health therapy have gone from stigmatized to ubiquitous. Wellness programs proliferate in workplaces. Numerous mobile apps facilitate mental health care from both human providers and artificial intelligence tools. A similar public image makeover is possible for legal services.

Educational institutions from other fields also have had success in these sorts of campaigns. For example, in 1988, the Harvard School of Public Health's Center for Health Communication launched a national media campaign to promote the use of a designated driver after drinking.[60] Harvard worked with "leading television networks and Hollywood production studios . . . to promote an emerging social norm that the driver should abstain from alcohol."[61] More than 160 entertainment programs and numerous public service announcements on all major broadcast networks featured the center's designated driver message.[62] According to a Gallup poll two months prior to the campaign, 62 percent of the respondents indicated the use of a designated driver, but immediately following the campaign, this percentage increased to 66 percent, and "[b]y mid-1989, it increased to 72 percent, a statistically significant increase compared to the precampaign figure."[63]

One law school acting on its own is not sufficient. American law schools span the nation, from small university towns to large metropolitan cities. Their network effect can be far reaching. Law schools hold significant intrinsic reputational value that goes wasted when they fail to bridge this public education gap. By acting together through a unified information campaign, law schools could make a tremendous impact on the public's understanding of law and legal services. This raises the question: who should lead the effort? It could start through a national organization like the Association of American Law Schools or the Law School Admission Council. It also could be driven by a cohort of top-tier schools, similar to the movement for abandoning the *U.S. News and*

World Report rankings sparked first by Yale Law School's departure and soon joined by most of the top-fourteen law schools among numerous others. Or the 150 law deans who united in support of the ABA's mandate for law school training in bias, cross-cultural competency, and racism might come together again for a collective public education campaign.

DIY Resources

A survey in 2019 uncovered more than 320 online self-help tools specifically targeted to individuals for do-it-yourself (DIY) legal help.[64] They assist both with criminal matters (for example, police stops or expungements of juvenile records) and civil issues (for example, family needs and health concerns). Most are free; some charge users a modest amount. The survey uncovered "tools targeted at a range of different user groups, including lawyers, law firms, corporations, in-house legal departments, court systems, community organizations, and individual users who are not trained as attorneys."[65] Slightly more than half help with justice problems, for example preparing legal documents, diagnosing legal problems, and resolving disputes.[66] Of course, the ability to use these tools requires access to stable, high-speed internet and a personal computer or mobile device. We know that millions living in the United States still lack both.

So, the same people who struggle to get the legal help they need— low-income individuals, minorities, those with lower levels of education or language barriers—likely find these tools illusive, too. While the tools proliferate, the survey found several shortcomings. First, the DIY tools offer limited functions and do not cover the most common justice problems faced by the public. Second, many were outdated and not user friendly. They survey concluded: "Digital legal technologies hold promise to empower individuals and communities to identify, understand, and take action on their justice problems and to use the rights that are theirs under law. At this stage in the growth of this field of activity, realizing that promise is not a technological challenge, but rather a social one."[67]

Online learning platforms also offer potential for educating the public about legal services. Coursera, for example, partners with more than 275 leading universities and companies to "bring flexible, affordable, job-relevant online learning to individuals and organizations worldwide."[68]

In late 2022, it counted more than 113 million students, a number that continues to grow.[69] Law schools and bar associations should join forces with companies like this.

An ABA study conducted in 2011 revealed that self-represented people turn to the judge for help during a proceeding more than any other resource.[70] As the study noted, this "suggests a basic misunderstanding of the role of the judge in our courts"—a judge who is supposed to play a neutral role and not lend assistance to either side in a case.[71] It also causes "substantial delays" and compromises "the effectiveness of our already overburdened and underresourced judicial system," according to research from law professor Stephan Landsman.[72]

Court facilitators and navigators help intervene on behalf of those who are self-represented. For example, while navigators cannot provide legal advice, they use computers located in the courthouse to retrieve information, research information about the law, collect documentation needed for individual cases, and respond to a judge's or court attorney's questions about the case.[73] In California, court facilitators work with licensed lawyers to provide information about court procedures and legal forms in family law matters. More than 345,000 individuals utilize facilitator services annually.[74] Individuals can find facilitators through the California Supreme Court's website, which lists them by county and provides contact details for scheduling an appointment. Washington State has a similar program in most counties.[75] During 2007, facilitators conducted approximately 57,000 customer sessions and made 108,000 customer contacts, with most reporting being very satisfied.[76] Nine out of ten agreed they felt more knowledgeable and prepared immediately after a visit with a facilitator, and 82 percent said the interaction left them with more trust and confidence in the courts.[77] Most judges and court administrators concluded the program had a positive impact on self-represented litigants, improved access to justice and the quality of justice, and increased court efficiency.[78] New York's court navigators program offers another tool for self-help. Initially launched in 2014, "college students, law students and other persons deemed appropriate . . . assist unrepresented litigants, who are appearing" in housing court in nonpayment, civil, and debt proceedings, all on a volunteer basis.[79] A 2016 study conducted by the American Bar Foundation, the National Center for State Courts, and the Public Welfare Foundation about the use of the volunteer navigators in Brooklyn's Housing Court found that tenants experienced greater success when working with a navigator.[80] For example, tenants with navigators were 87 percent more likely to have their legal defenses acknowledged, including the judge ordering the landlord to make repairs.[81] Arizona launched a comparable navigator program in 2015, partnering with Arizona State University to train and supervise undergraduates as navigators.[82]

* * *

Expanding educational opportunities for both the public and lawyers is an important tool for democratizing law. Similar to the court challenges via antitrust law and the First Amendment discussed in chapters 6 and 7, however, the educational reforms discussed here, alone, are insufficient. An all-hands-on-deck, multifaceted gameplan must be deployed. With all the approaches outlined in part II to this point, a central theme is innovation. Chapter 11 builds on the recommendations below and takes on the duty to innovate explicitly, unpacking how this obligation shapes the potential solutions for solving the access to justice crisis.

Recommendations

Key: Attorneys (A), Advocacy Groups (AG), Bar Authorities (BA), Individuals (I), Judges (J), Law Schools (LS), Legal Tech Industry (LTI), Legislators (L), Research Centers (RC)

Construct a User-Friendly National Directory or Portal for Legal Help (A, AG, BA, L, LTI, RC)

As MacArthur Genius Rebecca Sandefur's research shows, there is an "absence of coordination" among bar associations at the national and state levels in distributing the "resources available to support civil legal assistance."[83] A national portal for connecting individuals with the legal help is needed. This could be convened by the federal government, perhaps through a charge to the Legal Services Corporation (along with adequate funding). It could be led by a group of bar authorities, law schools, and/or research centers. Groups like Pro Bono Net and Law

Help already offer online tools of this nature. Suffolk Law School's Court Forms Online project (mentioned in chapter 9) is another small-scale effort to match individuals with online resources that could be expanded. In addition, the public must be convinced to actually use a directory or portal, which links to the recommendation below about public education campaigns.

Deploy DIY Justice Tools (A, BA, I, J, LS, LTI)

Numerous self-help resources are available for those willing to handle legal problems themselves. For example, Michigan Legal Help (www.MichiganLegalHelp.org) is a website for "people who are handling their legal problems without a lawyer." It is the product of a collaboration among the Michigan State Bar Foundation, the Legal Services Corporation, and the Michigan Supreme Court. The website provides education about legal problems and prepares individuals for court. Automated tools help users create individualized forms. It also directs users to lawyers, community services, or additional self-help tools as appropriate. Another example is LawHelp Interactive (www.lawhelpinteractive.org), a free resource that allows users across the country to create personalized legal documents and offers its tools to lawyers as well. For individual "self-helpers," the website asks users a series of questions about their legal problem and provides the relevant documents, and it provides the same service for lawyers on behalf of their clients. LawHelp Interactive covers topics including child support and custody, domestic violence, debt collection, foreclosures, evictions, and divorce. The website also offers court forms and legal documents for nonprofits and aids those seeking to "develop state-of-the art interactive forms for their states or for specific projects." More than one million individuals and organizations engaged with LawHelp Interactive in 2017. Like Michigan Legal Help, it is affiliated with the Legal Services Corporation. It is also part of the nonprofit Pro Bono Net. Other DIY resources supported by Pro Bono Net include immigration (www.immi.org and www.immigrationadvocates.org), citizenship applications (www.citizenshipworks.org), and legal risk screenings conducted by elder care professionals for their patients (www.probono.net/programs/risk-detector). More DIY tools like these should be made widely available and robustly promoted to the public by bar associations, courts, law schools, and members of the legal profession.

Implement (and Post in Courthouses) a National Bill of Rights for Self-Represented Parties (A, BA, J, LS, RC)

Upsolve founder Rohan Pavuluri has called for a national bill of rights for self-represented parties, both to inform individuals about what they can expect in the process and how they should be treated along the way. Two resources to draw from are the *American Code of Conduct for Trial Lawyers and Judges Involved in Civil Cases with Self-Represented Parties*, produced by the American College of Trial Lawyers, and a report from the Institute for the Advancement of the American Legal System, *Ensuring the Right to Be Heard: Guidance for Trial Judges in Cases Involving Self-Represented Litigants*. The bill of rights should provide for simplified processes, understandable forms and resources, and respect for all parties. This should be posted throughout justice spaces—both in physical courthouses and online remote courts. Equally important, judges and lawyers should pledge to uphold it.

Normalize Routine Legal Checkups (A, AG, BA, I, J, LS, LTI, RC)

A legal checkup raises awareness about legal needs and promotes recognition of legal assistance to solve problems. This concept is not new. In a 1974 book, *Manual for the Periodic Legal Checkups*, practitioner and law professor Louis Brown explained:

> Clients find that the checkups are educational for them and they are alerted to a number of legal aspects of their lives. Such things as inadequate insurance coverage for liability, failure to review a will executed many years before, failure to adopt a child who is living with a client, mixing of marital properties so as to cause problems in a decedent's estate or divorce, or failure of a person to take adequate security on a promissory note from one in whom the lender had great faith, are examples of facts which come up in a legal checkup. The legal profession

has yet to learn, and clients have yet to appreciate, that there is value in a professional diagnosis whether or not "problems" are surfaced.[84]

Brown envisioned that clients would meet with their lawyer on a periodic basis, just as they would meet with their doctor, dentist, or optometrist. (The ABA might reach out to the AMA to partner in an effort to instill the concept of a legal-wellness visit alongside the annual preventive health care physical.) While legal checkups have been promoted by bar associations, there has not been wide adoption because most people lack an all-purpose attorney. This could change with well-designed "expert system" technology to help users navigate and triage quickly. Even without a personal lawyer or a technology-driven framework, however, individuals can and should take stock of their "legal health" in these key areas: (1) birth/adoption of children/grandchildren; (2) caring for elders/special needs; (3) marriage/divorce; (4) moving to a new state; (5) real estate transactions; (6) retirement; and (7) wills and estate planning.

Promote Public Education Campaigns about Civics, Legal Problems and Solutions, and the Rule of Law (A, AG, BA, LS, RC)

Law schools are located across the country in communities of all sizes, urban and rural. This network holds great potential for shaping the public's understanding of law and legal services. Law schools should lead a unified public education campaign to remedy market failure. They should also consider offering online education broadly to the public. The *Bates* court placed this responsibility on the bar: "It is the bar's role to assure that the populace is sufficiently informed."[85] This directive equally applies to legal education. The Association of American Law Schools, with a membership of 176 schools, is well suited to lead such an effort, as are law school deans. Bar authorities should also become more involved with public education, fulfilling the call to action from the *Bates* opinion. Advocacy groups and research centers have an important role to play here as well.

Provide More Court Facilitators and Navigators (J, L, LS)

States like Arizona, California, New York, and Washington operate long-standing court facilitator and navigator programs. These efforts should be expanded throughout the nation.

Take Steps Toward Greater Court Transparency (J)

All courts should allow live-streaming and cameras in the courtroom, recordings, and transcripts of proceedings, notice of hearings, and other measures to promote public access and information.

11

Ethical Innovation

Everyone is innovative in the twenty-first century, so it seems. *Wired* magazine named "innovation" the most overused term in 2013.[1] It has become the ultimate buzzword, and its regular appearance in the legal profession is no exception. The word "innovation" is proudly displayed on firm websites and law school marketing brochures. The Legal Services Corporation hosts an annual "Innovations in Technology Conference." More than one hundred law firms and legal departments have created new positions for "innovation counsel" and "chief innovation officer."[2] Some even created structural incentives. For example, the law firm Reed Smith credits up to fifty innovation hours toward an attorney's yearly billable requirements.[3] A group of Austrian law firms created a Vienna-based "Legal Tech Hub" to facilitate innovation in legal advice.[4] To help support community legal aid, Justice Connect of Australia included a team of innovation professionals on every new project to offer advice about efficiencies and enhancements to expand access to legal help.[5] The Global Legal Hackathon annually brings "the legal industry together with tech and innovation, world-wide, with one purpose: rapid development of solutions for improving the legal industry world-wide."[6] More than twenty thousand individuals from seventy-five countries participated from 2018 to 2022.

Innovation outpaces law. Artificial intelligence, blockchain, data analytics, and other twenty-first-century advancements are already used by academic institutions, corporations, government entities, health care providers, and others, but they have introduced lingering questions about individual autonomy, identity, privacy, and security. Even as new laws address known threats, future technology developments and process improvements inevitably will present unforeseen externalities.

Innovation is essential to solving the justice crisis. How do we design laws and systems to ensure accountability, equality, and transparency in this environment of rapid change? Professional ethics—especially the regulation of legal expertise—offers a potential solution. This chapter offers examples and proposes guidelines for facilitating ethical innovation that avoids compromising legal rights or entitlements and instead furthers them.

Exponential Change and Protecting Human Rights

Technology is all the time more humanlike, even surpassing the capacity of the mind. Machines can not only beat humans at games like chess and Jeopardy!,[7] but they can also translate language,[8] read lips,[9] author news articles,[10] discriminate in advertising,[11] tweet in offensive language,[12] instantly translate two hundred languages,[13] and, as you saw in the preface, write eerily accurate book reviews without having actually read the content. In early 2023, law professors at the University of Minnesota gave ChatGPT exams in four classes.[14] They found, in blind grading, that it performed well enough to pass, averaging a C+ across all classes. Later that year a new version of ChatGPT reportedly passed the bar exam "by a significant margin," though a later study challenged that finding. Regardless, AI like ChatGPT is increasingly capable.[15]

Medical care is routinely offered by telehealth providers,[16] smartphone apps,[17] and life-like avatars or animatronic companion pets.[18] Legal services are not immune to automation either.[19] But much as we still need doctors to make judgment calls in life-or-death situations, machines cannot replace lawyers completely. At the same time, lawyers must embrace automation and related innovations. As law professor Ray Brescia explains:

> Given the rapid pace of evolutionary change brought on by technological advances, globalization, rapid urbanization, and climate change, as well as the displacement and economic inequality caused by these forces, the problems faced by society at large are problems lawyers should attempt to address if they are to remain relevant to the needs of the broader community.[20]

More than relevance is at stake, however. Lawyers should have an explicit ethical obligation to consider the impacts of innovation on their clients and the practice of law.

This bears on the lawyer's role both in considering ways artificial intelligence might replace some work that they once performed and in ensuring that these innovations do not compromise human rights. Lawyers must play an active role in certifying the information that machines rely on to develop artificial intelligence. In 1996, Richard Susskind advocated for this in his pioneering book *The Future of Law: Facing the Challenges of Information Technology*. He wrote: "There will be a need for some kind of system of certification of the information and services which become available—non-lawyers will want some comfort and assurance that the systems upon which they are relying (and clearly there are profound liability issues here) have indeed been developed by appropriately qualified lawyers."[21] This system will be fundamental to preserving the rule of law and will be a uniquely human job for lawyers, not machines.

Consider the system built by University of Toronto researchers and acquired by Google that facilitates facial recognition to organize photos and images on a smartphone. While accurate in some instances (and believed promising for use by other constituencies, including law enforcement) the product was "less accurate when used with women and people of color."[22] Naturally, questions emerged about how it might be used or misused and how it might perpetuate bias or discrimination.

Another example is the emerging phenomenon of "personalized law," where data is collected, "transferred, stored, organized, and analyzed in an efficient and timely manner, in order to tailor legal norms to individuals."[23] Personalized law might take the form of special conditions placed on driving for minors or drivers with a history of accidents, with sanctions administered by government authorities "in real time by enabling parking, issuing a ticket, or even remotely disabling a car following a warning."[24] This kind of personalization comes with distinct trade-offs. On the one hand, according to law professors Niva Elkin-Koren and Michal Gal, a legal system like this "may increase efficiency by improving law enforcement, reducing under- or overinclusive risk avoidance mechanisms, and reducing institutionalized discrimination."[25] On the other hand, it "may undermine important values, raising concerns regarding privacy, equality under the law, and civil liberties."[26] Lawyers, more than ever, will be needed to protect these values and to assure users about the accuracy and security of information used to develop artificial intelligence.

Scholars who are focused on big data's "disparate impact," or unintentional discrimination of minoritized and marginalized groups, offer a caution that applies to all innovation, especially technology-driven advancements like artificial intelligence: "If [we] are not careful, the process can result in disproportionately adverse outcomes concentrated within historically disadvantaged groups in ways that look a lot like discrimination."[27] Seemingly neutral processes, caution law professor Andrew Selbst and researcher Solon Barocas, "can reproduce existing patterns of discrimination, inherit the prejudice of prior decision makers, or simply reflect the widespread biases that persist in society. It can even have the perverse result of exacerbating existing inequalities by suggesting that historically disadvantaged groups actually deserve less favorable treatment."[28]

Researchers from the United Kingdom identify three possible scenarios for how artificial intelligence may facilitate what they term "augmented lawyering."[29] The first looks quite similar to what currently exists, basically human legal experts who use AI-enabled tools as consumers. In this world, the ability of lawyers to give legal advice may be "augmented by AI providing more efficient and effective outputs" for work like contract drafting and legal research.[30] This scenario represents "only a modest incremental change in the activities of the legal profession" and "a clear division of labor remains between lawyers who practice law and other professionals (data scientists, project managers, design thinkers)" who support lawyers.[31] The second possibility, according to these researchers, is that lawyers themselves may become "producers of AI-enabled legal services," what they call "the notion of 'lawyer-coders,' the idea that the majority of lawyers should become familiar with how to use AI models, if not learn how to code."[32] This would place a duty on lawyers "not only to give legal advice, but also to take a more systematic perspective to providing integrated legal solutions to their clients."[33] The final scenario envisions a "splintering of professionals beyond the traditional legal profession into multiple sub- or even new professions."[34] The idea here is that in addition to traditional lawyering, "new roles will be created that focus on the producer role for technology-enabled legal services, with an emergent specialization in legal operations, legal engineering, legal project management, legal products, and legal technology."[35] Their prediction? "This third scenario is quite plausible if changes

ETHICAL INNOVATION

in professional regulation around what constitutes unauthorized practice of law remain minimal or slow."[36]

Who should weigh these trade-offs and be responsible for preventing discrimination or other potential harms in innovation?

Assigning Responsibility

Government authorities seem like a logical place to turn for regulatory efforts aimed at protecting the public from known and unknown harms related to technology advancements and other innovations. In 2014, the White House issued a report concluding "that big data analytics have the potential to eclipse longstanding civil rights protections in how personal information is used in housing, credit, employment, health, education, and the marketplace."[37] The authors recommended the development of "a plan for investigating and resolving violations of law in such cases," placing responsibility on enforcement agencies like the Department of Justice, Federal Trade Commission, Consumer Financial Protection Bureau, and Equal Employment Opportunity Commission.[38] In 2018, Congressional hearings examined the misuse of social media and search engine platforms like Facebook, Google, and Twitter in the 2016 elections.[39] Other countries have engaged in similar efforts.

However, reliance on the state for protecting against algorithmic discrimination and bias presents serious risks. As law professor Sonia Katyal argues, "We are looking in the wrong place if we look to the state alone to address issues of algorithmic accountability."[40] She proposes other ways "to ensure more transparency and accountability that stem from private industry, rather than public regulation."[41] According to Katyal, "The issue of algorithmic bias represents a crucial new world of civil rights concerns. . . . Since we are in a world where the activities of private corporations, rather than the state, are raising concerns about privacy, due process, and discrimination, we must focus on the role of private corporations in addressing the issue."[42] She proposes private-actor-driven measures "including codes of conduct, impact statements, and whistle-blower protection" to protect civil rights.[43] As examples, she cites executives at "Amazon, Facebook, IBM, Microsoft, and Alphabet [who] have been attempting to design a standard of ethics around the creation of artificial intelligence" and work by "professional organizations like the

Association for the Advancement of Artificial Intelligence (AAAI) and the Association of Computing Machinery (ACM)."[44] Professional conduct rules could play a similar role for the legal profession.

One challenge for reliance on industry-sponsored "ethics" policies is the lack of any meaningful enforcement mechanism. At a summit on "New Work" held in early 2019, "a list of recommendations for building and deploying ethical artificial intelligence" was crafted by groups of attendees that included academics, policymakers, and corporate representatives.[45] The list contained ten goals that typically appear in these sorts of efforts: (1) transparency, (2) disclosure, (3) privacy, (4) diversity, (5) antibias, (6) trust, (7) accountability, (8) collective governance, (9) regulation, and (10) complementarity (i.e., treating technology "as a tool for humans to use, not a replacement for human work").[46] Social media and technology companies already have policies with similar components, as do institutions ranging from government bodies to health care providers to universities.

But policies to protect individuals through principles like transparency and trust haven't stopped innovations like data analytics from being misused. When representatives from Facebook, Google, and Twitter were summoned to testify before Congress in late 2018 about election interference and admitted that their platforms were vulnerable to misuse, all had long-standing measures in place to avoid these harms. Voluntary industry policies alone are not sufficient to protect individual rights.

The regulation of professional knowledge is a potential solution to this dilemma. Most disciplines (e.g., law, medicine, engineering, social or physical sciences, trades) define what constitutes competence within their specific fields via specialized education and training, certifications, and licensing. Often this is described as a code of ethics. As you know from chapter 3, the legal profession is governed by provisions based on the American Bar Association (ABA) Model Rules. These codes are different from a corporation's aspirational pledge; if lawyers violate the relevant ethics code under which they hold their license to practice, they may lose that privilege and, indeed, their very livelihood.

Systematized lawyer ethics can help protect human rights in the face of rapid innovation. The ABA House of Delegates has already recognized this in the context of artificial intelligence. In 2019, it passed a resolution urging "courts and lawyers to address the emerging ethical and legal issues related to the usage of AI in the practice of law including: (1) bias, explainability, and transparency of automated decisions made by AI; (2) ethical and beneficial usage of AI; and (3) controls and oversight of AI and the vendors that provide AI."[47] An ethical obligation related to innovation is a natural and obvious extension of this resolution.

Lawyers and judges will need to implement a framework for assuring users of AI-fueled legal tools that the information inputs are aligned with the rule of law, culturally competent, ethical, and unbiased. Civil rights scholar Sherley Cruz notes that genuine access to justice "requires that legal professionals work with legal technology designers to learn the preferences, values, and barriers of the audience, in order to create technological innovations that will benefit diverse end users."[48] She warns that if legal tech fails to consider diversity, it will "not only be ineffective, but it may also cause harm to already vulnerable communities."[49]

Some state courts, as well as the Conference of Chief Justices and the National Center for State Courts, have been leaders in driving legal services innovation to expand access to legal help.[50] Chief Judge Lippman, who implemented the fifty hour pro bono mandate described in chapter 9, called these efforts "beacons of hope . . . fueled in large measure by state judiciaries who, on access issues, are uniquely suited to initiate discussion, deliver the message, and generate large-scale change and innovation."[51] Some use their role as the chief judge or justice to spearhead innovation efforts.[52] As Lippman has written: "To be sure, some may not view the role of Chief Justices so expansively and may instead see their primary responsibility as limited to the adjudication of legal issues that come before our state high courts. But, as indispensable as that role is, being proactive in ensuring access to justice for all is foundational to the judicial role."[53] According to Marla Greenstein, executive director of the Alaska Commission on Judicial Conduct: "Judges can experiment, innovate, and grow. And by thoughtfully embracing innovation, judges will embody the integrity of the justice system."[54]

The Lawyer's Duty of Ethical Innovation

The duty of ethical innovation contemplated here is two-fold—both client centered and public facing. A majority of American jurisdictions, perhaps unwittingly, already have adopted a component of the client-centered aspect by adding to Model Rule 1.2's duty of competence an obligation to keep up with changes in technology in law practice, as noted in chapter 3. None has yet to formally embrace the public-facing component, that is, a duty to innovate to expand access to justice for the public, though many have devoted substantial resources toward exploring aspects of it through futures commissions and similar initiatives.

Some may contend that new ethics rules are not needed for governing innovation because existing ones are sufficient. While a special law for every innovation might be impractical, we do need regulatory structures to assess the benefits and risks of innovation.

Look no further than the voting corruption associated with social media during the 2016 and 2020 presidential election cycles as justification for some sort of oversight. We are increasingly immersed in a world of "fake news,"[55] "deep fakes,"[56] and "alternate facts."[57] Infusing a duty to innovate ethically into the professional rules governing the practice of law can help avoid the need for constantly updating legal structures as society progresses via globalization, technology, and related forces. This proposal to address innovation within legal ethics rules comes at a time when the legal profession is increasingly immersed in innovation—whether measured by the number of new tech-driven providers, the exponentially increasing financial investment in legal and justice tech, or, as noted in chapter 8, the ABA's 2020 Resolution supporting innovation to address the access-to-justice crisis.

Scholars range in their views on whether and how the ever-increasingly humanlike technology should be relied on for legal disputes. For example, First Amendment scholar Eugene Volokh in his article "Chief Justice Robots" contends that if "software can create persuasive opinions, capable of regularly winning opinion-writing competitions against human judges—and if it can be adequately protected against hacking and similar attacks—we should in principle accept it as a judge, even if the opinions do not stem from human judgment."[58] Dana Remus, former White House counsel for President Joe Biden, expressed a different view in an article she co-authored as a law professor with economist Frank Levy, "Can Robots Be Lawyers?"[59] They "showed that while technology is undoubtedly advancing and changing the nature of legal practice, it is displacing lawyers at a modest pace" and elsewhere she expressed "caution in the adoption of predictive-coding technologies" for law practice and the judiciary.[60] Law professor Aziz Huq, in his article "A Right to a Human Decision," advanced the position that there is only "a right to a well-calibrated machine decision" but not a decision by a human judge. In his view, "[m]achines have the capacity to classify and predict with fewer errors than humans. At least from a dynamic perspective, this suggests that legal rules should incentivize the creation of better machines rather than their substitution with humans."[61]

Whatever one's perspective on whether lawyers and judges *should* adopt innovations like artificial intelligence or machine learning, we must acknowledge that technology advancements like these are an inevitable part of modern society, including the practice of law and the resolution of disputes. And, in some instances, the legal help of a machine is better than no help at all; sometimes it may be better than what a human can provide.

Updated rules are especially warranted when a moment of crisis shatters the status quo, like when the 2020 coronavirus pandemic abruptly halted law practice in its traditional form, canceling office meetings and jury trials and other in-person interactions. Some lawyers and courts were prepared; others were not. Some clients received their legal advice through virtual consultations or mobile apps and had their cases decided by judges via Zoom hearings. Many others found themselves still without the justice they needed, especially those lacking a computer, mobile device, or reliable high-speed internet. The lawyers and judges at the forefront of ethical innovation before the pandemic were the ones best able to serve their clients once it hit.

Indeed, after enduring lockdowns imposed by the COVID-19 pandemic, we now know that the profession can adopt innovations overnight. The sudden and nonnegotiable need for innovation rendered the old guard defenseless. They no longer could hide behind precedent and professionalism as excuses for moving from the status quo. As one law firm innovator observed: "In just one week, we achieved what we've been trying to do for years."[62] Innovations in how lawyers work—like telecommuting and the use of the cloud for file storage—were implemented or expanded extensively. Courts around the country quickly moved to video hearings. In Texas alone, "the state's trial courts held video-powered hearings in more than 160,000 civil and criminal cases from late March to mid-June" of 2020, a feat that "would have been unimaginable prior to the COVID-19 outbreak" according to Chief Justice Hecht.[63] The overwhelming majority of states "had responded to in-person arguments being canceled by holding remote hearings" by that same time.[64] Federal courts were, notably, slower to respond, though the United States Supreme Court did audio-livestream oral arguments. It refused, however, to join the Michigan Supreme Court, the Supreme Court of Texas, and others in permitting videos or cameras in the courtroom.

The idea of regulation to instill ethical innovation may seem impractical, but consider the experience of regulatory bodies governing the practice of law over the past two decades, especially in Australia, England, and Wales, as discussed in chapter 8. Professional ethics rules framed new business structures for providing legal services through ABSs and law firms funded by nonlawyers. Even jurisdictions that have not overtly embraced regulatory reform nonetheless devote substantial resources to evaluation and promotion of innovation in legal services. In my work as a reporter for the ABA Futures Commission, we cataloged dozens of projects, programs, and more.[65] These measures validate the urgency for an overarching code of ethical innovation grounded in the lawyer's duties of competence as an officer of the legal system and as a public citizen.

To this end, ABA Model Rule 1.1 and the preamble should be revised to encompass the ethical obligations surrounding innovation. This is intended to cover both innovation in law itself and in the ways law mediates innovation in other areas. Such a move also would justify expanded support for innovation-based law school curricula, new roles for innovation counsel in law firms and legal departments, and continuing legal education in innovation for practicing lawyers and judges. Most importantly, formalizing a lawyer's ethical obligation in innovation promises to protect individual rights of autonomy, identity, privacy, and security more robustly than industry-borne pledges or policies. As the preamble explains, in addition to acting as "a representative of clients," the lawyer is "an officer of the legal system and a public citizen having special responsibility for the quality of justice."[66] Recall from chapter 10 that the preamble specifically provides as "a public citizen, a lawyer should seek improvement of the law, access to the legal system, the administration of justice and the quality of service rendered by the legal profession."[67] These areas of improvement arguably all require aspects of innovation.

Given that innovation often requires breaking the rules, one might question whether this duty proposed here could be misappropriated as a defense of otherwise problematic behavior. Successful innovation often is disruptive, if not illegal, before it becomes widely accepted—think of Uber's defiance of laws meant to protect the taxi industry or Airbnb's flouting of restrictions on home rentals. How can such a duty be reconciled with a lawyer's obligations to uphold the law? The duty to innovate as conceived here is not intended to supplant any ethical obligations owed elsewhere in the Model Rules, nor would it be a defense to actions taken that otherwise result in the intentional violation of rules.

Some may question the enforceability of a duty to innovate. Similar to the duty to keep abreast of technology changes, as discussed in chapter 3, there may be instances of discipline. A middle ground might be to make these amendments to the Model Rules aspirational in nature, similar to the recommendation in Model Rule 6.1 for lawyers to provide at least fifty hours of pro bono legal services. Even if not enforceable with discipline, recognizing an aspirational duty brings awareness and encourages compliance. A final related concern about enforcement might be that measuring the success and impact of innovation is expensive, time consuming, and distracting for lawyers who do not frequently encounter the need to innovate and should otherwise be focused on client needs at hand.[68] But incorporating a duty to innovate does not in itself require the implementation of a successful innovation. The duty to innovate is a process, both of assessing the potential benefits and harms for clients and of assessing the access to and delivery of justice. Learning from a "failed" innovation can be valuable. Moreover, researchers already have begun to measure innovation in various ways, including the WJP Rule of Law Index mentioned in the introduction to this book.[69] Indeed, formalizing an ethical duty to innovate may cultivate additional resources for assessing and improving innovation for individual justice solutions and the legal services industry as a whole.

* * *

In addition to embedding within the professional conduct rules an ethical obligation surrounding innovation, there are other ways a commitment to innovate might manifest in the context of access to justice. A few ideas follow in these recommendations, and we will continue to explore this theme in the final chapter of the book, which looks to the way forward.

Recommendations

Key: Attorneys (A), Advocacy Groups (AG), Bar Authorities (BA), Individuals (I), Judges (J), Law Schools (LS), Legal Tech Industry (LTI), Legislators (L), Research Centers (RC)

Add Innovation to the Duty of Competence (BA)

One mechanism to ensure that the rapid pace of change driven by consumer demand, globalization, and technology does not compromise the integrity of the justice system is to formalize a duty to innovate within professional ethics codes. Lawyers, in particular, have a critical role to play in both assessing the benefits and risks of innovation and in adopting new tools to help solve legal problems. All but ten states already mandate that lawyers "keep abreast of changes in the law and its practice." This mandate is not yet fully appreciated as a broad duty to engage in ethical innovation, but it should be. Just as the ABA amended Model Rule 1.1 in 2012 to extend the duty of competence to include an obligation to keep abreast with changes in technology, it should craft a similar amendment to encompass innovation. Comment 8 could be revised as follows: "To maintain the requisite knowledge and skill, a lawyer should keep abreast of changes *and innovations* in the law and its practice, including the benefits and risks associated with relevant *innovations such as* technology."[70] The duty to keep up with innovation in law practice covers both evaluating potential harm and engaging in innovation itself. Alternatively, the preamble to the Model Rules could be revised to include a new provision: *Every lawyer has a professional responsibility to engage in ethical innovation. The duty to innovate is an obligation to continually assess the intended, known, and unknown consequences of innovation in law and its practice, including the benefits and risks associated with relevant technology and other advancements. A lawyer also has an obligation to pursue ethical innovations for the improvement of the legal system.* Sometimes well-intentioned innovation results in unintended consequences. Lawyers might fear that an affirmative duty to innovate will result in discipline when harms result, even if the outcome was intended to improve the legal system in compliance with ethical obligations. A safe-harbor provision would ameliorate this: *When a lawyer engages in innovation pursuant to this Rule, and a harm occurs, the lawyer shall not be subject to discipline provided that the innovation was intended to comply with the lawyer's ethical obligations to the client, the profession, and the public.* Regulators could facilitate this sort of safe harbor by following the model from Australia's Victorian Legal Services Board's Innovation In-Box, offering a presumption against discipline to lawyers who proactively seek out compliance support.

Engage Ethically with Tech and AI Like ChatGPT (A, AG, BA, I, J, LS, LTI, RC)

When asked in late 2022 about the single most important factor for why people appear, or do not appear, at court, the chief justice of the Michigan Supreme Court Bridget Mary McCormack cited text remind-ers.[71] A simple technology-based nudge helps the public avoid delays in the justice process and even potentially criminal sanctions, like being held in contempt of court for failing to appear when required. This is an easy, but important illustration of ethical innovation to improve justice. With artificial intelligence and other advancements that increasingly embed legal decision-making within the technology, the role of lawyers and judges becomes more complex. Lawyers "need to oversee, control, review, and analyze AI output," a recommendation that comes from four lawyers who are also experts in legal tech solutions—Michael Simon, Alvin F. Lindsay, Loly Sosa, and Paige Comparato, co-authors of a *Yale Journal of Law and Technology* article published in 2018.[72] They sounded an alarm about innovation: "Without lawyers who have the knowledge as well as the ethical duty to test the answers provided by future AI legal systems, clients would be left with no option but to trust the answers given by the algorithms. As a result, clients might not learn of any errors until long after they have relied on erroneous or prob-lematic advice to their detriment."[73] I would add others among those responsible for leading on this front, including bar authorities, judges, and law schools.

Expand Effective Online Dispute Resolution (A, J, LTI)

After the widespread adoption of remote technology post-pandemic (which data shows has been positively received) there is no reason not to expand online dispute resolution. Alternative dispute resolution has long been a mechanism for resolving legal issues with reduced costs, increased efficiency, and improved results outside of traditional court proceedings. The concept, in essence, is any process agreed to by parties of a dispute in which a neutral person assists to reach an agreement, thus avoiding court litigation. One concern, however, is that parties may sacrifice constitutional rights and other protections if a resolution is reached outside of court. Ideally, courts provide oversight through "court-annexed" or sponsored online dispute resolution processes to ensure minimum due process.

Invest in Justice Tech (A, AG, BA, I, J, LS, LTI, RC)

The more than $13 billion raised for legal tech from 2016 to 2022 was not focused, predominantly, on access to justice. The Justice Technology Association (JTA), founded in 2022, aims to change this, with the following mission: "to democratize the consumer legal experience through the use of technology for the public good."[74] Specifically, they aspire to the following:

> We seek to grow, shape, and organize the emerging Justice Tech market to demonstrate how technology can provide affordable, accessible solutions to people facing everyday legal issues. We also support industry and policy leaders, businesses, and broader initiatives to empower consumers and advance access to, and engagement with, legal help. We aim to drive social impact by harnessing a collective voice for regulatory reform, building inclusive, interdisciplinary teams, sharing reliable data, and using technology to automate, simplify, and increase access to legal services.[75]

The Legal Services Corporation's investment in justice tech, alone, is insufficient. We need more independent advocacy groups like the JTA, along with venture capitalists and investors, to fund access-to-justice technology services and other innovations.

Prevent Disputes Before They Require Legal Help
(A, AG, LS, LTI, RC)

More resources should be devoted to what scholars Ethan Katsh and Orna Rabinovich-Einy call "dispute prevention," that is, "digital tools and systems that provide solutions to problems as well as the use of information technologies in new ways that anticipate and prevent disputes."[76] Richard Susskind similarly advocates for a concept of access to justice that provides for "dispute containment," "dispute avoidance," and "legal health promotion."[77] There is a role for justice tech in each of these phases to improve access to justice. As Susskind explains, this involves "much more than providing access to quicker, cheaper, and less combative mechanisms for resolving disputes. I am also speaking of the introduction of techniques that deeply empower all members of society—to contain disputes that have arisen, to avoid disputes in the first place and, more, to have greater insight into the benefits that the law can confer."[78] The goal, in the end, is for individuals "to be able to own and manage many of their own legal issues."[79]

12

The Way Forward

Those facing a legal problem rarely *want* a lawyer. They want their problem solved or, even better, they want to avoid the problem entirely.

But life is messy, and problems happen. We do not yet live in the world envisioned by Richard Susskind and others where preventive artificial intelligence and other innovations might resolve issues before they ever arise. For those in need of legal help now, or who want to take a more affirmative role in understanding their personal legal rights, entitlements, and needs, a range of tools already exist. Indeed, many of the tools and resources described throughout this book can be used for self-help.

A central question must be addressed before implementing any solution aimed at justice: does the effort actually democratize legal help? To democratize means to make something available to all.

If the effort does not expand access to and adoption of legal help in a measurable way, then it will perpetuate the very problems it aims to address. Think back to the Supreme Court's decision in *Bates v. Arizona State Bar*. The solution—removing the restriction on advertising for lawyers—did not achieve the intended goal, at least in part, because it was not tied to methods that make the information contained in the advertising accessible to everyone in need. As the case study in chapter 2 revealed, lawyer advertising fails to include information rational consumers want to know, like costs, and often reads at a level unintelligible to much of the public. The Supreme Court's idea to increase information about legal help proved well intentioned but ultimately misplaced. Solutions must be studied to ensure success.

When rules change, or new tech is adopted, we need to track the impact to make sure the intervention expands access to justice rather than maintains the status quo or makes things worse. For example, a 2021 study conducted by the Pew Research Center, in connection with the Conference of Chief Justices and the Conference of State Court Administrators, recommends data collection and analysis to "help guide

197

decisions on the use and performance" of technology-driven tools like electronic filing and virtual hearing platforms.[1] These organizations, along with others such as the American Academy of Arts and Sciences and the National Science Foundation "are actively working to improve state court data collection, create standards for research access, and leverage existing administrative data."[2] Legal tech industry members also have been active in measuring the legal services market and the impacts of technology on the delivery of legal services, for example the Clio Legal Trends Report referenced in chapter 8. Elizabeth Chambliss calls for judicial leaders "to support these efforts and encourage their states to implement standards for data collection and access [and] also engage with cybersecurity experts to implement privacy protections and best practices for data governance."[3] Legislative leaders can step up.

Democratizing justice requires not only empowered citizens equipped with knowledge about the legal system, but also engaged citizens who look out for the interests of all in addition to their own. Engaged citizenship means knowing the local government employees, legislators, and school board members where one lives and works. It means you vote *and* take responsibility to ensure that obstacles do not stand in the way of others when they go to cast their own ballots. Engaged citizenship also means actively contacting policymakers to demand the kinds of reforms listed throughout this book.

To fully enact this blueprint, we cannot neglect the mental health and well-being of those on the frontlines delivering justice as well as the individuals who engage with the justice system. Members of the legal profession suffer from depression and substance abuse at higher rates than other occupations. Facing a legal problem is stressful enough, on its own, and the process of resolving it should not impose further burdens.

We also need money for this blueprint to become reality. A lot of money. The Legal Services Corporation (LSC) 2022 Justice Gap Study documented that low-income individuals who qualify for LSC aid had 1.9 million civil legal problems in the prior year, but nearly half—49 percent—went unaddressed because of insufficient funding. Overall, "LSC-funded organizations are unable to provide any or enough legal help for an estimated 1.4 million civil legal problems (or 71 percent of problems) that are brought to their doors in a year."[4] Legislative bodies control budgets, and those budgets profoundly impact the availability of legal aid. Here's the plea from two justices of the Supreme Court of Texas to their legislators, a request that all lawmakers should heed when allocating funding for legal aid:

> For its own integrity's sake, the civil justice system must be available to every Texan victimized by domestic violence, to each veteran wrongly denied the benefits our country has promised, and to all families who have paid their bills but are nevertheless evicted from their homes. These situations occur in Texas. But under current funding sources, we can reach less than one-fourth of those in need. . . . Some consider [the Supreme Court of Texas] conservative. Conservative principles do not call for the rule of law to be denied to the most vulnerable members of our community. The civil justice system is where people can claim for themselves the benefits of the rule of law. It is where the promises of the rule of law become real. A society that denies access to the courts for the least among us denigrates the law for us all. For these reasons, securing funding for basic civil legal services has been a priority for the Supreme Court, one to which its members are unanimously committed.[5]

The Legal Services Corporation received $465 million in 2021 and requested $600 million in 2022 to address legal needs but got only $489 million. Circling back to chapter 1, remember that by comparison, if the LSC today was funded at the same rate as it was in 1980, factoring for inflation, it should receive more than *double* that amount annually.

Ultimately, the success of any blueprint depends entirely on those who collaborate and put it into action. The ideas compiled here require engagement from a broad range of constituents from within the legal profession and, necessarily, from beyond it.

Success also depends on our ability to learn from mistakes, experiment in the face of uncertainty, and keep our minds open to possibilities when faced with new information. As Adam Grant, in his book *Think Again*, reminds us:

> Every time we encounter new information, we have a choice. We can attach our opinions to our identities and stand our ground in the stubbornness of preaching and prosecuting. Or we can operate more like scientists, defining ourselves as people committed to the pursuit of truth—even if it means proving our own views wrong.[6]

For the legal profession, this means accepting that lawyers may not always be the solution.

* * *

Anyone, whether a lawyer or not, can take concrete steps to democratize law, both in finding help for one's own problems and by bringing legal assistance to those who need it. While not exhaustive, the blueprint laid out in part II offers concrete steps to democratize law and move us ever forward along Dr. King's arc of the moral universe.

Recommendations

Key: Attorneys (A), Advocacy Groups (AG), Bar Authorities (BA), Individuals (I), Judges (J), Law Schools (LS), Legal Tech Industry (LTI), Legislators (L), Research Centers (RC)

Be Engaged Citizens (A, AG, BA, I, J, LS, LTI, RC)

This recommendation builds on Richard Susskind's concept of the "empowered citizen." He proposed empowerment of individuals through information that allows them to solve their own legal issues and to discern when and how to hire a lawyer, if needed. I would take this a step further, calling on engagement not only for one's own legal problems but actively helping our colleagues, community members, coworkers, family, friends, and neighbors. Tom Gordon, the executive director of the consumer advocacy group Responsive Law, calls for an ongoing "grassroots movement" of individuals to motivate legislators and courts to implement reforms.[7] Groups like Voices for Civil Justice and All Rise for Civil Justice are also leading this effort. The Commission on the Practice of Democratic Citizenship, a project of the American Academy of Arts and Sciences, identified more than two dozen recommendations grouped among six strategies to reinvent American democracy for the twenty-first century, all of which bear on the commitment of engaged citizenship: a culture of shared commitment, connected communities, empowered voters, equal representation, responsive government, and social media as civic media.[8]

Foster Mental Health and Wellness (A, AG, BA, I, J, LS, LTI, RC)

All aspects of the justice system should take into account mental health and wellness. This involves efforts like mindfulness for law students, lawyers, and judges (see, for example, Jeena Cho's work, including her book with Karen Gifford, *The Anxious Lawyer,* and Scott Rogers's Institute for Mindfulness Studies at the University of Miami) as well as thoughtful design for those who encounter the justice system in everything from the space where a proceeding occurs (whether physical or virtual) to the usability of court forms.

Fully Fund the Legal Services Corporation and State and Local Legal Aid (L)

Congressional representatives Brian Fitzpatrick and Mary Gay Scanlon, co-chairs of the Congressional Access to Legal Aid Caucus, have pointed out that "LSC's funding has not increased significantly over the past 30 years. It is nowhere near what is needed to keep up with three decades of inflation and population growth—much less the increase in legal needs caused by recessions, medical crises, and other factors."[9] They noted that in 2022, lawyers at Houston's Lone Star Legal Aid were handling record-breaking numbers of evictions and Illinois's Land of Lincoln Legal Aid had to stop taking new eviction cases after two offices reached capacity.[10] Across all levels of government budgets—local, state, and federal—legislators must act to increase funding for legal aid.

Measure Reforms through National Standards on Empirical Data and Outcomes (AG, BA, LS, LTI, RC)

Many components of this blueprint are measurable. To the extent possible, outcomes derived from any established practices or new models for legal help must be assessed via data to evaluate effectiveness. Collecting and sharing these metrics is imperative. There is no "legal equivalent of public health departments, tracking the legal health of communities," as scholars Gillian Hadfield and Jamie Heine point out: "We don't have a national federally-funded research agency like the National Institute of Health, which distributes over $30 billion in 50,000 grants annually to medical researchers who collect, analyze, and are often required to share, data on disease, medical procedures and the impact of interventions. . . . As a result, systematic efforts to collect data about the health of legal systems for ordinary individuals are few and far between."[11] Absent this level of government funding for data analysis, it will take a consortium of advocacy groups, bar authorities, law schools, legal tech industry members, and research centers to work collectively on creating national standards and, importantly, assessing them.

Recognize the Inadequacies of the Criminal Justice System (A, AG, BA, I, J, LS, LTI, RC)

As noted in the introduction, the focus of this book has been civil legal needs. Many of the recommendations in this blueprint apply equally if not more so in the criminal justice context.[12]

"Think Again" (A, AG, BA, I, J, LS, LTI, RC)

Scholars like Rebecca Sandefur make profound impact because they cause us to, in Adam Grant's words, "think again." As we saw in part I of the book, Sandefur's research on unmet legal needs revealed that what many thought was the main barrier to access to legal help—the cost of the service—isn't actually the case. For most, lack of knowledge was the barrier. Sandefur's work also reveals that "[e]xisting legal services, even when they do meet apparent legal needs, may not be the simplest, cheapest, most lawful, or most effective way to meet legal need. Simply because lawyers appear impactful under the current state of affairs does not mean that they are the best solution to problems we observe."[13] Grant concludes his book *Think Again* with a list of thirty ways to practice the skill of revising our own mental conclusions. My favorite? "Keep a rethinking scorecard."[14] He urges us to not "evaluate decisions based only on the results; track how thoroughly different options are considered in the process."[15] As Grant concludes, "A bad process with a good outcome is luck. A good process with a bad outcome might be a smart experiment."[16] We need many smart experiments to solve the justice crisis.

Conclusion

And the point is, to live everything. Live the questions now.
—Rainer Maria Rilke, *Letters to a Young Poet*, 1903

Let's return to the questions I posed at the outset of the book. How do we educate and inform the public about the law so they can understand when the services of a lawyer are necessary or desirable? How do we effectively match clients to lawyers in a way that is affordable to the client but allows the lawyer to earn a living? When is a lawyer warranted, and when can an individual solve legal problems on their own, with a specialist who is not a licensed lawyer, or with the aid of burgeoning legal technology? In short, how do we democratize law?

You now have a blueprint filled with lots of possible answers to those questions. It is ambitious, at best, and probably impossible, to create a comprehensive plan for resolving the justice crisis. The need for legal help is vast and unmet, as documented in part I of this book. A century's worth of efforts to address the need have not been sufficient, as shown in part II. This doesn't mean we shouldn't keep trying. That history of endeavors, some successful and some not, laid the foundation for the blueprint set forth here.

In the wake of social justice protests and election challenges during the 2010s and 2020s, alongside travesties like the January 6 insurrection, now more than ever the American public must understand—and importantly, utilize—its justice system to enforce legal rights and entitlements.

The strategies charted out in this book advance the conversation but are not the final word. For every story I've told, for each study I've cited, there are dozens if not hundreds more that I could have included. (For more on that, take a look at the methodology and further resources section in the appendix.) Smart, dedicated people around the globe have been working hard for lifetimes to solve the justice crisis. I do not claim to have all the answers, or even all the questions.

My hope? That this book serves as a resource for those already at work and becomes the stimulus for many more to join the cause.

I have traveled the globe asking questions, finding answers, and asking more questions. The blueprint offered here will not eliminate legal needs entirely, but it charts out plans for moving ahead.

By documenting the gravity of the access-to-justice crisis and its roots, examining the efforts to fix it, and cataloging potential next steps, this book encourages the reader to turn the next page in the delivery of legal services. We must keep asking questions, challenging the solutions, and committing to bend the arc of the moral universe toward justice.

ACKNOWLEDGMENTS

Much of this book is drawn from research previously published in law journals, and I appreciate their permission to reprint portions of that work here. These publications include: "Attorney Advice and the First Amendment," *Washington & Lee Law Review* 68, no. 2 (2011): 717–64; "Cultivating Learners Who Will Invent the Future of Law Practice: Some Thoughts on Educating Entrepreneurial and Innovative Lawyers," *Ohio North University Law Review* 38 (2012): 847–54; "Democratizing the Delivery of Legal Services," *Ohio State Law Journal* 73 (2012): 1–46; "Democratizing Legal Education," *Connecticut Law Review* 42 (2013) 1281–318; "Legal Information, the Consumer Law Market, and the First Amendment," *Fordham Law Review* 82 (2014): 2843–68; "Commercialization of Legal Ethics," *Georgetown Journal Legal Ethics* 29 (2016): 715–27; "Legal and Ethical Impediments to Data Sharing and Integration Among Medical Legal Partnership," *Annals of Health Law* (2018): 183–204 (with J. Mantel); "The Legal Monopoly," *Washington Law Review* 93 (2018): 1293–338; "The Behavioral Economics of Lawyer Advertising: An Empirical Assessment," *Illinois Law Review* 1105 (2019): 1005–38 (with J. Hawkins); "Lawyer Ethics for Innovation," *Notre Dame Journal of Law, Ethics, and Public Policy* 35 (2021): 1–48; "Lawyer Lies and the First Amendment," *Yale Law Journal Forum* 31 (2021): 114–40; "Not the End of Lawyers, But a Beginning—The Place of Entrepreneurship and Innovation in Legal Ethics," *Leading Works in Legal Ethics*, Routledge (2023); and "The ReInvent Law Archive," *Legal Design: Dignifying People in Legal Systems*, Cambridge University Press (2024).

I am grateful to Clara Platter, Martin Coleman, Ann Boisvert, Mary Beth Jarrad, Veronica Knutson, Alexia Traganas, Sydney Garcia, Lia Hagen, and everyone at NYU Press for making this book a reality. They are at the top of a very long list of colleagues, co-authors, and friends who deserve thanks for helping support this project over the years, including Elizabeth Anker, Ben Barton, Len Baynes, Swethaa Ballakrishnen, Shelley Boyd, Lonnie Brown, Elizabeth Chambliss, Monika Gruter Cheney, Ben Cooper, Catrina Denvir, Michele DeStefano, Joanne and Larry Doherty, Tom Dougherty, Kathy Douglas, Calum Drummond, Meredith Duncan, Ben Edwards, Nora Freeman Engstrom, John Flood, Oliver Goodenough, Bob Gordon, Bruce Green, Jim Hawkins, William Henderson, Chase Hertel, Joan Howarth, William Hubbard, Dan Jackson, Hannah Brenner Johnson, Peter Joy, Sung Hui Kim, Josh Kubicki, Dan Linna, Swee Mak, Jessica Mantel, Milan Markovic, Judy Perry Martinez, John Mayer, Sarah McCormick, Fiona McLeay, Anne-Laure Mention, Terri Mottershead, Ellen Murphy, Jen Nelson, Jennie Pakula, Paul Paton, Rohan Pavuluri, Russ Pearce, Andy Perlman, James Peters, Amanda Perry-Peterson, Carla Pratt, Rebecca Purdom, Lucy Ricca, Deborah Rhode, Cassandra Robertson, Dan Rodriguez, Amy Salyzyn, Paula Schaefer, R. Amani Smathers, Richard Susskind, Laurel Terry, Steven Vaughan, Greg Vetter, Gina Warren, Amanda Watson, Julian Webb, Lisa Webley, Janet Welch, Tara Hawley Whitfield, Gretchen Whitmer, and David Wilkins. Special thanks to Emily Boynton, Johanna Leigh, Emory Powers, Katie Douglas-Rowald, and Katy Stein, and to the reference librarians at Michigan State University College of Law and University of Houston Law Center for help in research and editing. Maggie Loughran provided invaluable editing and feedback as the project neared completion. I am also indebted to the students in my *Entrepreneurial Lawyering, Professional Responsibility,* and *Twenty-First Century Law Practice* courses for asking questions, finding answers, and asking more questions—this book never would have been written without you inspiring me to seize my own entrepreneurial and innovative spirit.

Talking about this project helped it evolve, and I am appreciative of the feedback received from participants and audiences at various speaking engagements: University of Illinois College of Law Faculty Workshop in 2010; ABA Annual Conference on Professional Responsibility in 2010; Law and Society Annual Meeting 2010; University of the Pacific McGeorge School of Law in 2011; Connecticut Law Review Symposium on Future of Legal Education in 2012; Northeastern Law School Symposium on Experiential Education in Law in 2012; Vermont Law School in 2012; Ohio Northern Law Review Symposium in 2012; University of Tennessee College of Law Faculty Workshop in 2012; Association of American Law Schools Annual Meeting in 2012; Gruter Institute Conference on Innovation and Growth in 2012, 2013, and 2015; Stanford Law School in 2013 and 2015; Georgetown University Law Center in 2013; Fordham Law Review Symposium on Lawyers' Monopoly in 2013; George Mason Law School Research Roundtable in 2013; University of Florida Law School in 2013; Legal Services Board, London in 2013; Northeastern University Law School Faculty Colloquium in 2013; Pace Law School Annual Phillip A. Blank Lecture on Attorney Ethics in 2013; Association of Professional Responsibility Lawyers Annual Meeting in 2013; American Bar Association Annual Meeting in 2014; Washington & Lee Law School Faculty Workshop in 2014; University of Arizona Law School Faculty Speaker Series in 2014; American University Washington College of Law Faculty Workshop in 2014; South Carolina Law Review Symposium on Legal Education in 2014; National Conference of Bar Presidents in 2015; Fordham Law Review Symposium in 2015; ABA Standing Committee on Public Education in 2015; University of Maryland School of Law in 2015; Yale Law School Freedom of Expression Scholars Conference in 2015; Georgetown Journal of Legal Ethics Colloquium in 2016; The Antigua Forum in 2016 and 2017; Melbourne University Law School in 2019; Legal Innovation Festival Sydney in 2019; Lawfest Conference on Innovation and Technology New Zealand in 2019; College of Law Victoria in 2019; and UCLA Law School International Legal Ethics Conference 2022. Thanks as well to the anonymous peer reviewers who offered useful feedback.

I received generous funding to support this work from the Australian-American Fulbright Commission, the Fulbright Association, Ewing Marion Kauffman Foundation, Michigan State University College of Law Summer Research Grants, University of Houston Law Center Summer Research Grants, and the University of Houston Small Research Grants Program. My time as a Scholar-in-Residence at Stanford Law School's Center on the Legal Profession in 2015 and as the Fulbright Distinguished Chair in Entrepreneurship and Innovation at Royal Melbourne Institute of Technology in Australia in 2019 provided opportunities for research and writing.

Finally, to Wallace, James, Grace, and Rilke, you have my whole heart—thank you for living the questions with me.

APPENDIX 1

The Blueprint for Justice Checklist

Key: Attorneys (A), Advocacy Groups (AG), Bar Authorities (BA), Individuals (I), Judges (J), Law Schools (LS), Legal Tech Industry (LTI), Legislators (L), Research Centers (RC)

CHAPTER 6. ANTITRUST LAW
- ☐ Adjust Unauthorized Practice of Law Restrictions (BA, J, L)
- ☐ Explore the Reserved Activities Approach (BA)
- ☐ Include Lay Members with Meaningful Participation on Regulatory Boards (BA, J)
- ☐ Offer Alternative Fee Arrangements (A, BA, LTI)

CHAPTER 7. THE FIRST AMENDMENT
- ☐ Design Informative, Relatable, and Understandable Advertising (A)
- ☐ Extend the Duty of Candor in the Courtroom to the Court of Public Opinion (BA)
- ☐ Reform through Litigation, Like *Button*, *Bates*, and *Upsolve* (A, AG, I, J)

CHAPTER 8. REGULATORY AND LEGISLATIVE REFORM
- ☐ Adopt and Assess Regulatory Objectives (BA, J, L)
- ☐ Authorize Streamlined Licensing Paths for Discrete Specializations (BA, J, LS, L)
- ☐ Build More Regulatory Sandboxes (A, AG, BA, J, LS, LTI, RC)
- ☐ Call Upon Chief Justices (A, AG, J)
- ☐ Create a Civil Right to Counsel, aka "Civil Gideon" (AG, J, L)
- ☐ Ease Geographic Law Practice Restrictions (BA)
- ☐ Empower Innovations through Judicial Advisory Opinions (J)
- ☐ Legislate More Authorized Legal Service Providers and Legal Documentation Assistance (L)
- ☐ Make Federal Court Records Free to the Public (L)
- ☐ Remove Restrictions on Law Practice Ownership and Investment as well as Multidisciplinary Partnerships (BA)
- ☐ Simplify and Standardize Court Forms and Procedures, Prioritizing E-Filing and Online Hearings (J, L)

CHAPTER 9. EDUCATION FOR THE LEGAL PROFESSION

☐ Develop Meaningful Pipelines for a Profession that Reflects the Diversity of the Public (A, AG, BA, J, LS, RC)

☐ Incentivize Pro Bono Work (A, BA, J, LS)

☐ Infuse Law School Curriculum with Cultural Competency, Entrepreneurship and Innovation, Implicit Bias Training, Leadership Development, and Technology Skills (LS, LTI)

☐ Reduce the Costs and Time of Education, Especially for Limited Practice Lawyers (BA, LS)

☐ Require Continuing Legal Education for Lawyers and Judges in Cultural Competency, Entrepreneurship and Innovation, Implicit Bias Training, Leadership Development, and Technology Skills (A, AG, BA, J, LTI)

☐ Revise the Bar Licensure Process and Provide Ongoing Assessment of Competence for Law Students and Lawyers (BA, LS, RC)

CHAPTER 10. EDUCATION FOR THE PUBLIC

☐ Construct a User-Friendly National Directory or Portal for Legal Help (A, AG, BA, L, LTI, RC)

☐ Deploy DIY Justice Tools (A, BA, I, J, LS, LTI)

☐ Implement (and Post in Courthouses) a National Bill of Rights for Self-Represented Parties (A, BA, J, LS, RC)

☐ Normalize Routine Legal Checkups (A, AG, BA, I, J, LS, LTI, RC)

☐ Promote Public Education Campaigns about Civics, Legal Problems and Solutions, and the Rule of Law (A, AG, BA, LS, RC)

☐ Provide More Court Facilitators and Navigators (J, L, LS)

☐ Take Steps Toward Greater Court Transparency (J)

CHAPTER 11. ETHICAL INNOVATION

☐ Add Innovation to the Duty of Competence (BA)

☐ Engage Ethically with Tech and AI Like ChatGPT (A, AG, BA, I, J, LS, LTI, RC)

☐ Expand Effective Online Dispute Resolution (A, J, LTI)

☐ Invest in Justice Tech (A, AG, BA, I, J, LS, LTI, RC)

☐ Prevent Disputes Before They Require Legal Help (A, AG, LS, LTI, RC)

CHAPTER 12. THE WAY FORWARD

- ☐ Be Engaged Citizens (A, AG, BA, I, J, LS, LTI, RC)
- ☐ Foster Mental Health and Wellness (A, AG, BA, I, J, LS, LTI, RC)
- ☐ Fully Fund the Legal Services Corporation and State and Local Legal Aid (L)
- ☐ Measure Reforms through National Standards on Empirical Data and Outcomes (AG, BA, LS, LTI, RC)
- ☐ Recognize the Inadequacies of the Criminal Justice System (A, AG, BA, I, J, LS, LTI, RC)
- ☐ "Think Again" (A, AG, BA, I, J, LS, LTI, RC)

APPENDIX 2

Methodology and Further Resources

One of the most difficult tasks in writing a book is deciding not what to *include*, but what to *omit*. This book represents highlights, but not a comprehensive cataloging, of my research during the past decade. I've drawn from data, experiences, and scholarly works to document needs and offer solutions. If you want to learn more, I encourage you to explore the sources cited in endnotes and listed in the bibliography. The advocacy groups and research centers listed below offer additional guidance and resources.

ADVOCACY GROUPS
- American Civil Liberties Union
- Association of American Law Schools
- Corporate Legal Operations Consortium
- Conference of Chief Justices
- Justice Technology Association
- Legal Services Corporation
- NAACP Legal Defense Fund
- National Coalition for a Right to Civil Counsel
- Pro Bono Net
- Responsive Law
- Self-Represented Litigation Network

RESEARCH CENTERS
- ABA Center for Innovation
- American Bar Foundation
- American Academy of Arts and Sciences
- Centre for Legal Innovation, College of Law Australia
- Hague Institute for the Innovation of Law

214 | APPENDIX 2

- Institute for the Advancement of the Legal System
- Legal Services Board, United Kingdom
- National Center for Access to Justice
- National Institute for Justice, United States Department of Justice
- National Center for State Courts
- Pew Charitable Trusts Civil Legal System Modernization Project
- World Justice Project

Numerous law schools host and support centers related to access to justice and legal services innovation. For a detailed list, visit the Law School Innovation Index, www.legaltechinnovation.com/law-school-index. Hundreds of advocacy groups and research centers exist throughout the United States and around the globe, all devoted to advancing civil and criminal justice. The World Justice Project maintains a comprehensive, searchable database at www.worldjusticeproject.org/resource-hub/leading-organizations. Efforts exist at the state level throughout the country. The American Bar Association Center for Access to Justice Initiatives maintains a list at www.americanbar.org/content/dam/aba/administrative/legal_aid_indigent_defendants/ATJReports/ls_sclaid_atj_checklist.pdf.

Finally, while this book is not itself intended to be a guide about how to handle one's legal problems, www.LawHelp.org is a good place to start. This resource provides referrals to nonprofit legal aid organizations in every state and territory, free legal rights resources, court forms, and self-advocacy tools.

NOTES

PREFACE

1 D. Michael Dale and the A.L. Burruss Institute of Public Service and Research, *Civil Legal Needs of Low and Moderate Income Households in Georgia*, (2009) 27.

2 Ibid.

3 Robert Echols, "State Legal Needs Studies Point to 'Justice Gap,'" *ABA Dialogue* 9 (2005): 32, 34.

4 Ibid.

5 "About," Self-Represented Litigation Network, accessed January 22, 2023, www. srln.org.

6 Aaron Dewald, "Five Things I Learned at the Reinvent Law Conference in Silicon Valley," University of Utah S.J. Quinney College of Law (blog), March 9, 2013, www.law.utah.edu.

7 Michael Scutt, "Reinvent Law London 2013," *Internet Newsletter for Lawyers*, July 15, 2013, www.infolaw.co.uk.

8 Joanna Goodman, "Reinventlaw London: One Does Not Simply Start a New Law," *Legal IT Professionals*, June 26, 2014, www.legalitprofessionals.com.

9 Josh Blackman, "ReInvent Law Featured in New York Times," *Josh Blackman* (blog), August 1, 2014, www.joshblackman.com ("Kudos to my colleagues Dan Katz and Renee Newman Knake, and the ReInvent Law they founded, which was featured in the *New York Times*").

10 "'Top 10*' Law Schools Teaching the Technology of Law Practice," *Legal Skills Prof Blog*, August 18, 2014, www.lawprofessors.typepad.com.

11 "Organization Overview," *College of Law Practice Management*, accessed March 20, 2023, www.collegeoflpm.org.

12 "Legal Education Leading Edge Report," 2015, *Wolters Kluwer*, www.wklegaledu.com.

13 Richard Susskind famously predicted the disruption of law markets in his book *The End of Lawyers?*, in which he focuses primarily on changes in the United Kingdom. Thomas D. Morgan also extensively documents disruption of the profession with a focus on the United States market in his book *The Vanishing American Lawyer*.

14 On the debt bubble in legal education financing, see Matt Leichter, "Law School Debt Bubble: Aggregate Law School Grad Debt Grew $475 Million Between 2008 and 2010," *AmLaw Daily*, November 22, 2011, www.amlawdaily.typepad.com; Matt Leichter, "Law School Debt Bubble, Part II: Data Show Feds Will Lend $54.3

216 | NOTES

Billion to U.S. Law Schools by 2020," *AmLaw Daily*, December 5, 2011, www.am-lawdaily.typepad.com; and William Henderson and Rachel Zahorsky, "The Law School Bubble: How Long Will It Last If Grads Can't Pay Bills?," *ABA Journal* 98 (January 2012): 30.

15 On disgruntled law graduates, see Scott Jaschik, "Suing Over Jobs," *Inside Higher Ed*, August 11, 2011, www.insidehighered.com; Doug Lederman, "20 More Law Schools Targeted for Lawsuits Over Placement Rates," *Inside Higher Ed*, March 15, 2012, www.insidehighered.com. Would-be law applicants seem to be disgruntled at the time too—or at least disillusioned. See David Segal, "For 2nd Year, a Sharp Drop in Law School Entrance Tests," *New York Times*, March 19, 2012, www.nytimes.com.

16 David Segal, "What They Don't Teach Law Students: Lawyering," *New York Times*, November 20, 2011, www.nytimes.com.

17 See, e.g., Karen Sloan, "Reality's Knocking; The Recession is Forcing Schools to Bow to Reality," *National Law Journal* (September 2009): 1 (citing examples of economy-driven reform at law schools such as Duke, University of California, Irvine, and "Washington and Lee University School of Law [which] has thrown out its traditional third-year curriculum and replaced it with a series of legal simulations meant to prepare students to practice law in the real world"); Charlotte S. Alexander, "Learning to be Lawyers," *Maryland Law Review* 70 (2011): 467 (discussing the Fundamentals of Law Practice at Georgia State University College of Law, a course that "combine[s] instruction in lawyering skills, law practice management, and ethical decisions making while also giving students a structured framework within which to reflect on their own developing identities as lawyers"); "New York Law School Launches New Legal Practice Course," New York Law School, October 19, 2011, www.nyls.edu (announcing a new "first-year skills program, Legal Practice, which features a redesigned curriculum that provides students with a comprehensive introduction to lawyering skills at the beginning of their law school careers"). The 2012 Association of American Law Schools Annual Meeting featured the *Workshop on Changes in Law Practice; Implications for Legal Education*, organized by Susan Carle, Carol Needham, Carla Pratt, Mitt Regan, and me, where dozens of scholars presented innovative ways of responding to economic realities and other pressures through curriculum reform.

18 See, e.g., Hadfield, "Equipping the Garage Guys in Law," 484–85 (describing a joint session she holds "in which J.D. and M.B.A. students worked together to find a solution for a real company facing a very real business challenge"); Stanford Law School, "Stanford Law School Advances New Model for Legal Education," news release, *Stanford Law School News* (blog), February 13, 2012, www.law.stanford.edu (announcing that Stanford Law School is "successfully transforming its traditional law degree into a multi-dimensional J.D., which combines the study of other disciplines with team-oriented, problem-solving techniques together with expanded clinical training that enables students to represent clients and litigate cases while in law school").

19 Exceptions to this observation are law laboratories like the Harvard University Berkman Klein Center for Internet and Society's Law Lab (www.cyber.harvard.edu) and Stanford University's CodeX—Center for Legal Informatics (www.law.stanford.edu/).

20 Victoria Santoro, "Interested in the Future of Legal Tech? So Are These Law Schools," *Law Technology Today*, July 30, 2014, www.lawtechnologytoday.org.

21 *See* Victor Li, "Love Tech: ReInvent Law's Message Is Change for the Client's Benefit," *ABA Journal* 100, no. 4 (2014): 29–30.

22 Monica Bay, "Tech Circuit: Old, New, Borrowed and Blue at ReInvent Law; Like a Wedding with a Lot of Alcohol, a Joyful Cacophony of Noise, Disharmony and Optimism," *Legal Tech News*, February 11, 2014.

23 George Beaton, "Reflecting on Reinvent Law NYC, 2014," *Remaking Law Firms*, February 7, 2017, www.remakinglawfirms.com.

24 "ChatGPT is an AI language model produced by OpenAI. . . . GPT models, including ChatGPT, are 'autoregressive,' meaning that they predict the next word given a body of text. . . . Although ChatGPT was trained on a large general-purpose corpus [of text] and was optimized only for general-purpose dialog, it performs surprisingly well on specific technical tasks." Choi et al., "ChatGPT Goes to Law School," 1.

INTRODUCTION: MEANINGFUL ACCESS TO JUSTICE AND THE PROMISE OF ENTREPRENEURSHIP, INNOVATION, AND TECHNOLOGY

1 See Adam Carey, "End of the Line for $75 On-the-Spot Myki Penalty Fares," *Age*, May 26, 2016, www.theage.com.au.

2 Ibid.

3 Deborah Glass, *Investigation into Public Transport Fare Evasion Enforcement* (Melbourne: Victorian Ombudsman, 2016).

4 Lloyd K. Garrison et al., "Report of the Special Committee on the Economic Condition of the Bar," *American Bar Association Report* 63 (1938): 391.

5 World Justice Project, "WJP Rule of Law Index 2019: Global Press Release," Press Release, May 7, 2019, www.worldjusticeproject.org.

6 Agrast et al., *World Justice Project Rule of Law Index 2021*, 171.

7 Ibid.

8 Ibid.

9 Ibid.

10 World Justice Project, "WJP Rule of Law Index 2022: Global Press Release," Press Release, October 26, 2022, www.worldjusticeproject.org.

11 Ibid.

12 Ibid.

13 United Nations Department of Economic and Social Affairs, *Sustainable Development Goals*, accessed February 1, 2023, www.sdgs.un.org/about.

14 See generally, Sandefur, *Accessing Justice in the Contemporary USA*; Rhode, *Access to Justice*, 3 ("According to most estimates, about four-fifths of the civil legal needs

of the poor, and two- to three-fifths of the needs of middle-income individuals, remain unmet").

15 Sandefur, *Accessing Justice in the Contemporary USA*, 3.

16 Ibid.

17 Ibid.

18 Ibid.

19 Ibid.

20 Ibid.

21 For a discussion of advertising by so-called settlement mills, see Nora Freeman Engstrom, "Run-of-the-Mill Justice," *Georgetown Journal of Legal Ethics* 22, no. 4 (2009): 1492–93.

22 Hadfield, "Cost of Law," 43.

23 Stephanie Palmer-Derrien, "Legaltech Josef Partners with Fellow Startup Luna to Bring Lawyer-Bot to the Ecosystem," *Smart Company*, February 14, 2019, www.smartcompany.com.au.

24 Stephanie Palmer-Derrien, "Why Legaltech Josef's $1 million Raise was More About Securing Experts Than Cash," *Smart Company*, May 22, 2019, www.smart-company.com.au.

25 See Bob Ambrogi, "No Code Legal Automation Platform Josef Raises $3.5M to Fuel Further U.S. and In-House Expansion," *Law Sites*, November 28, 2022, www.lawnext.com.

26 See, e.g., Eilene Zimmerman, "More Lawyers Skip the Partner Track to Be Entrepreneurs," *New York Times*, B5, November 24, 2011, www.nytimes.com (describing two lawyers who left a large firm to start their own for lifestyle improvements, among others who have acted entrepreneurially).

27 Jerry Bowles, "Who Needs Lawyers? DoNotPay Lets You 'Sue Anyone' Free via a Chatbot," *Diginomica*, October 16, 2018, www.diginomica.com.

28 "About," DoNotPay.com, accessed September 1, 2022, www.donotpay.com.

29 See Ben Schreckinger, "My Lawyer, the Robot," *Politico*, January 9, 2023, www.politico.com.

30 See Matt Perez, "DoNotPay Offers $1M to Use 'Robot Lawyer' in Highest Court," *Law360*, January 9, 2023, www.law360.com.

31 Joshua Browder (@jbrowder1), "Good morning! Bad News," Twitter, January 25, 2023, www.twitter.com.

32 Joshua Browder (@jbrowder1), "I have realized that non-consumer legal rights products (e.g. defamation demand letters, divorce agreements and others), which have very little usage, are a distraction," Twitter, January 25, 2023, www.twitter.com.

33 See Mike Masnick, "Kathryn Tewson Invites DoNotPay To Use Its AI Lawyer in Court," *Tech Dirt*, February 14, 2023, www.techdirt.com.

34 Perez, "DoNotPay Offers $1M."

35 See Samantha Murphy Kelly, "ChatGPT Passes Exams from Law and Business Schools, *CNN*, January 26, 2023, www.cnn.com.

36 NYU Champions of Change, "The Entrepreneur Who is Disrupting the Legal Market," *Medium*, December 16, 2019, www.medium.com.

37 "LegalZoom Reports Fourth Quarter and Full Year 2021 Results," press release, March 10, 2022, www.investors.legalzoom.com.

38 "LegalZoom Reports Fourth Quarter and Full Year 2022 Financial Results," press release, February 23, 2023, www.investors.legalzoom.com.

39 Brynjolfsson and McAfee, *Race Against the Machine*, 56.

40 Joe Dysart, "A New View of Review: Predictive Coding Vows to Cut E-Discovery Drudgery," *ABA Journal*, October 1, 2011, www.abajournal.com ("Research has shown that, under the best circumstances, manual review will identify about 70 percent of the responsive documents in a large data collection. Some technology-assisted approaches have been shown to perform at least as well as that, if not better, at far less cost").

41 Brynjolfsson and McAfee, *Race Against the Machine*, 63.

42 Katsh, *Digital Justice*, 6.

43 See Lorraine Sanders, "Inside the Curious Bricks-and-Mortar Store for Legal Advice, Books, Tablets," *Fast Company*, March 27, 2013, www.fastcompany.com.

44 Parliament of the United Kingdom, Legal Services Act 2007, chap. 29, October 30, 2007, www.legislation.gov.uk/.

45 Jane O'Shea, "Tesco Legal Services," *Attorney Marketing Blog*, April 23, 2010, www.attorneymarketingnetwork.com (regulators see this as responding to a need "for an increase in cheaper and more accessible legal advice").

46 "Co-op Legal Services," *ZoomInfo*, accessed January 19, 2023, www.zoominfo.com.

47 John Hyde, "QualitySolicitors Leaves WHSmith Stores," *Law Society Gazette*, August 8, 2013, www.lawgazette.co.uk.

48 See Victor Li, "Law Firms Are Already Inside Some US Wal-Marts," *ABA Journal*, June 21, 2016, www.abajournal.com.

49 See "Our Locations," Axess, accessed April 13, 2022, www.axesslaw.com.

50 Quality Solicitors became part of LegalZoom in 2012. See Catherine Baksi, "LegalZoom in QualitySolicitors Tie-Up," *Law Gazette*, September 19, 2012, www.lawgazette.co.uk.

51 See Ribstein, "Death of Big Law," 795–96.

52 Bob Ambrogi, "Troubled 'Tech-Enabled' Law Firm Names Ethics Prof as Independent Monitor," *Law Sites*, July 31, 2018, www.lawnext.com.

53 US Department of Justice, "National Consumer Bankruptcy Law Firm Sanctioned for Harming Financially Distressed Consumers and Auto Lenders," Press Release, February 13, 2018, www.justice.gov.

54 "UpRight Law Announces Leadership Changes and Independent Monitor Appointment," Cision, July 30, 2018, www.prnewswire.com.

PART I. UNDERSTANDING THE JUSTICE CRISIS: ORIGINS OF THE UNMET NEED FOR CIVIL LEGAL SERVICES IN THE UNITED STATES

1 Hasbrouck, "Antiracist Constitution," 164.

2 Dobbs v. Jackson Women's Health Org., 142 S. Ct. 2228 (2022).

3 Jason Tashea, "Justice-as-a-Platform," *MIT Computational Law Report 2021*, www.law.mit.edu.

4 Luban, "Optimism, Skepticism, and Access to Justice," 499.

5 Ibid., 500.

6 Ibid.

7 Ibid.

8 Ibid., 513.

9 Sandefur, *Accessing Justice in the Contemporary USA*.

10 Sandefur, "Access to What?," 54.

11 Ibid.

12 Paul R. Tremblay, "Surrogate Lawyering: Legal Guidance, Sans Lawyers," *Georgetown Journal of Legal Ethics* 31 (2018): 379.

13 Young, "What the Access to Justice Crisis Means for Legal Education," 811.

14 Ibid.

15 Sandefur, "Access to What?," 54.

16 Ibid.

17 Greene and Renberg, "Judging Without a J.D.," 1311. States with judges who are not trained as lawyers "include Alabama, Alaska, Arizona, Colorado, Delaware, Georgia, Kansas, Louisiana, Maryland, Massachusetts, Michigan, Mississippi, Missouri, Montana, Nebraska, Nevada, New Mexico, New York, North Carolina, North Dakota, Oklahoma, Oregon, Pennsylvania, South Carolina, South Dakota, Tennessee, Texas, Utah, Virginia, West Virginia, Wisconsin, and Wyoming." Ibid., 1311n145.

18 Ibid., 1342–43.

19 Ibid., 1287.

20 Susskind, "Future of Courts."

21 Ibid.

22 *Remarks of the Right Honourable Richard Wagner, P.C., Chief Justice of Canada*, 7th Annual Pro Bono Conference, Vancouver, British Columbia, October 4, 2018.

23 "Innovation," *Merriam-Webster Dictionary*, accessed February 5, 2022, www.merriam-webster.com.

24 See Nick Skillicorn, "What Is Innovation? 15 Experts Share Their Innovation Definition," Idea to Value, accessed September 11, 2020, www.ideatovalue.com.

25 Bernabe, "Justice Gap vs. Core Values," 3–4 (footnotes omitted).

26 See, e.g., Estlund, "What Should We Do After Work?," 263–64 ("In particular, major technological innovations from the mid-1800s to the mid-1900s brought vast improvements in most people's lives and standards of living. Since the mid-twentieth century, technology has continued to destroy some jobs, to create others, to reduce misery and drudgery on and off the job, and to generate economic growth and prosperity") (footnotes omitted).

27 See Christensen, *Innovator's Dilemma*.

28 Williams, Platt, and Lee, "Disruptive Innovation," 4–5 (citing Clayton M. Christensen, *How Will You Measure Your Life?* Boston: Harvard Business Review Press [2012], 10–11).

29 Lepore, "Disruption Machine."

30 See, e.g., Rick Edmonds, "Naysayers Are Swarming on Clayton Christensen and His 'Gospel of Innovation,'" *Poynter*, June 19, 2014, www.poynter.org ("If business school professors were pop stars, Clayton Christensen would be Beyonce [*sic*]. His 1997 book, The Innovator's Dilemma, is wildly influential—in particular, it has been both the theoretical underpinning and rallying banner for would-be digital disruptors of legacy media").

31 David Sax, "End the Innovation Obsession: Some of Our Best Ideas Are in the Rearview Mirror," *New York Times*, December 7, 2018, www.nytimes.com.

32 Ibid.

33 Mitch Kowalski, *"McGill Study Reveals the 'Illusion' of Innovation at Canadian Law Firms,"* *Financial Post,* January 26, 2017, www.financialpost.com.

34 For an excellent discussion of the role of lawyer as accomplice in advising clients engaged in quasi-(il)legal behavior, see Yablon, "Lawyer as Accomplice," 309 (citing the example of Uber, whose "basic business model certainly involved the deliberate violation of laws with criminal penalties. . . . [But] was seeking to build a popular constituency for changes in the law, changes that it thought would be beneficial to consumers . . .").

35 Michael Hewlett and Jeffrey Billman, "A $100 Million Mess," *Assembly*, March 29, 2023, www.theassemblync.com.

36 Ibid.

37 Ibid.

38 Andy Main, "Beyond the Digital Frontier: Deloitte Publishes Its 10th Annual Tech Trends Report," *Deloitte*, March 11, 2019, www.deloittedigital.com.

39 Whalen, "Defining Legal Technology," 62.

40 Ibid.

41 Ibid.

42 Ibid.

43 Ibid.

44 Ibid.

45 Ibid.

46 Ibid.

47 Natalie Runyon, "How Justice Tech is Taking a Human-Centered Approach to Access to Justice Challenges," *Thomson Reuters*, August 9, 2022.

48 Katherine Hurley, Marcia Chong Rosado, Matt Zieger, Ben Wrobel, and Rustin Finkler, "Justice Tech for All: How Technology Can Ethically Disrupt the US Justice System," American Family Insurance Institute for Corporate and Social Impact (AmFam Institute), March 2021, 4.

49 Alexander, *New Jim Crow*.

50 Ibid., 245.

NOTES

51 National Registry of Exonerations, *2021 Annual Report*, April 12, 2022, 3, www.law.umich.edu.

52 Samuel R. Gross, Maurice Possley, and Klara Stephens, *Race and Wrongful Convictions in the United States*, National Registry of Exonerations, (Irvine, CA: Newkirk Center for Science and Society, University of California Irvine, 2017), ii.

1. UNMET LEGAL NEEDS

1 Martin Gramatikov, Rodrigo Nunez, Isabella Banks, Maurits Barendrecht, Jelmer Brouwer, Brittany Kauffman, and Logan Cornett, *Justice Needs and Satisfaction in the United States of America of 2021*, Hague Institute for Innovation of Law and Institute for the Advancement of the American Legal System, 2021, 19, www.hiil.org.

2 Ibid.

3 Ibid., 7.

4 Ibid.

5 Ibid.

6 Ibid.

7 Hansford, "Lippman's Law," 1142.

8 "The Legal Needs of Small Business: A Research Study Conducted by Decision Analyst," *LegalShield* 4, 2013, www.coruralhealth-wpengine.netdna-ssl.com.

9 Legal Services Corporation, "Executive Summary," *The Justice Gap: The Unmet Civil Legal Needs of Low-Income Americans (2022)*, www.justicegap.lsc.gov.

10 Legal Services Corporation, "Who We Are," accessed January 11, 2023, www.lsc.gov.

11 "The Neglected Middle Class," *California State Bar Journal*, June 2008, www.archive.calbar.ca.gov.

12 Rhode, "Access to Justice: Connecting Principles to Practice," 421. See also Susskind, *End of Lawyers?*, 235 (observing that "solving legal problems and resolving disputes is affordable, in practice, only to the very rich or those who are eligible for some kind of state support").

13 John T. Broderick, Jr., and Ronald M. George, "A Nation of Do-It-Yourself Lawyers," *New York Times*, January 2, 2010, www.nytimes.com.

14 The Task Force to Expand Access to Civil Legal Services in New York, *Report to the Chief Judge of the State of New York*, (November 2010), ww2.nycourts.gov.

15 The study reported that:

> "[Ninety-nine] percent of tenants are unrepresented in eviction cases in New York City, and 98 percent are unrepresented outside of the City. 99 percent of borrowers are unrepresented in hundreds of thousands of consumer credit cases filed each year in New York City. 97 percent of parents are unrepresented in child support matters in New York City, and 95 percent are unrepresented in the rest of the State; and 44 percent of homeowners are unrepresented in foreclosure cases throughout [the] State." Ibid., 1.

16 Ibid., 27.

NOTES | 223

17 Molly Crane-Newman, "No Lawyers Left to Represent Low-Income Manhattan and Brooklyn Tenants Facing Eviction," *Daily News*, April 17, 2022, www.nydailynews.com.

18 See Gillian Hadfield, "Lawyers, Make Room for Nonlawyers," *CNN*, November 25, 2012, www.cnn.com.

19 Ibid.

20 See D. Michael Dale and the A.L. Burruss Institute of Public Service and Research, *Civil Legal Needs of Low and Moderate Income Households in Georgia* (2009), 11. Of eight statewide legal needs surveys referenced in the Georgia report, Montana had the highest rate of legal needs at 3.47 annually, and Vermont had the lowest rate of legal needs at 1.1 annually. The Georgia report found that "[m]ore than 60 percent of low and moderate income households" face at least one, if not more, civil legal needs annually. Ibid., 1. Low income households, "(defined as up to $30,000 annual income for a four person household)[,] experience an average of three civil legal needs annually, totaling over two million civil legal needs per year" and moderate income households, "(defined as up to $60,000 annual income for a four person household)[,] experience an average of 2.63 civil legal needs per year, for a total number of problems exceeding four million per year." Ibid., 1–2.

21 Ibid.

22 *See* Bates v. State Bar of Arizona, 433 U.S. 350, 376 (1977). As the bar acknowledges, "the middle 70 percent of our population is not being reached or served adequately by the legal profession." Ibid. (citation and internal quotation marks omitted).

23 See generally Sandefur, *Accessing Justice in the Contemporary USA*; Dale, *Georgia Civil Legal Needs Report*, 27; American Bar Association Commission on the Future of Legal Services, *Report on the Future of Legal Services in the United States*, 12; Rhode, *Access to Justice*, 3 ("According to most estimates, about four-fifths of the civil legal needs of the poor, and two- to three-fifths of the needs of middle-income individuals, remain unmet"); Hadfield, "Cost of Law," 43 ("The ordinary family obtains no legal help or advice with legal problems, muddling alone through the crises of job loss, divorce, bankruptcy, immigration challenges, access to services and benefits, injuries, and conflicts with neighbors or schools or health-care providers or local officials").

24 Stephen Love, Karl Llewellyn, Osmond Fraenkel, and Malcolm Sharp, "Economic Security and the Young Lawyer: Four Views," *Illinois Law Review* 32 (1938): 671.

25 See, e.g., Lucas Mearian, "By 2020 There Will Be 5,200 GB of Data for Every Person on Earth," *Computerworld*, December 11, 2012, www.computerworld.com ("During the next eight years, the amount of digital data produced will exceed 40 zettabytes . . . estimated to be 57 times the amount of all the grains of sand on all the beaches on earth").

26 See, e.g., Steve Lohr, "Sizing Up Big Data," *New York Times*, June 20, 2013, www.nytimes.com.

224 | NOTES

27 Ribstein and Kobayashi, "Law's Information Revolution," 1171–72.

28 American Bar Association, "ABA National Lawyer Population Survey: 10-Year Trend in Lawyer Demographics (2022)," www.americanbar.org.

29 United States Census Bureau, "Data," accessed December 1, 2022, www.census.gov.

30 Wald, "A Primer on Diversity, Discrimination, and Equality in the Legal Profession," 1079.

31 Root, "Combating Silence in the Profession," 805.

32 Ibid.

33 April Simpson, "Wanted: Lawyers for Rural America," *Stateline*, June 26, 2019, www.pewtrusts.org.

34 Ibid.

35 Charlotte S. Alexander, "Legal Outcome Prediction, Access to Justice, and Legal Endogeneity," in *Beyond Legal Tech and the Future of Justice,* edited by David Freeman Engstrom, (New York: Cambridge University Press, 2023), 156.

36 Neil McCarthy, "Report: 42 Million Americans Do Not Have Access to Broadband," *Forbes*, February 7, 2020.

37 "New NTIA Data Show Enduring Barriers to Closing the Digital Divide, Achieving Digital Equity," *National Telecommunications and Information Administration*, accessed January 22, 2023, www.ntia.gov.

38 Legal Services Board, Solicitors Regulation Authority, and Community Research. "Social Acceptability of Technology in Legal Services: Research with Lawyers and the Public," (2022), www.legalservicesboard.org.uk.

39 Susskind, "Future of Courts."

40 Gorsuch, *Republic, If You Can Keep It*, 11.

41 William G. Ross, "The Ethics of Hourly Billing by Attorneys." *Rutgers Law Review* 44, no. 1 (1991): 8.

42 Gisbrecht v. Barnhart, 535 U.S. 789, 800 (2002) (citing Special Committee on Economics of Law Practice, *The 1958 Lawyer and His 1938 Dollar*).

43 Ross, "Ethics of Hourly Billing by Attorneys," 8.

44 Leigh McMullan Abramson, "Is the Billable Hour Obsolete?," *Atlantic*, October 15, 2015.

45 See "Billing for Professional Fees, Disbursements and Other Expenses," *ABA Commission on Ethics Professional Responsibility Formal Opinion 93–379* (1993) ("It is a common perception that pressure on lawyers to bill a minimum number of hours and on law firms to maintain or improve profits may have led some lawyers to engage in problematic billing practices").

46 See Thomas M. Reavley, "Rambo Litigators: Pitting Aggressive Tactics Against Legal Ethics," *Pepperdine Law Review* 17, no. 3 (1990): 639n15; see also Jonathan D. Glater, "Billable Hours Giving Ground at Law Firms," *New York Times*, January 30, 2009 ("Clients have complained for years that the practice of billing for each hour worked can encourage law firms to prolong a client's problem rather than solve it").

47 Aurora Abella-Austriaco, "The Future of the Billable Hour," *CBA Record*, January 2013, at 8.

48 Stephen Embry, "Is the Billable Hour Impacting Our Mental Health?," *ABA Law Practice Today*, October 15, 2019. See also Varsha Patel, "Review the Reliance on Billable Hours: What GCs Want from Law Firms in 2022," *Law.com*, January 12, 2022 ("The legal industry's love affair with the billable hour model needs to come to an end in order to truly tackle the sector's mental wellbeing problem").

49 See Lawrence Krieger and Kennon M. Sheldon, "What Makes Lawyers Happy?: A Data-Driven Prescription to Redefine Professional Success." *George Washington Law Review* 83, no. 2 (2015): 554–627.

50 See Robert Hilson, "Is the Billable Hour Responsible for the Legal Profession's Supply-Demand Gap?," *Logikcull*, June 16, 2016, www.logikcull.com.

51 Robert Gehrke, "A New App is Helping Some 450 Utahns Get a Second Chance," *Salt Lake Tribune*, November 23, 2022, www.sltrib.com.

52 Ibid.

53 Mark Tullis, "Noella Sudbury of Rasa Legal Named in *Inc. Magazine*'s 2023 Female Founders List," *TechBuzz Utah Tech News*, April 4, 2023, www.techbuzz.news.

54 Legal Services Corporation, "Who We Are," accessed January 11, 2023, www.lsc.gov.

55 Ibid.

56 Ibid.

57 Ibid.

58 Ibid.

59 Adediran, "Relational Costs of Free Legal Services," 359.

60 Ibid.

61 Ibid.

62 "Three Ways to Meet the 'Staggering' Amount of Unmet Legal Needs," *Your ABA*, July 2018, www.americanbar.org.

63 Gideon v. Wainwright, 372 U.S. 335 (1963).

64 See, e.g., Barton, *Fixing Law Schools*.

65 Emily Birken, "The Costs of Being Unbanked or Underbanked," *Forbes*, July 28, 2020, www.forbes.com ("According to a 2019 report by the Federal Reserve, 22 percent of American adults [63 million] are either unbanked or underbanked").

66 See Ylan Q. Mui, "Retailers Take on New Role: Banker," *Washington Post*, February 1, 2011, www.washingtonpost.com.

67 See Stephanie Clifford and Jessica Silver-Greenberg, "On the New Shopping List: Milk, Bread, Eggs and a Mortgage," *New York Times*, November 14, 2012, www.nytimes.com (Noting that on a recent shopping trip to Costco, Lilly Neubauer picked up "paper towels, lentils, carrots—and . . . a home mortgage. . . . She also bought home insurance from Costco, she said, again because it was cheaper there").

68 See Reena Jana, "Michael Graves, Champion of Accessible Design, Is Appointed to Obama Administration Post," *Smart Planet*, February 7, 2013, www.smartplanet.

226 | NOTES

com ("Beginning in 1999, Graves created the Michael Graves Design Collection for Target, one of the first collaborations between an innovative, well-recognized designer and a chain store. They shared the goal of making well-designed goods available to mass-market audiences"); Linda Tischler, "A Design for Living," *Fast Company*, August 1, 2004, www.fastcompany.com (According to Graves, "'In the mid-1990s, . . . products based on design didn't exist for everyday people with everyday budgets.' . . . 'I would love to democratize design,' he said").

69 Pink, *To Sell Is Human*, 31.

70 "Orbitz," *Wikipedia*, accessed March 20, 2013, www.en.wikipedia.org.

2. (NOT) FINDING LEGAL HELP

1 Sean Cole, "Call NOW!," *Life of the Law*, June 25, 2013, www.lifeofthelaw.org.

2 Ken Goldstein and Dhavan V. Shah, "Trial Lawyer Marketing Broadcast, Search and Social Strategies," U.S. Chamber Institute for Legal Reform, October 27, 2015, www.instituteforlegalreform.com.

3 See, e.g., Robertson, "Online Reputation Management in Attorney Regulation," 106–7 ("By 2014, however, those numbers had changed dramatically, with a significant shift from personal connections to online resources: a full 38 percent would search on the internet first, with only 29 percent turning to personal recommendations from friends and family"); Mike Blumenthal, "How People Find Lawyers in 2015," Moses & Rooth Attorneys at Law, accessed March 8, 2022, www.mosesandrooth.com (According to a 2015 survey of 1,500 people, 13.6 percent turn to friends and 9.4 percent turn to the internet, though participants ages eighteen to twenty-four and participants earning more than $150,000 a year were more likely to select an attorney through an internet search); Gyi Tsakalakis, "How Do People Find and Hire Attorneys?," *Lawyernomics*, April 30, 2013, www.lawyernomics.avvo.com (citing a 2013 survey of 1,183, 34.6 percent ask a friend and 32.4 percent use an internet search).

4 See generally James M. Altman, "Considering the ABA's 1908 Canons of Ethics," *Journal of the Professional Lawyer* (2008): 235. By 1924, nearly all states had adopted the Canons or a similar version.

5 Ibid., 321.

6 See Lori B. Andrews, *Birth of a Salesman: Lawyer Advertising and Solicitation* (Chicago: American Bar Association, 1980).

7 Bates v. State Bar of Arizona, 433 U.S. at 350.

8 Ibid., 384.

9 Ibid., 358.

10 Ibid., 376.

11 This test is based on Central Hudson Gas & Electric Corporation v. Public Service Commission of New York, 447 U.S. 557, 564 (1980). See also Mason v. Florida Bar, 208 F.3d 952, 954, 956 (11th Cir. 2000) (holding that a lawyer's truthful claim that he is "AV Rated, the Highest Rating in the Martindale-Hubbell National Law

Directory" is not a misleading or potentially misleading statement and rejecting the Florida Bar's argument that it had "an interest in encouraging attorney rating services to use objective criteria").

12 See, e.g., Florida Bar v. Went For It, Inc., 515 U.S. 618, 620 (1995) (holding that a thirty-day prohibition on direct mail solicitation by lawyers of personal injury or wrongful death clients withstood First Amendment scrutiny).

13 See, e.g., "Differences Between State Advertising and Solicitation Rules and the ABA Model Rules of Professional Conduct," American Bar Association, June 2, 2016, www.americanbar.org.

14 Wolfram, *Modern Legal Ethics*, 39.

15 See American Tort Reform Association Press Release, "Study: Trial Lawyers Spent $1.4 Billion on Advertising in 2021," February 22, 2022.

16 Victor Li, "Ad It Up," *ABA Journal*, April 2017, 38. See also "Marketing by the Numbers: Statistics on Legal Marketing in 2021 (And a Look at 2022)," *Justia*, December 20, 2021, www.onward.justia.com.

17 *Bates*, 433 U.S. at 350.

18 Ibid., 368, 372.

19 Ibid., 376–77 (internal punctuation and citation omitted).

20 Ibid., 350.

21 Ibid.

22 Ibid., 358 (quoting *In re* Bates, 555 P.2d 640, 648 (Ariz. 1976) (Holohan, J., dissenting).

23 See, e.g., Rhode, "Access to Justice: Connecting Principles to Practice," 421 ("Almost two decades ago, in a prominent report on professionalism, the American Bar Association concluded that the middle class's lack of access to affordable legal services was 'one of the most intractable problems confronting the profession today.' That problem remains . . .") (citation omitted).

24 See, e.g., Sandefur, *Accessing Justice in the Contemporary USA*; see also Echols, "State Legal Needs Studies Point to 'Justice Gap,'" 35 ("These findings indicate that for most of those with legal needs who did not seek help, the reason was *not* that they regarded the problem as unimportant. Rather, many did not understand that their problem had a potential legal solution . . .").

25 See Edenfield v. Fane, 507 U.S. 761, 778 (1993) (O'Connor, J., dissenting).

26 Buffalo is obviously substantially smaller than Austin and Jacksonville, but we selected it because it is the largest city in New York after New York City, which would have dwarfed Austin and Jacksonville. Also, despite its smaller size, Buffalo has a similar number of car accident attorneys as the other cities.

27 Michael G. Parkinson and Sabrina Neeley, "Attorney Advertising: Does It Meet Its Objective?" *Services Marketing Quarterly* 26 (2003): 23 ("Advertising is most important for 'one-shotters' or people who do not regularly use the services of an attorney").

28 Ibid., 26.

29 See "How to Get More Clients for Your Law Firm," *National Law Review*, March 22, 2022, www.natlawreview.com.

30 Jared Kimball, "8 Ways Lawyers Can Get Criminal Defense and DUI Clients," Zahavian Law Firm Marketing, July 31, 2019, www.zahavianlegalmarketing.com.

31 Larry Kim, "The 20 Most Expensive Keywords in Bing Ads," *WordStream*, November 23, 2021, www.wordstream.com.

32 Sam Carr, "The Most Expensive Google Keywords 2021," *PPC Protect*, January 28, 2021, www.ppcprotect.com.

33 Ibid.

34 Jim Hawkins and Renee Knake Jefferson, "The Behavioral Economics of Lawyer Advertising: An Empirical Assessment," *University of Illinois Law Review*, no. 3 (2019): 1024–25.

35 See New York Rules of Professional Conduct 7.1(e)(3) (2017) (stating that when referencing past success or results obtained require the disclaimer: "Prior results do not guarantee a similar outcome"). Texas does not mandate specific language but does require that the lawyer or firm have primary responsibility for the result, that any amount stated was received by the client, and that fees or expenses withheld be stated. Texas Disciplinary Rules of Professional Conduct 7.02(a) (2018). Florida requires that such references be "objectively verifiable." Rules Regulating the Florida Bar 4–7.13(b)(2) (2018).

36 Hawkins and Jefferson, "The Behavioral Economics of Lawyer Advertising," 1025.

37 See, e.g., Robertson, "Online Reputation Management in Attorney Regulation," 103–6; Laurel A. Rigertas, "How Do You Rate Your Lawyer? Lawyers' Response to Online Reviews of Their Services," *St. Mary's Journal on Legal Malpractice & Ethics* 4 (2014): 242.

38 See Oren Bar-Gill, "Bundling and Consumer Misperception," *University of Chicago Law Review* 73, no. 1 (2006): 45; see also Howard Beales, Richard Craswell, and Steven C. Salop, "The Efficient Regulation of Consumer Information," *Journal of Law & Economics* 24 (1981): 492 ("Information about price . . . allows buyers to make the best use of their budget . . ."). Price is so important in advertising that advertising scholars use price as a key factor in determining if advertising is informative or merely persuasive. See Alan Resnik and Bruce L. Stern, "An Analysis of Information Content in Television Advertising," *Journal of Marketing* 41 (1977): 50–51.

39 See Jeffrey O'Connell, Carlos M. Brown, and Michael D. Smith, "Yellow Page Ads as Evidence of Widespread Overcharging by the Plaintiffs' Personal Injury Bar— and a Proposed Solution," *Connecticut Insurance Law Journal* 6 (2000): 426–27 (finding in a study analyzing Yellow Page Ads of twelve major U.S. legal markets that "the number of ads that mentioned [(1) hourly rates, (2) the specific percentage of the fee exacted, (3) a flat fee, and (4) price competition] were all much less than one percent of the total of 1,425 ads").

40 *Bates*, 433 U.S. at 370–71.

41 See, e.g., Cedric Ashley, "Taking Ownership of Diversity." *Innovator* 2, no.1 (2016): 3 ("Many of the diversity and inclusion initiatives within the legal profession focus

on efforts to increase representation of diverse attorneys in settings that have historically lacked diversity. These efforts tend to be directed towards change within the institutional setting or securing employment within those environments for diverse lawyers").

42 See Myrick, Nelson, and Nielson, "Race and Representation," 714 (noting the "intriguing" results that African Americans, Asian Americans, and Hispanics were more likely to represent themselves compared to white individuals—20.79 percent African American, 25.58 percent Asian American, 21.38 percent Hispanic, and 8.37 percent White); Libgober, "Getting a Lawyer While Black," 76 (finding that in a study analyzing attorney response rates to potential client emails, those emails with a "white" name signal received a 40 percent response rate while those with a "Black" name signal received only a 19 percent response rate).

43 See, e.g., Davis, "Race and Civil Counsel in the United States," 451 ("Race has not been put forward as a central issue by the U.S. civil counsel movement, but the evidence demonstrating the racial disparities in access to counsel is deeply disturbing").

44 Richard L. Street, Kimberly J. O'Malley, Lisa A. Cooper, and Paul Haidet, "Understanding Concordance in Patient-Physician Relationships: Personal and Ethnic Dimensions of Shared Identity." *Annals of Family Medicine* 6, no. 3 (2008): 198.

45 Ana H. Traylor, Julie A. Schmittdiel, Connie S. Uratsu, Carol M. Mangoine, and Usha Subramanian, "The Predictors of Patient-Physician Race and Ethnic Concordance: A Medical Facility Fixed-Effects Approach," *Health Services Research* 45, no. 3 (2010): 793.

46 Ibid.

47 Cialdini, *Influence*, 174.

48 Ibid.

49 See, e.g., Jim Hawkins, "Selling ART: An Empirical Assessment of Advertising on Fertility Clinics' Websites," *Indiana Law Journal* 88 (2013): 1169–70 ("It is possible that pictures of white babies give social proof to white individuals considering fertility care but not to people who are of other races, driving up the number of white patients and driving down the number of patients from other races").

50 Troccoli, "I Want a Black Lawyer to Represent Me," 2.

51 Ibid., 3.

52 Michael T. Nietzel, "Low Literacy Levels Among U.S. Adults Could be Costing the Economy $2.2 Trillion A Year," *Forbes*, September 9, 2020, www.forbes.com.

53 Pat Rafferty, "Best Practices in Attorney Advertising," Texas Bar Continuing Legal Education, December 11, 2013, www.texasbarcle.com.

3. A BRIEF HISTORY OF LAWYER REGULATION

1 George B. Shepherd, "No African-American Lawyers Allowed: The Inefficient Racism of the ABA's Accreditation of Law Schools," *Journal of Legal Education* 53 (2003): 109.

230 | NOTES

2 Adjoa Artis Aiyetoro, "Truth Matters: A Call for the American Bar Association to Acknowledge Its Past and Make Reparations to African Descendants," *George Mason University Civil Rights Law Journal* 18 (2007): 62.

3 See Wright, "Code of Professional Responsibility," 2.

4 Ibid., 3.

5 See "Members of the House of Delegates," *Annual Report of the American Bar Association* 94 (1969): 6–18.

6 *See* "Rules of the State Bar," State Bar of California, accessed February 4, 2022, www.rules.calbar.ca.gov.

7 ABA Model Rules of Professional Conduct, Preamble & Scope Comment 10 (1983, as amended).

8 ABA Model Rule 1.1.

9 ABA Model Rule 2.1.

10 ABA Model Rule 1.4(b).

11 ABA Model Rule 2.1.

12 ABA Model Rule 1.6.

13 ABA Model Rule 1.3.

14 Barton, "The ABA, the Rules, and Professionalism," 424.

15 Zacharias, "What Lawyers Do When Nobody's Watching," 997 ("resource constraints prevent disciplinary authorities from fully enforcing all the professional rules[, and they] must choose among violators that come to their attention on the basis of such factors as the severity of the offense, the deterrent effect . . . the likely cost of prosecution, the nature of the offender, and the effect of enforcement or lack of enforcement on the image of the bar") (citations omitted).

16 Levin, "Emperor's Clothes," 8–9 (1998).

17 Rhode, "Profession and the Public Interest," 1512.

18 Zacharias, "What Lawyers Do When Nobody's Watching," 999.

19 Ibid. 999–1001 (citations omitted).

20 ABA Model Rule 1.1, Comment 8 (emphasis added).

21 For an ongoing update of jurisdictions adopting ABA Model Rule 1.1, Comment 8, or similar revisions, see "Tech Competence," *Lawsites*, accessed March 24, 2022, www.lawsitesblog.com.

22 *In re* Moore, 532 B.R. 614, 633 (Bankr. W.D. Pa. 2015) (finding that attorneys have an affirmative "obligation to monitor the court's docket to inform themselves as to the entry of orders") (citation omitted).

23 See Alaska Bar Association, Ethics Opinion 3 at 2 (2014) ("A lawyer engaged in cloud computing must have a basic understanding of the technology used and must keep abreast of changes in the technology").

24 See Colo. Bar Association, Formal Opinion 90 at 5 (2018) ("The frequency of advances in technology notwithstanding, Colorado lawyers 'should keep abreast of . . . changes in communications and other relevant technologies'") (quoting Colorado Rules Professional Conduct Rule 1.1, Comment 8).

25 See Ill. State Bar Association Professional Conduct, Advisory Opinion 16–06 at
    2 (2016) ("lawyers who use cloud-based services must obtain and maintain a suf-
    ficient understanding of the technology they are using to properly assess the risks
    of unauthorized access and/or disclosures of confidential information"); Ill. State
    Bar Association Professional Conduct, Advisory Opinion 18–01 at 2 (2018) ("It is
    appropriate and reasonable to expect lawyers to understand metadata and other
    ubiquitous aspects of common information technology. But it would be neither
    appropriate nor reasonable to charge all lawyers with an understanding of the lat-
    est version of tracking software that might be chosen, and then employed without
    notice . . .") (footnote omitted).

26 See Mo. Bar Association, Informal Advisory Opinion 2018–09 (2018) ("Because
    what constitutes adequate provider policies and practices in these areas may
    change as relevant technology evolves, Attorney is encouraged to consult with a
    qualified information technology professional, take continuing legal education
    courses on use of technology in practice, and/or engage in regular self-study of
    materials from reputable sources to maintain competence in the use of cloud
    computing in the practice of law").

27 See New Hampshire Bar Association, Opinion 2012–13/05 ("counsel has a general
    duty to be aware of social media as a source of potentially useful information
    in litigation, to be competent to obtain that information directly or through an
    agent, and to know how to make effective use of that information in litigation").

28 See N.C. State Bar, 2014 Formal Ethics Opinion 5 (2015) ("Rule 1.1 requires
    lawyers to provide competent representation to clients. Comment [8] to the
    rule specifically states that a lawyer 'should keep abreast of changes in the law
    and its practice, including the benefits and risks associated with the technology
    relevant to the lawyer's practice.' 'Relevant technology' includes social media");
    N. C. State Bar, 2018 Formal Ethics Opinion 5 (2019) ("The technology and
    features of social networks are constantly changing. It is impossible to address
    every aspect of a lawyer's ethical obligation when utilizing a social network to
    prepare or to investigate a client's legal matter. Every lawyer is required by the
    duty of competence to keep abreast of the benefits and risks associated with the
    technology relevant to the lawyer's practice, including social networks. Rule 1.1,
    cmt. [8]. Further, when using a social network as an investigative tool, a lawyer's
    professional conduct must be guided by the Rules of Professional Conduct").

29 See Ohio Board of Professional Conduct, Opinion 2017–05 at 2 (2017) ("Because
    of the nature of a VLO, a lawyer who chooses to maintain a virtual office must
    competently manage and maintain the technology used to run the practice and
    'keep abreast of . . . the benefits and risks associated with relevant technology.'
    Prof.Cond.R. [*sic*] 1.1, cmt. [8]. Consequently, a VLO lawyer should possess a gen-
    eral knowledge of the security safeguards for the technology used in the lawyer's
    practice, or in the alternate hire or associate with persons who properly can advise
    and inform the lawyer").

30 See Wisconsin Formal Ethics Opinion EF-15–01 at 3 (2017) ("Lawyers who use cloud computing have a duty to understand the use of technologies and the potential impact of those technologies on their obligations under the applicable law and under the Rules. In order to determine whether a particular technology or service provider complies with the lawyer's professional obligations, a lawyer must use reasonable efforts. Moreover, as technology, the regulatory framework, and privacy laws change, lawyers must keep abreast of the changes").

31 See State ex rel., Oklahoma Bar Association v. Oliver, 369 P.3d 1074 (Okla. 2016).

32 Ibid., 1075.

33 Ibid.

34 See Darla Jackson and Kenton Brice, "The Ethics of Using Cloud-Based Services and Products." *Oklahoma Bar Journal* 90 (2019): 14.

35 See, e.g., In the Matter of Reisman, No. 2013–21 (Oct. 9, 2013) (finding lawyer violated obligations related to client communication and competence for failing to preserve digital evidence based on a "lack of experience in electronic discovery"); James v. National Finance LLC, 2014 WL 6845560, at *12 (Del. Ch. Dec. 5, 2014) ("Professed technological incompetence is not an excuse for discovery misconduct").

36 See Mark D. Killian, "Court Approves CLE Tech Component," Florida Bar, October 15, 2016, www.floridabar.org; "Technology Training CLE Required Effective in 2019," North Carolina State Bar Continuing Legal Education, November 27, 2018, www.nccle.org.

37 Robert Ambrogi, "New York Becomes First State to Mandate CLE in Cybersecurity, Privacy, and Data Protection," *LawSites*, August 4, 2022, www.lawnext.com.

38 Pennsylvania Bar Association Committee on Legal Ethics and Professional Responsibility, *Ethical Obligations for Lawyers Working Remotely*, Formal Opinion 2020–300 (2020).

39 Ibid.

40 Julie Pattison-Gordon, "How Do—and Should—Judges Stay Up to Date on Technology?," *Government Technology*, August 29, 2022, www.govtech.com.

41 See "Town Court Justice in Chautauqua County Resigns After Being Charged with Administrative Deficiencies," News Release, New York State Commission on Judicial Conduct, December 13, 2018, www.cjc.ny.gov.

42 Ibid.

43 ABA Model Rule 8.4(g).

44 Wald, "Primer on Diversity," 1141.

45 Root, "Combating Silence in the Profession," 808.

46 Ibid., 858.

47 National Conference of Women's Bar Associations, "Status of Antidiscrimination Rules in Each State," accessed September 1, 2022, www.ncwba.org.

48 See Post, *Democracy, Expertise, Academic Freedom*, 96.

49 See Lanctot, "Does LegalZoom Have First Amendment Rights?," 262 (observing that a "significant part of the [First Amendment] problem is the legal profession's notorious inability to produce a principled definition of the practice of law").

50 Ibid.

51 Ibid., 265.

52 Some states over the years have assessed the merits of authorizing nonlawyers to perform certain services and tasks that currently require a law license. According to the 2012 Survey of Unauthorized Practice of Law Committees Report conducted by the ABA Standing Committee on Client Protection: "Twenty-one jurisdictions authorize nonlawyers to perform some legal services in limited areas."

53 Baxter, "Dereliction of Duty," 234–35.

54 Rhode, *Character*, 47.

55 Ibid.

56 See Ann Thompson, "Ohio Bar Set to Remove Requirement Students Disclose Things Like Mental Health, *91.7 WVXU*, December 26, 2022, www.wvxu.org.

57 Gorsuch, *Republic, If You Can Keep It*, 256 ("Indeed, by far and away most unauthorized practice of law complaints come from lawyers rather than clients and involve no specific claims of injury").

58 Rhode, "Policing the Professional Monopoly," 33.

59 Rhode and Ricca, "Protecting the Profession or the Public," 2589.

60 Ibid., 2604.

61 Chambliss, "Evidence-Based Lawyer Regulation," 323.

62 Moorhead, Paterson, and Sherr, "Contesting Professionalism," 795.

63 *Schedule 2 The Reserved Legal Activities*, Legal Services Act of 2007, UK Public General Acts, accessed January 19, 2023, www.legislation.gov.uk.

64 See Unauthorized Practice of Law Committee v. Parsons Technology, Inc., No. Civ. A. 3:97CV-2859, 1999 WL 47235, at *4–7 (N.D. Tex. Jan. 22, 1999), *vacated and remanded per curiam*, 179 F.3d 956 (5th Cir. 1999). For an opposing view, see Janson v. LegalZoom, 802 F. Supp. 2d 1053, 1063–65 (W.D. Mo. 2011) (holding that LegalZoom's legal document preparation service provided online constituted the unauthorized practice of law).

65 OpenAI, ChatGPT Jan 9 Version, accessed January 19, 2023, www.chat.openai.com.

66 Christensen, "Unauthorized Practice of Law," 216.

67 Wolfram, *Modern Legal Ethics*, 39.

68 American Bar Association Commission on the Future of Legal Services, *Report on the Future of Legal Services*.

69 Solomon, Rhode, and Wanless, "How Reforming Rule 5.4 Would Benefit Lawyers and Consumers," 8 (citations omitted).

70 Ibid.

71 Ibid.

72 Ibid., 9 (citations omitted).

73 Ibid., 7.

74 Robert Ambrogi, "Hello Divorce Raises $3.25M to Span More of the Divorce Lifecycle, Including Financial Planning," *LawSites*, October 19, 2022, www.lawnext.com.

75 ABA Model Rule 5.4(a), (b).

76 ABA Model Rule 5.4(d)(1), (2).

77 See ABA Canons of Professional Ethics, Canon 33 (1929), www.americanbar.org.

78 See Green, "Disciplinary Restrictions on Multidisciplinary Practice," 1126–28.

79 ABA Model Rule 5.4.

80 See, e.g., Wilkins, "Who Should Regulate Lawyers?," 853 ("Independence arguments have always had a privileged status in professional discourse. For example, the claim that there is an inherent link between the current disciplinary system and the status of lawyers as 'independent professionals' is firmly rooted in precedent, practice, and professional mythology").

81 ABA Model Rule 5.4, Comment 1; see also American Law Institute, *Restatement (Third) of the Law Governing Lawyers* § 10 Comment b (St. Paul: American Law Institute Publishers, 2000) ("Those limitations are prophylactic and are designed to safeguard the professional independence of lawyers. A person entitled to share a lawyer's fees is likely to attempt to influence the lawyer's activities so as to maximize those fees. That could lead to inadequate legal services"); American Law Institute, *Restatement (Third)*, § 10 Comment c ("Here also the concern is that permitting such ownership or direction would induce or require lawyers to violate the mandates of the lawyer codes, such as by subjecting the lawyer to the goals and interests of the nonlawyer in ways adverse to the lawyer's duties to a client").

82 American Law Institute, *Restatement (Third)* § 10.

83 American Law Institute, "About ALI," accessed September 1, 2022, www.ali.org.

84 ALM Staff, "The 2022 ALM Law 100: Ranked by Average Partner Compensation," *American Lawyer*, April 26, 2022, www.law.com.

85 "Job Market for Class of 2021 Law Graduates was One of the Strongest on Record," *NALP Bulletin*, September 2022, www.nalp.org.

86 Ibid.

87 Cheatham, "Lawyer When Needed," 81.

88 Ibid. (quoting the ABA's *Report of the Special Committee on Legal Clinics* published in 1940).

89 See, e.g., Gilbert and Lempert, "Nonlawyer Partner," 383 (noting that debate about reform to Model Rule 5.4 during a February 1983 ABA meeting was essentially shut down on the "fear of Sears," the idea that Sears could own a law firm). The ABA Commission on Evaluation of Professional Standards debated the nonlawyer ownership and investment question during the early 1980s but did not take action. See generally Wolfram, "ABA and MDPs," 1625; see also Andrews, "Nonlawyers in the Business of Law," 577.

90 See Schneyer, "'Professionalism' As Pathology," 137 ("I was disappointed that the 20/20 Commission decided not to recommend our proposal for adoption by the ABA House of Delegates. Our Draft Resolution and Draft Report remain in the ABA archives, but no relaxation of the ban on nonlawyer ownership of law firms by the ABA or state supreme courts seems likely in the short term—unless, of course, the ban is struck down in litigation").

91 *See* American Bar Association and Bureau of National Affairs, *Lawyers' Manual on Professional Conduct* (Washington, DC: American Bar Association, 2008), 91: 421 (noting that "[m]ost jurisdictions that base their ethics rules on the ABA Model Rules do not deviate appreciably from Rule 5.4(b) and Rule 5.4(d)"). The *Lawyers' Manual* describes the small variations in the rules of North Carolina, Illinois, Oklahoma, Washington, Florida, Kentucky, Utah, and the District of Columbia. American Bar Association and Bureau of National Affairs, *Lawyers' Manual on Professional Conduct*, 91:402–03.

92 Roger E. Barton, "Changing the Stakes: How Evolving Law Firm Ownership Rules Could (or Could Not) Re-shape the Legal Industry," *Reuters*, August 19, 2021, www.reuters.com.

93 American Bar Association House of Delegates, Resolution 402 (2022), www.americanbar.org.

94 See generally Henry Hansman and Reinier Kraakman, "The Essential Role of Organizational Law," *Yale Law Journal* 110 (2000): 387.

95 See NAACP v. Button, 371 U.S. 415, 428–29 (1963) (recognizing the First Amendment right of nonprofit corporations to provide legal services); see also Citizens United v. FEC, 558 U.S. 310, 365 (2010) ("[T]he Government may not suppress political speech on the basis of the speaker's corporate identity. No sufficient governmental interest justifies limits on the political speech of nonprofit or for-profit corporations").

96 American Law Institute, *Restatement (Third)*, § 10 Comment c. For further discussion of Model Rule 5.4's anticompetitive effect, see Gillers, "What We Talked About When We Talked About Ethics," 266–68. Gillers argues that Model Rule 5.4 "must be counted as serving the interests of some critical mass of lawyers, numerous and powerful enough" to stop reform and that the rule "exclude[s] a major source of capital for new firms." Ibid., 267–68. He notes: "In addition to the predictable downward pressure on fees that would accompany increased competition, lay investors might be willing to accept a lower return on their money." Ibid., 268. See also Rhode, "Policing the Professional Monopoly," 10.

97 Gillers, "What We Talked About When We Talked About Ethics," 247.

98 See ibid.

99 Ibid., 268.

100 Ibid.

101 See Solomon, Rhode, and Wanless, "How Reforming Rule 5.4 Would Benefit Lawyers and Consumers," 16 (citations omitted).

102 Ibid.

103 ABA Model Rule 5.4(d)(1).

104 Ibid.

105 See D.C. Rules of Professional Conduct 5.4, 5.7 (2007).

106 See Green, "The Disciplinary Restrictions on Multidisciplinary Practice," 1157.

107 Ibid.

108 See Krishnamurthy et al., "What We Know," 383 (showing that several studies have found that MLP programs have reduced ER visits for asthma patients follow-

236 | NOTES

ing housing interventions, improved pregnancy outcomes, and lowered rates of abuse).

109 See Maia Crawford, Tricia McGinnis, John Auerbach, and Kristin Golden, "Population Health in Medicaid Delivery System Reforms," *Milbank Memorial Fund*, 2 (2015), www.milbank.org.

110 See Krishnamurthy et al., "What We Know," 379 ("The MLP approach to health is designed as an integrated, upstream effort among health care, public health, and legal sectors that collectively work to improve social conditions for people and communities").

111 Ibid., 380 ("In the MLP approach, health care, public health, and civil legal aid services are integrated in a way that allows clinical staff at hospitals, clinics, and other sites to screen for health-harming legal needs, work in tandem with legal professional . . . and . . . refer patients to a civil legal aid team").

112 Ibid.

113 See ibid. (presenting a table with potential MLP interventions, such as "[s]ecure housing subsidies, protect against utility shut-off" and "[a]ppeal denial of food stamps, health insurance").

114 See ibid., 384–85 ("Medical-legal partnerships have shown significant community benefits by alleviating system-wide social conditions, such as housing reconstruction to meet city codes that affect community and population-wide health").

115 See Boumil, Feitas, and Feitas, *Multidisciplinary Representation of Patients*, 111 ("Patients trust medical providers with personal information and may speak to them about financial hardships, troubled relationships, and other socioeconomic stressors. This trust facilitates the identification of health-related social problems").

116 Ibid.

117 See ibid. ("Patients trust medical providers with personal information and may speak to them about financial hardships, troubled relationships, and other socio-economic stressors").

118 Ibid., 112.

119 See Krishnamurthy et al., "What We Know," 380 ("In the MLP approach, health care, public health, and civil legal aid services are integrated in a way that allows clinical staff at hospitals, clinics, and other sites to screen for health-harming legal needs, work in tandem with legal professionals . . .").

120 See Boumil, Feitas, and Feitas, *Multidisciplinary Representation of Patients*, 123–24.

121 ABA Model Rule 5.5(a).

122 See Hadfield and Rhode, "How to Regulate Legal Services," 1220.

123 See Cooter and Schafer, *Solomon's Knot*, 120 ("To produce innovations, money and ideas must come together like the rings in Solomon's knot"). *See also* Ribstein and Kobayashi, "Law's Information Revolution," 1218 (summarizing "many potential legal information innovations that are constrained by licensing laws [which]

shows how the rise of the legal information market intensifies arguments for reexamining lawyer licensing laws").

124 Cooter and Schafer, *Solomon's Knot*, 20, 136.

4. THE LEGAL MONOPOLY

1 See Joe Palazzolo, "Judges Step Up Electioneering as Outside Money Pours into Races," *Wall Street Journal*, October 13, 2014, www.wsj.com.

2 It should be noted that in a few states, some regulation of lawyers occurs via the legislature. For example, the states of Alaska, California, Maryland, Massachusetts, Michigan, Mississippi, Virginia, and Wyoming all have legal authority promulgated by a combination of judicial and legislative powers. See "Comprehensive Guide to Bar Admission Requirements," *National Conference of Bar Examiners and American Bar Association Section of Legal Education and Admissions to the Bar*, 2021, 1.

3 Levin, "Case for Less Secrecy in Lawyer Discipline," 19–20 (citations omitted).

4 See, e.g., Grievance Adm'r v. Fieger, 719 N.W.2d 123 (Mich. 2006); Jacoby & Meyers, LLP v. Presiding Justices of the First, Second, Third & Fourth Dep'ts, Appellate Div. of Supreme Court of N.Y., 488 F. App'x 526 (2d Cir. 2012), as amended (Jan. 9, 2013).

5 See Wolfram, *Modern Legal Ethics*, 23 (citation omitted).

6 See generally George J. Stigler, "The Theory of Economic Regulation," *Bell Journal of Economic and Management Science* 2, no. 1 (1971): 3.

7 Jolls, Sunstein, and Thaler, "Behavioral Approach to Law and Economics," 1504.

8 Leubsdorf, "Theories of Judging and Judge Disqualification," 42.

9 See Frank H. Easterbrook, "Antitrust and the Economics of Federalism," *Journal of Law and Economics* 26, no.1 (1983): 27, www.doi.org ("regulation often is procured by and designed for the benefit of those the regulation purports to control").

10 Ibid.

11 See, e.g., Hazard, Pearce, and Stempel, "Why Lawyers Should Be Allowed to Advertise," 1093.

12 Wolfram, *Modern Legal Ethics*, § 2.4, at 39 (observing that for regulators "resulting losses in economic efficiency" are acceptable if the "the restrictive rules prevent more harmful effects on clients and society").

13 See Rhode and Ricca, "Protecting the Profession or the Public?" 2605.

14 Rhode, "Policing the Professional Monopoly," 37.

15 Gellhorn, "Abuse of Occupational Licensing," 11.

16 See Luban, "Legal Ideals and Moral Obligations," 259 ("because lawyers are often better positioned than nonlawyers to realize the unfairness or unreasonableness of a law, lawyers often should be among the first . . . to counsel others that it is acceptable to violate or nullify it"); Stone, "Lawyer's Responsibility," 47 ("It is the legal profession that is most fundamentally responsible for helping the nation strike

238 | NOTES

the right balance [between national security and civil liberties] and for defending our freedoms").

17 NAACP v. Button, 371 U.S. 415, 429–30 (1963) (citations omitted). See also United Mine Workers of America, Dist. 12 v. Illinois State Bar Association, 389 U.S. 217, 223 (1967) (reinforcing that the First Amendment protections established in *Button* extend beyond "political matters of acute social moment" and that "[g]reat secular causes, with small ones, are guarded") (citations and internal punctuation omitted).

18 Freedman and Smith, *Understanding Lawyers' Ethics*, 23.

19 Gordon, "Role of Lawyers in Producing the Rule of Law," 450 ("Legal regulations and procedures are complicated and rapidly changing; so that sophisticated, experienced agents who know their way around the rule-systems and the courts are generally essential to effective representation within and operation of the system").

20 Pepper, "Counseling at the Limits," 1547–48.

21 Ibid. For a competing view on the value of a lawyer's role in selecting information for a client, see Louis Kaplow and Stephen Shavell, "Legal Advice About Information to Present in Litigation: Its Effects and Social Desirability." *Harvard Law Review* 102 (1989): 613–14 ("Our conclusions cast doubt on the social value of lawyers' role in selecting information for their clients, thereby challenging one of the fundamental premises of the legal system").

22 Edlin and Haw, "Cartels by Another Name," 1140.

23 Friedman, *Capitalism and Freedom*, 154–55; *see also* Christensen et al., "Will Disruptive Innovations Cure Health Care?"

24 Barton, "Institutional Analysis of Lawyer Regulation," 1239.

5. PRESERVING DEMOCRACY: THE ROLE OF COURTS AND THE ROLE OF LEGAL ETHICS

1 Alexis de Tocqueville, *Democracy in America* [1835] trans. Henry Reeve, 6th ed., 1876, 348.

2 See Nicholas Fandos, "White House Pushes 'Alternative Facts.' Here Are the Real Ones," *New York Times*, January 22, 2017, www.nytimes.com.

3 See Clare Foran, "Kellyanne Conway and the Bowling Green Massacre that Wasn't," *Atlantic*, February 3, 2017, www.theatlantic.com.

4 See Chris Cillizza, "Kellyanne Conway's Simply False Spin on 'COVID-19,'" *CNN*, April 16, 2020, www.cnn.com.

5 See Susan Hennessey and Benjamin Wittes, "Don't Convict Jeff Sessions of Perjury Just Yet: Not All Lies, Even Under Oath, Are Prosecutable Crimes," *Foreign Policy*, www.foreignpolicy.com.

6 See, e.g., Scott M. Karson, "With Truth on Trial, Judicial Branch Upholds Fragile Rule of Law," *New York Law Journal*, April 30, 2021, www.law.com.

7 See "Fact Check: Courts Have Dismissed Multiple Lawsuits of Alleged Electoral Fraud Presented by Trump Campaign," *Reuters*, February 15, 2021, www.reuters.

com ("Independent experts, governors and state election officials from both parties say there was no evidence of widespread fraud").

8   Jeremy Waldron, *Damned Lies*, 24 (New York University School of Law, Working Paper no. 21–11, 2021), www.ssrn.com.

9   See Jack Healy, "These Are the 5 People Who Died in the Capitol Riot," *New York Times*, February 22, 2021, www.nytimes.com.

10 See Michael S. Schmidt and Luke Broadwater, "Officers' Injuries, Including Concussions, Show Scope of Violence at Capitol Riot," *New York Times*, July 12, 2021, www.nytimes.com.

11 Ibid.

12 See Mike Valerio and Jordan Fischer, "Fourth Officer Who Responded to the US Capitol on January 6 Dies by Suicide," *KHOU 11*, August 3, 2021, www.khou.com.

13 United States v. Cua, No. 21–107, 2021 WL 918255, at *3 (D.D.C. Mar. 10, 2021).

14 Cass R. Sunstein, "On the Wrongness of Lies," 9 (Harvard Pub. L. Working Paper no. 21–05, 2020), www.ssrn.com.

15 See Allan Smith, "Michigan Republicans Eviscerate Trump Voter Fraud Claims in Scathing Report," *NBC News*, June 23, 2021, www.nbcnews.com.

16 Sherilynn Ifill, "Lawyers Enabled Trump's Worst Abuses," *New York Times*, February 12, 2021, www.nytimes.com.

17 Ibid.

18 See Jon Swaine and Aaron Schaffer, "Here's What Happened When Rudolph Giuliani Made His First Appearance in Federal Court in Nearly Three Decades," *Washington Post*, November 18, 2020, www.washingtonpost.com.

19 See *LDAD Collects 1000s of Signatures for Ethics Complaint Against Rudy Giuliani*, January 21, 2021, www.ldad.org.

20 *In re* Giuliani, 146 N.Y.S.3d 266, 268 (App. Div. 2021).

21 *In re* Giuliani, No. 21-BG-423 (D.C. July 7, 2021) (per curiam).

22 See Jacqueline Thomsen, "Can't Have It Both Ways: Sidney Powell's Defamation Defense Could Put Her in Ethical Bind, Experts Say," *National Law Journal*, March 23, 2021, www.law.com.

23 Ibid.

24 King v. Whitmer, 556 F.Supp.3d 680 (E.D. Mich. 2021).

25 Ibid.

26 Ibid.

27 See Letter from Gretchen Whitmer, Governor of the State of Michigan, to the State Bar of Texas, February 1, 2021, www.michigan.gov; Letter from Dana Nessel, Attorney General of the State of Michigan, to the State Bar of Texas, February 1, 2021, www.michigan.gov; Letter from Jocelyn Benson, Michigan Secretary of State, to the State Bar of Texas, February 1, 2021, www.michigan.gov.

28 Andrea Salcedo, "L. Lin Wood Spent Months Falsely Claiming Voter Fraud Cost Trump the Election. Now Georgia Is Investigating Whether He Voted Illegally," *Washington Post*, February 3, 2021, www.washingtonpost.com.

29 Adam Klasfeld, "Georgia State Bar Says There's a Glaring Problem with Lin Wood's Claim About How Mental Health Exam Request Went Public," *Law & Crime*, May 12, 2021, www.lawandcrime.com.

30 O'Rourke v. Dominion Voting Sys. Inc., Civil Action No. 20-cv-03747, 2021 WL 3400671, at *2 (D. Colo. Aug. 3, 2021).

31 28 U.S.C. § 1927 (2018).

32 See ABA Model Rule 4.1.

33 "Ethics of Positional Conflicts," ABA Ethics Opinion, May 2017, www.americanbar.org.

34 "Misrepresentation by an Attorney Employed by a Government Agency as Part of Official Duties," DC Bar Ethics Opinion 323, March 2004, www.dcbar.org.

35 The law firm Jones Day, for example, ceased all representation of Trump-related election-fraud challenges. See Josh Gerstein, "Another Law Firm Bails Out on Trump Campaign," *Politico*, www.politico.com; "Jones Day Statement Regarding Election Litigation," *Jones Day*, November 2020, www.jonesday.com.

36 ABA Model Rules of Professional Conduct, Rules 3, 3.3(a)(1).

37 Ibid., Rule 3.1 (prohibiting a lawyer from making an allegation in court "unless there is a basis in law and fact for doing so that is not frivolous").

38 ABA Model Rules of Professional Conduct, Rule 4.1(a).

39 ABA Model Rules of Professional Conduct, Rule 8.4(c).

40 See "Jurisdictional Rules Comparison Charts," *American Bar Association*, www.americanbar.org.

41 See "Sedley Alley: The Search for the Truth After Execution," *Innocence Project*, May 1, 2019, www.innocenceproject.org.

42 As Oxford Dictionaries defined the concept in naming it the 2016 word of the year, "post-truth" means "circumstances in which objective facts are less influential in shaping public opinion than appeals to emotion and personal belief." "Post-truth," *Oxford English Dictionary*, www.oed.com.

43 See ABA Model Rules of Professional Conduct, Rule 3.6.

44 Ibid., Rule 8.4(c).

45 See ibid., Rule 3.6, Comment 3.

46 Ibid., Preamble 1.

47 Ibid., Preamble 13.

48 Post, *Democracy, Expertise, and Academic Freedom*, xiii (explaining that "democratic competence" is a "constitutional value" and that "a First Amendment principle capable of sustaining the disciplinary practices that produce expert knowledge").

49 ABA Model Rules, Preamble 6.

50 Ibid.

51 *In re* Giuliani, No. 2021–00506, slip op. at 31 (N.Y. App. Div. June 24, 2021).

52 Ibid.

53 See ABA Model Rules of Professional Conduct, Rule 4.1, Comment 2, and accompanying text.

54 See McDonald v. Longley, 4 F.4th 229, 237 (5th Cir. 2021) (holding that the bar's engagement "in political and ideological activities that are not germane to its interests in regulating the legal profession and improving the quality of legal services" violated the First Amendment by compelling attorneys to join it); Boudreaux v. La. State Bar Association 3 F.4th 748, 756 (5th Cir. 2021) (holding that plaintiff attorneys plausibly pled that the bar association violated the First Amendment by engaging in "political and legislative activity" and compelling attorneys to join it). But see Schell v. Chief Justice & Justices Okla. Sup. Ct., 2 F.4th 1312, 1324 (10th Cir. 2021) (holding that mandatory bar dues do not violate the First Amendment rights of members).

55 Green, "Counterfeit Campaign Speech," 1489.

56 Ibid., 1450.

57 Ibid.

58 Hasen, "Constitutional Right to Lie in Campaigns and Elections?," 77.

PART II. DEMOCRATIZING LAW: THE BLUEPRINT

1 Saffer, *Designing for Interaction*, 220.

2 Gladwell, *Tipping Point*, 9.

3 See ibid., 139 (introducing the "Power of Context" as a "principle of epidemic transmission").

4 Ibid.

5 Ibid., 132.

6. ANTITRUST LAW

1 *See* Sherman Antitrust Act, 26 Stat. 209 (1890). In July of 1890, the United States Congress passed the Sherman Antitrust Act. Senator John Sherman (R-OH) authored the act, which passed the Senate 51–1, 21 Cong. Rec. 3153 (1890), and the House of Representatives 242–0, 21 Cong. Rec. 6314 (1890).

2 Senator Sherman, speaking on the Sherman Act, 21 Cong. Rec. 2457 (1890) (statement of Sen. John Sherman). Section I of the Sherman Act prohibits contracts or conspiracies in restraint of trade. Section II prevents monopolies or attempts to monopolize. Sherman Antitrust Act, 15 U.S.C. § 1, 2 (1890).

3 Northern Pacific Railroad Company v. United States, 356 U.S. 1, 4 (1958).

4 Ibid.

5 See Sherman Antitrust Act, 26 Stat. 209 (1890). The Clayton Act, enacted in 1914, extended the right to sue under the antitrust laws to the Federal Trade Commission.

6 Rice v. Norman Williams Company, 458 U.S. 654, 661 (1982).

7 United States v. Topco Associates, Inc., 405 U.S. 596, 610 (1972).

8 Ibid.

9 Klobuchar, *Antitrust*, 4.

10 Ibid., 351.

11 Parker v. Brown, 371 U.S. 341 (1943)

242 | NOTES

12 See McGowan and Lemley, "Antitrust Immunity," 356–57 ("If the Sherman Act, with its national mandate for competitive markets, were applied to all state regulations it would pose a serious threat to the states' very existence as meaningful government entities").

13 Areeda and Hovenkamp, *Antitrust Law* ¶ 215a, 339.

14 Goldfarb v. Virginia State Bar, 421 U.S. 773 (1975).

15 Ibid., 777–78.

16 Ibid., 786.

17 Ibid. (citation omitted).

18 Ibid., 776.

19 Ibid., 787 (citations omitted).

20 Ibid., 787 (citations omitted).

21 Ibid., 788.

22 Ibid., 790. ("The threshold inquiry in determining if an anticompetitive activity is state action of the type the Sherman Act was not meant to proscribe is whether the activity is required by the State acting as sovereign. . . . Here we need not inquire further into the state action question because it cannot fairly be said that the State of Virginia through its Supreme Court Rules required the anticompetitive activities of either respondent." *Goldfarb*, 421 U.S. at 790. "It is not enough that . . . anticompetitive conduct is prompted by state action; rather, anticompetitive activities must be compelled by direction of the State acting as a sovereign." *Goldfarb*, 421 U.S. at 791.)

23 Wolfram, *Modern Legal Ethics*, 40n29.

24 *Goldfarb*, 421 U.S. at 788n17.

25 Ibid., 792–93 (citations omitted).

26 Hoover v. Ronwin, 466 U.S. 558, 560 (1984).

27 Ibid., 565.

28 Ibid., 580. The majority characterized the admission denial as an act of the Arizona Supreme Court, rather than a state agency. See ibid., 588 (Stevens, J., dissenting) ("The majority's conclusion that the challenged action was that of the Arizona Supreme Court is, however, plainly wrong. Respondent alleged that the decision to place an artificial limit on the number of lawyers was made by petitioners—not by the State Supreme Court"). The dissent found significant the fact that the admission decision was made by a body with authority delegated by the court.

29 Ibid., 585.

30 Ibid., 598–99.

31 Ibid., 599 (citation and internal punctuation omitted).

32 See Palmer v. BRG of Georgia, Inc., et al., 111 S. Ct. 401 (1990).

33 See North Carolina State Board of Dental Examiners, 717 F.3d 359, 367 (4th Cir. 2013).

34 Ibid., 367.

35 See North Carolina State Board of Dental Examiners v. Federal Trade Commission., 135 S. Ct. 1101, 1120 (2015).

36 Ibid., 1107.

37 Ibid.

38 Ibid., 1105.

39 Ibid.

40 See "Statement of Interest on Behalf of the United States of America," TIKD Services LLC v. Florida Bar, Case No. 1:17-cv-24103-MGC, (S.D. Fla. Jan. 30, 2019), 11.

41 See Complaint for Declaratory and Injunctive Relief at 21–22, LegalZoom.com, Inc. v. N.C. State Bar, No. 11 CVS 15111 (N.C. Super. Ct. Sept. 30, 2011).

42 Complaint at 4, Express Lien, Inc. v. Cleveland Metro. Bar Ass'n, No. 2:15-cv-02519 (E.D. La. July 9, 2015).

43 Florida Bar v. TIKD Services, LLC, 326 So. 3d 1073, 1079 (Fla. 2021).

44 Ibid., 1082–83.

45 Ibid.

46 Edlin and Haw, "Cartels by Another Name," 1144.

47 ABA Task Force on the Model Definition of the Practice of Law, "Definition of the Practice of Law Draft," *American Bar Association*, September 19, 2002, www.americanbar.org.

48 Ibid.

49 "Letter from the United States Department of Justice and the Federal Trade Commission to Task Force on the Model Definition of the Practice of Law," *American Bar Association*, December 20, 2002, 3, www.justice.gov.

50 Ibid.

51 Ibid.

52 Stephen Mayson, "Independent Review of Legal Services Regulation: The Scope of Legal Services Regulation," *UCL Centre for Ethics and Law Working Paper LSR-2*, March 2020, 10–11.

53 Hadfield and Rhode, "How to Regulate Legal Services," 1215.

54 Helen Gunnarsson, "Conference Report: Supreme Court Decision Has Made Bar Regulators Cautious," *Bloomberg Law News*, November 19, 2019, www.bloomberglaw.com.

55 Fortney, "The Billable Hours Derby," 189 ("Corporate counsel are increasingly asking law firms to lower their bills and to use alternative fee arrangements . . . because the billable hours fee structure rewards inefficiency").

56 Dave Simpson, "Microsoft to Shift Away from Billable Hours," *Law360*, August 1, 2017, www.law360.com.

57 Clio, *Legal Trends Report 2022*, 54 ("Survey respondents were representative of the US population by age, gender, region, income, and race/ethnicity, according to US census statistics").

58 Ibid.

7. THE FIRST AMENDMENT

1 See U.S. Const. amend. VI ("In all criminal prosecutions, the accused shall enjoy . . . the Assistance of Counsel for his defense").

NOTES

2 See U.S. Const. amend. XV (forbidding discrimination in voting based on race); U.S. Const. amend. XIX (forbidding discrimination based on sex); U.S. Const. amend. XXIV (prohibiting poll taxes); U.S. Const. amend. XXVI (granting right to vote to citizens over 18 years of age).

3 U.S. Const. amend. I.

4 U.S. Const. amend. XIV.

5 See Abrams v. United States, 250 U.S. 616, 630 (1919) (Holmes, J., dissenting) ("[T]he ultimate good desired is better reached by free trade in ideas—that the best test of truth is the power of the thought to get itself accepted in the competition of the market . . .").

6 See Vincent Blasi, "The Checking Value in First Amendment Theory," *American Bar Foundation Research Journal* 2 (1977): 527.

7 See generally Thomas Scanlon, "A Theory of Freedom of Expression," *Philosophy and Public Affairs* 1 (1972): 215–22 (discussing the role of autonomy in the context of free expression).

8 See, e.g., Alexander Meiklejohn, *Free Speech and Its Relation to Self-Government*, New York: Harper & Brothers Publishers, 1948, 96–98 (credited with establishing the modern understanding of First Amendment political speech).

9 Frederick Schauer, "The Speech of Law and the Law of Speech." *Arkansas Law Review* 49, no. 4 (1997): 687 ("As lawyers, speech is our stock in trade").

10 See ABA Model Rule 1.6.

11 See ABA Model Rule 3.6.

12 See ABA Model Rule 1.2.

13 See ABA Model Rules 7.1, 7.2, 7.3.

14 See ABA Model Rule 3.5.

15 See ABA Model Rule 3.3.

16 See ABA Model Rule 4.1.

17 Post, *Democracy, Expertise, Academic Freedom*, 95.

18 Ibid.

19 Ibid., 33–34.

20 Ibid., 34 (emphasis in original).

21 NAACP v. Button, 371 U.S. 415, 447 (1963) (White, J., concurring in part and dissenting in part).

22 Brotherhood of Railroad Trainmen v. Virginia ex rel. Virginia State Bar, 377 U.S. 1, 8 (1964).

23 United Mine Workers, District 12 v. Illinois State Bar Association, 389 U.S. 217, 219 (1967).

24 United Transportation Union v. State Bar of Michigan, 401 U.S. 576, 585 (1971).

25 Bates v. Arizona State Bar, 433 U.S. at 350 (1977).

26 *In re* Primus, 436 U.S. 412, 414 (1978).

27 *In re* R.M.J., 455 U.S. 191, 204 (1982).

28 Peel v. Attorney Registration and Disciplinary Commission, 496 U.S. 91, 97 (1990).

29 *In re* R.M.J., 455 U.S. at 204.

30 Shapero v. Kentucky Bar Association, 486 U.S. 466, 469 (1988) (internal quotation marks omitted). But see Florida Bar v. Went For It, Inc., 515 U.S. 618 (1995) (upholding a Florida Bar rule banning lawyers from mailing letters to personal injury or wrongful death victims within thirty days of the accident).

31 NAACP v. Button, 371 U.S. 415 (1963).

32 Brown v. Board of Education II, 349 U.S. 294, 301 (1955).

33 *Button*, 371 U.S. at 428.

34 Ibid., 438 ("only a compelling state interest in the regulation of a subject within the State's constitutional power to regulate can justify limiting First Amendment freedoms"); Ibid. ("Precision of regulation must be the touchstone in an area so closely touching our most precious freedoms").

35 Ibid., 429–30 (footnotes omitted).

36 Ibid., 434–35.

37 *Brotherhood of Railroad Trainmen*, 377 U.S. 1.

38 Ibid., 7.

39 Ibid.

40 Ibid.

41 *United Mine Workers*, 389 U.S. 217.

42 Ibid., 223 (internal quotation marks omitted).

43 Ibid., 221–22 (footnote omitted).

44 United Transportation Union v. State Bar, 410 U.S. 576, 585 (1971).

45 *See* Legal Services Corp. v. Velazquez, 531 U.S. 533, 549 (2001) (holding that the federal government's prohibition against challenging the validity of welfare laws, by attorneys working for a congressionally created legal aid organization, is a violation of the First Amendment).

46 Ibid., 536–37 ("[T]he restriction . . . prohibits legal representation funded by recipients of LSC moneys if the representation involves an effort to amend or otherwise challenge existing welfare law"). Justices Kennedy, Breyer, Ginsburg, Stevens, and Souter formed the majority. Justice Scalia filed a dissenting opinion, in which Chief Justice Rehnquist and Justices O'Connor and Thomas joined. *See Velazquez*, 531 U.S. at 549 (Scalia, J., dissenting). The particular restriction under dispute "prevent[ed] an attorney from arguing to a court that a . . . state or federal statue by its terms or in its application is violative of the United States Constitution." *Velazquez*, 531 U.S. at 537 (majority opinion). It should be noted that other LSC restrictions on lobbying, class actions, attorney's fees, and solicitation have been upheld in the lower courts. See, e.g., Legal Aid Servs. of Or. v. Legal Servs. Corp., 608 F.3d 1084, 1087 (9th Cir. 2010) (upholding "restrictions on lobbying, soliciting clients, and participating in class actions").

47 *Legal Services Corp.*, 531 U.S. at 545.

48 Ibid.

49 Ibid.

50 Ibid.

246 | NOTES

51 Ibid., 546.
52 Ibid.
53 Ibid.
54 Ibid., 548.
55 Bigelow v. Virginia, 421 U.S. 809 (1975).
56 Greenhouse, *Becoming Justice Blackmun*, 117 (internal quotation marks omitted).
57 *Bigelow*, 421 U.S. at 811–12.
58 Ibid., 813.
59 Ibid., 815.
60 Ibid., 818.
61 Ibid., (quotation omitted).
62 Ibid., 822.
63 Ibid., 829.
64 Ibid., 770.
65 Ibid., 763.
66 Ibid., 769; see also 44 Liquormart v. Rhode Island, 517 U.S. 484, 503 (1996) ("The First Amendment directs us to be especially skeptical of regulations that seek to keep people in the dark for what the government perceives to be their own good").
67 *Virginia State Board of Pharmacy*, 425 U.S. at 770.
68 Ibid.
69 *Bates v. Arizona State Bar,* 433 U.S. at 372 (1977).
70 Ibid., 370.
71 See *In re* R.M.J., 455 U.S. at 203 (applying First Amendment commercial speech protection to lawyer advertising); Peel v. Attorney Registration and Disciplinary Commission of Illinois, 496 U.S. 91, 100 (1990) (same); Zauderer v. Office of Disciplinary Counsel, 471 U.S. 626 (1985) (holding that disciplinary rules could mandate disclosure regarding payment of costs in advertisement, but that the First Amendment protected attorneys so long as their advertisements were truthful and nondeceptive).
72 See, e.g., Timothy J. Muris, "California Dental Association v. Federal Trade Commission: The Revenge of Footnote 17." *Supreme Court Economic Review* 8 (2000): 287 ("The seminal commercial speech cases—Virginia State Board of Pharmacy v. Virginia Citizens Consumer Council, Inc. and Bates—turned on an analysis of the impact on consumers of banning advertising, just as would an antitrust analysis of an advertising ban. Indeed, commentators noted the identity of antitrust and First Amendment analysis. Under either antitrust law or the First Amendment, a restraint based on protection of the economic interests of any group, including professionals, would not stand").
73 See Turner v. American Bar Association, 407 F. Supp. 451, 478 (N.D. Tex. 1975) (citations omitted) ("The Plaintiffs have also attempted to couch their right to have unlicensed laymen represent them in Court in terms of the first amendment. Their argument is that the First Amendment guarantees the freedom of associa-

tion and right to petition their government for redress of grievances. An alliance between a defendant, or plaintiff for that matter, and an unlicensed layman for the purpose of litigation in Court is an association which has as its end the redress of grievances. Hence, the argument goes, the First Amendment guarantees the right of the Plaintiffs to have unlicensed attorneys in Court. . . . What this Court is holding is that the Constitution of the United States, in particular the First and Sixth Amendments, does not grant to the Plaintiffs the right to have an unlicensed layman represent them in Court proceedings").

74 See Lawline v. Am. Bar Association, 956 F.2d 1378, 1386 (7th Cir. 1992); see also Thomas v. Collins, 323 U.S. 516, 544 (1944) ("A State may forbid one without a license to practice law as a vocation, but I think it could not stop an unlicensed person from making a speech about the rights of man or the rights of labor, or any other kind of right, including recommending that his hearers organize to support his views. Likewise, the state may prohibit the pursuit of medicine as an occupation without its license, but I do not think it could make it a crime publicly or privately to speak urging persons to follow or reject any school of medical thought").

75 Ohralik v. Ohio State Bar Association, 436 U.S. 447 (1978).

76 *In re* Primus, 436 U.S. 412, 437–40 (1978).

77 Ibid.

78 See, e.g., Milavetz, Gallop & Milavetz, P.A. v. United States, 559 U.S. 229 (2010) (holding that a state may mandate an advertising disclosure for lawyers providing bankruptcy-related services); *Florida Bar*, 515 U.S. at 620 (holding that a thirty-day prohibition on direct-mail solicitation by lawyers of personal injury or wrongful death clients withstood First Amendment scrutiny); Zauderer v. Office of Disciplinary Counsel, 471 U.S 626, 655 (1985) (holding that disciplinary rules could mandate disclosure regarding payment of costs in advertisement, but that the First Amendment protected attorneys so long as advertisement was truthful and nondeceptive); *Ohralik*, 436 U.S. at 449 (upholding a ban on in-person solicitation of personal injury victims).

79 See, e.g., Republican Party of Minn. v. White, 536 U.S. 765, 788 (2002) (applying strict scrutiny to hold that a rule prohibiting attorneys and judges running for judicial office from speaking their views on legal or political issues violated the First Amendment); *Velazquez*, 531 U.S. at 547–49 (applying heightened scrutiny to hold that a federal statute prohibiting Legal Services Corporation attorneys from challenging the validity of welfare laws violated the First Amendment); *Zauderer*, 471 U.S. at 642–43 (holding that restrictions on attorney advertising and solicitation violated the First Amendment); *In re* R.M.J., 455 U.S. at 206 (same); *In re* Primus, 436 U.S. at 437–40 (same); *Bates*, 433 U.S. at 384 (same); *Button*, 371 U.S. at 437 (applying strict scrutiny to hold that rule prohibiting the NAACP from advising and assisting potential litigants to bring desegregation suits violates the First Amendment).

80 See *Bigelow*, 421 U.S. at 822 ("The advertisement . . . did more than simply propose a commercial transaction. It contained factual material of clear 'public interest'").

As Justice Blackmun explained in his written pre-argument memorandum for a later case, "The emphasis in *Bigelow* was on the public and its right to receive information." Greenhouse, *Becoming Justice Blackmun*, 119.

81 Hunter v. Va. State Bar, 744 S.E.2d 611, 614 (Va. 2013).

82 Ibid.

83 Ibid., 620.

84 Ibid., 617, 622.

85 Ibid., 622 (Lemon, J., dissenting in part).

86 Ibid.

87 Ibid.

88 See Margaret Tarkington, "A First Amendment Theory for Protecting Attorney Speech," *U.C. Davis Law Review* 45 (2011): 27.

89 See Daniel R. Fischel, "Lawyers and Confidentiality," *University of Chicago Law Review* 65 (1998): 1.

90 Ibid.

91 "About," Upsolve, accessed September 1, 2022, https://upsolve.org.

92 Upsolve, Inc. v. James, 22-cv-627 (PAC), 1 (S.D.N.Y. May. 24, 2022).

93 "About," Upsolve, accessed September 1, 2022, https://upsolve.org.

94 Ibid.

95 Ibid.

96 Upsolve, Inc. v. James, 22-cv-627 (PAC), (S.D.N.Y. May. 24, 2022) (quoting Dacey v. New York City Lawyers' Association, 423 F.2d 188, 189 [2d Cir. 1969]) (internal punctuation omitted).

97 Ibid.

98 Thomas A. Berry, "Upsolve Wins the Right to Give Basic Legal Advice," *Cato Institute*, June 1, 2022, www.cato.org.

99 See generally Omri Ben-Shahar and Carl E. Schneider, *More Than You Wanted to Know: The Failure of Mandated Disclosure* (Princeton: Princeton University Press, 2014).

100 See Florencia Marotta-Wurgler, "Will Increased Disclosure Help? Evaluating the Recommendations of the ALI's "Principles of the Law of Software Contracts," *University of Chicago Law Review* 78 (2011): 182.

101 Debra Pogrund Stark and Jessica M. Choplin, "A Cognitive and Social Psychological Analysis of Disclosure Laws and Call for Mortgage Counseling to Prevent Predatory Lending," *Psychology, Public Policy, & Law* 16 (2010): 98.

102 See Lauren E. Willis, "Decision Making and the Limits of Disclosure: The Problem of Predatory Lending: Price," *Maryland Law Review* 65, no. 3 (2006): 712.

103 See 16 C.F.R 255.2(b) (2018) ("An advertisement containing an endorsement relating the experience of one or more consumers on a central or key attribute of the product or service also will likely be interpreted as representing that the endorser's experience is representative of what consumers will generally achieve with the advertised product or service in actual, albeit variable, conditions of use.

Therefore, an advertiser should possess and rely upon adequate substantiation for this representation").

104 See, e.g., Susan Hart and Gillian Hogg, "Relationship Marketing in Corporate Legal Services." *Services Industry Journal* 18 (1998): 67 ("A further contribution of this research relates to the debate over the extent to which customers seek relationships with their suppliers. Our findings suggest that accessibility of the partner to the client is important, along with the partner's involvement with the case.... [T]he personal chemistry and the 'fit' between partner and client are rated of high importance").

105 Thomas A. Berry, "Upsolve Wins the Right to Give Basic Legal Advice," *Cato Institute*, June 1, 2022, www.cato.org.

106 Lahav, *In Praise of Litigation*, 6.

107 Ibid.

8. REGULATORY AND LEGISLATIVE REFORM

1 John Vickers, *Report on Competition in Professions* (Office of Fair Trading, 2000), www.webarchive.nationalarchives.gov.uk.

2 UK Parliament, Legal Services Act, chap. 29, October 30, 2007.

3 Nick Hilborne, "The SRA's First ABS—Still Going Strong, 10 Years On," *Legal Futures*, March 25, 2022, www.legalfutures.com.

4 Ibid.

5 Ibid.

6 See Marialuisa Taddia, "Funders Eye Equity Stakes in UK Law Firms," *Law360*, September 23, 2022, www.law360.com.

7 Hilborne, "The SRA's First ABS."

8 *See* Nick Robinson, "When Lawyers Don't Get All the Profits: Non-Lawyer Ownership, Access, and Professionalism," *Georgetown Journal of Legal Ethics* 21: 5 (2016).

9 Solomon, Rhode, and Wanless, "How Reforming Rule 5.4 Would Benefit Lawyers and Consumers," 10 (citations omitted).

10 Armour, Parnham, and Sako, "Augmented Lawyering," 127.

11 Ibid.

12 Crispin Passmore, "Spotlight on . . . the Impact of the Legal Services Act 2007," *Cost Lawyer Standards Board Newsletter*, January 2021, www.clsb.info.

13 Ibid.

14 Ibid.

15 See Parliament of Victoria, "Legal Profession Act, 2004," Act No. 99/2004, December 13, 2004, www6.austlii.edu.au.

16 Interview by Renee Knake Jefferson with Fiona McLeay, Commissioner, Victorian Legal Services Board, and Jennie Pakula, Manager of Innovation and Consumer Engagement, Victorian Legal Services Board, February 7, 2019.

17 Dubai International Financial Centre, "Sustained Growth for the DIFC Courts as Value of Commercial Claims Surge," Press Release, August 28, 2018, www.difc.ae.

18 See, e.g., Jon McNerney, "How Africa's Courtrooms Became as Advanced as Anywhere in the World," *Artificial Lawyer*, April 5, 2019, www.artificiallawyer.com.

19 Anna Zhang, "Is Singapore the Next Center for Legal Innovation?," *Law.com*, July 5, 2018, www.law.com.

20 "How Courts Embraced Technology, Met the Pandemic Challenge, and Revolutionized Their Operations," *Pew Charitable Trusts*, December 1, 2021, www.pewtrusts.org.

21 Ibid.

22 Ismail Sebugwaawo, "UAE: How Remote Court Hearings Changed Legal Practice," *Khaleej Times*, June 23, 2021, www.khaleejtimes.com.

23 Ibid.

24 Dominic Dudley, "Irish Judges Think Twice About Dubai Court Jobs and Make a Quick Exit," *Forbes*, August 3, 2022, www.forbes.com.

25 Ibid.

26 Staff, "Dubai Courts Revolutionises Its Judicial System With 'C3 Court,'" *Emirates News Agency*, May 1, 2018, www.wam.ae.

27 Ibid.

28 No single comprehensive list of legal services innovations exists, though several entities have created innovation indexes and inventories. See, e.g., "Legal Services Innovation Index," *Legal Tech Innovation*, accessed July 23, 2019, www.legaltechinnovation.com. The ABA Commission on the Future of Legal Services created an online Inventory of Innovations in 2016 that is no longer publicly available. At the time, it listed more than three hundred examples of legal services innovations compiled from public hearings, written testimony, and other submissions. The methodology and further resources section at the end of this book lists additional resources.

29 "About Us," *Hague Institute for Innovation of Law*, accessed February 2, 2022, www.hiil.org.

30 "Our History," *Hague Institute for Innovation of Law*, accessed February 2, 2022, www.hiil.org.

31 "About Us," Institute for the Advancement of the American Legal System, accessed January 15, 2023, www.iaals.du.edu.

32 See Canadian Bar Association, "C.B.A. Legal Futures Initiative, Futures: Transforming the Delivery of Legal Services in Canada," (Ottawa: Canadian Bar Association, 2014), www.cba.org.

33 See ABA Commission, *Report on the Future of Legal Services*; *see also* ABA Center for Innovation, accessed February 4, 2022, www.americanbar.org ("The ABA Center for Innovation is creating more accessible, efficient, and effective legal services in the United States and around the globe. We improve legal services through innovation, education, and collaboration"); Neil Rickman and James M. Anderson, *Innovations in the Provision of Legal Services in the United States* (Santa Monica: RAND Corporation 2011), www.rand.org.

34 "About," ABA Center for Innovation, accessed September 1, 2022, www.americanbar.org.

35 Ibid.
36 "Innovation Trends Report," ABA Center for Innovation, accessed January 25, 2023, www.americanbar.org.
37 "Justice System Metrics," ABA Center for Innovation, accessed January 25, 2023, www.legalinnovationmetrics.info.
38 Ibid.
39 See, e.g., ABA Commission, *Report on the Future of Legal Services*, App. 4 ("State and Local Bar Association Work on Access to Justice and the Future of Legal Services").
40 See State Bar of Michigan, "21st Century Law," accessed January 22, 2023, www.michbar.org.
41 See "Limited License Legal Technician Licensing and Admission," Washington State Bar Association, accessed February 2, 2022, www.wsba.org; Rhode, "Reforming American Legal Education and Legal Practice," 243.
42 Simon et al., "*Lola v. Skadden* and the Automation of the Legal Profession," 265 (footnotes omitted).
43 Lyle Moran, "Washington Supreme Court Sunsets Limited License Program for Nonlawyers," *ABA Journal*, June 8, 2020, www.abajournal.com.
44 Tom Gordon, "Comments to the Washington Supreme Court on Sunset of Limited License Legal Technician (LLLT) Program," *Responsive Law*, April 29, 2021, www.responsivelaw.com.
45 Karen Sloan, "Nonlawyer Licensing Movement Gains Steam with Oregon Approval," *Reuters*, July 20, 2022, www.reuters.com.
46 Talk Justice Podcast, "Mobilizing Non-Lawyers for Limited-Scope Legal Assistance in Alaska," January 17, 2023, www.lsc.org.
47 See Thomas M. Clarke and Rebecca L. Sandefur, "Preliminary Evaluation of the Washington State Limited License Legal Technician Program," March 2017, www.americanbarfoundation.org.
48 Christine Simmons, "Bar Groups Line Up Against Changes to Lawyer Regulation," *Law.com*, February 7, 2020, www.law.com.
49 See Stephanie Francis Ward, "Training for Nonlawyers to Provide Legal Advice Will Start in Arizona in the Fall," *ABA Journal*, February 6, 2020, www.abajournal.com.
50 See Roy Strom, "California Opens Door to More Legal Tech, Non-Lawyer Roles (1)," *Bloomberg Law*, July 2, 2019, www.news.bloomberglaw.com ("California has taken a step towards altering the role of lawyers after a state bar task force last week advanced controversial proposals for new ethics rules that would allow non-lawyers to invest in law firms and tech companies to provide limited legal services").
51 See Zacharia DeMeola, "Florida Joins Growing List of States Testing Legal Regulation Reforms," IAALS Blog, July 13, 2021, www.iaals.du.edu.
52 See Debra Cassens Weiss, "Nonlawyers Could Invest in Law Firms and Own Legal Businesses Under Utah Work Group's Proposal," *ABA Journal*, August 28, 2019, www.abajournal.com.

NOTES

53 Lyle Moran, "Utah Embraces Nonlawyer Ownership of Law Firms as Part of Broad Access-to-Justice Reforms," *ABA Journal*, August 14, 2020, www.abajournal.com.

54 Ibid.

55 Ibid.

56 Ibid.

57 Amy Salyzyn, "What's at Play? Learning About the Design and Impact of Legal Innovation Sandboxes," *The Journal of Things We Like (Lots)*, March 3, 2023, www.legalpro.jotwell.com.

58 Ibid.

59 See Office of Legal Services Innovation, Utah Supreme Court, November 2022, www.utahinnovationoffice.org.

60 Ibid.

61 Logan Cornett and Zachariah DeMeola, "Data from Utah's Sandbox Shows Extraordinary Promise, Refutes Fears of Harm," *IAALS Blog*, September 15, 2021, www.iaals.du.edu.

62 Ibid.

63 Ibid.

64 See Arizona Supreme Court, Administrative Office of the Courts, "Arizona Supreme Court Makes Generational Advance in Access to Justice," News Release, August 27, 2020, www.azcourts.gov.

65 See Arizona Code of Judicial Administration Section 7–209, "Alternative Business Structures," www.azcourts.gov.

66 Engstrom, Ricca, Ambrose, and Walsh, "Legal Innovation After Reform," 6.

67 Ibid.

68 Ibid., 7.

69 Ibid.

70 Ibid.

71 See Claire Newfeld, "Closing the 'Justice Gap': The First Ten Paraprofessionals Receive Licensure in Arizona," *Arizona State Law Journal*, February 3, 2022, www.arizonastatelawjournal.com.

72 Ibid.

73 Debra Cassens Weiss, "Colorado Will License Paraprofessionals to Perform Limited Legal Work," *ABA Journal*, March 30, 2023, www.abajournal.com.

74 Ibid.

75 See Lyle Moran, "Florida Supreme Court Rejects Bar Committee's Reform Proposals, Asks for Alternatives," *ABA Journal*, March 22, 2022, www.abajournal.com.

76 David Freeman Engstrom and Nora Freeman Engstrom, "Why Do Blue States Keep Prioritizing Lawyers over Low-Income Americans?," *Slate*, October 17, 2022, www.slate.com.

77 Ibid.

78 Ibid.

79 Ibid.

80 "Closing the Justice Gap Working Group," *State Bar of California*, accessed January 22, 2023, www.calbar.ca.gov.

81 Hecht, "Twilight Zone," 191.

82 Ibid.

83 American Bar Association House of Delegates, Resolution 115.

84 Ibid.

85 Ibid.

86 Conference of Chief Justices Issues Resolution Urging Regulatory Innovation, IAALS Blog, February 13, 2020, www.iaals.du.edu.

87 "Guiding Principles for Post-Pandemic Court Technology," *National Center for State Courts*, June 16, 2020, www.ncsc.org.

88 "Resolution 1 Encouraging State Courts to Adopt Innovative Practices in High-Volume Dockets," *Conference of Chief Justices and Conference of State Court Administrators*, accessed January 22, 2023, www.ccj.ncsc.org.

89 The term was initially coined by George Beaton in his eBook *New Law New Rules: A Conversation about the Future of the Legal Services Industry* (Melbourne: Beaton, 2013). The book has been described as "in itself an innovation—it is available only on e-readers, and its content is an aggregation of tweets and online postings by commenters on this topic, interspersed with analysis." Williams, Platt, and Lee, "Disruptive Innovation," 6.

90 Thomson Reuters, *Alternative Legal Service Providers 2021: Strong Growth, Mainstream Acceptance, and No Longer an "Alternative"* (Toronto: Thomson Reuters Publishing, 2021).

91 Ibid.

92 Ibid.

93 Ibid., 23.

94 Ibid., 2.

95 See Williams, Platt, and Lee, "Disruptive Innovation."

96 Ibid., 4.

97 Ibid., 5.

98 Jordan Furlong, "An Incomplete Inventory of NewLaw," Law21, May 13, 2014, www.law21.ca.

99 Williams, Platt, and Lee, "Disruptive Innovation," 7n18–19.

100 Bill Henderson, "World Class Innovation and Efficiency, Billed by the Hour (010)," *Legal Evolution*, June 18, 2017, (emphasis omitted), www.legalevolution.org.

101 Ibid.

102 Clio, *Legal Trends Report 2022*, 24.

103 Ibid.

104 Ibid., 28.

105 Nick Dolm, "713 percent Growth: Legal Tech Set an Investment Record in 2018," *Forbes*, January 15, 2019, www.forbes.com.

106 Ibid.

254 | NOTES

107 Debra Cassens Weiss, "Company That Promised to Revolutionize Legal Services Confirms Layoffs of Most of Its Legal Staff," *ABA Journal*, January 14, 2020, www.abajournal.com.

108 See Zach Warren, "LegalZoom Announces $500 Million Investment, Among Largest in Legal Tech History," LegalZoom, July 31, 2018, www.legalzoom.com.

109 See Savannah Dowling, "LegalTech Companies Snap Up $106M in VC During Active January," *Crunchbase*, January 31, 2019, www.news.crunchbase.com.

110 Robert Ambrogi, "At $1.2 Billion, It's Already a Record Year for Legal Tech Investment," *Above the Law*, September 16, 2019, www.abovethelaw.com.

111 Ibid.

112 Ibid.

113 Chris Metinko, "LegalTech Makes Its Case With Venture Capitalists, Tops $1B in Funding This Year," *CrunchBase*, September 23, 2021, www.news.crunchbase.com.

114 See Doug Austin, "Investor Funding is Down in 2022. How Long Will it Stay That Way?," *E-Discovery Today*, July 5, 2022, www.ediscoverytoday.com.

115 See Josh Constine, "Atrium Lays Off Lawyers, Explains Pivot to Legal Tech," *TechCrunch*, January 13, 2020, www.techcrunch.com.

116 "Dear Founders," *Legal Tech Fund*, accessed January 17, 2023, www.legaltechfund.com.

117 "How Courts Embraced Technology, Met the Pandemic Challenge, and Revolutionized Their Operations," *Pew Charitable Trusts*, December 1, 2021, www.pewtrusts.org, 9.

118 Ibid.

119 Ibid., 10.

120 Ibid., 9.

121 Ibid.

122 See, e.g., Perlman, "Towards the Law of Legal Services," 53 ("we can more effectively advance the interests of justice by authorizing people without a law degree to participate in the legal marketplace"); Terry, Mark, and Gordon, "Adopting Regulatory Objectives for the Legal Profession," 2692 ("In addition to the increased interest in regulatory reform theory in general, the regulatory objectives movement has taken place in the context of greater interest in the theory of lawyer regulation").

123 Perlman, "Towards the Law of Legal Services," 51.

124 Ibid.

125 Ibid.

126 "ABA Model Regulatory Objectives for the Provision of Legal Services," American Bar Association House of Delegates Resolution 105, adopted February 8, 2016, www.americanbar.org.

127 Ibid.

128 Ibid.

129 Ibid.

130 See Laurel Terry, "Examples of Regulatory Objectives for the Legal Profession," March 2, 2019, www.works.bepress.com.

131 Arizona Supreme Court Rule 20–0034, adopted August 27, 2020, www.azcourts. gov.

132 Utah Supreme Court Standing Order No. 15, adopted August 31, 2020, www. utcourts.gov.

133 Ibid.

134 Chambliss, "Evidence-Based Lawyer Regulation," 303.

135 Teena Wilhem, Richard L. Vining, Jr., Ethan D. Boldt, and Bryan M. Black. "Judicial Reform in the American States: The Chief Justice as Political Advocate," *State Politics & Policy Quarterly* 20 (2020).

136 McCormack, *Staying Off the Sidelines*, 188.

137 ABA House of Delegates Resolution 112A (2006).

138 Conference of Chief Justices and Conference of State Court Administrators, Resolution 5, "Reaffirming the Commitment to Meaningful Access to Justice for All," adopted 2015, www.ccj.ncsc.org.

139 Eric Cervone, "Bar Reciprocity for Military Spouses," *ABA After the Bar*, accessed December 12, 2022, www.americanbarassociation.org.

140 Marla N. Greenstein, "Judicial Innovations Lead to Inevitable Ethics Questions," *ABA Judges' Journal*, January 1, 2014, www.americanbar.org.

141 Ibid.

142 See "Consulting and Research," *National Center for State Courts*, accessed December 12, 2022, www.ncsc.org.

143 See "Penalty for Persons Who Negligently or Fraudulently Prepare Bankruptcy Petitions," 11 U.S.C § 110, accessed September 1, 2022, www.gpo.gov.

144 See "Bankruptcy Petition Preparer Guidelines," March 1, 2014, www.justice.gov.

145 Deborah L. Rhode, *Enhancing Access to Justice Through Alternative Regulatory Frameworks* (working draft) (citing Herbert Kritzer, *Legal Advocacy: Lawyers and Nonlawyers at Work. Ann Arbor: University of Michigan Press [1998]: 76, 108, 148, 190, 201*).

146 See "Frequently Asked Questions about Legal Document Assistants," *California Association of Legal Document Assistants*, accessed September 1, 2022, www.calda. org; *California Business & Professions Code* § 6400–6456 (1998), www.calda.org.

147 See *Nevada Revised Statutes Annotated* § 240A.030 (West 2014).

148 See "Legal Document Preparers," Arizona Courts, accessed September 1, 2022, www.azcourts.gov.

149 Ibid.

150 Nate Raymond, "Making PACER Court Records System Free Wouldn't Add to Deficit, CBO Says," *Reuters*, January 25, 2023, www.reuters.com. See also Jonah B. Gelbach, "Free PACER," in *Beyond Legal Tech and the Future of Justice*, edited by David Freeman Engstrom. New York: Cambridge University Press (2023): 328–48.

151 Greenstein, "Innovation and Ethics."

256 | NOTES

152 See Turner v. Rogers, 465 U.S. 431 (2011) (holding that Turner, who failed to pay child support, was not entitled to a public defender but that the state was required to provide notice of affirmative defenses, which could have been done with clear information or court forms).
153 Hagan, "Participatory Design," 120.
154 Ibid.

9. EDUCATION FOR THE LEGAL PROFESSION

1 Catherine Rampell, "The Lawyer Surplus State by State," *New York Times*, June 27, 2011, www.nytimes.com.
2 Joe Palazzolo, "Law Grads Face Brutal Job Market," *Wall Street Journal*, June 25, 2012, www.wsj.com.
3 Karen Sloan, "2021 Was the Year Everyone Wanted to Go to Law School," *Reuters*, December 28, 2021, www.reuters.com.
4 American Bar Association, "ABA Legal Education Section Releases Employment Data for Graduating Law Class of 2019," News Release, June 1, 2020, www.americanbar.org.
5 Stephanie Ward, "New Findings Published on Law School Debt," *ABA Journal*, September 21, 2021, www.abajournal.com.
6 Capers, "Law School as a White Space," 41.
7 Ibid.
8 Ballakrishnen, "Law School as a Straight Space," 1118.
9 See, e.g., Ethan Bronner, "A Call for Drastic Changes in Educating New Lawyers," *New York Times*, February 12, 2013, www.nytimes.com; Ethan Bronner, "Law Schools' Applications Fall as Costs Rise and Jobs Are Cut," *New York Times*, January 31, 2013, www.nytimes.com; Ethan Bronner, "To Place Graduates, Law Schools are Opening Firms," *New York Times*, March 8, 2013, www.nytimes.com, www.nytimes.com.
10 See, e.g., Morgan, *Vanishing American Lawyer*; Susskind, *End of Lawyers?*; Susskind, *Tomorrow's Lawyers*; Tamanaha, *Failing Law Schools*; Paul Caron, "The Future of Legal Education," *Iowa Law Review Symposium* 96 (2011): 1449; "ABA Task Force on the Future of Legal Education," American Bar Association, accessed January 14, 2022, www.americanbar.org; "Conference on the Future of the Law School Curriculum," Association of American Law Schools, June 11–14, 2011, www.aals.org.
11 Morgan, *Vanishing American Lawyer*.
12 Tamanaha, *Failing Law Schools*.
13 Lincoln Caplan, "An Existential Crisis for Law Schools," *New York Times*, SR10, July 15, 2012, www.nytimes.com.
14 Chambliss, "It's Not About Us," 1.
15 Ibid., (emphasis added; citations omitted).
16 Ibid.
17 Neither Apple cofounder and former CEO Steve Jobs, nor Facebook creator and CEO Mark Zuckerberg, graduated from college. See Colleen Mastony, "Steve

Jobs Isn't the Only Successful College Dropout," *Chicago Tribune*, August 27, 2011, www.articles.chicagotribune.com; Mark Smithers, "Dropping Out and Dropping In—Steve Jobs and Higher Education," *Rssing.com*, October 8, 2011, www.smithers87.rssing.com.

18 For a list of American law schools, see Professor Dan Linna's "Law School Innovation Index," *Legal Services Innovation Index*, accessed February 2, 2022, www.legaltechinnovation.com (identifying 40 schools of approximately 230 in the United States). For a list of Australian law schools, see Andrea Perry-Peterson and Michael Lacey, *"Legal Innovation" Education Courses in Australian Law Schools* (2018), accessed February 2, 2022, www.andreaperrypetersen.com.au.

19 Abby Young-Powell, "More Universities Are Teaching Lawtech—But Is it Just a Gimmick?," *Guardian*, April 12, 2019, www.theguardian.com ("Eager to be ahead of the curve, universities have started to offer specialist modules on the subject. But is it all a load of hype?").

20 See, e.g., Webb, "Regulating Lawyers in a Liberalized Legal Services Market," 569 ("If the LSA 2007 changes are to achieve their regulatory objectives, education has a potentially key role to play, in building and sustaining competence, in developing legal values and ethical infrastructure, and in fostering innovation. To do that, however, may require a radical rethink of at least some features of the education and training regime").

21 Minow, "Marking 200 Years of Legal Education," 2280.

22 See Eilene Zimmerman, "More Lawyers Skip the Partner Track to Be Entrepreneurs," *New York Times*, B5, November 24, 2011 (reporting on a pair of big firm lawyers who decided to launch their own firm for lifestyle reasons, and on the rising number of young lawyers who have lost work or have been unable to find it due to the economic recession and who reacted by taking more risks, including starting their own firms).

23 See ibid.

24 Brynjolfsson and McAfee, *Race Against the Machine*, 56 (emphasis added).

25 Ibid.

26 Ibid.

27 Ibid.

28 Saffer, *Designing for Interaction*, 220.

29 "Overview," *Stanford Center for Legal Informatics*, accessed April 13, 2022, www.law.stanford.edu.

30 "The Law Lab," Berkman Klein Center for Internet and Society at Harvard University, accessed August 19, 2022, www.cyber.harvard.edu.

31 "About," Laws Without Walls, accessed August 19, 2022, www.lawwithoutwalls.org. I had the privilege of participating in LawWithoutWalls—founded by Michele DeStefano—as an academic mentor from 2011 to 2013, where I advised students on "Projects of Worth" that resulted in proposals for a curriculum on emotional intelligence training and a mobile phone app for women lawyers to facilitate networking.

258 | NOTES

32 Course description, Technology, Innovation, and Law Practice, taught by Tanina Rostain and Roger Skalbeck, accessed April 13, 2022, www.law.georgetown.edu.

33 Ibid.

34 "How Courts Embraced Technology, Met the Pandemic Challenge, and Revolutionized Their Operations," *Pew Charitable Trusts*, December 1, 2021, www.pewtrusts.org, 35–36.

35 John Schwartz, "This Is Law School?" *New York Times*, August 1, 2014, www.nytimes.com.

36 "The Richmond Legal Business Design Hub," University of Richmond Law School, accessed January 14, 2023, www.law.richmond.edu.

37 "Law School Innovation Program," *Bloomberg Law*, accessed January 14, 2023, www.bloomberglaw.com.

38 "Directory of Law School Innovation Centers," *Above the Law*, accessed January 14, 2023, www.abovethelaw.com.

39 See "Mission," Institute for the Future of Law Practice, accessed April 13, 2022, www.futurelawpractice.org

40 "Conceptual Frameworks/Models, Guiding Values and Principles," National Centre of Cultural Competence, accessed September 1, 2022, www.nccc.georgetown.edu.

41 Annette Demers, "Cultural Competence and the Legal Profession: An Annotated Bibliography of Materials Published Between 2000 and 2011," *International Journal of Legal Information* (2011): 22, 24.

42 Tully, "Cultural (Re)Turn," 234.

43 Ibid.

44 Ibid.

45 Ibid.

46 Ibid.

47 See, e.g., "Embracing Leadership Development in Legal Education," *Law School Admission Council*, March 27, 2019, www.lsac.org ("Until relatively recently, though, most law programs did not specifically include leadership development as part of their curriculum").

48 See, e.g., Neil S. Siegel, "After the Trump Era: A Constitutional Role Morality for Presidents and Members of Congress," *Georgetown Law Journal* 107, no. 1 (2018): 109, 161 (discussing "a variety of potentially fruitful ways for law professors to theorize and teach about the role restraints, or lack thereof, that attach to political office").

49 See "Section on Leadership," *Association of American Law Schools*, www.aals.org.

50 See, e.g., Robert A. Gorman, "Proposals for Reform of Legal Education," *University of Pennsylvania Law Review* 119 (1971): 849 ("Unless legal education is drastically revamped to make the third year progressively illuminating and challenging, . . . I am convinced that law school could end after two years with no perceptible loss to students or the profession"); David F. Cavers, "Restructuring Law School Education into a Two-Calendar-Year Format Would Provide Both Educational and Financial Advantages," *American Bar Association Journal* 66 (1980): 973

(renewing his doubts about the three-year degree "first expressed in . . . 1963" and proposing a two-calendar-year curriculum as a response to "the great increase in law school applications" and "the great inflation in law school student costs and in beginning lawyers' earnings").

51 See "Early History of Columbia College Law School," *Columbia Law School Library*, accessed January 13, 2021, www.law.columbia.edu (an advertisement from 1860 announced a "course of study occup[ying] two collegiate years" for obtaining a "degree of L.L.B." at the law school).

52 Hazel Weiser, "More History of the Regulation of Legal Education So That We Understand Where We Are and How We Got Here," *SaltLaw Blog*, November 3, 2011, www.saltlaw.org.

53 "Accelerated J.D. Program," *University of Dayton School of Law*, accessed March 20, 2022, www.udayton.edu.

54 Estreicher, "Roosevelt-Cardozo Way," 610.

55 *See* John Johnson, "Obama: Make Law School Two Years, Not Three," *USA Today*, August 24, 2013, www.usatoday.com.

56 Ibid.

57 Kristina Dell, "Fast-Tracking Law School," *Time*, July 23, 2008, www.time.com.

58 Markovic, "Protecting the Guild," 163.

59 Ibid.

60 Ibid.

61 See Patricia E. Salkin, *May It Please the Campus: Lawyers Leading Higher Education*. New York: Touro University Press (2022): 27–28n72.

62 Adediran, "Racial Allies," 2153.

63 Ibid.

64 Howarth, *Shaping the Bar*, 99.

65 Ibid., 100.

66 See "Uniform Bar Examination," National Conference of Bar Examiners, accessed January 8, 2023, www.ncbex.org.

10. EDUCATION FOR THE PUBLIC

1 See "What Is Big Data?," IBM, accessed January 14, 2022, www-01.ibm.com.

2 See, e.g., Hon. Marcia S. Krieger, "A Twenty-First Century Ethos for the Legal Profession: Why Bother?," *Denver University Law Review* 86 (2009): 878–79 (stating that distrust of lawyers "is not at all surprising given the steady drumbeat of scandals involving . . . lawyers and judges"); Rachel M. Zahorsky, "It's Not Just Money Fears Blocking Access to Legal Help; Lawyer Distrust Is Growing," *ABA Journal*, December 1, 2012, www.abajournal.com ("Distrust of the private bar stands near the top of the list for many would-be clients . . .").

3 See ABA Model Rule 2.1 ("In representing a client, a lawyer shall exercise independent professional judgment and render candid advice"); ABA Model Rule 1.4(b) ("A lawyer shall explain a matter to the extent reasonably necessary to permit the client to make informed decisions regarding the representation").

4 ABA Model Rules, Preamble (6) (emphasis added).
5 ABA Model Rule 7.2, Comment 1.
6 ABA Model Code of Professional Responsibility, Ethical Consideration 2–1 (1969).
7 *Bates*, 433 U.S. at 358 (quoting *In re* Bates, 555 P.2d 640, 648 [Ariz. 1976] [Holohan, J., dissenting]).
8 See, e.g., Sandefur and Smyth, *Access Across America* ("States differ substantially in the resources available to support civil legal assistance, in the kinds of services that are available, and in the groups served by existing programs. Little coordination exists for civil legal assistance, and existing mechanisms of coordination often have powers only of exhortation and consultation. Thus, in most states, the public's civil legal needs are not routinely assessed and no entity can ensure that services in specific areas match the needs of the eligible populations in those areas").
9 Alexander, "Law-Related Education," 57.
10 Ibid.
11 Ibid., 97.
12 Kavanagh and Chorak, "Teaching Law as a Life Skill," 72.
13 Kamina A. Pinder, "Street Law: Twenty-Five Years and Counting," *Journal of Law & Education* 27 (1998): 232–33.
14 Kavanagh and Chorak, "Teaching Law as a Life Skill," 72.
15 Ibid., 73.
16 Ibid. (emphasis in original).
17 Ibid.
18 Ibid.
19 See "Directory of Registered Law School-Based Street Law Programs," StreetLaw, accessed December 29, 2022, www.streetlaw.org (listing more than two hundred registered schools).
20 "About Justice Teaching," Justice Teaching, accessed January 13, 2022, www.justice-teaching.org.
21 "The Marshall–Brennan Constitutional Literacy Project," American University Washington College of Law, accessed January 13, 2022, www.wcl.american.edu.
22 "Legal Bound," New York County District Attorney's Office, accessed January 7, 2013, www.manhattanda.org.
23 "High School Law Institute," New York University Law, accessed January 7, 2013, www.law.nyu.edu.
24 "Classroom Law Project," Classroom Law Project: Teaching Youth Participation in Democracy, accessed January 6, 2013, www.classroomlaw.org.
25 See "About," *iCivics*, www.icivics.org ("iCivics works to ensure every student in America receives a quality and engaging civic education and graduates from high school well prepared and enthusiastic for citizenship. [. . .] Today, more than 145,000 teachers and 9 million+ students in all 50 states utilize iCivics' innovative and free online resources").

NOTES | 261

26 See "Iconic Women in Legal History," *Texas Young Lawyers Association*, www.tyla. org.

27 See also Neil S. Siegel, "After the Trump Era: A Constitutional Role Morality for Presidents and Members of Congress," *Georgetown Law Journal* 107, no. 1 (2018): 173 (advocating for "newer forms of civic education and law teaching" to combat "the aggressive ideological agendas that politicians pursue").

28 Delaney Ramirez, "The People's Law School Now Solely Online," *Daily Cougar*, October 9, 2019, www.thedailycougar.com.

29 Amy Kincheloe, "Richard Alderman: A Lawyer for All People," *Texas Bar Journal* (2002): 912.

30 Julia Coffman, *Public Communication Campaign Evaluation: An Environmental Scan of Challenges, Criticisms, Practice, and Opportunities* (Harvard Family Research Project, 2002), 2.

31 Ibid.

32 Pink, *To Sell Is Human*, 3.

33 Ibid., 6.

34 Llewellyn, "The Bar's Troubles, and Poultices—and Cures?," 115 (emphasis in original).

35 Susskind, *End of Lawyers?*, 238–39.

36 Ibid., 239.

37 Ibid.

38 Ibid.

39 Rhode, *Access to Justice*, 391. See also Rhode, "Access to Justice: Connecting Principles to Practice," 402.

40 Rhode, "Whatever Happened to Access to Justice?," 908.

41 See "'How a Lawyer Can Help You' Statewide Public Education Campaign," Pennsylvania Bar Association, accessed February 6, 2013, www.pabar.org (describing purpose of campaign as to highlight "the importance of contacting a lawyer to ensure that [citizens'] rights are protected").

42 See "Public Education Campaign," Virginia State Bar, accessed February 6, 2013, www.vsb.org (indicating purpose of campaign as to "raise awareness of the value of the legal profession to the citizens of Virginia").

43 Ibid.

44 Ibid.

45 Ibid.

46 Ibid. ("The committee is considering developing the print ads into radio and/or TV spots, subject to available funding").

47 "K-12 Youth Education," American Bar Association, accessed February 6, 2013, www.americanbar.org.

48 See, e.g., *AALS Equal Justice Project, Pursuing Equal Justice: Law Schools and the Provision of Legal Services* (Washington, DC: Association of American Law Schools, 2002), 32–33.

49 See Rhode, "Public Interest Law," 2048.

50 Janet A. Weiss and Mary Tschirhart, "Public Information Campaigns as Policy Instruments." *Journal Policy Analysis & Management* 13, no. 1 (1994): 83.

51 Ibid., 99.

52 Whitney Randolph and K. Viswanath, "Lessons Learned from Public Health Mass Media Campaigns: Marketing Health in a Crowded Media World," *Annual Review of Public Health* 25, no. 1 (2004): 433.

53 Rhea K. Farberman, "Public Attitudes About Psychologists and Mental Health Care: Research to Guide the American Psychological Association Public Education Campaign," *Professional Psychology: Research & Practice* 28, no. 2 (1997): 128.

54 Ibid., 128 (internal quotation marks omitted).

55 Ibid.

56 Ibid., 135.

57 Ibid.

58 US Department of Labor, Bureau of Labor Statistics, "Charting the Projections: 2012–22," *Occupational Outlook Quarterly* 57 (2013): 10.

59 American Psychological Association, *A Summary of Psychologist Workforce Projections: Addressing Supply and Demand from 2015–2030* (Washington, DC: American Psychological Association, 2018).

60 Jay A. Winsten and William DeJong, "The Designated Driver Campaign," in *Public Communication Campaigns*, ed. Ronald E. Rice and Charles K. Atkin (Newbury Park: Sage Publications, 2001), 290.

61 Ibid., 290.

62 Ibid., 291.

63 Ibid., 292.

64 Rebecca L. Sandefur, Alice Chang, Taemesha Hyder, Sajid Khurram, Elizabeth Prete, Matthew Schneider, and Noah Tate, "Legal Tech for Non-Lawyers: Report of the Survey of US Legal Technologies," *American Bar Foundation* 3 (2019), www.americanbarfoundation.org.

65 Ibid.

66 Ibid.

67 Ibid.

68 "Our Vision," Coursera, accessed September 1, 2022, www.coursera.org.

69 Ibid.

70 American Bar Association Standing Committee on the Delivery of Legal Services, "Perspectives on Finding Personal Legal Services: The Results of a Public Opinion Poll," *American Bar Association* (2011), 28.

71 Ibid.

72 Landsman, "Growing Challenge of Pro Se Litigation," 449.

73 American Bar Association Standing Committee on the Delivery of Legal Services, "Perspectives on Finding Personal Legal Services," 28.

74 Judicial Council of California, "Background, Policy, and Services of the Child Support Commissioner and Family Law Facilitator Program," accessed September 1, 2022, www.courts.ca.gov.

75 See *Washington State Court Rules: General Rules,* "GR 27; Courthouse Facilitators," (2002), www.courts.wa.gov.

76 Thomas George and Wei Wang, *Washington's Courthouse Facilitator Programs for Self-Represented Litigants in Family Law Cases: Summary Report* (2008), www.courts.wa.gov.

77 Ibid.

78 Ibid.

79 See "Court Navigator Program," New York Courts, accessed September 1, 2022, www.courts.state.ny.us.

80 "Roles Beyond Lawyers: Evaluation of the New York City Court Navigators Program," Self-Represented Litigation Network, June 21, 2017, www.srln.org.

81 Ibid.

82 Arizona Commission on Access to Justice, *Arizona Commission on Access to Justice Report to the Arizona Judicial Council,* March 26, 2015, www.azcourts.gov.

83 See generally Sandefur and Smyth, *Access Across America* (documenting both nationally and by state whether and how individuals access free civil legal information, advice, or representation).

84 Louis M. Brown, "Lawyering Through Life—the Origin of Preventive Life," *Journal of the Legal Profession* (1986): 134–36 (footnotes omitted).

85 *Bates,* 433 U.S. at 375.

11. ETHICAL INNOVATION

1 See Michael O'Bryan, "Innovation: The Most Important and Overused Word in America," *Wired,* July 1, 2019, www.wired.com; Laura Bliss, "How 'Maintainers,' Not 'Innovators,' Make the World Turn," *Bloomberg City Lab,* April 8, 2016, www.citylab.com (noting "that the word 'innovation' is overused to the point of meaninglessness—and worse, that it can obfuscate the bleak realities of the status quo").

2 See Michele DeStefano, "The Law Firm Chief Innovation Officer: Goals, Roles and Holes (Parts 1 & 2)," *Globe Law & Business,* October 2018 (discussing interviews conducted with more than one hundred heads of innovation in law firms and legal departments).

3 See "Innovation Doesn't Magically Happen: Why Reed Smith's Innovation Hours Programme Should Be Applauded," *Legal IT Insider,* May 16, 2018, www.legaltechnology.com.

4 "Are Incubators Only for Big Law? Austrian Firms Show Collaboration Is the Answer," *Artificial Lawyer Blog,* July 3, 2019, www.artificiallawyer.com ("Most people assume that legal tech incubators and accelerators are only for larger law firms. But, a group of seven Austrian law firms, most with less than 100 lawyers, took a different approach and pooled their resources to create a new shared Legal Tech Hub in Vienna that has just completed its first incubator cohort . . . The founding members believed that the legal field is ready for change. They wanted to redesign

264 | NOTES

legal advice by joining forces to move forward the whole legal market to enhance services for their clients").

5 Interview by Renee Knake Jefferson with Kate Fazio, Head of Innovation and Engagement, Justice Connect, Melbourne, Victoria, Australia, May 10, 2019.

6 Global Legal Hackathon, accessed December 5, 2018, www.globallegalhackathon.com.

7 See Greg Satell, "Having Conquered Chess and Jeopardy!, IBM Takes on Humans in Debate," *Inc.*, August 4, 2018, www.inc.com.

8 See Jamie Condliffe, "AI Has Beaten Humans at Lip-Reading," *MIT Technology Review*, November 21, 2016, www.technologyreview.com.

9 Ibid.

10 See Jaclyn Peiser, "The Rise of the Robot Reporter," *New York Times*, February 5, 2019, www.nytimes.com.

11 See, e.g., Nitasha Tiku, "ACLU Says Facebook Ads Let Employers Favor Men over Women," *Wired*, September 18, 2018, www.wired.com.

12 See, e.g., James Vincent, "Twitter Taught Microsoft's AI Chatbot to Be a Racist Asshole in Less Than a Day," *Verge*, March 24, 2016, www.theverge.com.

13 See, e.g., Nathaniel Mott, "Meta's Latest AI Can Instantly Translate 200 Languages," *PC Mag*, July 6, 2022, www.pcmag.com.

14 See Choi et al., "ChatGPT Goes to Law School," 1.

15 Debra Cassens Weiss, "Latest Version of ChatGPT Aces Bar Exam With Score Nearing 90th Percentile," *ABA Journal*, March 16, 2023, www.abajournal.com; Eric Martinez, "Re-Evaluating GPT-4's Bar Exam Performance," May 8, 2023, www.ssrn.org.

16 See Julia Jacobs, "Doctor on Video Screen Told a Man He was Near Death, Leaving Relatives Aghast," *New York Times*, March 9, 2019, www.nytimes.com.

17 See Jennifer B. McCormick, Michael J. Green, and Daniel Shapiro, "Medication Nonadherence: There's an App for That!," *Mayo Clinic Proceedings*, October 2018, www.mayoclinicproceedings.org.

18 See Dave Muoio, "Researchers Adding AI, Medication Reminders to Companion Robots for Seniors," *MobiHealth News*, November 6, 2017, www.mobihealthnews.com ("Brown University researchers have announced a partnership with Hasbro to add medication reminders, basic artificial intelligence, and other capabilities to the toymaker's Joy for All Companion Pets, a collection of animatronic cats and dogs intended to relieve loneliness and improve mental health among older adults").

19 See, e.g., Joe Dysart, "A New View of Review: Predictive Coding Vows to Cut E-Discovery Drudgery," *ABA Journal*, October 1, 2011, www.abajournal.com ("Research has shown that, under the best circumstances, manual review will identify about 70 percent of the responsive documents in a large data collection. Some technology-assisted approaches have been shown to perform at least as well as that, if not better, at far less cost"); see also Thomas McMullan, "A.I. Judges: The Future of Justice Hangs in the Balance," *Medium*, February 14, 2019, www.medium.com.

20 Brescia, "Law and Social Innovation," 244.

21 Susskind, *Future of Law*, xxx.

22 Cade Metz, "Seeking Ground Rules for A.I.," *New York Times*, March 1, 2019, www.nytimes.com.

23 Elkin-Koren and Gal, "Chilling Effect," 405.

24 Ibid.

25 Ibid.

26 Ibid., 406; see also Jeremy Kun, "Big Data Algorithms Can Discriminate, and it's Not Clear What to Do About It," *Conversation*, August 13, 2015, www.theconversation.com.

27 Barocas and Selbst, "Big Data's Disparate Impact," 673.

28 Ibid.

29 Armour, Parnham, and Sako, "Augmented Lawyering," 131.

30 Ibid.

31 Ibid., 132.

32 Ibid.

33 Ibid.

34 Ibid.

35 Ibid.

36 Ibid., 133.

37 Executive Office of the President of the United States, *Big Data: Seizing Opportunities, Preserving Values* (2014), accessed February 2, 2022, www.obamawhitehouse.archives.gov.

38 Ibid.

39 See Anthony Cuthbertson and Emily Shugerman, "Twitter and Facebook Executives Testify Before Congress—as It Happened," *Independent*, September 5, 2018, www.independent.co.uk.

40 Katyal, "Private Accountability in the Age of Artificial Intelligence," 61.

41 Ibid.

42 Ibid., 54.

43 Ibid.

44 Ibid., 109.

45 Metz, "Seeking Ground Rules for A.I." Leaders of the groups ranged from academics to corporate representatives to venture capitalists to policy makers.

46 Ibid.

47 American Bar Association House of Delegates, Resolution 112.

48 Cruz, "Coding for Competency," 401.

49 Ibid.

50 See, e.g., Lippman, "Judiciary as the Leader of the Access-to-Justice Revolution," 1574–75 ("Momentum has been building around the country. The Conference of Chief Justices and the Conference of State Court Administrators have urged the nation's top judges to take a leadership role in their respective jurisdictions to prevent denials of access to justice.") (internal citation and quotation omitted).

51 Ibid., 1572.

52 Ibid., 1575 (citing examples of innovations in "Texas, under the leadership of its Chief Justice Wallace B. Jefferson, . . . Connecticut's Chief Judge Chase T. Rogers[,] . . . the State of Washington's Supreme Court . . . [and] Chief Justice Stuart Rabner in New Jersey").

53 Ibid.

54 Marla N. Greenstein, "Innovation and Ethics," *ABA Judges' Journal*, January 1, 2015, www.americanbar.org.

55 See, e.g., "Russia-Backed Facebook Posts 'Reached 126m Americans' During US Election," *Guardian*, October 30, 2017, www.theguardian.com; see also Danielle Kurtzleben, "Did Fake News on Facebook Help Elect Trump? Here's What We Know," *National Public Radio*, April 11, 2018, www.npr.org; Alex Ward, "4 Main Takeaways from New Reports on Russia's 2016 Election Interference," *Vox*, December 17, 2018, www.vox.com.

56 See, e.g., Chesney and Citron, "Deep Fakes," 1753.

57 See, e.g., Charles M. Blow, "A Lie by Any Other Name," *New York Times*, January 26, 2017, www.nytimes.com.

58 Volokh, "Chief Justice Robots," 1135.

59 Remus and Levy, "Can Robots Be Lawyers?," 556.

60 Remus, "Uncertain Promise of Predictive Coding," 1691.

61 Huq, "Right to a Human Decision," 619, 650–51.

62 Tom Dreyfus, "How the Legal Industry, Law Firms, and Josef Are Adapting to the New World," *Josef Blog*, April 14, 2020, www.joseflegal.com.

63 Lyle Moran, "Will the COVID-19 Pandemic Fundamentally Remake the Legal Industry?," *ABA Journal*, August 1, 2020, www.abajournal.com.

64 Ibid.

65 See, e.g., ABA Commission, *Report on the Future of Legal Services*, app. 2 ("Commission Work Plan and Methodology") (listing bar associations' commissions, reports, and other initiatives related to innovation).

66 ABA Model Rules, Preamble 1.

67 ABA Model Rules, Preamble 6.

68 See generally Greiner, "New Legal Empiricism and Its Application to Access-to-Justice Inquiries," 64.

69 Other measures include (1) "Legal Services Innovation Index," *Legal Services Innovation Index*, www.legaltechinnovation.com; (2) Susan Urahn, "The Modernization Our Civil Legal System Needs," Pew, November 6, 2018, www.pewtrusts.org; and (3) "Supporting Justice Innovations," Hague Institute for Innovation of Law, accessed February 2, 2022, www.hiil.org.

70 ABA Model Rule 1.1, Comment 8 (compare to original text: "[8] To maintain the requisite knowledge and skill, a lawyer should keep abreast of changes in the law, including the benefits and risks associated with relevant technology . . .").

71 See Rhonda Wood, Bridget McCormack, and Beth Walker, "Episode 16: Equal Access to Justice," *Lady Justice: Women of the Court Podcast*, April 18, 2022, www.ladyjustice.podbean.com.

72 Simon et al., "*Lola v. Skadden* and the Automation of the Legal Profession," 301.
73 Ibid.
74 "Our Mission," Justice Technology Association, accessed January 15, 2023, www.justicetechassociation.org.
75 Ibid.
76 Katsch, *Digital Justice*, 3.
77 Susskind, *Online Courts*, 67–69.
78 Ibid., 70.
79 Ibid.

12. THE WAY FORWARD

1 "How Courts Embraced Technology, Met the Pandemic Challenge, and Revolutionized Their Operations," *Pew Charitable Trusts*, December 1, 2021, www.pewtrusts.org.
2 Chambliss, "Evidence-Based Regulation," 302.
3 Ibid.
4 Legal Services Corporation, "Executive Summary," *The Justice Gap: The Unmet Civil Legal Needs of Low-Income Americans (2022)*, section 6, www.justicegap.lsc.gov.
5 Chief Justice Wallace B. Jefferson and Justice Nathan L. Hecht Letter to Texas State Senator Royce West, June 1, 2011.
6 Grant, *Think Again*, 76.
7 Tom Gordon, "Expanded Grassroots Support Needed to Move US Regulatory Reform Needle," *Passmore Consulting Blog*, August 29, 2022, www.passmoreconsulting.co.uk.
8 See "Commission on the Practice of Democratic Citizenship," American Academy of Arts and Sciences, accessed January 10, 2023, www.amacad.org.
9 Brian Fitzpatrick and Mary Gay Scanlon, "It's Time for Congress to Step Up Funding for the Legal Services Corporation," *Hill*, February 15, 2022, www.thehill.com.
10 Ibid.
11 Hadfield and Heine, "Life in the Law-Thick World," 21–22.
12 See, e.g., Katherine Hurley, Marcia Chong Rosado, Matt Zieger, Ben Wrobel, and Rustin Finkler, "Justice Tech for All: How Technology Can Ethically Disrupt the US Justice System," (Village Capital and American Family Insurance Institute for Corporate and Social Impact, March 2021), 4.
13 Sandefur, "What We Know," 444.
14 Grant, *Think Again*, 257.
15 Ibid.
16 Ibid.

BIBLIOGRAPHY

44 Liquormart v. Rhode Island, 517 U.S. 484 (1996).

American Bar Association Commission on the Future of Legal Services. *Report on the Future of Legal Services in the United States.* American Bar Association, 2016.

Abrams v. United States, 250 U.S. 616 (1919).

Adediran, Atinuke O. "Racial Allies." *Fordham Law Review* 90, no. 5 (2022): 2151–219.

———. "The Relational Costs of Free Legal Services." *Harvard Civil Rights-Civil Liberties Law Review* 55 (2020): 357–407.

Agrast, Mark, Juan Botero, Joel Martinez, Alejandro Ponce, and Christine Pratt. *World Justice Project Rule of Law Index 2021.* The World Justice Project, 2021.

Agrast, Mark, Juan Botero, and Alejandro Ponce. *World Justice Project Rule of Law Index 2022.* The World Justice Project, 2022.

Alexander, Mark C. "Law-Related Education: Hope for Today's Students." *Ohio Northern University Law Review* 20, no. 1 (1993–1994): 57–98.

Alexander, Michelle. *The New Jim Crow: Mass Incarceration in the Age of Colorblindness.* New York: New Press, 2010.

Andrews, Thomas R. "Nonlawyers in the Business of Law: Does the One Who Has the Gold Really Make the Rules?" *Hastings Law Journal* 40, no. 1 (1989): 577–656.

Areeda, Phillip E. and Herbert Hovenkamp. *Antitrust Law: An Analysis of Antitrust Principles and Their Application.* Philadelphia: Wolters Kluwer Law & Business, 2006.

Armour, John, Richard Parnham, and Mari Sako. "Augmented Lawyering." *University of Illinois Law Review* 2022, no. 1 (2022): 71–138.

Ballakrishnen, Swethaa S. "Law School as Straight Space." *Fordham Law Review* 91, no. 4 (2023): 1113–38.

Barocas, Solon, and Andrew D. Selbst. "Big Data's Disparate Impact." *California Law Review* 104, no. 3 (2016): 671–732.

Barton, Benjamin. "The ABA, the Rules, and Professionalism: The Mechanics of Self-Defeat and a Call for a Return to the Ethical, Moral, and Practical Approach of the Canons." *North Carolina Law Review* 83, no. 2 (2005): 411–80.

———. *Fixing Law Schools: From Collapse to the Trump Bump and Beyond.* New York: NYU Press, 2019.

———. "An Institutional Analysis of Lawyer Regulation: Who Should Control Lawyer Regulation-Courts, Legislatures, or the Market?" *Georgia Law Review* 37, no. 4 (2003): 1167–250.

BIBLIOGRAPHY

Bates v. State Bar of Arizona, 433 U.S. 350 (1977).

Baxter, Ralph. "Dereliction of Duty: State-Bar Inaction in Response to America's Access-to-Justice Crisis." *Yale Law Journal Forum*, no. 132 (2022): 228–58.

Bernabe, Alberto. "Justice Gap vs. Core Values: The Common Themes in the Innovation Debate." *Journal of the Legal Profession* 41, no. 1 (2016): 1–18.

Bigelow v. Virginia, 421 U.S. 809 (1975).

Boumil, Marcia M., Debbie F. Feitas, Cristina F. Feitas. "Multidisciplinary Representation of Patients: The Potential for Ethical Issues and Professional Duty Conflicts in the Medical-Legal Partnership Model." *Journal of Health Care Law & Policy* 13, no. 1 (2010): 107–38.

Brescia, Raymond H. "Law and Social Innovation: Lawyering in the Conceptual Age." *Albany Law Review* 80, no. 1 (2016): 235-310.

Brotherhood of Railroad Trainmen v. Virginia ex rel. Virginia State Bar, 377 U.S. 1 (1964).

Brynjolfsson, Erik, and Andrew McAfee. *Race Against the Machine: How the Digital Revolution Is Accelerating Innovation, Driving Productivity, and Irreversibly Transforming Employment and the Economy.* Lexington, MA: Digital Frontier Press, 2011.

Capers, Bennett. "The Law School as a White Space." *Minnesota Law Review* 106, no. 1 (2021): 7-57.

Central Hudson Gas & Electric Corporation v. Public Service Commission of New York, 447 U.S. 557 (1980).

Chambliss, Elizabeth. "Evidence-Based Lawyer Regulation." *Washington University Law Review* 97, no. 2 (2019): 297–350.

———. "It's Not About Us: Beyond the Job Market Critique of U.S. Law Schools." *Georgetown Journal of Legal Ethics* 26, no. 1 (2013): 423–42.

Cheatham, Elliot E. "A Lawyer When Needed: Legal Services for the Middle Classes." *Columbia Law Review* 63, no. 6 (1963): 973–86.

Chesney, Bobby, and Danielle Citron. "Deep Fakes: A Looming Challenge for Privacy, Democracy, and National Security." *California Law Review* 107, no. 6 (2019): 1753–819.

Cho, Jeena and Karen Gifford, *The Anxious Lawyer: An 8-Week Guide to a Joyful and Satisfying Law Practice Through Mindfulness and Meditation.* Chicago: Ankerwycke, 2016.

Choi, Jonathan H., Kristin E. Hickman, Amy B. Monahan, and Daniel Schwarcz. "ChatGPT Goes to Law School." *Social Science Research Network (SSRN)* (2023).

Christensen, Barlow F. "The Unauthorized Practice of Law: Do Good Fences Really Make Good Neighbors—Or Even Good Sense?" *American Bar Foundation Research Journal* 5, no. 2 (1980): 159–216.

Christensen, Clayton. *The Innovator's Dilemma: When New Technologies Cause Great Firms to Fail.* Boston, MA: Harvard Business Review Press, 1997.

———. "Will Disruptive Innovations Cure Health Care?" *Harvard Business Review*, (September–October 2000).

Cialdini, Robert B. *Influence: The Psychology of Persuasion.* New York: HarperCollins Publishers, 2007.

Citizens United v. FEC, 558 U.S. 310 (2010).

Cooter, Robert D., and Hans-Bernd Schafer. *Solomon's Knot: How Law Can End the Poverty of Nations.* Princeton: Princeton University Press, 2012.

Cruz, Sherley. "Coding for Competency: Expanding Access to Justice with Technology." *University of Tennessee Law Review* 86, no. 2 (2019): 347–402.

Davis, Martha F. "Race and Civil Counsel in the United States: A Human Rights Progress Report." *Syracuse Law Review* 64, no. 3 (2014): 447–768.

Dobbs v. Jackson Women's Health Organization, 142 S. Ct. 2228 (2022).

Edenfield v. Fane, 507 U.S. 761 (1993).

Edlin, Aaron, and Rebecca Haw. "Cartels by Another Name: Should Licensed Occupations Face Antitrust Scrutiny?" *University of Pennsylvania Law Review* 162, no. 5 (2014): 1093–164.

Elkin-Koren, Niva, and Michal S. Gal. "The Chilling Effect of Governance-by-Data on Data Markets." *University of Chicago Law Review* 86, no. 2 (2019): 403–32.

Engstrom, David Freeman, Lucy Ricca, Graham Ambrose, and Maddie Walsh. "Legal Innovation After Reform: Evidence from Regulatory Change." *Stanford Law School Deborah L. Rhode Center on the Legal Profession* (September 2022).

Estlund, Cynthia. "What Should We Do After Work? Automation and Employment Law." *Yale Law Journal* 128, no. 2 (2018): 254–326.

Estreicher, Samuel. "The Roosevelt-Cardozo Way: The Case for Bar Eligibility After Two Years of Law School." *N.Y.U. Journal of Legislation and Public Policy* 15, no. 3 (2012): 599–618.

Feldman, Robin. "Artificial Intelligence: The Importance of Trust and Distrust." *Green Bag* 21, no. 3 (2018).

Florida Bar v. TIKD Services, LLC, 326 So. 3d 1073 (Fla. 2021).

Florida Bar v. Went For It, Inc., 515 U.S. 618 (1995).

Fortney, Susan Saab. "The Billable Hours Derby: Empirical Data on the Problems and Pressure Points." *Fordham Urban Law Journal* 33, no. 1 (2005): 171–92.

Freedman, Monroe H., and Abbe Smith. *Understanding Lawyers' Ethics.* New York: LexisNexis, 2010.

Friedman, Milton. *Capitalism and Freedom.* 1962. Chicago: University of Chicago Press, 2002.

Gellhorn, Walter. "The Abuse of Occupational Licensing." *University of Chicago Law Review* 44, no. 1 (1976): 6–27.

Gladwell, Malcolm. *The Tipping Point: How Little Things Can Make a Big Difference.* New York: Little, Brown, 2000.

Gilbert, Susan, and Larry Lempert. "The Nonlawyer Partner: Moderate Proposals Deserve a Chance." *Georgetown Journal of Legal Ethics* 2, no. 2 (1988): 383–410.

Gideon v. Wainwright, 372 U.S. 335 (1963).

Gillers, Stephen. "A Profession, if You Can Keep It: How Information Technology and Fading Borders Are Reshaping the Law Marketplace and What We Should Do About It." *Hastings Law Journal* 63, no. 4 (2012): 953–1022.

———. "What We Talked About When We Talked About Ethics." *Ohio State Law Journal* 46, no. 2 (1985): 243–76.

Goldfarb v. Virginia State Bar, 421 U.S. 773 (1975).

Gordon, Robert W. "The Role of Lawyers in Producing the Rule of Law: Some Critical Reflections." *Theoretical Inquiries in Law* 11, no. 1 (2010): 441–68.

Gorsuch, Neil. *A Republic, If You Can Keep It.* New York: Crown Forum, 2019.

———. "Access to Affordable Justice." *Judicature* 100, no. 3 (2016): 46–56.

Grant, Adam. *Think Again: The Power of Knowing What You Don't Know.* New York: Viking, 2021.

Green, Bruce A. "The Disciplinary Restrictions on Multidisciplinary Practice: Their Derivation, Their Development, and Some Implications for the Core Values Debate." *Minnesota Law Review* 84, no. 6 (2000): 1115–58.

Green, Rebecca. "Counterfeit Campaign Speech." *Hastings Law Journal* 70, no. 6 (2019): 1445–90.

Greene, Sara Sternberg, and Kristen M. Renberg, "Judging Without a J.D." *Columbia Law Review* 122, no. 5 (2022): 1287–385.

Greenhouse, Linda. *Becoming Justice Blackmun: Harry Blackmun's Supreme Court Journey.* New York: Times Books, Henry Holt, 2005.

Greiner, D. James. "The New Legal Empiricism and Its Application to Access-to-Justice Inquiries." *Dædalus* 148, no. 1 (2019): 64–74.

Hadfield, Gillian. "Equipping the Garage Guys in Law." *Maryland Law Review* 70, no. 2 (2011): 484–98.

———. "The Cost of Law: Promoting Access to Justice Through the (Un) Corporate Practice of Law." *International Review of Law and Economics* 38, Supplement (2013): 43–63.

Hadfield, Gillian, and Deborah Rhode. "How to Regulate Legal Services to Promote Access, Innovation, and the Quality of Lawyering." *Hastings Law Review* 67, no. 5 (2016): 1191–224.

Hadfield, Gillian, and Jaime Heine. "Life in the Law-Thick World: The Legal Resource Landscape for Ordinary Americans." In *Beyond Elite Law: Access to Civil Justice in America*, edited by Sam Estreicher and Joy Radice. New York: Cambridge University Press, 2016.

Haan, Sarah C. "The Post-Truth First Amendment." *Indiana Law Journal* 94, no. 4 (2019): 1351–406.

Hagan, Margaret. "Participatory Design for Innovation in Access to Justice." *Dædalus* 148, no. 1 (2019): 120–27.

Hansford, Justin. "Lippman's Law: Debating the Fifty-Hour Pro Bono Requirement for Bar Admission." *Fordham Urban Law Journal* 1144, no. (2014): 1141–88.

Hasbrouck, Brandon. "The Antiracist Constitution." *Boston University Law Review* 102, no. 1 (2022): 87–166.

Hasen, Richard L. "A Constitutional Right to Lie in Campaigns and Elections?" *Montana Law Review* 74, no. 1 (2013): 53–78.

Hazard, Geoffrey, Russell Pearce, and Jeffrey Stempel. "Why Lawyers Should Be Allowed to Advertise: A Market Analysis of Legal Services." *New York University Law Review* 58, no. 5 (1983): 1084–114.

Hecht, Nathan L. "The Twilight Zone." *Dædalus* 148, no. 1 (2019): 190–2.

Hoover v. Ronwin, 466 U.S. 558 (1984).

Howarth, Joan. *Shaping the Bar: The Future of Attorney Licensing*. Stanford: Stanford University Press, 2023.

Hunter v. Virginia State Bar, 744 S.E.2d 611 (Va. 2013).

Huq, Aziz Z. "A Right to a Human Decision." *Virginia Law Review* 106, no. 3 (2020): 611–88.

Jolls, Christine, Cass R. Sunstein, and Richard Thaler. "A Behavioral Approach to Law and Economics." *Stanford Law Review* 50, no. 5 (1998): 1471–550.

Katsh, Ethan, and Orna Rabinovich-Einy. *Digital Justice: Technology and the Internet of Disputes*. New York: Oxford University Press, 2017.

Katyal, Sonia K. "Private Accountability in the Age of Artificial Intelligence." *UCLA Law Review* 66, no. 1 (2019): 54–141.

Kavanagh, Matthew M., and Bebs Chorak. "Teaching Law as a Life Skill: How Street Law Helps Youth Make the Transition to Adult Citizenship." *Journal for Juvenile Justice & Detention Services* 18, no. 1 (2003) 71–78.

Klobuchar, Amy. *Antitrust: Taking on Monopoly Power from the Gilded Age to the Digital Age*. New York: Alfred A. Knopf, 2021.

Krishnamurthy, Bharath, Sharena Hagins, Ellen Lawton, and Megan Sandel. "What We Know and Need to Know about Medical-Legal Partnership." *South Carolina Law Review* 67, no. 2 (2016): 377–88.

Lahav, Alexandra. *In Praise of Litigation*. London: Oxford University Press, 2018.

Landsman, Stephan. "The Growing Challenge of Pro Se Litigation." *Lewis & Clark Law Review* 13, no. 2 (2009): 439-460.

Lanctot, Catherine J. "Does LegalZoom Have First Amendment Rights?: Some Thoughts About Freedom of Speech and the Unauthorized Practice of Law." *Temple Policy and Civil Rights Law Review* 20, no. (2011): 255–96.

Legal Services Corp. v. Velazquez, 531 U.S. 533 (2001).

Leubsdorf, John. "Theories of Judging and Judge Disqualification." *New York University Law Review* 62, no. 2 (1987): 237–92.

Levin, Leslie C. "The Case for Less Secrecy in Lawyer Discipline." *Georgetown Journal of Legal Ethics* 20, no. 1 (2007): 1–50.

——. "The Emperor's Clothes and Other Tales About the Standards for Imposing Lawyer Discipline Sanctions." *American University Law Review*, no. 48 (1998): 1–84.

Lepore, Jill. "The Disruption Machine: What the Gospel of Innovation Gets Wrong." *New Yorker*, June 16, 2014, www.newyorker.com.

Libgober, Brian. "Getting a Lawyer While Black: A Field Experiment." *Lewis & Clark Law Review* 24, no. 1 (2020): 53–108.

Lippman, Hon. Jonathan. "The Judiciary as the Leader of the Access to Justice Revolution." *New York University Law Review* 89, no. 5 (2014): 1569–88.

Llewellyn, K. N. "The Bar's Troubles, and Poultices—and Cures?" *Law & Contemporary Problems* 5, no. 1 (1938): 104–34.

Luban, David. "Legal Ideals and Moral Obligations: A Comment on Simon." *William and Mary Law Review* 38, no. 1 (1996): 255–68.

———. "Optimism, Skepticism, and Access to Justice." *Texas A&M Law Review* 3, no. 3 (2016): 495–514.

Markovic, Milan. "Protecting the Guild or Protecting the Public? Bar Exams and the Diploma Privilege." *Georgetown Journal of Legal Ethics* 35, no. 2 (2022): 163–202.

McCormack, Bridget Mary. "Staying Off the Sidelines: Judges as Agents for Justice System Reform." *Yale Law Journal Forum* 131 (2021): 175–89.

McGowan, David, and Mark A. Lemley. "Antitrust Immunity: State Action and Federalism, Petitioning, and the First Amendment." *Harvard Journal of Law & Public Policy* 17, no. 2 (1994): 293–400.

Milavetz, Gallop & Milavetz, P.A. v. United States, 559 U.S. 229 (2010).

Minow, Martha. "Marking 200 Years of Legal Education: Traditions of Change, Reasoned Debate, and Finding Differences and Commonalities." *Harvard Law Review*,130, no. 9 (2017): 2279–97.

Moorhead, Richard, Alan Paterson, and Avrom Sherr. "Contesting Professionalism: Legal Aid and Nonlawyers in England and Wales." *Law & Society Review* 37, no. 4 (2003): 765–808.

Morgan, Thomas D. *The Vanishing American Lawyer*. New York: Oxford University Press, 2010.

Myrick, Amy, Robert L. Nelson, and Laura Beth Nielson. "Race and Representation: Racial Disparities in Legal Representation for Employment Civil Rights Plaintiffs." *New York University Journal of Legislation & Public Policy* 15, no. 3 (2012): 705–58.

NAACP v. Button, 371 U.S. 415 (1963).

North Carolina State Board of Dental Examiners v. FTC, 574 U.S. 494 (2015).

Northern Pacific Railroad Company v. United States, 356 U.S. 1 (1958).

Ohralik v. Ohio State Bar Association, 436 U.S. 447 (1978).

State ex rel., Oklahoma Bar Association v. Oliver, 369 P.3d 1074 (Okla. 2016).

Palmer v. BRG of Georgia, Inc., et al., 498 U.S. 46 (1990).

Parker v. Brown, 371 U.S. 341 (1943).

Peel v. Attorney Registration and Disciplinary Commission of Illinois, 496 U.S. 91 (1990).

Pepper, Stephen L. "Counseling at the Limits of the Law: An Exercise in the Jurisprudence and Ethics of Lawyering." *Yale Law Journal* 104, no. 7 (1995): 1545–610.

Perlman, Andrew M. "Towards the Law of Legal Services." *Cardozo Law Review* 37, no. 1 (2015): 49–112.

Pink, Daniel H. *To Sell Is Human*. New York: Riverhead Books, 2012.

Post, Robert C. *Democracy, Expertise, Academic Freedom: A First Amendment Jurisprudence for the Modern State*. New Haven: Yale University Press, 2012.

In re Primus, 436 U.S. 412 (1978).

Remus, Dana A. "The Uncertain Promise of Predictive Coding." *Iowa Law Review* 99, no. 4 (2014): 1691–724.

Remus, Dana A., and Frank Levy. "Can Robots Be Lawyers? Computers, Lawyers, and the Practice of Law." *Geographic Journal of Legal Ethics* 30, no. 3 (2017): 501–58.

Republican Party of Minnesota v. White, 536 U.S. 765 (2002).

Rhode, Deborah. *Access to Justice.* New York: Oxford University Press, 2005.

———. "Access to Justice: Connecting Principles to Practice." *Georgetown Journal of Legal Ethics* 17, no. 3 (2004): 369–422.

———. *Character: What It Means and Why It Matters.* New York: Oxford University Press (2019).

———. "Policing the Professional Monopoly: A Constitutional and Empirical Analysis of Unauthorized Practice Prohibitions." *Stanford Law Review* 34, no. 1 (1981): 1–112.

———. "The Profession and the Public Interest." *Stanford Law Review* 54, no. 6 (2002): 1501–22.

———. "Public Interest Law: The Movement at Midlife." *Stanford Law Review* 60, no. 6 (2008): 2027–86.

———. "Reforming American Legal Education and Legal Practice: Rethinking Licensing Structures and the Role of Nonlawyers in Delivering and Financing Legal Services." *Legal Ethics* 16, no. 2 (2013): 243–57.

———. "Whatever Happened to Access to Justice?" *Loyola of Los Angeles Law Review* 42, no. 4 (2009): 869–913.

Rhode, Deborah, and Lucy Burford Ricca. "Protecting the Profession or the Public? Rethinking Unauthorized Practice Enforcement." *Fordham Law Review* 82, no. (2014): 2587–610.

Ribstein, Larry E. "The Death of Big Law." *Wisconsin Law Review 2010*, no. 3 (2010): 749–816.

Ribstein, Larry E., and Bruce H. Kobayashi, "Law's Information Revolution." *Arizona Law Review* 53, no. 4 (2011): 1169–220.

Rice v. Norman Williams Company, 458 U.S. 654 (1982).

In re R.M.J., 455 U.S. 191 (1982).

Robertson, Cassandra Burke. "Online Reputation Management in Attorney Regulation." *Georgetown Journal of Legal Ethics* 29, no. 1 (2016): 97–152.

Root, Veronica. "Combating Silence in the Profession." *Virginia Law Review* 105, no. 4 (2019): 805–63.

Saffer, Dan. *Designing for Interaction: Creating Smart Applications and Clever Devices.* San Francisco: New Riders, 2006.

Sandefur, Rebecca L. *Accessing Justice in the Contemporary USA: Findings from the Community Needs and Services Study.* Chicago: American Bar Foundation, 2014.

———. "Access to What?" *Dædalus* 148, no. 1 (2019): 49–55.

———. "What We Know and Need to Know About the Legal Needs of the Public." *South Carolina Law Review* 67, no. 2 (2016): 443–60.

Sandefur, Rebecca L., and Aaron C. Smyth. *Access Across America: First Report of the Civil Justice Infrastructure Mapping Project.* American Bar Foundation, 2011.

Schneyer, Ted. "'Professionalism' As Pathology: The ABA's Latest Policy Debate on Nonlawyer Ownership of Law Practice Entities." *Fordham Urban Law Journal* 40, no. 1 (2012): 75–138.

Shapero v. Kentucky Bar Association, 486 U.S. 466 (1988).

Simon, Michael, Alvin F. Lindsay, Loly Sosa, and Paige Comparato. "*Lola v. Skadden* and the Automation of the Legal Profession." *Yale Journal of Law & Technology* 20 (2018): 234-310.

Solomon, Jason, Deborah Rhode, and Annie Wanless. "How Reforming Rule 5.4 Would Benefit Lawyers and Consumers, Promote Innovation, and Increase Access to Justice." *Stanford Law School Center on the Legal Profession White Paper* (April 2020).

Stone, Geoffrey R. "A Lawyer's Responsibility: Protecting Civil Liberties in Wartime." *Washington University Journal of Law and Policy* 22, no. 1 (2006): 47–56.

Susskind, Richard. *The End of Lawyers? Rethinking the Nature of Legal Services*. Oxford: Oxford University Press, 2008.

———. "The Future of Courts." *The Practice Magazine*, Harvard Law School Center on the Legal Profession (July/August 2020).

———. *The Future of Law: Facing the Challenges of Information Technology*. Oxford: Oxford University Press, 1996.

———. *Online Courts and the Future of Justice*. Oxford: Oxford University Press, 2021.

———. *Tomorrow's Lawyers: An Introduction to Your Future*. Oxford: Oxford University Press, 2013.

Tamanaha, Brian Z. *Failing Law Schools*. Chicago: University of Chicago Press, 2012.

Terry, Laurel S., Steve Mark, and Tahlia Gordon. "Adopting Regulatory Objectives for the Legal Profession." *Fordham Law Review* 80, no. 6 (2012): 2685–760.

Thomas v. Collins, 323 U.S. 516 (1944).

Topco Associates, Inc., United States v., 405 U.S. 596 (1972).

Troccoli, Kenneth P. "I Want a Black Lawyer to Represent Me: Addressing a Black Defendant's Concerns with Being Assigned a White Court-Appointed Lawyer." *Minnesota Journal of Law and Inequity* 20, no. 1 (2002): 1–52.

Tully, L. Danielle. "The Cultural (Re)Turn: The Case for Teaching Culturally Responsible Lawyering." *Stanford Journal of Civil Rights & Civil Liberties* 16, no. 2 (2020): 201–57.

Turner v. Rogers, 465 U.S. 431 (2011).

United Mine Workers of America, District 12 v. Illinois State Bar Association, 389 U.S. 217 (1967).

United Transportation Union v. State Bar of Michigan, 401 U.S. 576 (1971).

Virginia State Board of Pharmacy v. Virginia Citizens Consumer Council, Inc., 425 U.S. 748 (1976).

Volokh, Eugene. "Chief Justice Robots." *Duke Law Journal* 86, no. 6 (2019): 1135–92.

Wald, Eli. "A Primer on Diversity, Discrimination, and Equality in the Legal Profession or Who is Responsible for Pursuing Diversity and Why." *Georgetown Journal of Legal Ethics* 24, no. 4 (2011): 1079–142.

Webb, Julian. "Regulating Lawyers in a Liberalized Legal Services Market: The Role of Education and Training." *Stanford Law & Policy Review* 24, no. 2 (2013): 533–70.

Whalen, Ryan. "Defining Legal Tech and Its Implications." *International Journal of Law and Information Technology* 30, no. 1 (2022): 47–67.

Wiley, John Shepard. "A Capture Theory of Antitrust Federalism." *Harvard Law Review* 61, no. 5 (1986): 1327–42.

Wilkins, David B. "Who Should Regulate Lawyers?" *Harvard Law Review* 105, no. 4 (1992): 799–887.

Williams, Joan C., Aaron Platt, and Jessica Lee. "Disruptive Innovation: New Models of Legal Practice." *Hastings Law Journal* 67, no. 1 (2015): 1–84.

Wolfram, Charles. "The ABA and MDPs: Context, History, and Process." *Minnesota Law Review* 84, no. 6 (2000): 1547–624.

———. *Modern Legal Ethics*. St. Paul, MN: West Publishing Company, 1986.

Wright, Edward L. "The Code of Professional Responsibility: Its History and Objectives." *Arkansas Law Review* 24, no. 1 (1970): 1–18.

Yablon, Charles M. "The Lawyer as Accomplice: Cannabis, Uber, Airbnb, and the Ethics of Advising 'Disruptive' Businesses." *Minnesota Law Review* 104, no. 1 (2019): 309–84.

Young, Kathryne M. "What the Access to Justice Crisis Means for Legal Education." *UC Irvine Law Review* 11, no. 3 (2021): 811–50.

Zacharias, Fred. "What Lawyers Do When Nobody's Watching: Legal Advertising as a Case Study of the Impact of Underenforced Professional Rules." *Iowa Law Review* 87, no. 3 (2002): 971–1022.

Zauderer v. Office of Disciplinary Counsel, 471 U.S. 626 (1985).

INDEX

AAAI (Association for the Advancement of Artificial Intelligence), 187

ABA. *See* American Bar Association

ABA Model Rules. *See* Model Rules of Professional Conduct, ABA

ABS ("alternative business structure"), 8–9, 65, 119–21, 129–30

Accessing Justice in the Contemporary USA (Sandefur), 217n14, 223n23, 227n24

access to justice, 4, 15–16, 18, 26, 32, 114, 198

"Access to Justice" (Rhode), 217n14, 222n12, 223n23, 227n23

ACLU (American Civil Liberties Union), 88, 111–12

ACM (Association of Computing Machinery), 187

Adediran, Tinu, 35, 162–63

advertising, lawyer, 38, 39, 227n27, 228n39; *Bates v. Arizona State Bar*, 40–44, 46, 48, 223n22; direct mail, 227n12; disclaimers, 44–45; "How a Lawyer Can Help You" campaign, 171–72; images, 46–48, 229n49; informative, relatable, understandable, 116–17; internet, 40, 43, 45–48; price information, 45–46, 228n38; readability, 46–48

African Americans, 4, 21–22, 32, 46, 91; in ABA, 49, 51; Black people, 17, 24, 30, 47, 229n42

AI. *See* artificial intelligence

Aiyetoro, Adjoa Artis, 49

Alaska, 31, 53, 56, 127, 188, 220n17, 230n23, 237n2

Alderman, Richard, 169

Alexander, Michelle, 24

algorithmic bias, 186

ALSPs (alternative legal service providers), 133, 144–45

"alternative business structure" (ABS), 8–9, 65, 119–21, 129–30

alternative fee arrangements, 101

alternative legal service providers (ALSPs), 133, 144–45

AMA (American Medical Association), 75–76

Amazon, 45, 186

American Academy of Arts and Sciences, 198, 200

American Bar Association (ABA), 21, 30, 32, 88, 148, 176, 189; Canons of Ethics, 39, 49, 226n4; Center for Innovation, 125–26, 155, 250n33; Commission on Billable Hours, 33; Commission on the Future of Legal Services, 9, 125, 126, 140; Council of the Section of Legal Education and Admission to the Bar, 157, 237n2; criticism of, 149; Ethics 20/20 Commission, 63; House of Delegates, 50–51, 53, 55, 63, 71, 132, 138–39, 143, 156–57, 187–88; Kutak Commission, 51; members, 2–3, 49–51; on middle class without affordable legal services, 27, 227n23; Model Code of Professional Responsibility, 49–51; Model Regulatory Objectives for the Provision of Legal Services, 138–39, 141; practice of law and, 99–100;

279

280 | INDEX

American Bar Association (*cont.*)
on professionalism, 27, 49–56; reports, 2, 125; Standing Committee on Client Protection, 233n52; youth education and, 172. *See also* Model Rules of Professional Conduct, ABA

American Bar Association Journal (*ABA Journal*), xiv, 215n14, 217n21, 219n40, 219n48, 227n16, 251n43, 251n49, 251n52, 252n53, 252n73, 252n75, 254n107, 256n5, 258–59n50, 259n2, 264n15, 264n19, 266n63

American Bar Foundation, 127, 167

American Civil Liberties Union (ACLU), 88, 111–12

American Medical Association (AMA), 75–76

American Law Institute, 62, 234n81, 234n82, 234n83, 235n96

American Psychology Association (APA), 173, 174

Am Law 200, 35

Antitrust (Klobuchar), 91

"Antitrust and the Economics of Federalism" (Easterbrook), 237n9

antitrust law: attorney fee schedules, 92–94; attorney licensing, 94–95; federal, 73, 90–92; fee schedules and, 33; recommendations, 99–101; Sherman Act and, 90–95, 98; teeth whitening services and, 95–99

Anxious Lawyer (Cho and Gifford), 201

APA (American Psychology Association), 173, 174

Archer, Dennis, 50

Arizona, 56, 63, 66, 127, 128, 131, 146–47, 220n17; legal paraprofessionals, 130, 142; state bar, 40–44, 46, 48, 95, 99, 110–11, 118, 167, 180, 197, 223n22; supreme court, 94, 120, 129, 130, 145

Arizona State University, 177

artificial intelligence (AI), 20, 182, 185, 189–90, 197; AAAI, 187; bots, 5–6, 32,

59, 129, 151, 183, 194, 217n24; ethical innovation and, 194; justice tech and, 6–7; responsibility with, 186–88

Ashley, Cedric, 228n41

Asian Americans, 30–31, 46, 229n42

Association for the Advancement of Artificial Intelligence (AAAI), 187

Association of American Law Schools, 158, 159, 172, 174, 180

Association of Computing Machinery (ACM), 187

ATHENA award, National Newspaper Association, 171

Atrium, 135, 136

"Attorney Advertising" (Parkinson and Neeley), 227n27

Australia, 6, 65, 131, 182, 191, 194; with alternative legal service providers, 133; regulatory reform, 122, 123, 124; tram fines in, 1–2, 5

Axiom, 134

Axios-Momentive Poll (2022), 78–79

Ballakrishnen, Swethaa, 148

bar association, 21, 164–65. *See also* American Bar Association; National Bar Association; state bar associations; *specific bar associations*

"bar authorities," 21, 88

bar exam, 57, 88, 95, 159–60, 164–65; AI and, 7, 183; passing, 94, 126, 143, 147, 161

Barocas, Solon, 185

Barton, Ben, 52, 76

Bates, John, 40–41, 110

Bates v. State Bar of Arizona, 433 U.S. 350 (1977), 40–44, 46, 48, 99, 110–11, 118, 167, 180, 197

Baxter, Ralph, 57

Bay Area Legal Services, Florida, 136

Beaton, George, 217n23

Benson, Jocelyn, 80

Berkman Klein Center for Internet and Society Law Lab, Harvard Law School, 152, 217n19

Bernabe, Alberto, 19

bias, 23, 74, 160, 175, 184–85, 187–88; algorithmic, 186; implicit, 162, 163, 164; racism, cross-cultural competency and, 156–57; self-serving, 72–73

Biden, Joe, 78–79, 189

Bigelow v. Virginia, 421 U.S. 809 (1975), 108, 109

billable hours, 33–34, 63, 101

"Billable Hours Giving Ground at Law Firms" (Glater), 224n46

BIPOC (Black, Indigenous, People of Color), 23

Birken, Emily, 225n65

Black, Hugo, 90, 106

Black, Indigenous, People of Color (BIPOC), 23

Blackmun, Harry, 41, 94, 108, 109, 110, 111

Black people, 17, 24, 30, 47, 229n42. *See also* African Americans

Bleich, Jeff, 27

blockchain, 20, 182

Bloomberg Law, 156

Blumenthal, Mike, 226n3

"BookFlip," 8

bots, AI, 5–6, 32, 59, 129, 151, 183, 194, 217n24

Boumil, Marcia M., 236n115, 236n117

Boundless, 135

Brann, Matthew W., 79

Brescia, Ray, 183

Brotherhood of Railroad Trainmen v. Virginia ex rel. Virginia State Bar, 377 U.S. 1 (1964), 105–6

Browder, Joshua, 6, 7, 218n32

Brown, Louis, 179–80

Brown, Paulette, 51

Brown v. Board of Education II, 349 U.S. 294, 301 (1955), 105

Brynjolfsson, Erik, 7–8, 151

Bureau of Labor Statistics Occupational Outlook Handbook, 174

Burger, Warren E., 93

California, 51, 76, 128, 131, 145, 162; state bar, 27; supreme court, 36, 176

Canada, 125, 129, 133

candor, duty of, 79, 82–85, 117–18

Canons of Ethics, ABA, 39, 49, 226n4

"Can Robots Be Lawyers?" (Remus and Levy), 189–90

Cantil-Sakauye, Tani, 142

Capers, Bennett, 148

Capitol attack, US, 78, 79, 83, 203. *See also* January 6 insurrection

CCJ (Conference of Chief Justices), 132, 137, 142, 143, 188, 197–98

Center for Innovation, ABA, 125–26, 155

Central Hudson Gas and Electric Corporation v. Public Service Commission, 447 U.S. 557 (1980), 108

Chambliss, Elizabeth, 58, 140, 149, 198

Character (Rhode), 57–58

chatbots, 32, 59, 129

ChatGPT, 59, 151, 183, 194, 217n24

Cheatham, Elliot, 234n87

Chesney, Bobby, 266

child support, 27, 28, 178

Cho, Jeena, 201

Chorak, Bebs, 168

Christensen, Barlow, 59–60

Christensen, Clayton, 19, 221n30

churning, 33

citizens, public, 166, 198, 200. *See also* education, for the public

citizenship, engaged citizenship, 12, 198, 200

Citron, Danielle, 266

civil courts, 3, 26, 123, 153

"civil Gideon," 36, 143

civil justice, 4, 200; gap, 34–36, 41, 42, 56; system, 3, 23, 24, 27–28, 199

civil legal services, 27–28, 35, 132, 199

Clarke, Frank, 123

CLEAR company, 37–38

Clinton, Hillary, 50

Clio, 101, 134–35, 198

cloud computing, 53, 136, 230n23, 231nn25–26, 232n30

CodeX, Stanford Law School, 152, 217n19

cognitive empowerment, 103

Colorado, 53, 81, 130–31, 139, 144, 156, 173, 220n17

Colorado Bar Association, 230n24

Columbia Law School, 158–59

"Combating Silence in the Profession" (Root), 31

commercial speech cases, First Amendment, 108–16

Commission on the Future of Legal Services, ABA, 9, 125, 126, 140

Commission on the Practice of Democratic Citizenship, 200

Comparato, Paige, 194

competence: cultural, 156–57, 163, 164; democratic, 56, 83, 103; innovation and, 193–94; for law students and lawyers, 164–65; technology, 53–55

Computerworld (magazine), 223n25

Conference of Chief Justices (CCJ), 132, 137, 142, 143, 188, 197–98

Conference of State Court Administrators (COSCA), 132, 137, 142, 143

conflicts of interest, 33, 52, 56, 62, 65, 73, 76, 97

Congress, US, 34–35, 108

Congressional Access to Legal Aid Caucus, 201

Connecticut, 36, 55, 127, 143, 173

Constitution, US, 13, 14, 102. *See also* First Amendment

Consumer Financial Protection Bureau, 186

consumer law market, 29, 30, 37, 41, 70, 121

contingency fees, 32–33

continuing legal education, 54, 55, 80, 145, 161–62, 164

Conway, Kellyanne, 77

Coolidge, Calvin, 13

Co-op Group, Legal Services branch, 9

Cooter, Robert, 70, 236n123

COSCA (Conference of State Court Administrators), 132, 137, 142, 143

Costco, 37

"Cost of Law" (Hadfield), 223n23

"The Costs of Being Unbanked or Underbanked" (Birken), 225n65

Counsel on Call, 134

Coursera, 175

court facilitators, 176, 181

court forms, standardizing, 146

Court Forms Online, Suffolk Law School, 153, 178

court navigators, 176–77, 181

Court of Appeals, US, 13, 33, 84, 96

COVID-19 pandemic, 28, 54, 77, 123, 134, 137, 160, 190–91

criminal justice, 3, 24, 31, 36, 125, 138, 202

criminal sanctions, 24, 57, 90, 96, 113, 115, 194

Crotty, Paul, 115–16

Cruz, Sherley, 188

cultural competency, 156–57, 163, 164

"culturally responsive lawyering," 157

data, 166, 184–86, 197–98, 201–2, 223n25

Davis, Martha F., 229n43

Dean, John, 50

delay, harm of, 31, 32–33, 67, 79, 142, 176, 194

democracy, 80, 200

democracy, lawyers with: with accountability for election-denial lies, 81–85; election-fraud lies, 78–82, 84; lies and vulnerability, 77–79

democratic competence, 56, 83, 103

democratization: legal education, 147–58; public education through information campaign, 169–75

Denmark, 3

Department of Homeland Security, US, 144

Department of Justice, US, 90, 97, 99–100, 144, 186

"A Design for Living" (Tischler), 225n68
DeStefano, Michele, 152
DIFC (Dubai International Financial Center), 122–24
diploma privilege, 160
disability, people with disabilities, 31, 32, 35, 55, 67, 148
disciplinary knowledge, 56, 57, 103
Disciplinary Rules of Professional Conduct, Texas, 228n35
discrimination: in civil justice, 4; harassment and, 55–56
disputes: prevention, 196; resolution, 8, 32, 57, 119, 138, 195, 222n12
disruptive innovation, 19–20, 150
distributive justice, 17
diversity, 50, 56, 122, 139, 162–63, 228n41
DIY (do-it-yourself), 19, 27; justice tools, 9, 178–79; resources, 175–77
Dobbs v. Jackson Women's Health Organization, 142 S. Ct. 2228 (2022), 14
document review, technology-assisted, 8, 219n40
do-it-yourself. *See* DIY
Dominion Voting Systems, 80
DoNotPay, 6, 57
double-billing, 33
Dubai International Financial Center (DIFC), 122–24

Easterbrook, Frank H., 73, 237n9
economy, 2, 237n9. *See also* expenses
eCourts, 21
Edlin, Aaron, 75
education: *Brown v. Board of Education II*, 105; continuing legal, 54, 55, 80, 145, 161–62, 164; youth, 172. *See also* law schools; legal profession, education for
education, for the public: democratized through information campaign, 169–75; DIY resources, 175–77; lawyers as public citizens, 166; LRE, 168–69; recommendations, 177–81

e-filing, 146, 153
elections: denial lies and accountability of lawyers, 81–85; lawyer lies about fraudulent, 78–82, 84
Elkin-Koren, Niva, 184
Embry, Stephen, 225n48
End of Lawyers? (Susskind), 222n12
enforceable justice, 17
engaged citizenship, 12, 198, 200
England, 32, 58, 65, 100, 119–22, 124, 129, 154, 191
Engstrom, David, 131
Engstrom, Nora, 131, 218n21
Ensuring the Right to Be Heard (IAALS), 179
Entrepreneurial Lawyering, ReInvent Law curriculum, 155
entrepreneurship, 150–53, 155, 163, 164
Equal Employment Opportunity Commission, 144, 186
"Equipping the Garage Guys" (Hadfield), 28
Estlund, Cynthia, 220n26
Estreicher, Samuel, 159
Ethical Consideration 2–1, ABA Model Rules, 166–67
ethical innovation: AI and, 194; human rights, change and, 183–86; lawyers with, 188–93; recommendations, 193–96; with responsibility assigned, 186–88
ethics, 22, 63, 75, 133, 166–67, 232n30; ABA Canons of Ethics, 39, 49, 226n4; *Modern Legal Ethics*, 40, 237n12
ethnicity, 4, 30–32, 35, 46–47, 51, 55, 57, 148
"Evidence-Based Lawyer Regulation" (Chambliss), 58, 140, 198
exonerations, 24, 82
expenses, 29, 37, 40, 62, 112; billable hours, 33–34, 63, 101; NewLaw, legal and justice tech, 135–36; pricing information for lawyers, 45–46; unmet legal need with time and, 32–34
Express Lien, 97

284 | INDEX

Failing Law Schools (Tamanaha), 149
Fairfax County Bar Association, 92, 93
Fast Company (magazine), 8, 155, 225n68
"fear of Sears," 63, 234n89
federal court records, free to public, 145
federalism, 73, 91, 237n9
Federal Reserve, 225n65
Federal Rules of Civil Procedure, 81, 82
Federal Trade Commission (FTC), 90, 95, 96, 99, 101, 117, 186
fees, 32–33, 65, 81, 92–94, 101
Feitas, Cristina F., 236n115
Feitas, Debbie F., 236n115
Fielder, Gary, 81
fine schemes, for trams, 1–2, 5
Finland, 3
First Amendment, 12, 56, 76, 81, 84, 140; *Bates v. Arizona State Bar,* 40–44, 46, 48, 99, 110–11, 118, 167, 180, 197, 223n22; *Bigelow v. Virginia,* 108, 109; *Brotherhood of Railroad Trainmen v. Virginia ex rel. Virginia State Bar,* 105–6; commercial speech cases, 108–16; Fourteenth and, 102; *Hunter v. Virginia State Bar,* 112–14, 117; lawyers speech and, 103–4, 112, 117; *Legal Services Corporation v. Velazquez,* 107–8; *NAACP v. Button* and, 105–8, 111, 118; *Ohralik v. Ohio State Bar Association,* 111–12; recommendations, 116–18; *In re Primus,* 111–12, 247n79; *United Mine Workers, District 12 v. Illinois State Bar Association,* 106; UPL and, 88; *Upsolve v. James,* 114–16, 118; *Virginia State Board of Pharmacy v. Virginia Citizens Consumer Council, Inc.,* 109–10
Fitzpatrick, Brian, 201
Fixing Law Schools (Barton), 225n64
Florida, 43, 54, 71, 98, 128, 131, 136–37, 144, 162
Florida Bar, 98, 226n11, 228n35
Florida Bar v. TIKD Services, LLC, 326 So. 3d 1073 (Fla. 2021), 98

Florida Justice Teaching Program, 168
Flynn, Sam, 5, 6, 7, 8
Forbes (magazine), 135, 225n65
Fortney, Susan Saab, 101
Fourteenth Amendment, 102
Freedman, Monroe, 74–75
free speech. *See* First Amendment
Friedman, Milton, 75–76
Friedman, Rose, 75–76
FTC. *See* Federal Trade Commission
Furlong, Jordan, 134
Futures (Canadian Bar Association), 125
The Future of Law (Susskind), 184

Gal, Michal, 184
Gellhorn, Walter, 74
gender, 4, 46, 47, 55
geographic practice restrictions, lawyers, 56, 69–70, 143
Georgetown Iron Tech Lawyer Contest, 153
Georgetown University Law Center, 133, 152–53, 156, 168
Georgia, 9, 31, 56, 80, 95, 220n17
Georgia Civil Legal Needs of Low and Moderate Income Households in Georgia, 223n20
"Getting a Lawyer While Black" (Libgober), 229n42
Gideon v. Wainwright, 372 U.S. 335 (1963), 36
Gillers, Stephen, 64–65, 235n96
Giuliani, Rudy, 79–80, 82, 83
Gladwell, Malcolm, 87
Glass, Deborah, 2
Glater, Jonathan D., 224n46
Global Legal Hackathon, 182
Goldfarb v. Virginia State Bar, 421 U.S. 773 (1975), 91, 94, 95, 98, 101, 102
Google, 43, 184, 186, 187
Gordon, Robert W., 75
Gordon, Tom, 200
Gorsuch, Neil, 32

Grady, Kenneth, 34
Grant, Adam, 199, 202
Graves, Michael, 225n68
Green, Bruce, 66
Green, Rebecca, 84
Greene, Sara, 17, 220n17
Greenstein, Marla, 188

Hadfield, Gillian, 28, 100, 201–2, 223n23
Hagan, Margaret, 146
Hague Institute for Innovation of Law (HiiL), 124–25
Hand, Learned, 13
Hansford, Justin, 26
harassment, discrimination and, 55–56
Hart, Susan, 249n104
Harvard Law School, 150, 152, 156, 217n19
Harvard School of Public Health, 174
Hasbrouck, Brandon, 14
Hasen, Richard, 84
Haw, Rebecca, 75
Hawaii, 56
Hawkins, Jim, 206, 229n49
Hazard, Geoffrey, 237n11
health, 14, 77, 129, 174, 183, 201–2; MLP and, 67–69, 112, 236n114; social determinants of, 66, 68, 236n115. *See also* mental health
Hecht, Nathan, 131, 191
Heine, Jamie, 201–2
Hello Divorce, 61
Henderson, Bill, 134
HiiL (Hague Institute for Innovation of Law), 124–25
Hispanics, 4, 30, 32, 46, 229n42
Hoffer, Eric, 87
Holmes, Oliver Wendell, 102
Holy Cross Ministries, 129
Hoover v. Ronwin, 466 U.S. 558 (1984), 94, 95
Horowitz, Andreessen, 7
hourly billing, 33–34, 63, 101, 224nn45–46, 225n48, 243n55

"How a Lawyer Can Help You" campaign (Pennsylvania Bar Association), 171–72
Howarth, Joan, 164
"How Do People Find and Hire Attorneys?" (Tsakalakis), 226n3
"How People Find Lawyers in 2015" (Blumenthal), 226n3
"How to Regulate Legal Services" (Hadfield and Rhode), 236n122
Hubbard, William, 3, 125
human rights, ethical innovation and, 183–86
Hunter, Horace Frazier, 112–13
Hunter v. Virginia State Bar, 744 S.E.2d 611 (Va. 2013), 112–14, 117
Huq, Aziz, 190
Hyatt Legal Services, 9

IAALS (Institute for the Advancement of the Legal System), 124–25, 129, 141, 179
Icertis, 135
iCivics program, 169
Iconic Women in Legal History website, 169
Ifill, Sherilynn, 79, 85
IFLP (Institute for the Future of Law Practice), 156
Illinois, 53, 56, 106, 139, 162, 201
images, lawyer advertising, 46–48, 229n49
implicit bias training, 162, 163, 164
Inc. (magazine), 34
inclusion, diversity and, 50, 56, 139, 228n41
inflation, 33, 35, 199, 201
injustice, 2–5, 15
innovation, 18, 124–26, 144, 155; competence and, 193–94; disruptive, 19–20, 150; with education for legal profession, 163, 164; ethical, 183–96; justice tech, 5–7; in law schools, 150, 152–53, 156; legal profession resisting, 7–10; legal services and non-regulatory, 133–37; technology and, 20–21, 182, 220n26

Innovation by Design Award, *Fast Company*, 155
"Innovations in Technology Conference," LSC, 182
Innovation Trends Report (ABA Center for Innovation), 126
"Innovative Law Firms," NewLaw, 134
The Innovator's Dilemma (Christensen), 221n30
In Praise of Litigation (Lahav), 118
Institute for the Advancement of the Legal System (IAALS), 124–25, 129, 141, 179
Institute for the Future of Law Practice (IFLP), 156
"An Institutional Analysis of Lawyer Regulation" (Barton), 238n24
Internal Revenue Service, 144
internet, 5, 19, 39, 58, 75, 226n3; access, 31–32, 127, 175, 190; advertising, 40, 43, 45–48
In the Matter of Reisman, No. 2013–21, 232n35
investment: in justice tech, 135–36, 195–96; in law firms and nonlawyer ownership, 19, 56, 60–65, 128–29, 139, 145–46
"Is the Billable Hour Impacting Our Mental Health?" (Embry), 225n48
I Want a Black Lawyer to Represent Me (Troccoli), 47

January 6 insurrection, 78, 79, 83, 203. *See also* Capitol attack
JD (Juris Doctor) degree, 138, 147, 158
Jefferson, Wallace B., 266n52
Jim Crow, new, 24
job market, 148, 151
Jobs, Steve, 150
Jolls, Christine, 72–73
Jones Day, 240n35
Josef Legal, 5–6, 7
JTA (Justice Technology Association), 195–96

judges (justices), 17, 55, 164, 179, 220n17; CCJ, 132, 137, 142, 143, 188, 197–98; lawyer-judges and regulators, 70, 71, 72, 73, 76. *See also* Supreme Court, US
"Judging Without a J.D." (Greene and Renberg), 220n17
judicial advisory opinions, 144
Juris Doctor (JD) degree, 138, 147, 158
justice, 17, 90, 97, 99–100, 144, 186, 222n12, 227n23; *Accessing Justice in the Contemporary USA*, 217n14, 223n23, 227n24; access to, 4, 15–16, 18, 26, 32, 114, 198; tech, 5–7, 22, 23, 135–36, 195–96. *See also specific types of justice*
Justice Connect, 182
Justice Gap Study, LSC (2022), 198
justices. *See* judges
Justice System Metrics Project website, 126
Justice Technology Association (JTA), 195–96

Kansas, 56, 220n17
Kaplow, Louis, 238n21
Katsh, Ethan, 196
Katyal, Sonia, 186
Kavanagh, Matthew, 168
Kay, Alan, 87
Kelley, Peter, 123
Kennedy, Anthony, 96, 107–8
Kentucky, 9, 56
Kentucky Bar Association, 245n30
King, Martin Luther, 15–16
Klobuchar, Amy, 91
Kobayashi, Bruce H., 236n123
Kowalski, 221n33
Krieger, Marcia S., 259n2
Krishnamurthy, Bharath, 235n108, 236n110, 236n119
Kubicki, Josh, 155
Kutak Commission (Special Commission on Evaluation of Professional Standards), ABA, 51

Lahav, Alexandra, 118
Land of Lincoln Legal Aid, 201
Landsman, Stephan, 176
Latinx, 17, 30
law. *See specific topics*
"Law and Business Companies," NewLaw, 134
"Law Firm Accordion Companies," NewLaw, 134
law firms, 20, 134, 224n46. *See also* non-lawyer ownership, investment in law firms and
LawHelp Interactive website, 178
law-related education (LRE), 168–69
Law School Admission Council, 156, 174
"Law School as a White Space" (Capers), 148
Law School Innovation Program, Bloomberg Law, 156
law schools, 56, 121, 130, 168–70, 175, 178; applications, 36, 258–59n50; Association of American Law Schools, 158, 159, 172, 174, 180; bias, cross-cultural competency and racism, 156–57; candidates, 147–49; curriculum, 37, 163; debt, 148, 159; innovation in, 150, 152–53, 156; lawyers educated after, 161–62; leadership development, 157–58, 163, 164; with legal education democratized, 147–58; with public education campaigns, 180
"Law's Information Revolution" (Ribstein and Kobayashi), 236n123
LawWithoutWalls, University of Miami Law School, 152
"Lawyer as Accomplice" (Yablon), 221n34
lawyer-judges, regulators and, 70, 71, 72, 73, 76
Lawyernomics conference, 226n3
lawyer regulation, ABA Model Code of Professional Responsibility, 49–51; ABA Model Rules of Professional Conduct, 51–56; discrimination and

harassment, 55–56; geographic practice restrictions, 69–70, 143; multi-disciplinary partnership bans, 65–69; nonlawyer ownership and investment in law firms, 60–65; regulatory capture, 72–74, 75, 76; technology competence, 53–55; UPL, 56, 57–60, 66; "Who Should Regulate Lawyers?," 234n80
lawyers (attorneys). *See specific topics*
Lawyers and Justice (Luban), 15
Lawyers Defending American Democracy, 80
"Lawyer's Responsibility" (Stone), 237n16
lay members, on regulatory boards, 101, 157
LDA (legal documentation assistance) programs, 144–45
leadership development, 157–58, 163, 164
legal aid, 28, 29, 136, 201. *See also* Legal Services Corporation
legal assistance, 2–5, 27, 37, 41, 42
legal assistance, finding: *Bates v. Arizona State Bar* and, 40–44, 46, 48; case study, 43–44; internet searches, 39, 40, 43; lawyer advertising and, 38–48
Legal Business Design Hub, 155
legal checkups, routine, 179–80
legal documentation assistance (LDA) programs, 144–45
Legal Force, 8
"Legal Ideals and Moral Obligations" (Luban), 237n16
legal monopoly, 70–76, 147
legal needs, unmet, 26, 217n14, 223n20, 223n23, 227n24; government aid and private pro bono, 34–36; lawyers, 31, 36–37; overwhelming, 27–29; personal connection, 30–31; proximity, 31–32; technology, 37–38; time and expense, 32–34
legal paraprofessionals, 127, 130, 142

288 | INDEX

legal problems, 223n23, 227n24; low income and, 26–27; public education campaigns, 171, 173, 175, 178, 180. *See also* legal needs, unmet

legal profession, 16, 22, 41, 60, 61, 237n16; innovation resisted by, 7–10; mental health and, 33–34, 58, 198, 201, 225n48. *See also* judges

legal profession, education for: costs and licensing requirements, 158–60; diversity of public and, 162–63; law school, 147–58, 161–62; pro bono requirements, 160–61; recommendations, 162–65; who chooses to become lawyers, 147–49

Legal Profession Act, Australia, 122

legal service providers, 133, 139, 144–45

legal services, 9, 125–27, 140, 147, 204; advertising and, 40–41; civil, 27–28, 35, 132, 199; DIY, 19; justice tech with, 5–7; middle class without affordable, 27, 227n23; non-regulatory innovation in, 133–37; not provided by lawyers with regulation, 137–41; technology and, 38

Legal Services Act (LSA), 8–9, 61, 119, 122, 154

Legal Services Corporation (LSC), 107, 136, 177, 178, 182; founding of, 34–35; funding for, 198–99, 201; survey, 26–27

Legal Services Corporation v. Velazquez, 531 U.S. 533 (2001), 107–8

"Legal Services Innovation Index," 250n28, 257n18, 266n69

legal tech, 22–23, 135–36, 182

Legal Tech Fund, 136

Legal Tech Hub, 182

Legal Trends Report, Clio, 101, 134–35, 198

legal writing, 157, 158

LegalZoom, 7, 58, 97, 120–21, 129, 135, 219n50, 232n49, 233n64

legislative reform. *See* regulatory reform, legislative and

legislature, lawyer regulation via, 237n2

Lepore, Jill, 19

Letters to a Young Poet (Rilke), 203

Levin, Leslie, 71–72

Levine, Erin, 61

Levy, Frank, 189–90

LGBTQAI+, 23–24, 148

Libgober, Brian, 229n42

licensing, 94–95, 126–28, 141–42, 158–60, 164–65

"Life in the Law-Thick World" (Hadfield and Heine), 201

Lillie, Mildred, 50

limited license legal technicians (LLLTs), 126–28, 141–42

limited practice, 19, 163, 164

Lincoln, Abraham, 39

Lindsay, Alvin F., 194

Linna, Dan, 156

Lippman, Jonathan, 160–61, 188

Liu, Brian, 7, 8

Liu, Goodwin, 36

Llewellyn, Karl, 170

LLLTs (limited license legal technicians), 126–28, 141–42

Lone Star Legal Aid, 201

Louisiana, 56, 220n17

low income, 26–27, 36, 67, 126, 131; access to justice and, 4, 32, 114, 198; poverty and, 2, 4, 11, 28, 35, 70; with unmet legal needs, 217n14, 223n20, 223n23

LRE (law-related education), 168–69

LSA (Legal Services Act), 8–9, 61, 119, 122, 154

LSC. *See* Legal Services Corporation

Luban, David, 15–16, 237n16

Maine, 55, 162

Malaysia, 124

Manual for the Periodic Legal Checkups (Brown, L.), 179–80

market potential, legal needs, 28

market sustainability, 37

Markovic, Milan, 160

Marshall, Thurgood, 91
Marshall-Brennan Constitutional Literacy Project, 168
Maryland, 36, 143, 220n17
Massachusetts, 55, 153, 220n17
Massachusetts Institute of Technology, 15
McAfee, Andrew, 7–8, 151
McCormack, Bridget Mary, 142, 194
McGill University, 20
Mearian, Lucas, 223n25
medical legal partnership (MLP), 67–69, 112
mental health, 78; legal profession and, 33–34, 58, 198, 201, 225n48; services, 28, 173, 174
"Michael Graves, Champion of Accessible Design, Is Appointed to Obama Administration Post" (Jana), 225n68
Michigan, 126, 178, 220n17
Michigan State University, 120, 122, 153–56
Michigan Supreme Court, 142, 178, 191, 194
middle class, 27, 28, 38, 63, 227n23
Middle East, regulatory reform, 122–23, 124
Minnesota, 127, 162
Minow, Martha, 150
Mississippi, 56, 220n17
Missouri, 9, 53, 137, 162, 220n17, 231n26
MLP (medical legal partnership), 67–69, 112
Model Code of Professional Responsibility, ABA, 49–51
Model Regulatory Objectives for the Provision of Legal Services, ABA, 138–39, 141
Model Rules of Professional Conduct, ABA: 8.4 (Misconduct), 55, 82; Ethical Consideration 2–1, 166–67; 5.4 (Professional Independence of a Lawyer), 60–69, 116, 128–29, 139, 145–46, 234n81, 234n89, 235n91; 5.5 (Unauthorized Practice of Law; Multijurisdictional

Practice of Law), 69; 4.1 (Truthfulness in Statements to Others), 82, 117; lawyer regulation and, 51–56; 1.1 (Competence), 53, 157, 191, 193; preamble, 51, 83, 191, 193; reform, 85; 6.1, 192; 3.1 (Meritorious Claims & Contentions), 82; 3.3 (Candor Toward the Tribunal), 82; 3.6, 82–83; violation of, 187
Modern Legal Ethics (Wolfram), 40
MoneyCenter, Walmart, 37
Montana, 56, 137, 220n17, 223n20
"More Universities Are Teaching Lawtech" (Young-Powell), 257n19
Morgan, Thomas D., 215n13
Moss, Randolph D., 78
multidisciplinary partnerships, 56, 65–69, 121, 128, 145–46
Myrick, Amy, 229n42

NAACP, 88
NAACP Legal Defense Fund, 79
NAACP v. Button, 371 U.S. 415 (1963), 105–8, 111, 118
NALP (National Association for Law Placement), 62
National Bar Association (NBA), 21–22, 88
national bill of rights for self-represented parties, 179
National Center for State Courts, 127, 144, 176, 188
National Coalition for a Right to Civil Counsel, 36, 88
National Conference of Bar Examiners, 164
national directory, user-friendly, 177–78
National Institute of Health, 201–2
National Jurist, 158
National Newspaper Association, 171
National Registry of Exonerations, 24
National Science Foundation, 198
National Standards on Empirical Data and Outcomes, 201–2

290 | INDEX

National Telecommunications and Information Administration, 32
Native Americans, 30, 31, 51
NBA (National Bar Association), 21–22, 88
Nebraska, 220n17
Nelson, Robert L., 229n42
Nessel, Dana, 80
Netherlands, 3
Neukom, William, 3
Neureiter, N. Reid, 81
Nevada, 56, 145, 220n17
New Hampshire, 53, 71, 231n27
New Jersey, 162
NewLaw, 133–37, 146
New Law New Rules (Beaton), 253n89
New Mexico, 127, 220n17
New York City, 1, 13, 36, 109, 143, 222n15, 227n26
New York County District Attorney's Legal Bound Program, 168
New York State, 55–56, 61, 115, 127, 162, 220n17, 228n35; Buffalo, 43, 227n26; civil justice system, 27–28; Court of Appeals, 160–61
New York State Bar, 80
New York Times (newspaper), 27, 155
New York University Law School, High School Law Institute, 168
Nielson, Laura Beth, 229n42
Nixon, Richard, 50
nonlawyer ownership, investment in law firms and, 19, 56, 60–65, 128–29, 139, 145–46
North Carolina, 21, 53, 54, 56, 95, 127, 162, 220n17
North Carolina State Bar, 10, 97, 231n28
North Carolina State Board of Dental Examiners v. FTC, 574 U.S. 494 (2015), 95
North Dakota, 31, 220n17
Northern Pacific Railroad Company v. United States, 356 U.S. 1 (1958), 90

Northwestern Pritzker School of Law, 156, 159
Norway, 3
Notarize, 135

Obama, Barack, 159
O'Connor, Sandra Day, 42, 50, 168–69
Ohio, 53, 58, 97, 231n29
Ohralik v. Ohio State Bar Association, 436 U.S. 447 (1978), 111–12
Oklahoma, 56, 220n17
Online Courts and the Future of Justice (Susskind), 17
online dispute resolution, 138, 195
online hearings, 123, 146
"Online Reputation Management in Attorney Regulation" (Robertson), 226n3
Open Courts Act, 145
open justice, 17
OpenTable, 45
Oregon, 71, 127, 136, 162, 220n17
Oregon Classroom Law Project, 168
O'Steen, Van, 40–41, 110

PACER (Public Access to Court Electronic Records), 145
Palmer v. BRG of Georgia, Inc., et al., 498 U.S. 46 (1990), 95
parallel track, for injustice, 2–5
Parker, Linda V., 80
Parker v. Brown, 371 U.S. 341 (1943), 91
"participatory design," 146
Passmore, Crispin, 121–22
Patel, Varsha, 225n48
Patent and Trademark Office, 144
Pavuluri, Rohan, 115, 179
Pearce, Russell, 237n11
Pennsylvania, 10, 54, 56, 79, 220n17
Pennsylvania Bar Association, 54, 171–72
People's Law School, 169
Pepper, Stephen, 75
Perlman, Andrew M., 254nn122–23

personal connection, 30–31, 47, 226n3

Peters, James, 120

Pew Research Center, 123, 137, 141, 153, 197

Pink, Daniel, 170

police officers, 1, 78

"Policing the Professional Monopoly" (Rhode), 233n58, 235n96, 237n14

political speech, 108–10, 113, 115

populations, 2, 3, 27, 30–32, 41, 42

Posner, Zach, 136

Post, Robert, 56, 83, 103

post-truth, 82

poverty, 2, 4, 11, 28, 35, 70. *See also* low income

Powell, Lewis, 94

Powell, Sidney, 80

practice of law, 99–100

Pre-Law Pipeline Program, University of Houston, 148

Premier Property Lawyers, 119–20

In re Primus, 436 U.S. 412 (1978), 111–12

pro bono, 34–36, 38, 52, 160–61, 163, 192

Pro Bono Net, 177–78

procedural justice, 17

professional discipline, lawyers, 10, 21, 33, 41, 52, 54, 55, 72, 79, 80, 84, 112–13, 120, 160, 192, 194

professionalism, 22, 27, 42, 44, 49–56, 61

"Profession and the Public Interest" (Rhode), 203n17

proportionate justice, 17

pro se, 27

"Protecting the Profession or the Public" (Rhode and Ricca), 74, 233n59

proximity, as unmet legal need, 31–32

psychology, 31, 173, 174

Public Access to Court Electronic Records (PACER), 145

public citizens, 166, 198, 200. *See also* education, for the public

public education campaigns, legal problems, 171, 173, 175, 178, 180

public information campaign, legal education democratized through, 169–75

Public Welfare Foundation, 127, 177

Quality Solicitors, 9, 219n47, 219n50

Rabinovich-Einy, Orna, 196

Race Against the Machine (Brynjolfsson and McAfee), 7, 151

"Race and Civil Counsel in the United States" (Davis), 229n43

"Race and Representation" (Myrick, Nelson, and Nielson), 229n42

"racial allies," 162–63

racism, 67, 156–57, 175

"Rambo Litigators" (Reavley), 224n46

Ramo, Roberta Cooper, 50

Rasa Legal, 34

readability, lawyer advertising, 46–48

Reavley, Thomas, 33, 224n46

Reflections on the Human Condition (Hoffer), 87

"Reforming Rule 5.4" (Rhode), 233n69

regulation. *See* lawyer regulation

regulators, lawyer-judges and, 70, 71, 72, 73, 76

regulatory boards, lay members on, 101

regulatory capture, 72–74, 75, 76

regulatory constraints, 30, 73

regulatory enforcement, 3

regulatory objectives, adopt and assess, 141

regulatory reform, 7, 12, 76, 191, 195

regulatory reform, legislative and: international examples, 119–24, 125; legal services not provided by lawyers, 137–41; legal tech, justice tech and NewLaw, 135–36; non-regulatory innovation in legal services, 133–37; recommendations, 141–46; US experience, 125–32

regulatory sandbox, 128–31, 139–40, 142

Rehnquist, William, 110

ReInvent Law Lab, Michigan State University, 153–56
Remus, Dana, 189–90
Renberg, Kristen, 17
Report on the Economic Condition of the Bar (ABA), 2
Report on the Future of Legal Services (ABA Commission), 125, 223n23
A Republic, If You Can Keep It (Gorsuch), 32, 233n57
research centers, 25, 88–89
reserved activities, 58–59, 100
resources, DIY, 175–77
Responsive Law, 127, 200
Restatement (Third) of Law Governing Lawyers, 62, 64
Resy, 45
"Review the Reliance on Billable Hours" (Patel), 225n48
Rhode, Deborah, 27, 74, 100, 121, 158; "Access to Justice," 217n14, 222n12, 223n23, 227n23; *Character*, 57–58; "Policing the Professional Monopoly," 233n58, 235n96, 237n14; "Profession and the Public Interest," 203n17; "Protecting the Profession or the Public," 74, 233n59, 237n13; on public education programs, 171; "Public Interest Law," 262n49; "Reforming American Legal Education," 251n41; "Reforming Rule 5.4," 233n69; "Whatever Happened to Access to Justice," 262n40
Ribstein, Larry E., 236n123
Ricca, Lucy, 74
"A Right to a Human Decision" (Huq), 190
rights, 3, 5, 36, 88, 179, 183–86, 190
Rilke, Rainer Maria, 203
Robertson, Cassandra Burke, 226n3
RocketLawyers, 135
Roe v. Wade, 50
"Role of Lawyers in Producing the Rule of Law" (Gordon R. W.), 238n19

Ronwin, Edward, 94
Root, Veronica, 31, 55
Ross, William, 33
Rostain, Tanina, 152–53
Rule of Law Index, WJP, 3–4, 192. *See also* World Justice Project
Rules of Professional Conduct, 115, 228n35

SAID Business School, 133
salaries, 29, 34, 62–63, 112
Salyzyn, Amy, 128
Sandefur, Rebecca, 4, 16, 32, 177, 202
Scanlon, Mary Gay, 201
Schafer, Hans-Bernd, 70
Scotland, 124
"Secondment Firms," NewLaw, 134
Selbst, Andrew, 185
self-representation, 176, 179
Sessions, Jeff, 77
Shaping the Bar (Howarth), 164
Sherman Act, 90–95, 98
Silver-Greenberg, Jessica, 225n67
Simon, Michael, 194
Singapore, 123
Sixth Amendment, 102
Slater and Gordon, 122
small business owners, 26, 29, 37, 121, 130
Small Claims Tribunal, DIFC, 122–23
smart contracts, 23, 32
Smart Planet (online magazine), 225n68
Smith, Abbe, 74–75
Smith, Mary L., 51
Smith, Reed, 182
social determinants of health, 66, 68
social media, 40, 53, 55, 186–87, 189, 200, 231nn27–28
Social Security Administration, 144
social security disability insurance (SSDI), 67
Sokolove Law, 40
Solicitors Regulatory Authority (SRA), 120–21
Solomon, Jason, 233n69

Solomon's Knot (Cooter and Schafer), 70

Sosa, Loly, 194

South Carolina, 127, 220n17

South Dakota, 55, 56, 220n17

Special Commission on Evaluation of Professional Standards (Kutak Commission), ABA, 51

speech: commercial, 108–16; lawyer, 83, 84, 103–4, 112, 117; political, 108–10, 113, 115. *See also* First Amendment

The Spirit of Liberty speech (Hand), 13

SRA (Solicitors Regulatory Authority), 120–21

SSDI (social security disability insurance), 67

Standing Committee on Client Protection, ABA, 233n52

Stanford Center on the Legal Profession, 60, 61

Stanford Law School, 121, 130, 152, 156, 217n19

state-action doctrine, 73, 91–94, 96, 111

state bar associations, 6, 12, 33. *See also specific state bars*

state sovereignty, federalism and, 73, 91

Stempel, Jeffrey, 237n11

Stevens, John Paul, 94–95

Stone, Geoff, 160, 237n16

Street Law, 168–69

substantive justice, 17

Sudbury, Noella, 34

Suffolk Law School, Massachusetts, 153, 156, 178

Summers, Berni, 120

Sunstein, Cass, 72–73

Supreme Court, US, 6, 12, 13, 32, 33, 38, 64, 104, 168–69, 191; antitrust law and, 90–96, 98–99; decisions, 14, 36, 40–44, 48, 50, 91, 95, 102, 105, 107–8, 110, 197; First Amendment and, 102, 106–11. *See also specific legal cases*

supreme courts, 36, 92, 127, 128, 139–40, 176; Arizona, 94, 120, 129, 130, 145;

Michigan, 142, 178, 191, 194; Texas, 126, 131, 191, 199

"surrogate lawyering," 16

Survey of Unauthorized Practice of Law Committees Report (2012), 233n52

Susskind, Richard, 17–18, 146, 170–71, 184, 196, 197, 200

sustainable justice, 17

Sweden, 3

Taft, William, 13

"Taking Ownership of Diversity" (Ashley), 228n41

Tamanaha, Brian, 149

Target, 37, 225n68

Task Force to Expand Access to Civil Legal Services, 27–28

Tech Lawyer Accelerator Program, University of Colorado School of Law, 156

technology, 15, 29, 30, 153, 156, 163, 164, 191, 194; advances, 37–38, 87, 175, 180, 198, 230n24, 231n28; cloud computing, 53, 136, 230n23, 231nn25–26, 232n30; competence, 53–55; document review, 8, 219n40; innovation and, 20–21, 182, 220n26; justice, 5–7, 22, 23, 135–36, 195–96; with legal profession resisting innovation, 7–10; legal tech, 22–23, 135–36, 182; online hearings, 123, 146; online justice tools, 31–32; post-pandemic court, 132, 133, 137. *See also* artificial intelligence; internet; *specific technologies*

Technology Innovation Grants, LSC, 136

teeth whitening services, antitrust and, 95–99

Tennessee, 56, 136, 220n17

Tenth Annual Tech Trends Report 2019 (Deloitte), 21

terminology, 14–24

Terry, Laurel, 254n122

Tesco, 8–9, 61

Texas, 9, 43, 56, 59, 79, 127, 137, 190, 220n17; Disciplinary Rules of Professional Conduct, 228n35; Lone Star Legal Aid, 201; supreme court, 126, 131, 191, 199

Texas Young Lawyers Association, 169

Thaler, Richard, 72–73

Think Again (Grant), 199, 202

TIKD Services, LLC, 98

Tocqueville, Alexis de, 77

tools, justice, 9, 31–32, 178–79

To Sell is Human (Pink), 170

training, legal, 17, 103, 155

tram fines, in Australia, 1–2, 5

transparency, 17–18, 76, 132, 138, 152, 181–83, 186–88

travel, 37–38, 45

Tremblay, Paul, 16

Troccoli, Kenneth, 47

Trump, Donald, 36, 77–78, 79, 80, 82, 147

Tsakalakis, Gyi, 226n3

Tully, L. Danielle, 157

Twenty-First Century Law Practice Summer Program, Michigan State University, 154

Uber, 37, 192, 221n34

unauthorized practice of law (UPL), 97, 127, 144, 186; adjust restrictions on, 99–100, 130; First Amendment and, 88; lawyer regulation, 56, 57–60, 66; with lay members on regulatory boards, 101; LegalZoom with, 233n64; reserved activities, 100; teeth whitening and, 98; TIKD with, 98; *Upsolve v. James*, 115

unbanked, or underbanked, 225n65

Understanding Lawyers' Ethics (Freedman and Smith, A.), 75

United Arab Emirates, 123–24

United Kingdom (UK): England, 32, 58, 65, 100, 119–122, 124, 129, 154, 191; parking tickets, 6; Scotland, 124; Wales, 32, 58, 65, 100, 119–22, 124, 191

United Mine Workers, District 12 v. Illinois State Bar Association, 389 U.S. 217 (1967), 106

United Nations, 4

United States (US), 27, 30–31; Capitol attack, 78, 79, 83, 203; Congress, 34–35, 108; Court of Appeals, 13, 33, 84, 96; Department of Homeland Security, 144; Department of Justice, 90, 97, 99–100, 144, 186; regulatory and legislative reform in, 125–32; Rule of Law Index and, 3–4; Virgin Islands, 56. *See also* Constitution, US; Supreme Court, US; *specific states*

University of Chicago, 160, 170

University of Colorado School of Law, 156

University of Dayton, 159

University of Denver, 125

University of Houston, 43, 148

University of Houston Law Center, 169

University of Miami Law School, 152, 156

University of Minnesota, 183

University of Oxford Legal Executive Institute, 133

University of Toronto, 184

University of Westminster, England, 154

UPL. *See* unauthorized practice of law

UpRight Law, 10

Upsolve v. James, 114–16, 118

U.S. News and World Reports, 158, 174–75

Utah, 63, 66, 127–31, 139–40, 146–47, 220n17

Verbit, 135

Vermont, 56, 127, 223n20

Victorian Legal Services Board, Australia, 122, 194

Virginia, 56, 71, 220n17

Virginia Commonwealth University, 171

Virginia State Bar, 91–95, 98, 101–2, 105–6, 112–13, 171–72

Virginia State Board of Pharmacy v. Virginia Citizens Consumer Council, Inc., 425 U.S. 748 (1976), 109–10

INDEX | 295

Virgin Islands, United States, 56
"Virtual Firms," NewLaw, 134
virtual law office (VLO), 231n29
Voices for Civil Justice, 200
Volokh, Eugene, 189

Wagner, Richard, 18
Wald, Eli, 31, 55
Waldron, Jeremy, 78
Wales, 32, 58, 65, 100, 119–22, 124, 191
Walker, Ernest, 81
Walmart, 9, 37
Wanless, Annie, 233n69
Washington, DC, 65–66, 160, 168
Washington State, 36, 126, 139, 141–42, 143, 176, 181
Washington State Bar Association, 97, 126
Washington Supreme Court, 127
Webb, Julian, 257n20
Weddington, Sarah, 50
West Virginia, 71, 220n17
Whalen, Ryan, 22–23
"What Lawyers Do When Nobody's Watching" (Zacharias), 230n15
"What Should We Do After Work?" (Estlund), 220n26
White, Byron, 94
Whitmer, Gretchen, 80
"Who Should Regulate Lawyers?" (Wilkins), 234n80

WHSmith stores, 9
"Why Lawyers Should be Allowed to Advertise" (Hazard, Pearce, and Stempel), 237n11
Wilkins, David B., 234n80
Williams, Joan, 134
Wired (magazine), 182
Wisconsin, 53, 160, 220n17
Wisconsin Formal Ethics Opinion, 232n30
WJP (World Justice Project), 3–4, 192
Wolfram, Charles, 40, 60, 72, 237n12
women, 14, 31, 35, 49–50, 109, 111–12, 148, 169
Wood, L. Lin, 80
Working Group on Access to Legal Services for Low-Income Texans, 126
World Health Organization, 77
World Justice Project (WJP), 3–4, 192
Wyoming, 220n17

Yablon, Charles M., 221n34
Yale Law School, 56, 175
Young, Kathryne, 16
Young, William, 123
youth education, ABA and, 172

Zacharias, Fred, 230n15
Zahorsky, Rachel M., 259n2
Zimmerman, Eilene, 218n26
Zuckerberg, Mark, 150

ABOUT THE AUTHOR

RENEE KNAKE JEFFERSON is the Doherty Chair in Legal Ethics and a Professor of Law at the University of Houston. She is also a member of the Michigan State University Board of Trustees. In 2019, she held the Fulbright Distinguished Chair in Entrepreneurship and Innovation at Royal Melbourne Institute of Technology in Australia, and during 2015, she was a Scholar-in-Residence at Stanford Law School's Center on the Legal Profession. From 2014 to 2016, she served as a co-reporter for the American Bar Association Presidential Commission on the Future of Legal Services. Jefferson also is an elected member of the American Law Institute and a graduate of the University of Chicago Law School.